BABA

MEN and FATHERHOOD in SOUTH AFRICA

Edited by Linda Richter and Robert Morrell

HSRC PRESS

Compiled within the Child, Youth and Family Development Research Programme, Human Sciences Research Council

Published by HSRC Press
Private Bag X9182, Cape Town, 8000, South Africa
www.hsrcpress.ac.za

ISBN 0-7969-2096-6

Cover by Farm
Print management by comPress

Distributed in Africa by Blue Weaver
PO Box 30370, Tokai, Cape Town, 7966, South Africa
Tel: +27 (0) 21 701 4477
Fax: +27 (0) 21 701 7302
email: orders@blueweaver.co.za
www.oneworldbooks.com

Distributed in Europe and the United Kingdom by Eurospan Distribution Services (EDS)
3 Henrietta Street, Covent Garden, London, WC2E 8LU, United Kingdom
Tel: +44 (0) 20 7240 0856
Fax: +44 (0) 20 7379 0609
email: orders@edspubs.co.uk
www.eurospanonline.com

Distributed in North America by Independent Publishers Group (IPG)
Order Department, 814 North Franklin Street, Chicago, IL 60610, USA
Call toll-free: (800) 888 4741
All other enquiries: +1 (312) 337 0747
Fax: +1 (312) 337 5985
email: frontdesk@ipgbook.com
www.ipgbook.com

Contents

Preface

What do we know about fathers in South Africa? What fatherhood roles should we be trying to encourage? These are some of the questions addressed in this, the first book to focus specifically on fathers and fatherhood in South Africa. The volume contributes to an emerging international literature on fathers, making the case, amongst others, for men to make a greater contribution to the wellbeing of children.

One of the central challenges facing researchers working on this topic is to distinguish between fathers and fatherhood. Many people equate a father with the man who makes the biological contribution to the creation of the child. Around the world, though, the term father is used to refer to many people who take on the role of father with respect to children, families and the wider community. This is fatherhood. In this book we argue that biological fathers should be encouraged to be close to their children and responsibly take on the fatherhood role. However, other men need to, can and should do this when the biological father has died, has abandoned or fails to recognise his children. We also argue that children benefit from the love, care and attention of men and that fatherhood should be given greater social credibility.

Fatherhood is understood in different and contested ways, which is why we have called this book, *Baba*. The term '*baba*' is a polite form of address to an older African man. It suggests connectedness and a particular kind of protective and respectful relationship between a younger and older person. The content of the relationship is not specified. The biological relationship between *baba* and the person who is addressing him is also not defined.

In this collection, authors examine fathers and fatherhood from many angles. In the first section, some of the major conceptual and theoretical questions are posed and an attempt is made to map the field. Writers address the following questions: How does fatherhood feature in the way men understand masculinity? How many men are fathers in South Africa? How did apartheid affect fathers and patterns of fatherhood? What is the role of poverty in shaping fatherhood? How do experiences of fatherhood affect the parenting practices of South African men? What do children want from their fathers?

In the second section, fathers and fatherhood are examined from an historical perspective. These chapters show how race and class shaped fatherhood in South Africa in the second half of the twentieth century. They show that understandings of fatherhood have changed over time. Men have struggled and sometimes failed to meet the expectations of fatherhood. Yet, some men have fulfilled their fatherly roles in surprising if contradictory ways.

In the third section of the book, authors discuss the way in which fathers appear in the media. They show that men as fathers are often ignored or portrayed in narrow ways which inhibit alternative forms of fatherhood from emerging. The way in which the fatherhood role can be understood is discussed from different perspectives, which suggests that international perspectives should be blended with local understandings to promote fatherhood and create the opportunities to interact with children in caring ways accessible to all men.

How do men experience fatherhood and what obstacles bar men from expanding their engagement with children? In the fourth section, contributors offer answers to this and related questions. They discuss the law, its intention and its effects. They show how men in different contexts are generating new ways of relating to children, but also show that the material context remains important in proscribing what is possible.

In the final section, the book offers examples of local and international programmes that have been initiated to promote fatherhood and to work with fathers.

This book demonstrates the centrality of fatherhood in the lives of men and in the experiences of children. It argues that fathers can make a major contribution to the health of South African society by caring for children and producing a new generation of South Africans for whom fathers will be significant by their presence rather than their absence. In becoming *baba*, South African men can also go a long way towards healing themselves.

This book grew out of the Fatherhood Project, initiated in 2003 by the Child, Youth and Family Development Programme at the Human Sciences Research Council. The project was launched through a travelling exhibition of photographs, together with events organised by partner organisations in the project. The photographic exhibition, and a selection of posters drawn from it, continues to be shown around the country at conferences and other occasions at which the constructive involvement of men in the care and protection of children is promoted.

The exhibition consists of about 120 photographs which were selected from hundreds of images collected in various ways: professional photographers submitted prints; student photographers worked with us to capture men's everyday interactions with children; and we gave disposable cameras to children aged 10–13, in Soweto, Johannesburg and in a rural area outside Durban so they could capture images of men in their lives who they considered to be fathers.

Some of these photographs – are included on the section-divider pages of this book. We would like to thank all the photographers for allowing us to use their images.

Acronyms and abbreviations

ADAPT	Agisanang Domestic Abuse Prevention and Training
ARV(s)	anti-retroviral(s)
ASSA	Actuarial Society of South Africa
Bt20	Birth to Twenty
CASE	Community Agency for Social Enquiry
CBOs	community-based organisations
CBS	Central Bureau of Statistics
CGE	Commission on Gender Equality
CINDI	Children in Distress
COSATU	Congress of South African Trade Unions
CYFD	Child Youth and Family Development programme
DHS	Demographic and Health Survey
ERPAT	Empowerment and Re-affirmation of Paternal Abilities programme
FEDUSA	Federation of Unions of South Africa
FIFA	Federation of International Football Associations
GEAR	Growth, Employment and Redistribution Strategy
GETNET	Gender, Education and Training Network
GHS	General Household Survey
HIV/AIDS	Human Immuno-deficiency Virus/ Acquired Immuno-deficiency Syndrome
HIVAN	Centre for HIV/AIDS Networking
HSRC	Human Sciences Research Council
IDASA	Institute for Democracy in South Africa
IECD	Integrated Early Chidhood Development
IMCI	Integrated Management of Childhood Illness
LFS	Labour Force Surveys
MAPP	Men as Partners Programme
MRC	Medical Research Council
MIPAA	Men in Partnership Against AIDS
MRM	Moral Regeneration Movement
NACTU	National Council of Trade Unions
NBS	National Bureau of Statistics

NCC	National Council of Churches
NCPD	National Council for Population and Development
NICHD	National Institute of Child Health and Human Development
NGM	National Gender Machinery
NGO	non-governmental organisation
NSO	National Statistical Office
OECD	Organisation for Economic Co-operation and Development
OHS	October Household Surveys
OSW	Office on the Status of Women
PPA	Planned Parenthood Association
PSLSD	Project for Statistics on Living Standards and Development
SAfAIDS	Southern Africa HIV and AIDS Information Dissemination Service
SALDRU	Southern Africa Labour & Development Research Unit
SAMF	South African Men's Forum
SANGOCO	South African NGO Coalition
STD	sexually transmitted diseases
UN	United Nations
UNAIDS	Joint United Nations Programme on HIV and AIDS
UNDP	United Nations Development Programme
UNICEF	United Nations Childrens Fund
WISER	Wits Institute for Social and Economic Research

Opening lines

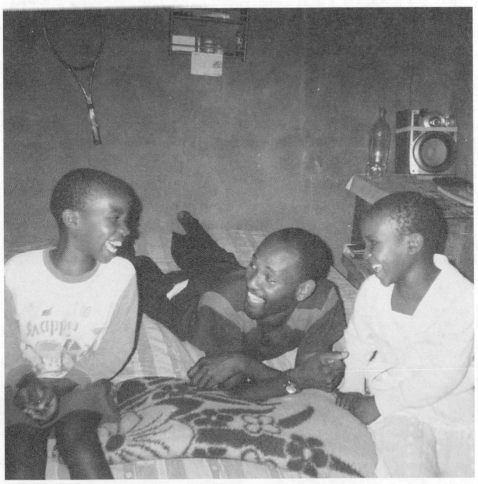

Untitled by Noluthando Gabela, aged 10, KZN

CHAPTER 1

Introduction

Robert Morrell and Linda Richter

Baba is defined by the *South African Pocket Oxford Dictionary* as 'a polite form of address to an older African man' (Oxford, 2002, p. 55). The word comes from *isiZulu*. The definition suggests a broad usage that centres on a generational and gendered hierarchy and that rests on a foundation of respect. The word is widely used in South Africa to establish or confirm a relationship with an older man. It locates the user in an almost filial relationship to the older man and it requires that the receiver of such a greeting bestow upon the user reciprocal dignity. The term has currency beyond South Africa. For example, the honorific, *baba*, is used for men who are deemed saintly in the Himalayas (*Sunday Tribune Herald*, 20 June 2004).

We decided to use the term *baba* as the organising motif of this book for a number of reasons. In the first instance, it suggests that fatherhood is not simply a matter of biology. In the second, it locates the book in a South African context and indicates that debates about fatherhood in South Africa will reflect a diversity of local views and experiences. A corollary is that attempts to understand fatherhood in South Africa will neither begin nor end with definitions created in distant, northern, industrial contexts. More than anything else, *baba* is a term that evokes a particular type of relationship. We are wary of specifying the content or the constituent parts of this relationship because they can and do change over time and according to context. The important point is that *baba* is a term for an older man (though age need not necessarily be calculated in years) who is fulfilling, or is called to fulfil, a role of care, protection and provision in relation to 'children'. (Again, a child is not necessarily only someone who is very young).

The fluidity of fatherhood

Fatherhood is a social role. The importance of this role fluctuates over time and the content of the role shifts. No better indication of this can be found than in the pages of the newly launched *Bl!nk* magazine, a publication intended for the new, young, black middle-class guy. One of the launch issue's contributors describes the magazine as 'celebrating blackness' (2004, p. 12), while *Bl!nk* itself advertises itself as 'The key to being a man'. And what is the key? Benedict Maaga, selected for an interview and presumably a model of the new black man, has no doubt that being a father is the key. 'I was lucky enough to be able to attend the birth [of his first daughter].' He describes the experience as 'one of those rare privileges', a 'truly emotional' and 'life-changing' experience (*Bl!nk*, 2004, p. 15). Zam Nkosi, TV presenter and the man on the launch issue's front cover, similarly affirms fatherhood: 'It is a pleasure to be a dad, it's an incredible opportunity to learn, it's to learn emotions, realisations, it's a lot' (*Bl!nk*, 2004, p. 27).

Not all fathers are proud to be fathers, and unfortunately not all fathers want to participate in the lives of their children. In fact, most South African men do not seem especially interested in their children. They seldom attend the births of their own, they don't always acknowledge that their children are their own, and they frequently fail to participate in their children's lives. In the early 1990s, of the 22 000 children born in Chris Hani Baragwanath hospital in Johannesburg, half had no male support (Erasmus, 1998, p. 205). And when a sample of 171 Pedi women were asked if they wanted the father to be present at the birth of their children, most said 'no'. Of the third who said said 'yes', many answered in the affirmative because they felt that the presence of the father would ensure that they were not blamed if anything went wrong with the birth (Chalmers, 1987).

Some South African men, though, are beginning to reassess the value of fatherhood. This is part of an international process, in which two kinds of response by men can be discerned. One response is to demand rights for fathers, while the other approaches the question of parenting from a more holistic position and emphasises the interests of children. An example of the first kind of response is the radical activism of the kind undertaken by the UK-based Fathers for Justice. Dramatic acts to gain media attention are undertaken by fathers who have been deprived of access to their children in situations of divorce and separation. Across Europe fathers are beginning to mobilise to protest the bias in laws that presume the centrality of the mother, and the relative unimportance of the father, in the lives of children (Geary & Ghoshi, 2004). The position taken by these organisations is often confrontational. Many of the men involved in father-activism are still caught up in acrimonious disputes with their ex-partners and their actions thus often appear to be misogynistic. For this reason fathers' rights organisations share, with other men's rights organisations such as the Promise Keepers, a reputation for anti-feminism. However, it is difficult to discount the case made by fathers' rights organisations. Increasingly, men are being denied access to their children. In order to make their case, fathers publicly mobilise equality and rights discourses to gain access to their children. The problem has been that before divorce, as critics point out, these same fathers have often often not been particularly concerned about the depth and extent of their relationship with their children and have tended to leave the bulk of childcare to their female partners (Messner, 1997). A way out of these binary oppositions and gladiatorial politics is suggested by the second kind of response, from organisations like FathersDirect in the United Kingdom, for example. This work proceeds from an explicit commitment to gender equity. It does not challenge the importance of mothering or mothers' rights to children, and it highlights the importance of working collectively for the interests of children. While it is undoubtedly still true that in many instances men (and women) use their children as weapons in partnership disputes, this movement has attempted to chart a different course by supporting gender equity programmes and by putting the interests of the child first (see Chapter 23 in this volume).

Current international movements to promote fatherhood include innovative changes in state policy in various areas of the world. In the Scandinavian countries, for example, paternity leave has been dramatically extended, encouraging men to be primary caregivers for their children. In Iceland, a parent-leave system that allows mothers and fathers to take leave for up to six months was introduced over 10 years ago. While on leave, parents receive 80 per cent of their salary in compensation. Employers are involved in the system and the policy seeks to accommodate the demands of both family and work. A combination of work and leave can be negotiated with the employer. Once an agreement has been reached between parent and employer, it is illegal for the employer to sack the parent-employee until the full parent leave has been taken. In 2000, the system was modified and the period of paid leave available was extended from six to nine months. This leave time has to be used before the child reaches the age of 18 months, and is shared between the parents along the following lines: three months are for the mother, three for the father, and three months can be divided between the couple as they choose. From the outset, between 80 and 90 per cent of fathers have used their right to parent leave fully or partially. Generally, mothers tend to use the three months' shared leave, although around 15 per cent of fathers in Iceland use some of this time (I. Gíslason, Centre for Gender Equality, Iceland, personal communication by e-mail, 15 October 2004).

As Jacqui Gallinetti shows, South Africa's laws and policies with regard to fathers have not yet followed the lead taken by social welfare states in the north (see Chapter 16). Modest attempts have been made to extend parental leave but this has not explicitly aimed to increase father involvement in childcare. Rather, the move emanates from equity arguments generated by the country's human rights culture. Fathers can now also take 'family responsibility' leave to attend to serious family business – but this comes nowhere near to the Scandinavian systems. Unfortunately, the South African legal system remains father-unfriendly as Grace Khunou illustrates in her study of the experiences of divorced fathers (see Chapter 21).

South African trade unions and other civil society organisations have attempted to raise the debates about paternity leave (Appolis, 1998; de Villiers, 1998). Thus far, though, the debates have not been taken up seriously by business. Nonetheless, Alan Hosking's chapter shows promising stirrings of debate in this area (see Chapter 17).

There are many reasons why fatherhood has not yet become a policy issue in South Africa, not least that there are many other claims made upon the over-stretched social agenda of the state. To fully appreciate the specific context in which fatherhood has been experienced and understood in South Africa, one needs to examine the sociological and historical determinants of fatherhood in the country.

Fathers and fatherhood in South Africa

About half of all men over 15 years of age are fathers according to Dorrit Posel and Richard Devey (see Chapter 4). We don't know with more certainty the number of fathers in the country because, up until now, the state's data-collection agencies have not considered such data to be important and have not collected it. The experiences of South Africa's fathers have been powerfully influenced by history. For much of the twentieth century, different experiences of work fundamentally shaped what was possible for black and white fathers. Black, particularly African, fathers were, for the most part, separated from their children by the need to work in distant places on terms of migrant contracts that permitted only annual visits home. The work was physically hard and the environment brutal; it produced men who were inured to pain, hardship and violence (Breckenridge, 1998; Morrell, 2001). Caring, for the most part, was considered to be the task exclusively of women (Burns, 1998). This was not inevitable, however. Francis Wilson, (see Chapter 3), shows how patterns of fathering were shaped by migrant labour as well as the poverty which the racialised labour market produced. The experience men had of fatherhood under these circumstances was limited and, as shown by Linda Richter and Mamphela Ramphele, they frequently abandoned and neglected their children (see Chapter 6).

Yet this was not African men's only experience of fathering. Lindsay Clowes shows that in the 1950s African fathers in urban areas had a better chance of establishing themselves in the household and enjoying a relationship with their children (see Chapter 9). Admittedly, the representation of fathers in advertisements in the pages of *Drum* may be only a very proximate reflection of actual fatherly involvement. Nonetheless, it remains highly significant that this popular and widely-read magazine saw fit to represent men in domestic environments and involved with their children. Jeanne Prinsloo argues that the situation is now much changed and fathers are seldom reflected in the mass media (see Chapter 11). She suggests that this is because men continue to be characterised in the public rather than the domestic realm. This, in turn, bolsters broader patriarchal power relations that assign the unrecognised responsibility for childcare to women.

There is a stereotype that men are not interested in children and that fathers are naturally ill-suited to parenting (see Chapter 5 by Linda Richter). We cannot enter the 'born or made' debate here, though this often underpins debates about fathers and children. However, we do note that research in this field shows that social positions, such as being a father and husband, have physiological effects on men (Gray, Kahlenberg, Barrett, Lipson, & Ellison, 2002). This illustrates that the social and physical states of men cannot be separated, and we cannot initiate the debate about the capacity of men to father from an unreflective, 'naturalised' position. In the most authoritative comment on this issue to date, Marsiglio and Pleck state that 'researchers would be remiss to discourage explorations of the "possible" biosocial dimensions of fathering [parenting]' (2005, p. 262). The importance of natal links cannot be ignored.

Children (adopted, deserted or abandoned) have a strong desire to find their biological fathers. Take the case of Sthandiwe Gumede, who was abused and abducted at an early age and then discovered that her mother had died of AIDS. The driving force in her life is 'to find her father or relatives so that she has family again' (*Sunday Times*, 14 November 2004). Many South African children are in similar positions. From data collected in the longitudinal Birth to Twenty study, caregivers of 26 per cent of 11-year-olds reported that the child had no contact with his/her father, and hadn't had any contact, either from birth, or from early childhood (Richter 2004). In *Steering by the stars*, Mamphela Ramphele describes boys who would rather run away from home than face the shame of not having their father's name when they go for initiation (2002).

But what do men themselves think about being a father? Little is said about this in the international literature (Jarrett, Roy, & Burton, 2002) and almost nothing has been written on the topic in South Africa. In a national survey of young people of 18 to 32 years of age, men and women were asked to rank what they considered to be the distinguishing characteristics of adulthood. More than 70 per cent of young South Africans, of all race groups and both genders, ranked aspects of parenthood in their top four defining features – Capable of supporting one's family (72.7%); Capable of keeping one's family safe (72.2%); Capable of running a household (71.8%), and Capable of caring for children (70.1%) (Emmett et al., 2004). The results show clearly that parenthood and family are important to young South Africans, and young men are increasingly speaking out about their desire to be good fathers. The Human Sciences Research Council's (HSRC) Fatherhood Project has acted as a catalyst, releasing strong support for men as fathers.

Historically, it has been important for fathers to be responsible and to provide for their children. Migrant workers' expectations of themselves included that they would have, and support, a homestead with a wife and children in the rural areas (Moodie, 1984). Even in contexts where men are not earning and are unable to meet the provider expectations of fathers, men hold on to the idea that being a good man involves being a good father (Silberschmidt, 1999). But fatherhood patterns are changing as the country and its economy changes. Marlize Rabe's contribution (see Chapter 20) shows that mine workers continue to believe that providing for one's children and family is a critical part of being a father; but workers who now have their families living with them are beginning to extend their fatherhood practice more into caring and engaging in play and school-preparation activities.

Despite the widely held view that being a father and providing for one's children is important, many South Africans neglect their paternal responsibilities. In Umlazi, Durban, for example, only 7 000 out of 67 000 people (the vast majority of them men) ordered by the court to pay maintenance complied in 2002. In the same year, district courts received 372 000 complaints of maintenance default (*Daily News*, 1 September 2004). It is not only those who cannot pay who default. Echoing international trends, there are many cases of men who refuse to pay maintenance, largely because of conflict with the children's mother (Meyer & Bartfeld, 1996). Such high-profile figures as footballer Lucas Radebe and Metro FM DJ Glen Lewis are named as defaulters in a *Mail & Guardian* exposé (*Mail & Guardian*, 15–21 October 2004).

Many children grow up without a father's presence in their homes or in their lives. In some quarters, this is identified as a contributory cause of childhood vulnerability – including vulnerability to HIV infection (Campbell, 2003). This is one of the reasons why movements such as the South African Men's Forum (SAMF) and the Moral Regeneration Movement (MRM) have begun to put their energies into fatherhood work as shown by Desmond Lesejane (Chapter 14) and Dean Peacock and Mbuyiselo Botha (Chapter 22).

Is there currently a crisis of fatherhood?

Fathers as a constituency and fatherhood as an issue in South Africa came dramatically into public view through the case of Lawrie Fraser. In the mid-1990s he contested the right of his ex-partner, Adri Naude, to give up their child for adoption without consulting him. The pair had never married and, by law, Fraser had no rights. Fraser contested the case all the way to the Constitutional Court. Its ruling extended the rights of unmarried fathers with regard to their children. The media gave extensive coverage to the case which lasted several years and culminated in Fraser receiving a four-year prison sentence for conspiring to kidnap his own son, Timothy, who by this time had been adopted and was living in Malawi.

There are now several organisations working with fathers and on fatherhood issues. Indeed, it was in recognition of the need to support men as fathers that the Child Youth and Family Development programme at the HSRC was prompted to launch the Fatherhood Project in December 2003. Conceived as a form of action research, a set of a priori principles was used to devise an advocacy platform, and strategies put in place to assemble available information and generate new knowledge about men as fathers, with the intention of trying to increase men's care and protection of children.[1] The project was prompted by three converging issues:

- The very high rates of child sexual abuse in South Africa, most of which is perpetrated by men. More than 25 000 children are sexually abused each year in South Africa. Few, if any, of the available programmes to reduce child sexual abuse in South Africa target men, either as individuals or to change norms, including those which inhibit men from acting against other men who sexually abuse children (Richter, Dawes & Higson-Smith, 2004).
- The absence of very large numbers of men from households in which children are growing up and low levels of father support for children's care. According to South Africa's Central Statistics Services (Budlender, 1998), about 42 per cent of children lived only with their mother in 1998, in comparison to one per cent of children who lived only with their father at that time. Findings

from a longitudinal birth cohort study in Soweto-Johannesburg show that father support for children is tenuous if a couple is not married, and grows weaker over time. Only 20 per cent of fathers who were not married to the child's mother at the time of the child's birth, were in contact with their children by the time the children reached the age of 11 (Richter, 2004).

- The increased care needs of children as a result of deaths and family disruption from the AIDS epidemic require men to take responsibility for children's wellbeing. The AIDS epidemic is significantly unsettling the care of children as breadwinners and caregivers lose their jobs or are unable to work at home, as they become over-burdened with the care of others, and as they become ill and die (Richter, Manegold & Pather, 2004). Much of the burden of care for children displaced by the impact of AIDS falls to women, including older women. Potentially more South African fathers could step into the breach and care for their children. Demographic and Health surveys indicate that South Africa has the lowest rate, in the African countries examined, of maternal orphans living with their surviving parent – 41 per cent as compared to 65 per cent in Zambia, for example (Ainsworth & Filmer, 2001).

The AIDS pandemic has undoubtedly weakened family structures and highlighted the question of fatherhood. Adult deaths have continued to rise since 1998, with a shift in the age distribution caused by a large increase in the death of young adults, particularly marked among women. In the case of women between 20 and 49 years of age, there has been a 190 per cent increase in deaths from 1998 to 2003 (Bradshaw et al., 2004). The phenomenon of so-called 'AIDS orphans' – estimated in 2003 to number 360 000 children (UNAIDS, UNICEF & USAID, 2004) – testifies not only to the deaths of mothers but also to the absence of fathers. In their chapter, Philippe Denis and Radikobo Ntsimane discuss the phenomenon of absent fathers among Pietermaritzburg orphans (see Chapter 19). They show that children whose mothers are either ill or deceased are worse off if their fathers are also absent. Mark Hunter also picks up the theme of absent fathers by focusing on the decline in marriage among African men in KwaZulu-Natal (see Chapter 8). He shows that high rates of unemployment have contributed to these declining rates of marriage. Men are unable to pay *ilobolo* (bridewealth) and therefore cannot meet the traditional expectations of a man who intends to marry. These are men without *amandla*, men without power, diminished men.

In the literature on men, it has been argued that there is a crisis of masculinity (Faludi, 1999). This is measured by, among other things, high rates of male suicide, the declining academic performance of boys, and changes in the gendered nature of work which challenge male hierarchical entitlement. Most writers on this subject argue that the idea of a crisis is somewhat alarmist and conceals the persistence of male power (Hatty, 2000; Lemon, 1995; Mac an Ghaill, 1996). Specifically with regard to boys in schools, feminists have argued that boys are doing satisfactorily but that the major change is that girls have made some advances (Epstein, Elwood, Hey

& Maw, 1998; Younger & Warrington, 1996). Despite these cautions there is recognition, particularly in South Africa, that men (and especially young males) are in trouble (Chant, 2000; Everatt & Sisulu, 1992).

In South Africa there are two factors to consider when thinking about men and fatherhood in the context of masculinity. The first is the persistence of high levels of unemployment which affects young black men disproportionately. And the second is the historical legacy of racial emasculation by which African men were infantilised (Morrell, 1998). To restore the value of fatherhood in constructions of masculinity it is necessary to tackle both of these factors. In his chapter, Nhlanhla Mkhize suggests that the project to restore the dignity of fatherhood might best be achieved by retrieving communal understandings of the fatherhood role (see Chapter 15). These valorise the relationship between men (not necessarily only biological fathers) and the families in which children find themselves. He de-emphasises the individual experiences and interests of fathers and stresses rather the way in which meaning is relationally constructed and morality is communally negotiated. His approach finds an echo in Azeem Badroodien's chapter on how boys in reformatories came to establish relationships with 'fathers', the men in whose custody they were placed, and how these relationships came to influence their adult lives (see Chapter 7). Badroodien recounts how coloured boys gained white fathers, a complicated process, particularly in the apartheid era and in racially defined, single-sex environments. Nonetheless, his research shows how important the men are who take on the fatherhood role in the lives of the children that accept them as a 'father'. Despite the importance of fathers in the lives of children, Solani Ngobeni cautions against what he calls the essentialisation of the father – the assumption that mother-care is not good enough, and that children need fathers to adequately develop (see Chapter 12).

Fathers and children

Fatherhood is essentially a human, social and cultural role. In Chapter 10, Graham Lindegger explores Carl Jung's notion of the father as an archetype. The archetype is a biological or species disposition towards a mental image that maps our expectations of fatherhood, both as children and fathers. These images are expressed in the paternal metaphors that seep through religious, moral and social systems. However, for the individual, these images are modulated by experience and they change across generations. Linda Richter and Wendy Smith explore children's views of fatherhood and their experiences of fathering through essays written by children and children's answers to semi-structured questionnaires (see Chapter 13). Children express a general 'father need', in which they simultaneously contrast the deficiencies of many men in fulfilling the father role in the way they are expected to by children, and the enormous value that children place on their relationships and interchanges with father-figures.

Baba: Men and fatherhood in South Africa concludes with a programmatic call by Tom Beardshaw, (see Chapter 24). He identifies a range of activities – from research to activism, from supporting fathers and mothers to assisting organisations (including the state) to promote good fathering and to assist fathers in matters of policy and law – which will encourage and sustain work that is already under way. While noting the lack of national studies of fathering, Beardshaw stresses the importance of respecting local understandings and practices of fatherhood. In this book we explore the situation of South Africa's fathers and illustrate how the practice of fatherhood has been, and remains, deeply influenced by the particular history of this country. The challenge for policy makers is to blend different approaches to fatherhood in a way that does not make fathering seem an unattainable ideal or an impossible responsibility. At the same time, fathers need to be encouraged and helped to involve themselves more in the lives of their children and to support their children financially and emotionally. By the same token, mothers need to be encouraged to create space for men to become more involved in childcare. Changing patterns of neglect and abuse will be neither easy nor quick. But national developments are underway which will hopefully contribute. Poverty and racial oppression, which contributed to paternal malpractice, are being addressed. Added to this, international and local organisations have already started to work to foster a process of building healthy families and engaged fathers.

Rob Morrell and his daughter Tamarin, *c.* 1983

Robert Morrell is Professor in the Faculty of Education, University of KwaZulu-Natal. He trained in History at the Universities of Rhodes, Witwatersrand and Natal. He has taught at the Universities of Transkei, Durban-Westville and Natal. He researches issues of gender and education, and is particularly interested in questions of masculinity. He is the editor of *Changing Men in Southern Africa* (Pietermaritzburg/ London: University of Natal Press/ Zed Books, 2001) and co-editor (with Lahoucine Ouzgane) of *African Masculinities* (New York/Pietermaritzburg: Palgrave/University of KwaZulu-Natal Press, 2004).

Linda Richter is the Executive Director of the Child, Youth and Family Development programme at the Human Sciences Research Council. She also holds honorary appointments at the Universities of KwaZulu-Natal, Witwatersrand, and Melbourne, Australia. Linda was trained as a clinical developmental psychologist but has worked in research environments for most of her career, investigating issues of risk and resilience in children, youth and families. She is co-author of *Mandela's Children: Growing up in Post-Apartheid South Africa* (New York: Routledge, 2001) and joint editor of *The Sexual Abuse of Young Children in Southern Africa* (Cape Town: HSRC Press, 2004).

Dev Griesel, husband of Linda, with their son Stefan, *c.* 1988

Note

1   See http://www.hsrc.ac.za/fatherhood

References

Ainsworth, M., & Filmer, D. (2001). *Poverty, AIDS and children's schooling: A targeting dilemma*. Washington: World Bank Research Working Paper 2885.

Appolis, P. (1998). Workers as fathers, *Agenda*, 37, 78–81.

Bl!nk, Launch issue, November 2004.

Breckenridge, K. (1998). The allure of violence: Men, race and masculinity on the South African goldmines, 1900–1950. *Journal of Southern African Studies, 24,* 669–693.

Bradshaw, D., Laubscher, R., Dorrington, R., Bourne, D., & Timaeus, I. (2004). Unabated rise in number of adult deaths in South Africa. *South African Medical Journal, 94,* 278–279.

Budlender, D. (1998). *Women and men in South Africa*. Pretoria: Central Statistical Services.

Burns, C. (1998). A man is a clumsy thing who does not know how to handle the sick: Male nurses in South Africa: A history of absence. *Journal of Southern African Studies, 24,* 695–717.

Campbell, C. (2003). *'Letting them die': Why HIV/AIDS interventions programmes fail*. Oxford/Bloomington: James Currey/Indiana University Press.

Chalmers, B. (1987). The father's role in labour – Views of Pedi women'. *South African Medical Journal, 72,* 138–140.

Chant, S. (2000). Men in crisis? Reflections on masculinities, work and family in North-West Costa Rica. *The European Journal of Development Research, 12,* 199–218.

de Villiers, C. (1998). Qualified parental rights for unmarried fathers. *Agenda, 37,* 82–85.

Emmett, T., Richter, L., Makiwane, M., du Toit, R., Brookes, H., Potgieter, C., Altman, M., & Makhura, P. (2004). *The status of youth report 2003*. Johannesburg: Umsobomvu Youth Fund.

Epstein, D., Elwood, J., Hey, V., & Maw, J. (1998). *Failing boys? Issues in gender and achievement.* Buckingham: Open University Press.

Erasmus, P. (1998). Perspectives on black masculinity: The abortion debate in South Africa. *South African Journal of Ethnology, 21,* 203–206.

Everatt, D., & Sisulu, E. (Eds.). (1992). *Black youth in crisis: Facing the future.* Johannesburg: Ravan.

Faludi, S. (1999). *Stiffed: The betrayal of the American man.* New York: William Morrow and Company.

Geary, J, & Ghoshi, A. (2004). In the name of the fathers. *Time,* 27 September.

Gray, P., Kahlenberg, S., Barrett, E., Lipson, S., & Ellison, P. (2002). Marriage and fatherhood are associated with lower testosterone in males. *Evolution and Human Behavior, 23,* 193–201.

Hatty, S. (2000). *Masculinities, violence and culture.* Thousand Oaks, CA: Sage.

Jarrett, R., Roy, K., & Burton, L. (2002). Fathers in the 'Hood': Insights from qualitative research on low-income African-American men. In T. Le-Monda & N. Cabrera (Eds.). *Handbook of father involvement: Multidisciplinary perspectives* (pp. 211–248). Mahwah, NJ: Lawrence Erlbaum.

Lemon, J. (1995). Masculinity in crisis? *Agenda, 24,* 61–71.

Mac an Ghaill, M. (1996). What about the boys? Schooling, class and crisis masculinity. *Sociological Review, 44,* 381–397.

Marsiglio, W., & Pleck, J. (2005). Fatherhood and masculinities. In M. Kimmel, J. Hearn and R. Connell (Eds.). *Handbook of studies on men and masculinities.* Thousand Oaks, CA: Sage.

Messner, M. (1997). *Politics of masculinities: Men in movements.* Thousand Oaks, CA: Sage.

Meyer, D. & Bartfeld, J. (1996). Compliance with child support orders in divorce cases. *Journal of Marriage and the Family, 58,* 201–212.

Moodie, T. with Ndatshe V. (1984). *Going for gold: Men, mines and migration.* Johannesburg: Witwatersrand University Press.

Morrell, R. (Ed.). (2001). *Changing men in Southern Africa.* Pietermaritzburg/London: University of Natal Press/Zed Books.

Morrell, R. (1998). Of boys and men: Masculinity and gender in southern African Studies. *Journal of Southern African Studies, 24,* 605–30.

Ramphele, M. (2002). *Steering by the stars: Being young in South Africa.* Cape Town: Tafelberg.

Richter, L. (2004). Psychosocial studies in Birth to Twenty: Focusing on families. Johannesburg: Birth to Twenty Dissemination Day 8 May 2004. (http://www.wits.ac.za/birthto20).

Richter, L., Dawes, A., & Higson-Smith, C. (2004). *The sexual abuse of young children in southern Africa.* Pretoria: Human Sciences Research Council Press.

Richter, L., Manegold, J., & Pather, R. (2004). *Family and community interventions for children affected by AIDS.* Pretoria: Human Sciences Research Council Press.

Silberschmidt, M. (1999). *'Women forget that men are the masters': Gender antagonism and socio-economic change in Kisii District, Kenya.* Copenhagen: Nordiska Afrikainstitutet.

SA Pocket Oxford Dictionary (3rd Edn). (2002). Cape Town: Oxford University Press.

UNAIDS, UNICEF, & and USAID (2004). *Children on the brink 2004: A joint report of new orphan estimates and a framework for action.* New York: UNICEF.

Younger, M., & Warrington, M. (1996). Differential achievement of girls and boys at GCSE: Some observations from the perspective of one school. *British Journal of Sociology of Education, 17,* 299–314.

CHAPTER 2

Fathers, fatherhood and masculinity in South Africa

Robert Morrell

The connection between fathers and masculinity seems patently obvious. Fathers are men. Men have a gender identity that we call masculinity; therefore there must be some clear link. In this chapter, I examine the link between fathers and masculinity and draw on South African examples to illustrate what is, in fact, a complex subject. I begin this exploration by distinguishing between fathers and fatherhood. In section two I examine the connection between childhood, manhood and fatherhood. In the final section, I investigate how fatherhood is positioned in debates about good and bad fathers from the perspective of the politics of masculinity.

Fathers and fatherhood

In the western world, it is widely understood that a man becomes a father when he impregnates a woman. This explanation makes a biological happening the sole criterion of becoming a father. There are some problems with this understanding. In the first instance, artificial insemination and a range of other technologically advanced procedures now make it possible to create human life without direct impregnation. Although human cloning may not yet be a reality, Dolly the sheep reminds us that this is a real possibility. *In vitro* fertilisation is now common. The law recognises that in some instances when a man's sperm fertilises an ovum, he is not the father. This is the case, for example, when sperm is donated to a sperm bank. In short, modern technologies are forcing new definitions of what a father is.

There are other reasons why we should avoid assuming that the status of 'father' is simply the result of a biological process. Anthropological literature is filled with examples where the provider of the sperm – the 'father' – is not considered important in the life of the ensuing child or the mother. In many African contexts, being a father has more to do with kinship ties than with medically established paternity. Polygamy complicates matters and the identity of the father is often decided by who is married to the mother or agrees to be 'the father'. In the celebrated case of aboriginal spirit children in Australia, the 'biological father' is considered so unimportant that conception is believed to have been achieved without coitus or the involvement of a corporeal man (Merlan, 1986).

In cautioning against linking biology and procreation too closely or unquestioningly with the idea of 'a father', this chapter draws on studies of masculinity that reject the view that masculinity can be inferred unproblematically from the body. Masculinity is neither biologically determined nor automatic. It is socially constructed, can take many different forms and can change over time. There are many different, culturally sanctioned ways of being a man; not one universal masculinity. In turn, this reminds us that masculinity is acted or performed. Boys and men choose how to behave and this choice is made from a number of available repertoires. Such choices are never entirely free, because the available repertoires differ from context to context and because the resources from which masculinity is constructed are unevenly distributed. Some men have more power (in terms, for example, of body, money, material resources, social ties) than others (Connell, 1995).

In order to make explicit the difference between biological fathers and the social role of fathering, the term fatherhood is commonly used. Unlike 'father', which, despite the cautions above, is generally associated with a sexual moment and the child that may issue from it, fatherhood stresses the importance of social relationships and choice.

Fatherhood is a role that is understood and exercised in different ways. One does not need to be the biological father to accept the fatherhood role and act as a father towards one or more children. Particularly in the context of the developing world, other categories of father – economic and social – are important (Engle, 1997). Economic fathers are men who contribute to the upkeep of a child. Social fathers include a range of men who live with and/or care for children who may not be their offspring. Such men might be in situations of formal adoption, or in a living relationship with the mother of the children, or a member of an extended family who has taken on the role and responsibilities of caring for children (for example, a man's brother might see himself as having the responsibility of father when his male sibling is out of work, or because he is the older son). Not all men accept the role of fatherhood. Abandonment, flight and denial are ways of avoiding fatherhood, as illustrated in Chapter 6 in this collection.

Child and father

There are many people who believe that a child, especially a boy, needs his father (see Biddulph, 1997). This is often understood to mean that a boy needs in his life the man that fathered him. The expectation that a father should be with his boy or girl child fits into a belief system which overestimates the influence of biological parents on their children, and underestimates other forces that shape a child. The focus should be on the need of all young children for adult care and protection, and on the quality of the relationship between the adult/s and the child. As Kieran McKeown comments in the context of Ireland, 'fathers who have warm, close and nurturing relationships with their children can have an enormously positive influence on their development. The converse of this also applies' (McKeown, Ferguson & Rooney, 1999, p. 92). Furthermore, studies show that, under certain circumstances, living with a father is not in the interests of a child. A New Zealand study of young fathers, for example, found that it was not in the interests of the child to be in touch with the biological father if he was a drug-user, engaged in crime or was himself living out the consequences of a troubled childhood (Jaffee, Caspi, Moffitt, Taylor & Dickson, 2001).

If we assume that a child does not 'need' a biological father, does he (or she) need an adult man who fulfills the fatherhood role? This is a controversial and unresolved issue which involves evaluating recent changes in family structure including the development of gay and lesbian parenting and the rise of single-parent, female-headed families (also see Chapter 5 in this volume). The question has become more urgent in the era of HIV/AIDS, where many households are deprived of the presence of adults by death or acute illness. In these circumstances, siblings sometimes take over parenting duties. In this collection as a whole, the argument has been made that biology is secondary to the provision of love and support (see Miller, 1981/1997). Whether this comes from adults or young people who are forced by circumstance to take over parenting seems unimportant, though the special bond that can exist between fathers and children needs to be kept in mind. Probably the answer to the question is that, ideally, children should have adult men around them, to care for them, love them and to provide role models.

There are many approaches to parenting. Although the media tend to present one particular institutional context – the nuclear family – and prescribe particular gendered parenting roles, there is a great deal of variation. African conceptions of parenting stress the needs of the child and the importance of adults meeting children's, especially young children's, needs. The saying that 'every child is my child' articulates the idea that a child needs to be supported, loved and guided by adults, that s/he is a member of a community (and not just an isolated individual), and that adults have a collective responsibility for the upbringing of a child. This ideal does not, however, provide a guarantee of the child's good health and care. A child who is not recognised by his or her father can be left without connections to clan and family. A further consequence is that s/he will not inherit from the father and, in patrilineal contexts, this undermines the security of the child.

Manhood and fatherhood

Fatherhood is associated with manhood. When one is 'a man' one is expected to be able to take on the fatherhood role. But the point at which one becomes a man is reached along different routes and the process is often contested. Young males tend to want to be considered men earlier than older males (who are the ones who generally metaphorically anoint the process) are prepared to concede. Tensions can therefore result.

Manhood is a desired estate and marks the moment when a male ceases to be a minor. Such a transition has historically been associated with rights such as marriage, the vote, gun ownership, and opening a bank account. Young men often understand manhood as the time when rights are conferred on them and when their role elicits respect. The transition does not happen in a political vacuum. Under apartheid, for example, adult African men were denied many of the rights enjoyed by white men. Further, rights granted to men can be at the expense of women and children and, for this reason, feminists have long been cautious about endorsing manhood as a desirable stage of masculinity.

Achieving manhood involves physical growth and some definitions of manhood require a mature male body (Miescher & Lindsay, 2003). But most definitions of manhood stress some act or choice on the part of the young male as well as social acceptance by adult men. For this reason, rites of passage are often emphasised in the transition from childhood to manhood.

In examining the relationship of fatherhood to manhood, I focus on two issues: the physical act of begetting a child, and the processes of accepting and performing a fatherhood role. In a heterosexualised world, the ability to ejaculate has particular meaning for many young boys. It is a signifier of physical maturity. It makes the claim that one can father a child and thus become a member of the adult male world. But the claim has to be supported by more than just physical capacity. Converting this physical development into a cogent claim for manhood has historically involved obtaining and exercising skills. In the realm of sexuality – as opposed to the development of a sexually mature body – a set of social skills associated with the creation of intimacy is required. In many cultures this is recognised and space is made for experimentation or sexual play to occur. Amongst Zulu-speakers, for example, girls and boys were historically encouraged to interact and to explore different ways, including sexually, of relating to one another. But full intercourse was prohibited. Thigh sex (*ukusoma*) was sanctioned and this involved a boy ejaculating between the thighs of the girl. Only after initiation into manhood and the negotiation of bride wealth was vaginal penetration permitted. Fines and other social sanctions were imposed on transgressors. This example serves to show that, at least in some cultures, a sexually mature body did not provide automatic entry into the estate of manhood (or fatherhood).

In their desire to 'become men', and pressured by peers to claim this status, boys may mobilise their sexuality and power over girls to establish this claim. Such moments generally involve disagreements and struggles between younger and older males, which can spill over into the public realm. In the period after the Soweto 1976 uprising, for example, young males gained status and power by virtue of their involvement in militant anti-apartheid action. The rise of the 'young lions' disrupted existing gender hierarchies and contributed to the bloody struggles in the late 1980s and early 1990s when 15 000 people were killed in Natal.

Young girls can also be the victims of the unbridled assertion of manhood by young males. Shortly after the Second World War, the disappearance of the restraining influence of elders in Ciskei resulted in young men aggressively and violently claiming sexual rights over local girls (Mager, 1998). Males are thus able to claim manhood at a young age and without the approval of adult men.

Such developments are not unique to South Africa. In a research project in the US, for example, it was found that about one fifth of teenage males believe that impregnating a young woman would make them feel 'more like a man' (Marsiglio quoted in Thornberry, Smith & Howard, 1997, p. 518). Similar findings are suggested by research conducted in Johannesburg. In a 2003 survey of over 2 000 men, one out of five admitted to having had forced sex with a woman without her consent and another three per cent said they would be sexually violent (Andersson & Mhatre, 2003). Such attitudes are likely to result in males having full sex at a young age and fathering children. This phenomenon is widely observed in the US context where rates of fatherhood among young, black, working-class boys is much higher than among equivalent middle-class boys (Hanson, Morrison & Ginsburg, 1989). This simply makes the point that the performance of masculinity for boys with resources depends less on heterosexual success with girls than it does for those who do not have the same life prospects.

Fathers in society and the politics of fatherhood

As already indicated, fatherhood is not always considered to be good building material for a feminist project. At the very heart of feminism is the idea that patriarchy – the rule of the father – is the cause of women's oppression. Developed by Kate Millett, the idea, although qualified, contested and debated, remains powerful within feminist theory (Jackson & Jones, 1999, pp. 13–18). Even allowing for the difference between a patriarch (a male leader in the biblical sense that implies age, seniority and paternal rights) and a pater (a 'father'), it is important to consider the gendered status of fathers.

Is fatherhood necessarily implicated in gender inequality? Do men use their position as fathers to oppress women? Or does the assumption of fatherhood produce men who are more responsible, more tolerant, and more supportive of gender equality? These are key questions in considering how fatherhood is related to constructions of masculinity. Some theories make the case that within family contexts, the power of the father necessarily operates to the detriment of women. Women's autonomy is limited, their professional prospects are subordinated to the demands of child-bearing and raising and to the professional aspirations of the father; domestic labour is unevenly distributed, and the father makes decisions about reproduction and the domestic economy. There is a conflation, in this view, of two different estates, those of husband and father, although in many societies these do indeed coincide.

If fatherhood is understood as the social role that men undertake to care for their children, then the question seems less ideologically weighted. But here, too, there are important debates. The most prominent concern in research on fathers in the recent period has been the phenomenon of the absent father (see Chapter 19 in this volume). There are two meanings that can be given to absence. The physical absence of fathers – caused by situations of divorce, domestic instability, work and social dislocations, including wars – has been identified as a major problem. In the US context, work on fatherhood has identified absent fathers as one of a number of factors associated with poor educational outcomes amongst children, difficulties with psychosocial development, anti-social behaviour and delinquency, and disrupted employment trajectories (Lamb, 2002). Similarly, work on masculinity has, from different standpoints, examined the way in which boys have been affected by physically absent fathers. Robert Bly (1992), through his mythopoetic work, has created support for the idea that absent fathers are responsible for a crisis of masculinity (Kimmel, 1995). This work has been taken further and popularised by men all over the world who have sought to gain access to their children under conditions of separation and divorce. In South Africa, possibly the most visible moment in what might be called a fathers' movement was when Lawrie Fraser attempted to gain access to his biological child, the son of Pretoria musician Adriana Naude. When Naude gave the child up for adoption without consulting Fraser, he contested this and in 1996 succeeded in establishing the rights of unmarried fathers before the Constitutional Court. By 1997, however, his son was in Malawi with adoptive parents. The son was kidnapped and Fraser was subsequently convicted of conspiracy for his part in the crime. His exploits resulted in extensive media coverage and contributed to the promulgation of the Natural Father's Act. He also drew attention to the plight of fathers, although it is arguable whether he ultimately gave legitimacy to the cause of unmarried fathers.

There are two problems with the absent father argument. The first is that it is difficult to show that the physical absence of the biological father is as serious for the child as is often argued (Cooksey & Fondell, 1996). Indeed, as has been argued before, the presence of the father can have negative consequences for the child (Jaffee et al., 2001). The second problem is that men have used the argument that children need their (biological) fathers to pursue anti-feminist campaigns designed to return women to their dependence on men or to reduce their autonomy (Connell, 1995; Messner, 1997).

The position of a father cannot be measured simplistically in terms of his physical absence or presence (see Chapter 18 in this volume). A father might well be physically present, but emotionally absent, or physically absent but emotionally supportive. This is the other meaning of 'father absence'. Emotional absence can be devastating for children. In South Africa, the emotionally absent father features in many contemporary novels. In Damon Galgut's *The Beautiful Screaming of Pigs* (1991), the central character of the novel, Patrick, describes his father thus: 'For myself, I don't believe he had a heart at all: this swollen, implacable man who wore shirts open to the belly' (Galgut, p. 13). Patrick goes on to recall how his father

> liked more than anything, to go away, and it was often that I would return from school to find the house all empty of his presence, streaming with light. On such occasions my mother would be happier than usual, allowing herself the indulgence of a smile. (p. 14)

He also describes how his father would go on hunting trips:

> He would go in the company of men: loud, hairy, intense as he. I had seen them often, my father's friends, as they congregated on the lawn outside. Beers in their hands, their worn boots creaked as they moved. They were – and behaved like – people in no doubt of themselves. (pp. 14–15)

J. M. Coetzee gives a similar, unappealing account in *Boyhood* (1997). As with Galgut's portrayal, the father is a misogynist, self-interested and concerned with making his son a man. The world Coetzee describes is of a father present in body alone.

> He [the narrator] had never worked out the position of his father in the household. In fact, it was not obvious to him by what right his father is there at all. In a normal household, he is prepared to accept, the father stands at the head: the house belongs to him, the wife and children live under his sway. But in their own case … it is the mother and children who make up the core, while the husband is no more than an appendage, a contributor to the economy as a paying lodger might be. (p. 12)

In these accounts, the fathers consist of a combination of unequal and careless relationships with women, children and people of colour or other religions and beliefs; unquestioning self-belief and bluster; and a preference for physically demanding homosocial contexts. This form of masculinity is often considered to be dominant among white South African men. Even though other expressions of masculinity exist, it is the values and behaviours of these men that are accepted as 'normal' and, indeed, even lauded.

In an African context, fathers are often presented as absent not least because of the migrant labour system which physically took men away. But the stern patriarch, present but dominant and uncaring, is also part of the story. Zazah Khuzwayo's novel, *Never Been at Home* (2004), captures this image.

> My father lived far away in a township on the north coast, where he was working as a policeman. He was very tall, dark and had a handsome face, but he was very fat and ate like a pig. He would demand food at any time. He had a black belt in karate and drove a white car, an old Volvo manual. The people in the village respected him. (p. 1)

Her father frequently beat his wife and daughters. He demanded obedience from them and latitude (to have extramarital relationships) for himself. He did not provide for his wife and children, preferring to give money to his mother and his township girlfriends. He was callous and often cruel. Zazah reflects disillusionment as she describes her father when she becomes a young woman.

> He was a devil to us and an angel to his family. He spent the rest of that money on his bitches. … He was a sex maniac full of lust. He even wanted to sleep with his own children. He could not talk to us as a parent. (p. 88)

Another image of the African man as father – intimately engaged with childcare and responsibility – was in fact an important feature in media representations in the 1950s in the black newspaper *Drum* (see Chapter 9). While *Drum* dropped this portrayal in the 1960s and replaced it with images of men at work, relating to one another rather than to women and children, the idea that African men were and are not interested in children is challenged (see also Chapter 3). In Lauretta Ngcobo's novel *And They Didn't Die* (1990), for example, the main male figure, Siyalo, is presented in the most positive terms as a father. A migrant worker in Durban, Siyalo only comes home once a year. The child he has with his wife, Jezile, is malnourished and in danger of dying. 'Seeing Jezile (his wife) in that tender little face flooded his heart with love for both of them; how much he loved Jezile; how much he wished to protect her from pain and inconvenience' (pp. 88–9). Siyalo gets the idea of stealing milk from a local white farmer's cows to keep his child alive. At the idea, '[H]e worked himself into a frenzy; he pranced around and shouted for joy' (p. 136). In this representation, the emotional connection between father and child, even in difficult circumstances involving physical separation, is powerfully represented. Read from a masculinity perspective, Ngcobo's novel presents the African father as a role model, providing protection, taking responsibility and investing emotionally in his children. Here the responsible acceptance of the fatherhood role is critical to the survival and sustainability of the family (wife and children, and also more distant members).

Questions of masculinity arise when approaching the phenomenon of black American fathers. Publicly identified as irresponsible and sexually precocious, a great deal of research has identified them as absent as well (Hanson et al., 1989). Recent studies, however, have found that despite being physically non-resident, the levels of interaction between father, child and mother may be high. This suggests that these men are more responsible and caring than was previously assumed (Barret & Robinson, 1982; Mott, 1990). One reason why many fathers don't take up their fatherhood role is lack of resources. Poverty is the most important factor undermining the role of fatherhood and the involvement of fathers (see Chapters 3, 6, and 18). Fathers who are unable to meet what they consider to be a father's responsibility to provide for their family, are more likely to deny or flee the fatherhood role (Coles, 2002; McAdoo & McAdoo, 1995).

Men, young and old, in contexts as varied as the migrant labour economy of South Africa and inner city locations in the United States, express aspects of fatherhood in different ways. Nonetheless, conscious choices are made that have implications for gender relations, the health and prospects of children and, indeed, for efforts to promote gender equity. Under these circumstances it is again important to ask the question, how can fatherhood contribute to the construction of peace-loving, democratic, tolerant and respectful masculinities?

In asking questions about how fatherhood can be conceived as part of a broader project to enhance the development of children and gender equity (including the development of non-toxic masculinities), it is helpful to ask, what are good fathers?

For the last four decades and more, in countries across the world, the state has been intervening to shape the rights and duties of fathers. Such interventions have ostensibly been to promote the interests of the child but, in some instances, they have run counter to gender equity principles and have prejudiced the position of fathers from minority sections of the population (black and poor) (Curran & Adams, 2000). In some countries, however, fatherhood interventions have occurred against the backdrop of gender equity commitments. Amongst the most impressive initiatives to promote fatherhood is the Norwegian government's paternity leave allowance. Initiated in 1987, it has expanded steadily to enable fathers to spend time with infants. Fathers are encouraged to spend time with their children from birth, with the strongest incentives reserved for spending time alone with the child. In this arrangement, funded by the state, it is possible for a father to take time off from work without suffering crippling economic losses. The number of fathers who have elected to be with their children has surprised policy makers (Brandth & Kvande, 2001). And the results have been that fathers have become invested in the lives and routines of their children. Such investment has, in turn, had implications for masculinity. The classic struts of masculinity – work, sport and body – are being replaced with child-centred rhythms and new measures of accomplishment (Brandth & Kvande, 2002). Such interventions are promoting the idea that a good father spends time with his children from the time of their birth and places their emotional interests at the top of his list of priorities. Good fathers are themselves healthy men because they have a good relationship with their children.

Another definition of a good father might emphasise taking responsibility for paternity, supporting the child and being a good role model. This definition places less stress on emotional engagement and more on the material aspects of fatherhood. In communities that are poor and in societies that have limited resources, men are frequently the main source of money in a family. In many parts of Africa, therefore, a 'big man' only commands respect when he is able to provide (Dover, 2001; Miescher & Lindsay, 2003). The good father in these contexts is a man who does his utmost to secure life opportunities for his children. By contrast, a bad father is somebody who denies his obligations to his children and shows little heed for the responsibilities of fatherhood.

For many years, countries have attempted to limit 'bad father' practices. Laws against absconding fathers have been and continue to be made. But the state has found it difficult to bring fathers to heel, and the mechanisms that exist to force fathers to meet their obligations are ineffective and are often stretched to the limit. For this and other reasons, in many countries infractions are now treated as criminal offences (Carlson & McLanahan, 2002). Many fathers neglect their financial responsibilities – they don't pay even when they can (Meyer & Bartfeld, 1996). On the other hand, many men are unable to fulfil expectations of being a provider (Greene & Biddelcom, 2000). This is particularly the case when fathers have many children, and is compounded in contexts where labour markets are shrinking and job opportunities are declining. In such situations the shame of being a 'bad father' drives men away from their children.

In South Africa, laws that seek to force men to meet their financial obligations to their children have existed for many years (see Chapter 16). It is only recently that a new direction in policy – one that attempts to build a relationship between father and child – has been advocated. Following the granting of paid maternity leave to mothers in 1991, Family Responsibility Leave was introduced in 1997. This grants an employee whose child is being born, is sick or dies leave for up to three days (du Toit et al., p. 506). Efforts to obtain greater paternity benefits for men, first articulated by trade unions in the 1990s, are ongoing (Appolis, 1998; de Villiers, 1998).

Fatherhood policy-making in South Africa is complicated by the different situations in which men find themselves. Middle-class men can generally adopt a fatherhood role that includes being a provider, protector and caregiver. Not all men have this privilege, and the tendency of law courts to award custody to mothers uncritically has had grievous effects on the relationships of many fathers with their children. In addition, middle-class men seldom encounter material constraints on their choices. For many working-class and particularly unemployed fathers, money and resources are scarce. Some men cannot provide for their children, and/or find themselves working at great distances from their children. More generally, the effect of apartheid is very evident on the different positions in which white and black fathers find themselves.

But there is no need for separate policies for middle- and working-class men. There is an obvious case to be made for encouraging men to be both responsible and caring. The difficulty comes with the diverse ways in which men construct masculinity. On the one hand, in conditions of poverty where ethnic identities are mobilised as a way of creating social cohesion and repelling the disintegrative effects of globalisation, fatherhood is more likely to be associated with protector and provider roles (see, for example, Heald, 1999). On the other hand, where material circumstances are secure (because men have reliable and sufficient incomes), fathers may be expected to participate in more engaging ways with their children. In this context, where time and money are not an issue, the new father – caring, domestically engaged and demonstrably loving – is more likely to be the model.

Conclusion

Fatherhood is an integral element in the construction of masculinities, but it is interpreted in different ways. The mere fact of having a child may be used to claim the status of manhood. For men who accept that fathering goes beyond their contribution to conception, there are many ways of interpreting fatherhood. Fatherhood may be understood as conferring a responsibility to provide and protect. Over decades, men have accepted this interpretation and have sought paid work to provide for their children. In the case of many black men, this has forced them to seek work far from their children and to endure privations and hardships. This is a largely unspoken aspect of the history of migrant labour. A more present kind of fatherhood, in which one's children become part of one's identity – 'I am my children' – is another way of interpreting fatherhood. These are not mutually exclusive positions but history and material conditions place constraints on how men understand and express fatherhood. Masculinities which value both responsibility and caring should be fostered. Such masculinities should steer away from the claim that fatherhood gives men power over women and children and justifies authority and tyranny. Fatherhood can make a contribution to the lives of men. It can give meaning to their lives and open up unexplored channels of emotional engagement. When men accept the fatherhood role, in whatever form, they also contribute to the broader goals of gender equity. Fatherhood should be a role that integrates men into families, rather than separating them from children, women and other men.

Robert Morrell is Professor in the Faculty of Education, University of KwaZulu-Natal. He trained in History at the Universities of Rhodes, Witwatersrand and Natal. He has taught at the Universities of Transkei, Durban-Westville and Natal. He researches issues of gender and education and is particularly interested in questions of masculinity. He is the editor of *Changing Men in Southern Africa* (Pietermaritzburg/ London: University of Natal Press/Zed Books, 2001) and co-editor (with Lahoucine Ouzgane) of *African Masculinities* (New York/Pietermaritzburg: Palgrave/University of KwaZulu-Natal Press, 2004).

References

Andersson, N., & Mhatre, S. (2003). 'Do unto others – and pay the price', *SA Crime Quarterly, 3,* accessed at http://www.iss.co.za/Pubs/CrimeQ/No.3/2Andr.html

Appolis, P. (1998). Workers as fathers. *Agenda, 37,* 78–81.

Barret, R., & Robinson, B. (1982). A descriptive study of teenage expectant fathers. *Family Relations, 31,* 349–352.

Biddulph, S. (1997). *Raising boys.* Sydney: Finch.

Bly, R. (1992). *Iron John.* New York: Vintage.

Brandth, B., & Kvande, K. (2001). Flexible work and flexible fathers. *Work, Employment and Society, 15,* 251–267.

Brandth, B. & Kvande, E. (2002). Reflexive fathers. *Gender, Work and Organisation, 9,* 186–203.

Carlson, M., & McLanahan, S. (2002). Fragile families, father involvement, and public policy. In C. Tamis-LeMonda & N. Cabrera (Eds.). *Handbook of father involvement: Multidisciplinary perspectives* (pp. 461–488). Mahwah, New Jersey: Lawrence Erlbaum.

Clowes, L. (2004). To be a man: Changing constructions of manhood in *Drum Magazine,* 1951–1965. In L. Ouzgane and R. Morrell (Eds.). *African masculinities: Men in Africa from the late 19ᵗʰ century to the present.* New York: Palgrave.

Coetzee, J. M. (1997). *Boyhood.* London: Secker & Warburg.

Coles, R. (2002). Black single fathers: Choosing to parent full-time. *Journal of Contemporary Ethnography, 31,* 411–439.

Connell, R. (1995). *Masculinities.* Cambridge: Polity Press.

Cooksey, E., & Fondell, M. (1996). Spending time with his kids: Effects of family structure on fathers' and children's lives. *Journal of Marriage and the Family, 58,* 693–707.

Curran, L., & Adams, L. (2000). Making men into dads: Fatherhood, the state and welfare reform. *Gender and Society, 14,* 662–678.

de Villiers, C. (1998). Qualified parental rights for unmarried fathers. *Agenda, 37,* 82–85.

Dover, P. (2001). *A man of power: Gender and HIV/AIDS in Zambia.* Unpublished doctoral dissertation, Uppsala University, Sweden.

du Toit, D., Bosch, D., Woolfrey, D., Godfrey, S., Rossouw, J., Christie, S., Cooper, C., Giles, G., & Bosch, C. (2003). *Labour Relations Law.* Durban: Lexis Nexis Butterworths.

Engle, P. (1997). The role of men in families: Achieving gender equity and supporting children. *Gender and Development, 5,* 31–40.

Galgut, D. (1991) *The beautiful screaming of pigs.* London: Abacus.

Greene, M., & Biddlecom, A. (2000). Absent and problematic men: Demographic accounts of male reproductive roles. *Population and Development Review, 26,* 81–115.

Hanson, S., Morrison, D., & Ginsburg, A. (1989). The antecedents of teenage fatherhood. *Demography, 26,* 579–596.

Heald, S. (1999). *Manhood and morality: Sex, violence and ritual in Gisu Society.* New York: Routledge.

Jackson, S., & Jones, J. (1999). *Contemporary feminist theories*. Edinburgh: Edinburgh University Press.

Jaffee, S., Caspi, A., Moffitt, T., Taylor, A., & Dickson, N. (2001). Predicting early fatherhood and whether young fathers live with their children: Prospective findings and policy reconsiderations. *Journal of Child Psychology and Psychiatry, 42*, 803–815.

Khuzwayo, Z. (2004). *Never been at home*. Cape Town: David Philip.

Kimmel, J. (1995). The effectiveness of childcare subsidies in encouraging the welfare to work transition of low-income single mothers. *American Economic Review* (Papers and Proceedings), *85*, 271–275.

Kimmel, M. (2000). *The gendered society*. New York: Oxford University Press.

Kimmel, M. S. (Ed.). (1995). *The politics of manhood: Profeminist men respond to the mythopoetic men's movement (and the mythopoetic leaders answer)*. Philadelphia: Temple University Press.

Lamb, M. (2002). Nonresidential fathers and their children. In C. Tamis-LeMonda & N. Cabrera (Eds.). *Handbook of father involvement: Multidisciplinary perspectives* (pp. 169–184). Mahwah, NJ: Erlbaum.

Mager, A. (1998). Youth organisations and the construction of masculine identities in the Ciskei and Transkei, 1945–1960. *Journal of Southern African Studies, 24*, 653–667.

McAdoo, J., & McAdoo, J. (1995). The African-American father's roles within the family. In M. Kimmel and M. Messner (Eds.). *Men's lives* (pp. 485–494). Boston: Allyn & Bacon.

McKeown, K., Ferguson, H., & Rooney, D. (1999). *Changing fathers? Fatherhood and family life in modern Ireland*. Wilton, Cork: Collins Press.

Merlan, F. (1986). Australian Aboriginal conception beliefs revisited. *Man, 21*, 474–493.

Messner, M. (1997). *Politics of masculinities: Men in movements*. Thousand Oaks: Sage.

Meyer, D., & Bartfeld, J. (1996). Compliance with child support orders in divorce cases. *Journal of Marriage and the Family, 58*, 201–212.

Miescher, S., & Lindsay, L. (2003). Introduction. In L. Lindsay and S. Miescher (Eds.). *Men and masculinities in modern Africa* (pp. 1–29). London: Heinemann.

Miller, A. (1997). *The drama of the gifted child: The search for the true self*. New York: Basic Books (original in English, 1981).

Mott, F. (1990). When is a father really gone? Paternal-child contact in father-absent homes. *Demography, 27*, 499–517.

Ngcobo, L. (1990). *And they didn't die*. Pietermaritzburg: University of Natal Press.

Thornberry, T., Smith, C., & Howard, G. (1997). Risk factors for teenage fatherhood. *Journal of Marriage and the Family, 59*, 502–522.

Wood, K., & Jewkes, R. (2001). Dangerous love: Reflections on violence among Xhosa township youth. In R. Morrell (Ed.). *Changing men in Southern Africa*. (pp. 317–336) Pietermartizburg/London: University of Natal Press/Zed Books

CHAPTER 3
On being a father and poor in southern Africa today

Francis Wilson

Fathers also are often devoted to their children, and make much of them when small, carrying them about in their arms, fondling them, playing with them, and teaching them to dance. (Monica Hunter writing about life in Pondoland, 1936, cited in Reynolds, 1984, p. 12)

My children are not living...In order for us to live we should eat. But now I am not working it is just like these hands of mine have been cut off and I am useless. Now life for my children will be difficult, they will scarcely eat. Now that I am not working – I do not know what I shall do or what I shall take and put against what. (Unemployed man interviewed in Lesotho, Thabane & Guy, 1984)

These two statements, separated by half a century, tell us much about what has happened to poverty and to the changing nature of fatherhood as experienced by men who are poor in southern Africa. Pondoland in 1936 was not by any stretch of imagination a wealthy place yet; although many men went off to earn money on the mines of the Witwatersrand or in the sugar-cane fields of Natal, there was a rich network of family, kinship and neighbourhood connections. Despite battering from white invaders to the south and north, rural people in this remote area lived in a cohesive society on land which, whilst not sufficient, at least ensured that for a significant part of the population there was maize for the family to harvest and milk throughout most of the year for children to drink; and for the adults, nutritious sorghum beer and *amasi*.[1] In this context one can easily imagine the joy of young fathers teaching their children to dance or visualise the frequent sight of 'a child of three or four climbing over his father and mauling him with impunity' (Hunter, 1936, cited in Reynolds, 1984).

Fast forward 50 years to Lesotho, another rural labour reserve of the South African economy. By the mid-1980s there were few economic resources of any kind in Lesotho, as was the case in all of the 'Bantustans', the so-called homelands of apartheid South Africa. If one could not get a job as a migrant worker on the mines or in some other sector of the modern economy, how could one feed one's children? The extent to which people in southern Africa, particularly in the rural areas, have moved from poverty to full-blown destitution is not easy to quantify; but it is important to note that it is possible to be poor, in the sense of having not much by way of income or material resources, and yet to be reasonably secure within a supportive community where there is generally enough food to eat and where parents have their children growing up around them. Destitution, on the other hand, implies a degree of poverty where the source of the next meal is uncertain and where fathers (and sometimes mothers) have to travel long distances to look for work.

In this chapter, I focus not only on households that have inadequate income but also on those whose lack of income requires the father to be frequently absent from home in order to earn enough to feed his family. Not all poor households in South Africa have members who are migrant workers. But as migrants generally earn relatively low wages – not all of which are remitted home – it is safe to say that virtually all migrants come from households that are poor. This wide overlap between poverty and migration requires us to consider the double impact of these two states on fatherhood.

How widespread is migration, in the sense of adults living away from home to earn income? No reliable figures on this aspect of life have been collected for South Africa as a whole since 1993. But in analysing data from the survey conducted in that year (Project for Statistics on Living Standards & Development, 1994), Pieter le Roux found that 87 per cent of white and Indian children under the age of 19 lived with both parents in the household. But for African children this was true for only 34 per cent. Part of the reason for this, clearly, was the fact that one parent, and sometimes both parents, were absent in order to earn money. In the rural areas, no fewer than 22 per cent of children had neither parent in the household whilst only 32 per cent had both in the household. Moreover, nearly half (46%) had only one parent in the household (le Roux, 1994). Bearing in mind that these figures include data collected on white-owned commercial farms where most children live with their parents, we can surmise that the situation in the old Bantustans was even worse than the above figures suggest. According to these figures, in 1993 more than two-thirds of children lived with one (probably the father) or both parents away for most of the year. Nothing suggests that the situation has improved since then. Benedict Carton (2001) provides a vivid picture of life in the Thukela River valley of KwaZulu-Natal where the younger men, between 20 and 40 years of age, are away for most of the year, returning only at Christmas and Easter to assert their masculinity in ways that are profoundly destabilising to the community. Assuming that most men have their children between the ages of 25 and 35, we can deduce that in the Thukela valley, as in most of the rural labour reserves, the fathers are away from their children during the crucial years of early childhood, up to the age of 15. The degree of havoc caused in the rural areas by the combination of poverty and the migrant system was graphically described by Buntu Mfenyana at the time of the Carnegie Inquiry when he described how 'Knifings, rape, abductions, drunkenness, and all the other aberrations which we tend to associate with urban townships like Soweto, have become part of the daily life in the so-called "rural areas"', and he went on to point out that he was 'duty-bound to hammer and stress the on-going vital connection between the reserves and the cities' (Mfenyana, 1984).

The figures for the major metropolitan areas are slightly better, but still indicate severe social disruption: 15 per cent of children lived without either parent in the home; 42 per cent had one parent there; and another 42 per cent lived with both parents. Quite where the parents of the apparent orphans were, is not clear. Some (2%) were dead (although HIV/AIDS was not yet a major fact of South African life in 1993) and others had abandoned their children or left them with relatives or neighbours. For the 42 per cent of children living with just one parent it is likely that the missing person is a father, although not so much a migrant as a man for whom his child's home is not his own.[2] Anecdotal evidence rather than scientific research would suggest that there is a significant difference between the relationship of fathers to their children in the single-parent households of the rural areas and similar households in town. It is a matter requiring further, in-depth, research. For the time being, however, we can note the important distinction which Iona Meyer observed between a migrant worker's children at home in the rural area with his wife (*inkazana*), and the children born of the woman (*ishweshwe*) with whom he lives in town (Meyer, 1961). The former are his responsibility for whom he must provide; the latter have little if any claim on his resources. Of course, much has changed since the early 1960s when Iona Meyer did her fieldwork, but her observation serves to highlight one important fact; namely, that in a country where the system of oscillating migration has been so widespread, so entrenched, and has endured for so long, it is hardly likely that a nuclear family of father and mother living at home with their children will be the norm. In this context it is hardly surprising that in 1993, two-thirds (66%) of black children were not living at home with both parents, compared to only 13 per cent of white children in the same situation (le Roux, 1994).

Turning now to the experience of poverty, we start with the obvious observation that in South Africa it is a scourge which primarily afflicts those who are black. In 1995, 61 per cent of the black population was classified as poor whilst only one per cent of the white population fell into the same category. These figures reflected the fact that average annual household income in 1995 for black families was R12 400, and for white families it was R60 000. A significant proportion (38%) of coloured households (whose average income was R19 400) was also classified as poor. There was a geographic dimension to poverty as well. Of those living in the rural areas, no less than 71 per cent were classified as poor compared with 'only' 29 per cent in urban areas. This means that, while poverty in the urban areas and among other racial groups was not to be ignored, it was amongst black South Africans in the rural areas that it was most concentrated.

How then have things changed in the 10 years of democratic governance in South Africa? We know from statistics and from observation that electricity has been rolled out to poor households in urban and many rural areas. The statistics also suggest that much has been done to provide clean drinking water within 200 metres of households – which is the stated RDP goal (Department of Water Affairs and

Forestry, 1994). But hugely important though this 'social income' is, not least for women who are saved the daily toil of carrying heavy buckets of water for long distances, it does not feed children. Moreover, unemployment has increased. Although there has been a net rise in the number of jobs in the formal sector, the net increase of people coming into the labour market has been even greater. The most recent estimate is that in March 2003, the proportion of the black population willing and able to work but who could not find employment was 43 per cent (Labour Force Survey, cited in United Nations Development Programme, 2003).

More significant from this perspective perhaps, are social grants for children. In 2002 some 3.8 million Child Support Grants were being distributed nationally, the overwhelming proportion (94%) of them to black households. Nearly three-quarters (71%) of the grants went to single-parent homes. There is a means test thus, in theory at least, all very poor children under the age of seven stand to benefit from the grant which, in 2004, was R170 per child per month. It is still too early to tell how effectively the policy is being carried out in practice, although early evidence from Cape Town suggests that, in the metropolitan areas, the bureaucracy is reasonably efficient. Whether the same will be true of the remoter rural regions of the Eastern Cape, Limpopo and elsewhere, remains to be seen, although one study in deep rural KwaZulu-Natal suggests that many eligible children are indeed receiving their grants. However, analysis of the 2002 census in the Hlabisa district, run under the auspices of the Africa Centre for Health and Population Studies, finds a disturbing bias against fatherhood in the sense that, 'Holding constant father's status, children with resident mothers were significantly more likely to be in the Child Support Grant System' (Case, Hosegood, & Lund, 2003).

Be that as it may, the available data regarding income for those who are poor show a depth of poverty well below the level at which current childhood grants would ensure sufficient resources for a reasonable upbringing. So skewed is the distribution of income in South Africa that in 1993 it was found that the poorest 10 per cent of households accounted for less than half of one per cent (0.4%) of total income whilst the poorest half of the population earned less than one-tenth (8.9%) of total income (Wilson, 2003). More recent figures suggest that, if anything, the gap between poor and rich has widened during the first years of democracy (Leibbrandt, 2004). Whilst the proportion of the population in deep poverty (<$2 per person per day) increased only marginally between 1996 and 2001, the proportion of the population in slightly less acute, nonetheless debilitating poverty (< R250 – measured in 1996 terms – per month), rose significantly from 50 per cent to 58 per cent of the population (Leibbrandt, 2004). This is an increase of no less than 16 per cent in five years.

Another way of looking at these figures is to reflect that one-quarter (25.6%) of South African households in 2000 had to make ends meet with a total income that varied anywhere between zero and a maximum of R1 200 per month (Labour Force Survey, cited in UNDP, 2003). In these households the Child Support Grant

(R110 per month for each child under seven) would increase daily expenditure for the average poor family by less than R4 for each young child, a welcome addition to the family budget, but not sufficient to enable much saving for shoes, blazers or school fees for the older children. Or if these necessities are paid for, because they have to be, then there may not be enough to buy sufficient food every day. Children's grants or no children's grants, grinding poverty in the sense of inadequate income to meet the basic needs of human existence remains a searing feature of life in South Africa today for a significant proportion of households, particularly those that are black.

How then does the experience of poverty affect fathers and their role vis-à-vis their children? In a study of Mossel Bay and surrounding areas in 1999, it was found that in black households there was a strong and significant relationship between children missing meals due to lack of funds and adults' self-reported depression. This was true not only for women but also for men (Case & Wilson, 2000). This is hardly surprising but it is interesting to have it so emphatically confirmed by scientific analysis. Fathers as well as mothers become depressed when there is not enough money in the home to feed their children. '…[I]t is just like these hands of mine have been cut off and I am useless' (Thabane & Guy, 1984), said the unemployed man in Maseru speaking for fathers living everywhere under economic circumstances beyond their control.

If there is not enough money for food, what of the other necessities for children growing up? They need shoes and a warm jersey (which they grow out of far too quickly); they need school fees, books and possibly a blazer; they need dental care and medical attention. They don't *need* – in the sense of *have* to have as a matter of life and death – pocket money or football boots, but children who do not have a little sum of money, however small, of their own to spend and some equipment for playing games must count as having a deprived childhood. And what about money for educational excursions to the science museum or the planetarium? Or the opportunity to see a play by John Kani or to hear Miriam Makeba sing? As one thinks of all these things, one realises anew just how much fathers (and mothers) who are poor are prevented from sharing the inherited riches of humanity with their children by the simple harsh fact of not having enough money.

But there is a further dimension to be considered. It is the extent to which poverty in South Africa at the beginning of the twenty-first century goes hand in hand with a dislocated social structure. I began this chapter by contrasting life in Pondoland in 1936 with the harsher realities facing a father in Lesotho half a century later. Here, a process of rural impoverishment combined with increasing dependence on migrant remittances, has left fathers with little alternative but to leave home to look for, money. This has created a black social structure throughout much of rural South Africa (and Lesotho) where poverty is combined with the almost permanent absence of fathers from the home. As Moodie (2001) points out, in both Lesotho and Pondoland the rural homestead proprietorships, the central pillars of the social architecture that sheltered people, have been destroyed by a combination of social, political and economic forces. This means that the concept of *ubudoda*,[3] competent and benevolent management of the household, which men traditionally – even as migrants to the gold mines – had as their ideal, has been shattered. Its meaning is no longer understood by young men, even in rural Pondoland (Moodie, 2001).

This fragmented social structure in the rural areas is mirrored in black urban townships where, possibly for different reasons, fathers are absent from households where children are growing up. Many women, it seems, are choosing to be single mothers. 'Of course I want children', said one young woman to anthropologist Virginia van der Vliet, 'but I don't want to be married to one' (van der Vliet, 1984). However, many women have the choice forced upon them. In both the townships around the gold mines, and in Cape Town, there is evidence of the 'desperate struggle' between town women (the *iishweshwe* of an earlier generation) and country wives for men's wages and for urban accommodation (Moodie, 2001; Ramphele, 1993). And there are, of course, fully urbanised men with no country wife who do not live with the children they have fathered. There is little doubt that the migrant labour system, as it has been enforced upon the black population of South Africa over the past century and more, has had a devastating impact on the structure of households in both rural and urban areas. Just how people have found ways of fulfilling their family obligations in quite remarkable ways within these structures lies beyond the scope of this chapter. What is of concern here are the stresses that these social structures place upon fatherhood, particularly in households that are poor.

Amongst the coloured population there is also severe social dislocation but this seems to have been caused more by the destruction wrought by Group Areas removals in the 1960s and 1970s than by a systemic migrant pattern. It is worth noting, though, that in 1993 the proportion of coloured children growing up without a father in the house was no less than 37 per cent (le Roux, 1994). In a haunting paper presented to the Carnegie Conference in 1984, Don Pinnock described the devastating impact on growing up of a social structure that had been broken by events over which members of the community had no control. In the case of District Six, the events were the forced removals of households to little box houses in different new townships established by the apartheid government on the remote edges of the city. In District Six,

> It was always the extended family which was the catch-net of the urban poor. Within it were people who could be trusted implicitly, those who would give assistance without counting the cost. In major calamities like losing one's job or a death in the family, it was kinfolk who rallied to support first, and those whose support lasted longest. Kin were also people who helped to find employment, accommodation, and who bribed or bailed one out of the clutches of the law. They were, in short, indispensable. (Pinnock, 1984, p. 3)

But it was precisely this web of support that was destroyed by the forced removals which left District Six a shell and turned a similar black community in Sophiatown into the whites-only suburb of Triomf. Oscar Wolheim, the first warden of the Cape Flats Distress Association (cited by Pinnock), described the consequences:

> Like a man with a stick breaking spiderwebs in a forest. The spider may survive the fall, but he can't survive without his web. When he comes to build it again he finds the anchors are gone, the people are all over and the fabric of generations is lost. Before, there was always something that kept the community ticking over and operating correctly … there was the extended family, the granny and grandpa were at home, doing the household chores and looking after the kids. Now, the family is taken out of this environment where everything is safe and known. It is put in a matchbox in a strange place. All social norms have suddenly been abolished. Before, the children who got up to mischief in the streets were reprimanded by neighbours. Now there's nobody and they join gangs because that's the only way to find friends. (Pinnock, 1984 p. 3)

And so the seeds of South Africa's violence, both within and beyond the household, were sown by the dual time bombs of the migratory labour system and Group Areas removals. The extent of violence in the wider society, outside of the household, is of course only too well known. Whether we are talking of armed robbery, hijacking, murder or rape, we know that South Africa has one of the highest crime rates in the world. Analysis of these crimes lies beyond the scope of this chapter but clearly their existence is not unrelated to the frustrations of poverty, the social dislocations of urbanisation exacerbated by migrant labour and the forced removals of the apartheid era, and the huge divide between rich and poor reflected in a Gini coefficient that is one of the highest if not the highest amongst countries with data, in the world[4] (Brown & Folscher, 2003).

But what is less well documented is the barely visible but no less real intra-household violence, not least the abuse of children and women by men within the home. Anecdotal evidence would suggest that violence against children often involves the boyfriend of the mother or the stepfather rather than the father himself, but the fact that 66 per cent of African children are not living at home with both parents, most of them without their father, would suggest that for a large proportion of poor children the possibility of experiencing violence at the hands of the man in their home is not insignificant.

This leads us to the broader issue of men as role models. For some young women, men are not to be taken seriously as husbands. The single parent home now seems to be a matter of choice for a significant proportion of mothers, albeit under duress. What a far cry this is from the ideal of *ubudoda* of earlier years, when men were seen by all as being responsible for the competent and benevolent management of the household. But what does this mean for the children growing up in a world where, for many of them, the father figure is either absent or a role-model that leaves much to be desired? For girls, it must leave them with a distrust of men so deep that, in extreme cases, marriage is out of the question. And for boys? The consequences can be even more destructive as they seek to navigate the turbulence of growing up without the guidance of someone whom they love and trust and who is there when they need him.

Of course there are thousands of youngsters, boys as well as girls, living in poor homes in South Africa who are being brought up with a value system that will serve them and the wider community well as adults. But it would be a mistake to assume that the astonishing resilience of our society to everything that was thrown at it during the twentieth century will necessarily endure without radical action to heal the social fragmentation which has occurred. More than 30 years ago a medical doctor living and working in a remote rural part of KwaZulu-Natal described the impact of the migratory labour system and warned of its long-term consequences.

> Economic or even social analysis of migratory labour will fail to reveal the full picture of its cost in terms of human misery. To learn this you must listen to the lonely wife, the anxious mother, the insecure child … It is at family level that the most pain is felt, and we cannot forget that the African cultural heritage enshrines a broader, more noble concept of family than that of the west. The extended family has proved a marvellous security for those for whom, otherwise, there was no security at all. The extended family is a net wide enough to gather the child who falls from the feeble control of neglectful parents; it receives the widow, tolerates the batty, gives status to grannies. Migratory labour destroys this by taking away for long months together, the father, the brother, the lover and the friend. Each must go, and no one fools themselves that these men can live decent lives in a sexual vacuum. The resultant promiscuity is but one aspect of the mood of irresponsibility. For your migrant is concerned with nobody but himself; his own survival is the only survival that he can influence by any act that he performs. He may be well fed; doubtless he is. He may be well cared for; doubtless he is. He may have the companionship of others like himself. Yet the food he eats cannot fill the bellies of his children, nor the blanket he sleeps under warm any but himself. His care, his love, his family loyalty cannot reach out to his wife nor caress his children, nor extend to the grandmother who brought him up…Deprived of their natural guides, children of migrants grown through an insecure, uncertain childhood to an adult life whose sole preoccupation may be to escape the system. There must be a harvest of aggression, with the weeds of violence growing rank within it. The dreadful society is the community of the careless, of those who, treated like boys, behave like boys; of those who, having had no responsibility laid upon them, owe none to any man. In that chill

climate will there be any place for trust? Any hope for human
intercourse at all? (Barker, 1970, p. 55)

'The conclusion', said a Xhosa-speaking father, in the migrant barracks in Cape
Town in 1984, discussing the problem of remaining faithful to his wife under such
circumstances, 'is that in the towns we are spilt just like water on the ground'
(Reynolds, 1984, p. 22).

If that was not bad enough, southern Africa since then has been visited by the plague
of HIV/AIDS. Between 1992 and 2000, the proportion of pregnant mothers visiting
the clinics who were found to be HIV-positive rose from less than two per cent to
nearly 25 per cent (loveLife, 2001). In the country as a whole, the annual number of
deaths in 2004 is estimated to exceed the total number of all non-AIDS deaths
including those by violence and old-age. By 2010 overall life expectancy is expected
to fall, unless intervention becomes effective. If there are no fundamental changes in
lifestyle, overall life expectancy will fall from the pre-epidemic high of 65, to 41 years
of age (ING Barings, 2000). And the total number of deaths from AIDS-related
causes, without effective intervention or without lifestyle changes, is projected to
reach nine million persons – roughly nine times as many people as died in the Irish
famine in the middle of the nineteenth century. Whilst many young children are
perishing from the scourge, we know that the most vulnerable groups are young men
and women in the prime of life. Fathers are most likely to be dying just as their
children are growing up.

The devastating consequences of HIV/AIDS on the capacity of fathers to fulfil the
obligations which they feel they owe to their children has been sensitively explored
and movingly documented in a small qualitative study (Coetzee & Swartz, 2004) in
Cape Town of fathers, all of whom were HIV-positive and over 26 years of age.
The findings are difficult to summarise but the following points are amongst the
sharpest that emerge:
*   All the fathers emphasised the severe lack of basic resources without which
    they found it extremely hard to live (p. 121);
*   The illness forced fathers into difficult and life-threatening choices: for
    example, the needs of the sick father had to be weighed against the needs of
    the sick child, the need to rest against the need to work and earn money;
*   The consequences of the stigma attached to the disease are brutal;
*   Anti-retroviral therapy is of critical importance in providing a platform enabling
    fathers to renew their engagement as fathers and to increase family cohesion;
*   Fathering was extremely important and meaningful to all those interviewed,
    indeed, they described their experience of fathering as 'a vocation of the
    highest spiritual significance and meaning' (p. 125, see also Chapters 18 and 19
    in this volume).

Given these findings, it is all the more shameful to note that in South Africa at the end of 2004 it was estimated that of all those who were HIV-positive, no more than four per cent were receiving anti-retroviral therapy (Bourne, 2004).

In neighbouring Botswana, where the government has been active from the very beginning with high-profile campaigns to prevent AIDS, and which in 2004 committed itself to providing free anti-retroviral therapy to all those needing it, the situation seems to be even worse in terms of the proportion of the population affected. But then Botswana, like South Africa, is locked into the migrant labour system, which remains entrenched in the gold mining industry. Thousands of men continue to be drawn from all over southern Africa, most particularly from the Eastern Cape, Lesotho and Mozambique but also from Botswana and Swaziland, and housed on a single-sex basis. And as Mark Lurie from the Medical Research Council pointed out,

> If you wanted to spread a sexually transmitted disease, you'd take
> thousands of young men away from their families, isolate them in
> single-sex hostels, and give them easy access to alcohol and commercial
> sex. Then to spread the disease around the country, you'd send them
> home every once in a while to their wives and girlfriends. (Lurie, cited
> in Schoofs 2001)

The impact of HIV/AIDS on fathers and their children has not yet been researched in detail. But it requires little imagination to think of the consequences of increasing poverty – more widows, more fatherless children, more orphans. Of course the migratory labour system is not the only factor leading to the spread of HIV as its prevalence from Asia to Zimbabwe testifies, but both common sense and the available evidence suggest that it has certainly exacerbated the situation.

Furthermore it is true that pass laws or no pass laws, a system as pervasive and deep-rooted as South Africa's migratory labour structure cannot vanish overnight. Neither can its consequences, as any observer of the gold mining industry or of the rural areas or of the graveyards can confirm. Nor, too, can we wish away the destruction caused by the forced removals endured only a generation ago.

The issue now facing us is how to restore a sense of fatherhood, how to re-create *ubudoda*, (suitably modified by the twenty-first century requirements of women's liberation) after the social havoc caused in southern Africa through the nineteenth and twentieth centuries by conquest, colonialism, racist capitalism, apartheid, and now, by HIV/AIDS.

It is a tough challenge, but there is no way of avoiding it.

Francis Wilson grew up in the Eastern Cape, and was trained in Physics (at the University of Cape Town [UCT]) and Economics (Cambridge). He has been teaching in the School of Economics at UCT for the past 38 years apart from sabbaticals in Harvard, Lyon (working in a lorry factory), New Delhi (Jawaharlal Nehru University), Oxford (All Souls and Balliol), Princeton and Sussex (Institute of Development Studies). In 1975 he founded SALDRU, the Southern Africa Labour & Development Research Unit, which he directed until 2000 when he started Data First (a resource unit For Information Research & Scientific Training) within the university's new Centre for Social Science Research. His main areas of work have been in labour (mine, migrant, farm), some South African history, data collection and in poverty about which, to find out more, he directed the second Carnegie Inquiry into Poverty and Development in Southern Africa during the 1980s.

Frances Wilson with his son,
David, Cape Town, 1969

Notes

1   A thick, naturally soured milk.

2   In South Africa as a whole, of the 47 per cent of African children living with one parent the vast majority, somewhere between 42 per cent and 45 per cent, were recorded as living without their fathers at home.

3   Manhood.

4   The Gini coefficient measures the degree of inequality in a society. In South Africa, in 2001, the national Gini coefficient was estimated to be 0.73.

References

Barker, A. (1970). Community of the careless. *South African Outlook*, April, 51–55.

Bourne, D. (2004) Letter to the *Sunday Times*, 11 December.

Brown, S., & Folscher, A. (Eds.). (2003). *Taking power in the economy*. Cape Town: Institute for Justice and Reconciliation.

Carton, B., (2001). Locusts fall from the sky: Manhood and migrancy in KwaZulu. In R. Morrell (Ed.). *Changing men in Southern Africa* (pp. 129–140). Pietermaritzburg: University of Natal Press.

Case, A., Hosegood, V., & Lund, F. (2003). *The reach of the South African Child Support Grant: Evidence from KwaZulu-Natal*. CSDS Working Paper No. 38, University of Natal, Durban.

Case, A., & Wilson, F. (2000). *Health and wellbeing in South Africa: Evidence from the Langeberg survey*. Princeton University, unpublished paper.

Coetzee, Z., & Swartz, L. (2004). Fathers with HIV/AIDS: The struggle for occupation. In R. Watson & L. Swartz (Eds.), *Transformation through occupation* (pp. 119–128). London: Whurr Publishers.

Department of Water Affairs and Forestry (DWAF). (1994). *Water Supply and Sanitation Policy*. Government White Paper. Cape Town: DWAF.

ING Barings (2000). *Economic impact of AIDS in South Africa: A death cloud on the horizon*. Johannesburg.

Leibbrandt, M. (2004). South African poverty and inequality: Measuring the changes. In S. Brown & A. Folscher (Eds.). *Taking power in the economy: Gains and directions* (pp. 76–91). Cape Town: Institute for Justice and Reconciliation.

le Roux, P. (1994). *Parental care and family structure: Some interesting findings from the SA Living Standards Survey*. Cape Town: University of the Western Cape.

loveLife (2001). *Impending catastrophe revisited: An update on the HIV/AIDS epidemic in South Africa*. Johannesburg: loveLife.

Meyer, I. (1961). Town children and country children. In P. Meyer (Ed.). *Townsmen or tribesmen* (Chapter 17 of Part 4, pp. 270–282). Cape Town: Oxford University Press

Mfenyana, B. (1984). *Among the discarded*. Paper No. 78. Cape Town: Second Carnegie Inquiry into Poverty and Development in Southern Africa.

Moodie, D. (2001). Black migrant labourers and the vicissitudes of male desire. In R. Morrell (Ed.). *Changing men in Southern Africa* (pp. 297–315). Pietermaritzburg: University of Natal Press.

Pinnock, D. (1984). *Breaking the web: Economic consequences of the destruction of extended families by Group Areas relocations in Cape Town*. University of Cape Town: SALDRU Monographs.

Ramphele, M. (1993). *A bed called home: Life in the migrant labour hostels of Cape Town*. Cape Town: David Philip

Reynolds, P. (1984). *Men without children*. Paper No. 5. Cape Town: Second Carnegie Inquiry into Poverty and Development in Southern Africa.

SALDRU. (1994). *Project for Statistics on Living Standards & Development*. Cape Town: SALDRU.

Schoofs, M. (2001). African gold giant finds history impedes a fight against AIDS. *Wall Street Journal*, 26 June.

Thabane, M., & Guy, J. (1984). *Unemployment and casual labour in Maseru*. Paper No. 124. Cape Town: Second Carnegie Inquiry into Poverty and Development in Southern Africa.

United Nations Development Programme (UNDP). (2003). *Labour Force Survey. Human Development Report*. Oxford: Oxford University Press.

van der Vliet, V. (1984). *Staying single: A strategy against poverty?* Paper No. 116. Cape Town: Second Carnegie Inquiry into Poverty and Development in Southern Africa.

Wilson, F. (2003). Understanding the past to reshape the future: Problems of South Africa's transition. In P. Davis & M. Thomas (Eds.). *The economic future in historical perspective* (pp. 297–313). Oxford: Oxford University Press.

CHAPTER 4

The demographics of fathers in South Africa: an analysis of survey data, 1993–2002

Dorrit Posel and Richard Devey

Introduction

In this chapter, we investigate two sets of empirical questions about biological fathers in South Africa.[1] First, how many and which men are fathers? Second, we ask what proportion of children, and specifically children aged 15 years and younger,[2] do not live with their fathers or have fathers who are deceased?

In addressing these questions, we examine and evaluate possible sources of data in South Africa, and we show why the available national data to count and describe fathers are limited. It is possible to arrive at only crude estimates to answer the first question and we can say little about how measures and characteristics of fathers have changed over time. The collection of this kind of information in the future would enrich our understanding of fertility trends. It would also result in the recognition of men, and thereby the promotion of the role of men, as parents (Morrell, Posel & Devey, 2003).

The data available permit a more comprehensive, albeit still qualified, response to our second question. We find that between 1993 and 2002, a large and growing proportion of children in South Africa did not have either a father who was alive or a father who was a resident member of their household. In 2002, children were more likely to be living apart from their biological father than they were to be living with him. Our study also highlights clear differences across population groups: of all children in South Africa, African children are the most likely to be living without their fathers, either because their fathers are living elsewhere or because their fathers are deceased.

Levels of paternal absence in South Africa seem particularly high in comparison to estimates for many other countries in sub-Saharan Africa. If the absence of a father from the household has significant economic and psychological implications for the wellbeing of a child, then these data are indeed cause for concern. In interpreting the statistics, however, it is important to recognise that binary measures of paternal absence will mask considerable variation in both the involvement of biological fathers, and the presence of social or substitute fathers, in the lives of children (Mott, 1990; Greene & Biddlecom, 2000). Furthermore, part of the recorded increase in paternal absence in South Africa is likely to be the result of changes over the period in survey design, particularly with respect to how household membership, and hence absence from the household, has been defined in household questionnaires.

Counting fathers in South Africa

There are a number of sources of data on individuals, and the households of which they are part, in South Africa. The first of these is the range of nationally representative household surveys conducted by Statistics South Africa (Stats SA) since 1993. These surveys include the Project for Statistics on Living Standards and Development (PSLSD) conducted in 1993, the October Household Surveys (OHS) conducted annually from 1993 to 1999, the biannual Labour Force Surveys (LFS) introduced in 2000, and a General Household Survey (GHS) conducted in 2002.

Household surveys in South Africa have regularly asked questions (often an entire module) on biological reproduction. However, the questions have been asked only of women (of reproductive age) in the household. In some of the surveys, it is possible to identify all women who are biological mothers because women have been asked how many times they have ever given birth and if these children are still alive.[3] In other surveys, the question is narrower and women are asked only about children born in the previous year.[4]

None of the surveys, however, includes a question that makes it possible to directly identify all men who are (or who have been) biological fathers. One explanation for not collecting information on fathers but on mothers is that whereas paternity can be questioned, maternity cannot. Women are unlikely to conceal or deny their motherhood, but men may not know whether they are fathers or they may wish to deny it (for example, to avoid maintenance claims). Men may therefore under-report the number of births of their own children, particularly children outside marriage or from previous marriages (Rendall, Clarke, Peters, Ranjit, & Verropoulou, 1999; Greene & Biddlecom, 2000; Ratcliffe, Hill, Harrington, & Walraven, 2002). Another explanation may be in the purpose of asking questions about motherhood. Here, the interest is in fertility rates and in infant or child mortality rates and information on fatherhood is not directly needed for these calculations (Morrell et al., 2003).

However, there are good reasons also for identifying men who are fathers and birth rates for fathers. Counting fathers means recognising the role that men can or do play as parents (Morrell et al., 2003). Furthermore, although South African data reveal a fertility decline among women (see for example Moultrie & Timaeus, 2003), we can say little about the number and characteristics of men who are fathers and about changes over time. For example, we cannot explore whether there is a relationship between education, employment status and fatherhood, or whether the age distribution of fathers is shifting. The determinants of male fertility may also be different to those of female fertility, and a description and understanding of men's reproductive experiences therefore 'would allow for a fuller understanding of fertility trends and dynamics in any population' (Ratcliffe et al., 2002, p. 573).

With no direct question identifying biological fathers in the national household surveys, the only way to classify men as fathers is to make inferences using data collected through other questions (Morrell et al., 2003). One possibility is to infer the extent of fatherhood from information that identifies women who are biological mothers. Table 1 shows that in 1993, 1998 and 2002, some 57 per cent, 61 per cent and 62 per cent respectively of all women aged 15 to 49 years were biological mothers (they were reported as having given birth to children who were still alive at the time of the survey). If we assume a unique matching between all women who are mothers and all men who are fathers in the same age group, then a growing proportion of men aged 15 to 49 years were fathers over the period – almost 63 per cent and 65 per cent in 1993 and 1998 respectively (there are fewer men than women in South Africa thus accounting for the higher estimated percentages for men).

However, there are several problems with these data. First, there may not be a one-to-one mapping between mothers and fathers – a man may have fathered children with more than one woman, and a woman may have had children with more than one man. Second, it is only possible to identify *which individual men* are fathers for a specific subset of fathers: men who are reported as being partnered with, and part of the same household as, biological mothers. We are not able to describe the characteristics of a large number of men who are fathers but who are not a member of the same household as the mother of their children, perhaps because of divorce, desertion or migration.[5] Our estimates assume also that being the partner of a mother means being a father, which is not always the case.

Table 1 Counting fathers using measures of biological mothers

Of those aged 15 to 49 years	1993 (PSLSD)	1998 (OHS)	2002 (GHS)
Percentage of women who are mothers	57.5	61.1	62.0
Number of women who are mothers	6 536 046	7 374 934	7 979 749
Number of men	10 443 847	11 360 553	11 869 496
Estimated percentage of men who are fathers	62.6	64.9	67.2
Of those aged 15 years and older			
Percentage of women who are mothers	–	65.7	–
Number of women who are mothers	–	9 554 498	–
Number of men	–	13 033 485	–
Estimated percentage of men who are fathers	–	73.3	–

Notes: The 1993 survey addressed birth-related questions to women 15–49 years of age. The 2002 survey addressed birth-related questions to women 13–49 years of age. This explains why we cannot estimate the number of all men (15 years and older) who are fathers in 1993 and 2002. The 1998 survey addressed birth-related questions to women of all ages.

Another possible means of identifying fathers is to use information collected in household surveys on the kin relation between household members and the head (or acting head) of the household.[6] A range of relationships is specified, including parent, grandparent, child, grandchild and spouse of the head of household. Men are likely to be fathers if they are: the grandparent or parent of the head of household; the head or spouse of the head and there are children or grandchildren of the head living in the household; or an adult son of the household head and there are grandchildren living in the household.[7]

According to these characteristics, some 47 per cent, 43 per cent and 40 per cent respectively of men aged 15 to 54 years can be counted as fathers in 1993, 1998 and 2002 (see Table 2).[8] Taking the data at face value therefore suggests that the percentage of men, specifically men aged 15 to 54 years, who are fathers declined over the period. These estimates therefore contradict the trend identified in Table 1. However, because fathers will also be measured with error in Table 2, it is not possible to evaluate which is the real trend.

Table 2 Counting fathers using information on relationship to household head

Likely fathers	1993 (PSLSD)	1998 (OHS)	2002 (GHS)
Percentage of men (15–54 years)	47.1	43.1	39.5
Number of men (15–54 years)	4 495 585	4 906 696	4 984 784
Percentage of men (15 years and older)	50.0	46.4	42.9
Number of men (15 years and older)	5 508 170	6 046 898	6 196 925

First, there is scope for misclassification when inferring relationships through the head of the household. Consider, for example, a hypothetical household in which both an adult son and a grandchild of the head are resident. Using the characteristics identified above, the resident adult son of the head would be identified as a father. But it is possible that the grandchild is not the child of the resident son but of another (non-resident) son (or daughter) of the head. In fact, the resident adult son may have no children of his own.

Second, kin relations are not formally defined in the questionnaires and it may be that in answering the question on the relationship to household head, respondents were referring not only to biological kin but also to kin defined by social relations of co-residence, reciprocity and norms. Included in these estimates of fathers, therefore, may be men who are not biological fathers but who have become social fathers to children.

Third, and perhaps most important, these estimates count only a particular subset of men who are fathers, namely fathers who are in the same household as their children (or grandchildren) *and* who are heads of household or the spouse/parent/grandparent/child of the head. They therefore exclude men who live in separate households to their children, men who are divorced and men whose adult offspring have formed their own households. They also omit men who are fathers but who are brothers, uncles (or perhaps not even related) to the head of the household in which they live. These omissions would explain why the count of fathers here is considerably lower than that inferred from a measure of biological mothers.

In Table 3, we have augmented our estimates by combining information on a man's relationship to the head of household with whether he is married to, and part of the same household as, the mother. The proportion of men who are fathers still declines over time, but the count of fathers is more inclusive across all years, and hence the percentages are higher than in Table 2. For example, men will be identified as fathers even if their adult children are living in another household, provided these men are married to, and living with, women who are mothers. But excluded from the measure will be men who are fathers but who are not part of the same household as the mother of their children, or their children and grandchildren. As we show in section 2, with high levels of paternal absence in South Africa, this may represent a sizeable number of 'hidden' fathers.

In sum, it is not possible to simply count how many men are fathers in South Africa and to identify trends over time, or to say anything meaningful about the characteristics of fathers and the households in which they live, using available national household survey data.[9] We can only arrive at a best estimate of fathers through a series of inferences and data manipulations.[10]

Table 3 Counting fathers combining partnership with a mother and relationship to household head

Likely fathers	1993 (PSLSD)	1998 (OHS)	2002 (GHS)
Percentage of men (15–54 years)	50.21	46.53	45.0
Number of men (15–54 years)	4 792 836	5 290 163	5 671 758
Percentage of men (15 years and older)	53.04	51.44	47.9
Number of men (15 years and older)	5 846 200	6 711 083	6 916 679

Another possible source of data on fathers in South Africa is the Demographic and Health Survey (DHS). The first DHS in the country, conducted in 1998, was designed to collect information on maternal and child health. The survey therefore sampled only women and provides no direct measure of paternity. In 2003, however, the second DHS administered an additional questionnaire to men asking them directly whether they had children (and how many). The public release of these data will provide an important new source of information on fathers in South Africa.

A number of other countries in Africa have also included a men's questionnaire in their Demographic and Health Survey (DHS), and some estimates of biological fathers are presented in Figure 1. The figure shows considerable variation across the countries, with our measures of fathers in South Africa for 1993, 1998 and 2002 falling within this broad range, and mostly in the lower tail of the distribution.

Figure 1 Percentage of men (aged 15 to 54 years) who are fathers, for selected African countries

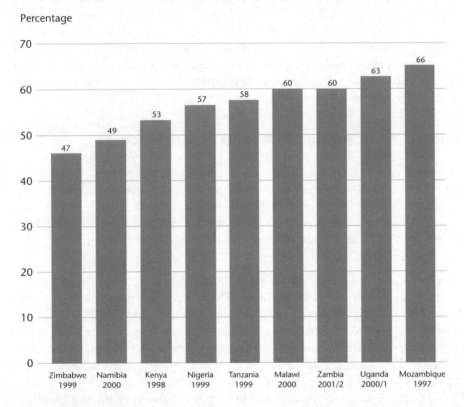

Notes: The data are weighted. Percentages have been calculated by dividing the reported number of men (aged 15–54 years) with one or more living child by the total number of men (aged 15–54 years). The men are selected as a systematic sub-sample from households with at least one woman aged 15 to 49 years.

Sources: Gaspar, et al. p. 112 (Mozambique, 1997); Uganda Bureau of Statistics and ORC Macro, (2001), p. 91; Central Statistical Office (Zambia), Central Board of Health (Zambia), and ORC Macro, (2003), p. 112; National Statistical Office (Malawi) and ORC Macro, (2001), p. 93; National Bureau of Statistics (Tanzania) and Macro International Inc., (2000), p. 81; National Population Commission (Nigeria), (2000), p. 95; National Council for Population and Development, Central Bureau of Statistics (Office of the Vice President and Ministry of Planning and National Development) (Kenya), and Macro International Inc., (1999), p. 86; Ministry of Health and Social Services (Namibia), (2003), p. 99; Central Statistical Office (Zimbabwe) and Macro International Inc., (2000), p. 95.

However, a major limitation with using DHS data to count and describe fathers is that the men surveyed are selected as a systematic sub-sample from households containing women of reproductive age (15 to 49 years). Fathers who are not co-resident with women in this age range, therefore, will not be identified. Collecting information on fathers in South Africa, therefore, should not be confined to DHSs. Rather, questions could be included regularly in the national household surveys. Comprehensive socio-economic information collected in these surveys on individuals and the household of which they are part would enrich a future empirical research agenda on fathers, and the standard inclusion of questions identifying men who are fathers would make it possible to study changes in fatherhood over time. The challenge is to develop questions that best capture men's reproductive experiences and minimise reporting errors.

Children living without fathers in South Africa

Surveys in South Africa do not directly identify which men (and therefore how many men) are fathers. But in some of the household surveys, household members are asked to report whether their fathers (and mothers) are part of the same household, absent in that they are living in another household, or deceased. In this section, we explore how many children in South Africa live 'without' their fathers, using household survey data for the period 1993 to 2002.

There is a considerable body of international literature that investigates the contributions that fathers make to their children's development (see, for example, Mott, 1990; Cooksey & Craig, 1998; Cherlin, 1999; Bartfeld, 2000; Nyamukapa, Foster & Gregson, 2003). Many studies within this literature explore the economic and psychological implications for children of growing up without their fathers. Two important considerations highlighted in this research, which have relevance particularly for interpreting available South African data, concern the nature of absence of the father, and whether and in what ways absent or deceased biological fathers are replaced by new father-figures in the household.

Fathers who are alive are viewed as being absent if they are not part of the same household as their children. But this measure of absence may mask a range of contact between the father and the child:

> At one extreme, a father may never be present in the home or may leave and never be seen again. At the other extreme, even though a father may not live in the home, he may have extensive and continuing contact with his children, thus accomplishing many of the typical fatherhood roles ascribed to men. (Mott, 1990, p. 501)

What an absent father means is complicated further in South Africa particularly because of the migrant labour system and the implications this had for the living arrangements of many Africans. African labour migrants historically were not permitted to settle permanently at (urban) places of employment nor could they migrate with spouses and family members. Labour migrants, who were predominantly men, would therefore not be physically living in their household of origin for a large part of the year. But, given the restrictions on African urbanisation and the contractual nature of urban employment, many labour migrants migrated 'temporarily'; they remained members of their household of origin, to which they would return each year and which was their 'permanent' home (Posel, 2003). Labour migration therefore would have been associated with a considerable degree of paternal flux.

Although formal restrictions on African urbanisation were lifted in the late 1980s, patterns of temporary labour migration, particularly from rural areas, continued. Between 1993 and 1999 a growing number of rural African households reported labour migrants, particularly women, as non-resident members of the household (Posel & Casale, 2003).

Household surveys conducted in South Africa, however, have not been consistent in the way in which they define household membership, and therefore in defining what is meant by an absent father or household member more generally. The 1993 PSLSD allowed individuals to be identified as members of a household even if they were not physically living in the household for most of the year. Those men who are temporary labour migrants would therefore be included as household members rather than as 'absent'. Consequently, we would expect that children whose fathers are labour migrants *would not* be identified as children with absent fathers.

In contrast, the other nationally representative household surveys adopt a stricter residency requirement for household membership (Posel, 2003). Individuals must be resident in the household for most of the year to be assigned household membership. In these surveys, absent fathers include men who may view themselves (and are viewed by others) as being members of the household, but who do not meet the residency requirement for household membership established in the questionnaire. Children with fathers who are labour migrants therefore *would* be counted as children with absent fathers.

The reported absence or death of a father may also mask the involvement of other father figures in the lives of children. Many children in South Africa live with extended families. In households where biological fathers are not present, other men may assume the role of social father (see, for example, Lloyd & Blanc, 1996) although we have no way of measuring this using available household survey data. Statistics that capture and compare the extent of paternal absence or death over time in South Africa therefore need to be interpreted with considerable caution. The measure of absent fathers is likely to be a blunt and noisy reflection of the contact between fathers, or social fathers, and children. We might also expect underreporting of the number of children with deceased fathers, particularly in light of the stigma associated with HIV infection (see Jackson, 2002; Monk, 2002; Nyblade et al., 2003).

In Table 4, we present estimates of the presence of fathers of children aged 15 years and younger, using available household survey data for the period 1993 to 2002. Taking the data at face value, the proportion of children whose fathers were reported as either absent or dead increased from approximately 43 per cent in 1993 to 57 per cent in 2002. In 2002, less than half of the children in South Africa lived with their fathers.

Table 4 Presence of fathers of children (aged 15 years and younger), 1993–2002

	1993 (PSLSD)	1996 (OHS)	1998 (OHS)	2002 (GHS)
Number of children whose fathers are deceased	1 104 364	1 362 253	1 481 428	1 776 183
Percentage of all children with fathers deceased	7.5	9.2	9.5	11.5
Number of children with absent (living) fathers	5 292 568	6 140 479	–	7 073 041
Percentage of children with absent (living) fathers	36.0	41.6	–	45.8
Total number of children	14 720 825	14 759 509	15 579 324	14 434 928

Notes: In 1998, we can establish whether or not a child's 'own father' is still alive but not whether he is absent from the household. Although the 1998 DHS allows for estimates of paternal absence and death, the sampling frame – households containing at least one woman aged 15–49 years – may exclude relevant households, for example grandparent and orphan households; for this reason the DHS is not included in this series. In the GHS, two per cent of children are reported with fathers who are of unknown status. It seems probable that these fathers are either absent or deceased but we do not adjust our estimates of children accordingly.

The presence of fathers varied widely across population groups. Table 5 illustrates that African children were consistently and considerably more likely than other children to have fathers who were reported as absent or deceased. Furthermore, the increase in the proportion of children living without fathers between 1993 and 2002 was largest among African children. By 2002, less than 40 per cent of all African children aged 15 years or younger were reported as living with their fathers, compared to almost 90 per cent of white children. Differences in access to economic resources and services (particularly health services), and in rates of adolescent pregnancy, are likely to be important in accounting for disparities across groups. Higher levels of paternal absence among African children would also reflect greater labour migration to work or to find work among Africans, primarily in rural areas.[11]

Fathers of rural African children were the most likely to be reported as absent. In 2002, an estimated 55 per cent of rural African children had absent fathers; a further 12.5 per cent had fathers who were deceased (Table 6). A higher proportion of

African children living in urban areas, however, were paternal orphans. There is no clear explanation for this finding, and it is an area for future research. One possible explanation that could be explored is that when husbands or partners die, women move with their children to urban areas, perhaps to find employment.[12]

Table 5 Presence of fathers of children (aged 15 years and younger) by population group, 1993–2002 (percentages)

	1993 (PSLSD)	1996 (OHS)	1998 (OHS)	2002 (GHS)
African				
Deceased father	8.4	10.0	10.6	12.8
Absent (living) father	40.0	45.5	–	50.2
Indian				
Deceased father	1.7	4.8	3.1	5.0
Absent (living) father	10.6	16.6	–	8.4
Coloured				
Deceased father	5.6	7.3	5.3	7.4
Absent (living) father	31.1	34.3	–	37.2
White				
Deceased father	2.1	3.4	3.0	2.4
Absent (living) father	7.5	12.8	–	10.9

Table 6 Presence of fathers of African children (aged 15 years and younger), 1993–2002

	1993 (PSLSD)	1996 (OHS)	1998 (OHS)	2002 (GHS)
Rural				
Number of children with deceased fathers	755 000	821 593	928 597	971 218
Percentage of children with deceased fathers	8.6	10.6	11.3	12.5
Number of children with absent fathers	3 385 088	3 782 151	–	4 276 243
Percentage of children with absent fathers	38.4	49.0	–	55.0
Total number of children	8 817 864	7 726 371	8 252 513	7 776 734
Urban				
Number of children with deceased fathers	255 496	393 645	438 639	666 989
Percentage of children with deceased fathers	7.8	9.0	9.5	13.2
Number of children with absent fathers	1 431 872	1 722 800	–	2 165 451
Percentage of children with absent fathers	43.8	39.4	–	42.7
Total number of children	3 266 098	4 373 030	4 595 105	5 067 372

Figure 2 Presence of fathers of children (younger than 15 years) for selected African countries

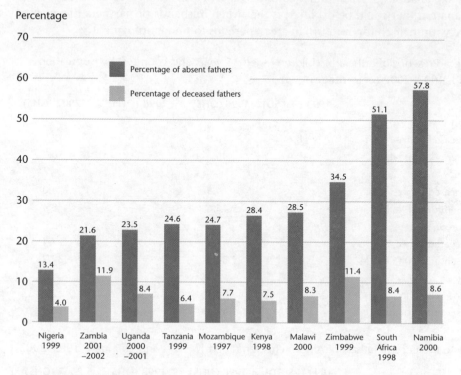

Note: The data are weighted.

Sources: MOHSS (Namibia), 2003, p. 12; Department of Health, South Africa, 1999, p. 11; CSO (Zimbabwe) & MI, 2000, p. 10; NSO (Malawi) & ORC Macro, 2001, p. 11; NCDP, CBS (Office of the Vice President and Ministry of Planning and National Development) (Kenya), & MI, 1999, p. 12; Gaspar et al., 1998, p. 18; NBS (Tanzania) & MI, 2000, p. 12; UBOS & ORC Macro, 2001, p. 12; CSO (Zambia), Central Board of Health (Zambia), & ORC Macro, 2003, p. 14; National Population Commission (Nigeria), 2000, p. 15.

In Figure 2, we compare estimates of children with absent and deceased fathers for South Africa with those for a range of other countries in the region. To facilitate inter-country comparisons, all statistics for this graph have been derived from country-specific DHSs.[13] Estimates of paternal absence[14] (specifically for children who live with women of reproductive age) range from approximately 13 per cent to 58 per cent. The measure obtained from the 1998 DHS in South Africa clearly falls in the upper tail of this distribution. In fact, if paternal absence in sub-Saharan Africa is viewed as 'substantial' (Greene & Biddlecom, 2000), then the estimate for South Africa is strikingly high.

Conclusion

There are currently no data available in South Africa with which we can count and describe all men who are fathers, or identify changes over time. But we can establish that very high and growing proportions of children, and particularly African children, do not live in households with their fathers. In fact, children are more likely *not to live* with their fathers than with them. In 2002, approximately 57 per cent of all children, and 63 per cent of African children specifically, were reported as having fathers who were 'absent' or deceased.

Estimates of children living with absent or deceased fathers may underestimate the presence of fathers in the lives of children. Absent fathers may continue to retain contact with their children, and may even remain non-resident members of the household in which their children live. Fathers who are reported as absent or deceased may also be substituted with social fathers or father figures in the household. Clearly more research, both qualitative and quantitative, is needed to probe further the nature of absence, to explore how and why fatherhood in South Africa is changing, and to investigate the implications of high and rising levels of paternal absence for the wellbeing of children.

Dorrit Posel is an Associate Professor in Economics at the University of KwaZulu-Natal. She studied Economics at the former University of Natal and at the University of Massachusetts, Amherst. Her research examines the economics of households and the movement of individuals between households and labour markets. Particular areas of interest include labour migration, labour force participation and intra-household resource allocation.

Richard Devey is a Research Fellow in the School of Development Studies, University of KwaZulu-Natal. He teaches research methods and specialises in quantitative research, including analysis of national household surveys. Current research interests include: measuring the relationship between changes in social and economic indicators and satisfaction levels of South Africans; definition and measurement of the informal economy; and measurement of fathers and mothers in South Africa. He is presently supervising projects on community-based conservation initiatives, and the definition and measurement of single mothers.

Notes

1   Thanks to Robert Morrell and Linda Richter for their valuable comments and support. We acknowledge permission to access data by the Southern African Labour and Development Research Unit (1993, PSLSD) and Statistics South Africa (1996 OHS; 1998 OHS; and 2002 GHS). The results presented in this chapter are based on our own data compilations and calculations.

2   The South African Constitution defines a child as an individual less than 18 years of age. In this chapter, we use a narrower definition, where an individual is not a child if he or she is eligible either to be a member of the labour force or to be measured for fertility characteristics.

3 See, for example, Section 10.2 of the PSLSD questionnaire and Section 2 of the 1998 OHS questionnaire.

4 See, for example, Section 2 of the 1999 OHS questionnaire.

5 In 1993, for example, less than 60 per cent of all women identified as mothers reported that they were married and that their spouse was part of the same household.

6 This information is collected in all the household surveys with the exception of the LFSs.

7 The 1993 PSLSD includes a far larger set of responses identifying relationships to household head than the 1998 OHS. For example, unlike the OHSs more generally, and the 1998 OHS specifically, the PSLSD includes possible responses of 'aunt/uncle' and 'niece/nephew'. Although this information could have been used to identify fathers in 1993, we omitted it from the calculations so as to make our measures for 1993 and 1998 comparable. Similarly, the PSLSD included 'mother-or-father-in-law' as a possible response, whereas the 1998 OHS included in-laws in the more general category of 'other relative'. Again for reasons of comparability, we excluded fathers-in-law from our estimate of fathers in 1993.

8 As we explain in more detail in the next section, the 1993 PSLSD uses a different definition of the household to the OHSs and the GHS. People can be identified as household members even if they have only spent 15 days of the previous year in the household. In the OHSs and GHS, people must have been 'normally' resident for at least four nights a week in the household in order to be included in the household. To make our estimates of fathers in 1993 and 1998 comparable, we restricted the PSLSD data to resident household members only. However, when non-resident household members (such as migrant workers) are included, the 1993 estimates of men who are fathers in Table 2 increase for men aged 15 to 54 years to 50.6 per cent (5,633,099 men), and for all men 15 years and older to 53.3 per cent (6,811,138 men).

9 The National Census, conducted every five years, is a further source of individual and household level data in the country. However the Census is equally deficient in providing information on how many, and which, men are fathers. Like the household surveys, the Census asks how many children, if any, have been born alive to women of reproductive age and also identifies the relationship to head of all household members, but there is no question identifying men as fathers.

10 Errors in our estimates of fathers are likely to vary across population groups. The overwhelming majority of labour migrants in South Africa are African; therefore measures that require men to be co-resident with their partners and children will under-count the number of fathers particularly in African households. We have therefore not provided disaggregated estimates of fathers by population group, although with comprehensive data, this clearly would be important to investigate.

11 Note that the increase in paternal absence from 1993 to 1996, when the definition of household membership changed, is particularly pronounced among African children living in rural areas.

12 In this regard, it is perhaps significant that the proportion of all African children who are living in urban areas has increased significantly over the period, from 27 per cent in 1993 to almost 40 per cent in 2002.

13 As noted earlier, the DHS sample only includes households that contain women age 15 to 49 years. DHS estimates for children with absent or deceased fathers therefore reflect a specific sample of children and may not be representative of all children in a country. For example, the DHS sample will exclude children who live only with fathers or men more generally. We might therefore expect that DHS statistics will overestimate paternal absence. This may help explain why the measure for paternal absence derived from the 1998 DHS in South Africa is somewhat higher than that derived from a nationally representative sample in 2002 (and reported in Table 4).

14 DHS questionnaires ask of all children in the household whether the child's natural father is alive, and if so, whether he lives in the household.

References

Bartfeld, J. (2000). Child support and the post-divorce economic well-being of mothers, fathers and children. *Demography, 37*, 203–213.

Central Statistical Office (Zambia), Central Board of Health (Zambia), and ORC Macro. (2003). *Zambia Demographic and Health Survey 2001–2002*. Calverton, Maryland, USA: Central Statistical Office, Central Board of Health, and ORC Macro.

Central Statistical Office (Zimbabwe) and Macro International Inc. (2000). *Zimbabwe Demographic and Health Survey 1999*. Calverton, Maryland, USA: Central Statistical Office and Macro International Inc.

Cherlin, A. J. (1999). Going to extremes: Family structure, children's well-being, and social science. *Demography, 36*, 421–428.

Cooksey, E. C., & Craig, P. H. (1998). Parenting from a distance: The effects of paternal characteristics on contact between nonresidential fathers and their children. *Demography, 35*, 187–200.

Department of Health, Medical Research Council (MRC), and Measure DHS+. (1999). *South African Demographic and Health Survey 1998*. Pretoria, South Africa and Calverton, Maryland, USA: Department of Health, Medical Research Council and Measure DHS+.

Gaspar, M. C., Cossa, H. A., Ribeiro dos Santos, C., Manjate, R. M., & Schoemaker, J. (1998). *Mozambique Demographic and Health Survey 1997*. Calverton, Maryland, USA: Instituto Nacional de Estatistica and Macro International Inc.

Greene, M. E., & Biddlecom, A. E. (2000). Absent and problematic men: Demographic accounts of male reproductive roles. *Population and Development Review, 26*, 81–115.

Jackson, H. (2002). *AIDS Africa*. Harare: SAfAIDS.

Kaufman, C. E., de Wet, T., & Stadler, J. (2001). Adolescent pregnancy and parenthood in South Africa. *Studies in Family Planning, 32*, 147–160.

Lloyd, C. B., & Blanc, A. K. (1996). Children's schooling in sub-Saharan Africa: The role of fathers, mothers and others. *Population and Development Review, 22*, 265–298.

Ministry of Health and Social Services (MOHSS) [Namibia]. (2003). *Namibia Demographic and Health Survey 2000*. Windhoek, Namibia: MOHSS.

Monk, N. (2002). Enumerating children orphaned by HIV/AIDS: Counting a human cost. *Discussion paper presented at the XIV International AIDS Conference, Barcelona, Spain, 7–12 July 2002*. Boston, MA: Francois-Xavier Bagnound Foundation. [Online] http://www.albinasactionfororphans.org/learn/inform.html (accessed 30 April 2004).

Morrell, R., Posel, D., & Devey, R. (2003). Counting fathers in South Africa: Issues of definition, methodology and policy. *Social Dynamics, 29*, 73–94.

Mott, F. L. (1990). When is a father really gone? Paternal–child contact in father-absent homes. *Demography, 27*, 499–517.

Moultrie, T. A., & Timaeus, I. M. (2003). The South African fertility decline: Evidence from two censuses and a demographic and health survey. *Population Studies, 57*, 265–283.

National Bureau of Statistics (Tanzania) and Macro International Inc. (2000). *Tanzania reproductive and child health survey 1999*. Calverton, Maryland, USA: National Bureau of Statistics and Macro International Inc.

National Council for Population and Development (NCPD), Central Bureau of Statistics (CBS) (Office of the Vice President and Ministry of Planning and National Development) (Kenya), & Macro International Inc (MI) (1999). *Kenya demographic and health survey 1998*. Calverton, Maryland, USA: NCPD, CBS, & MI.

National Population Commission (Nigeria). (2000). *Nigeria demographic and health survey 1999*. Calverton, Maryland, USA: National Population Commission & ORC/Macro.

National Statistical Office (Malawi), & ORC Macro. (2001). *Malawi demographic and health survey 2000*. Zomba, Malawi and Calverton, Maryland, USA: National Statistical Office & ORC Macro.

Nyamukapa, C. N, Foster, G. & Gregson, S. (2003). Orphans' household circumstances and access to education in a maturing HIV epidemic in eastern Zimbabwe. *Journal of Social Development in Africa, 18*, 7–32.

Nyblade, L., Pande, R., Mathur, S., MacQuarrie, K., Kidd, R., Banteyerga, H., Kidanu, A., Kilonzo, G., Mbwambo, J., & Bond, V. (2003). *Disentangling HIV and AIDS stigma in Ethiopia, Tanzania and Zambia*. Washington: International Center for Research on Women.

Posel, D. (2003). The collection of national household survey data in South Africa (1993–1999): Rendering labour migration invisible. *Development Southern Africa, 20*, 361–368.

Posel, D., & Casale, D. (2003). What has been happening to internal labour migration in South Africa, 1993–1999? *The South African Journal of Economics, 71*, 455–479.

Ratcliffe, A. A., Hill, A. G., Harrington, D. P., & Walraven, G. (2002). Reporting of fertility events by men and women in rural Gambia. *Demography, 39*, 573–586.

Rendall, M. S., Clarke, L., Peters, H. E., Ranjit, N., & Verropoulou, G. (1999). Incomplete reporting of men's fertility in the United States and Britain: A research note. *Demography, 36*, 135–144.

Uganda Bureau of Statistics (UBOS) & ORC Macro. (2001). *Uganda Demographic and Health Survey 2000–2001*. Calverton, Maryland, USA: UBOS and ORC Macro.

CHAPTER 5

The importance of fathering for children

Linda Richter

> An important question that has not been resolved is whether men's
> contribution in families has a unique aspect to it. Are gender differences
> in parenting a matter of culture, choice and preference or of innate skill
> and inherited propensity? Is there a mother template to which fathers
> must measure up? Or, is there a parent template that both parents must
> achieve if effective parenting is to occur? Of course, the third possibility
> is that there is a mother template for parenting and a father template.
> This question can only be answered with careful and systematic
> research. (Day, 1998, p. 28)

It is clear that there is a worldwide change occurring in the way men's roles in the family and the care of children are conceived (Brown & Barker, 2004). Partly this emanates from the politics and scholarship of identity, partly it is prompted by the changing nature of employment associated with post-industrial economics and globalisation, as well as by changes in the nature and composition of families (Lupton & Barclay, 1997). For example, female-headed households are increasing all over the world. However, another driver of the growing attention given to men's relationships to the home and family is the increasing importance attached to children, both economically, because it is a critical period for the development of human and social capital, and emotionally. Declining fertility and family size has been accompanied by the creation, and even re-creation, of *the child* and *childhood* as a life-stage with particular needs and conditions (James, Jenks & Prout, 1998; Zelizer, 1994). Very widespread increases in father absence have elevated fathers 'from relative obscurity to a central position in efforts to understand and promote children's well-being. New types of fathers are being acknowledged – in step-, recombined and cohabiting families. All of these family types call for men – even those not biologically related – to increase their involvement in the lives of children' (Tamis-LeMonda & Cabrera, 1999, p. 3). Marsiglio observes that changing concepts of fathers, and the implications for children, are currently embedded in a debate 'fueled by the diverse interests of those associated with the feminist movements, men's rights organisations, gay/lesbian associations, and the new right' (1995a, p. 20). To this list one needs to add advocates for children.

In understanding these changes, and in thinking about interventions to promote the wellbeing of children, some key questions attend the role and importance in children's development of maternal and paternal behaviour, as opposed to a more

general category of parental behaviour. These include the following. Do children need the care of a mother (a woman) and/or a father (a man)? Is it best that these people are specifically the child's biological progenitors? Or do children simply need appropriate parental behaviour? Can parental behaviour be provided by any devoted adults, or, given the importance of stability for children, is childcare best provided by adults connected to one another by emotional and social ties and obligations – that is, a partnership? Do the gendered roles of fathers and mothers in most societies create conditions in which both mothering and, in particular, fathering bestows particular benefits on children?

In this chapter, I review the evidence that attests to the importance of fathers in the lives of children. In the course of the review, attention is drawn to problems with the evidence, particularly the fact that most research has been conducted in the west (Engle & Breaux, 1998; Nsamenang, 1997; Townsend, 2002). Almost no research on fathering has been conducted in South Africa. In addition, almost all the data have been collected from stable nuclear families despite our knowledge that this family form is not normative anywhere in the world (Coontz, 2000). In reality, in South Africa and elsewhere, there is a wide range of fathering relationships, varying from residential biological fathers married to a child's mother, to concerned teachers who take an interest in and encourage children (Mkhize, 2004). For this reason, the term *social fatherhood* has emerged to describe the many ways in which a child can be connected to an adult male, including legal ties and ties based on the emotional connection between them (Day, 1998; Marsiglio & Day, 1997). As Bachrach and Sonenstein (1998) point out: 'men are now more likely than ever to live separately from their children and to father outside marriage. Many men experience fatherhood as a sequence of relationships with children, some biologically theirs and some the children of spouses or partners' (1998, p. 1). As a result of these changes, we have to renew our images of who fathers are and what they do, incorporating as we do so the increasing diversity of fatherhood.

Fathering

It is generally acknowledged that our knowledge of parenting has been constructed from what is called the 'maternal template', or a view of parenting determined by what mothers usually do for children (Marsiglio, Amato, & Day, 2000). By the same token, justification for the importance of fathering is frequently advanced on the basis of a deficit model of single female parenting, and the adverse effects of father absence – for example, findings that single mothers are less authoritative and provide less discipline and supervision to their children than married parents (Steinberg, 1987), and that single mothers have restricted social networks in comparison to two-parent families (Cochran, Larner, Riley, Gunnarsson, & Henderson, 1990).

Fathers can provide for and be involved with their children in many different ways, and there are cultural, social and individual differences in how fatherhood is defined and expressed. Several authors emphasise the fact that fathers' contributions go beyond hands-on care of children. 'As such, we take into account the resources fathers can provide for their children, including human capital (e.g., skills, knowledge, and traits that foster achievement in US society), financial capital (e.g., money, income and experiences purchased with income), and social capital (e.g., family and community relations that benefit children's cognitive and social development)' (Marsiglio & Day, 1997; p. 2).

What is clear is that men in the role of fathers can have both direct and indirect effects on children's development and adjustments. For example, it is almost universally true that two-parent households, where fathers are present, are better off than single-mother households (Jarrett, 1994). Not only are men generally better paid than women, and therefore bring more income into a household if they are employed, but they may also be able to access more resources for children in the community because of their prestige and status as men. This creates the difficulty of distinguishing between effects on children due to socio-economic status and effects due to family structure. Nonetheless, the conclusion has been reached that the presence of the father's income tends to be associated with improved child status and that female-headed households with children are poorer (Engle & Breaux, 1998). On the basis of an ethnographic study in Botswana, Townsend concluded that 'Children are not necessarily disadvantaged by the absence of their father, but they are disadvantaged when they belong to a household without access to the social position, labour and financial support that is provided by men' (2002, p. 270).

Despite the importance of men's financial contribution, children are not invariably better off in male-headed households, as men's decisions about income distribution do not always benefit children (Kennedy & Peters, 1992). Nonetheless, fathers' economic provision for children goes beyond the mere supply of funds, but is also linked to symbolic aspects of power and status, values relating to work, and connections to the wider community (Marsiglio & Day, 1997). Marsiglio and Day also argue that 'Financial capital, distributed in the context of a caring and appropriately supervised parent/child relationship, may be substantially more effective in reducing the effects of lower education, poverty and higher crime rates than the dispersing of money only' (1997, p. 18).

Beyond money, there are indications that children who live with their fathers or with the male partners of their mothers may be better protected than children who live in single women-headed households (Dubowitz, Black, Kerr, Starr, & Harrington, 2000; Guma & Henda, 2004). The mere fact of having a father who acknowledges and lives with a child may confer social value on children, especially in societies such as South Africa, where close to 60 per cent of children do not live with their fathers (Budlender, 1998). Of course, male presence in households also has costs. Domestic violence rates, which affect children significantly, vary between 20 and 60 per cent around the world (Heise, Pitanguy & Germain, 1994). Nonetheless, 'Fiscal support and the fulfillment of the provider role by males have the typical effect of lifting children out of or preventing their descent into poverty. Buffering the poverty experience can increase the life chances of children irrespective of ethnicity or class' (Johnson, 1997, p. 10). A study of Xhosa secondary school students' reports about parental behaviour found that resident genetic fathers spent proportionately more money on their children, and spent more time with them than other categories of fathers. However, resident step-fathers spent more money and time on the children of their current partner than genetic fathers who had never lived with their children or lived with them for only a short period of time. This finding demonstrates how very important men's proximity to children is for their care of them as is the strength and proximity of men's relationships with the mother of a child (Anderson, Kaplan, Lam, & Lancaster, 1999).

Another way in which fathering can affect children's behaviour and development is through men's impact on mothers. For example, women who live with partners report being less stressed about childcare issues. In addition, children in single-parent homes have more domestic and other responsibilities at an earlier age, presumably to compensate for the domestic work that an additional parent might provide (McLoyd et al., 1994). In addition, an absent father is not available to compensate for inappropriately neglectful or punitive maternal behaviour. The results of Anderson et al's study in South Africa (1999) suggests that men's investment in children might be primarily a strategy to improve their relationship with the mother of the children, which indicates the potential importance of men's investment in children for their mother.

Particular father roles and types of father involvement can be discerned from the increasing literature on fathering (Lamb, 1997). Researchers have looked at, amongst others:
- How much time men spend doing childcare tasks;
- What kind of childcare and domestic activities men take on;
- In what way fathering behaviour differs from mothering behaviour; and
- What differential effects fathers and mothers have on children's behaviour (Clarke-Stewart, 1978).

Time

The amount of time men spend in childcare approximates notions of 'mothering', and it is in this area that men are frequently portrayed as 'deficient women' (Brown & Barker, 2004). In most parts of the world, men spend considerably less time with children and in childcare activities than women (Population Council, 2001). Results from the South African Time Use Survey show that men spend less than a tenth of the time, compared to women, performing childcare tasks for children under seven years of age (Budlender, Chobokoane & Mpetsheni, 2001). It needs to be borne in mind that the amount of time men spend in childcare does not necessarily reflect the influence or interest men have in their children's lives, particularly if they make important decisions about a child, such as their access to schooling or health care. In addition, there are important race, culture and class differences regarding the time men spend in childcare.

Michael Lamb and his colleagues refined the simple *hours spent* approach to looking at men's involvement and care of children by proposing the following categories of fathering behaviour: engagement (that is, interaction between father and child), accessibility or availability, and responsibility for the child's care (Lamb, Pleck, Charnov & Levine, 1985). However, in addition to any particular activities in which fathers may engage, there is widespread agreement that there are many ways in which a father's influence may be felt when he is present; chiefly, that his children may benefit from the economic and social resources that he controls or to which he has access (Anderson et al., 1999; Day, 1998).

Childcare and domestic activities

In many societies, the father's role is traditionally defined as breadwinner or provider. It is no surprise then that men are generally found to have lower levels of engagement in childcare tasks, especially for young children (Lewis & Lamb, 2004). A summary of early ethnographic studies of 186 cultures conducted a long time ago found that in fewer than 5 per cent of cultures did men regularly care for preschool children, although fathers in nearly half the cultures surveyed were often in close proximity to their children (Barry & Paxson, 1971). This pattern is true also in South Africa. A recent study of time-use by men and women showed that of those parents who had children under the age of seven years who were living with them, women spent an average of 87 minutes a day in active childcare (washing, dressing and so on) compared to seven minutes a day spent by men doing the same category of tasks (Budlender, Chobokoane & Mpetsheni, 2001). In many studies, the largest discrepancy between maternal and paternal involvement is found on the 'responsibility' dimension of childcare – planning, anticipation, enactment, and follow-up on children's needs, with findings suggesting that fathers assume almost no responsibility, as defined by Lamb et al. (1985), for their children's care. Although men's proportional share of childcare rises when their female partners work, the data suggests that this is not because men are doing more; rather, that women are doing less (Pleck, 1997).

Urbanisation, changing patterns of employment and work by men and women, and attitudinal shifts in gender, are altering these patterns and more men are performing household tasks and taking responsibility for childcare (Tamis-LeMonda & Cabrera,

1999). For example, in 1993 in the United States, more than 1.6 million pre-schoolers were cared for by their fathers while their mothers were at work. Men are more likely to provide care when family income is low and when there is no overlap of maternal and paternal work schedules (Casper & O'Connell, 1998). Called the 'availability hypothesis', this data suggest that the more time a father has to care for his children, the more likely he is to do so (Levine & Pittinsky, 1997). Informal observations in South Africa indicate that men are increasingly attending health centres with children who require immunisation or health care, walking children to and from school, and providing care at home because their female partners are employed, often with non-standard hours of work. Young men are also heard to voice the opinion that they would like to be more involved in their children's lives, and more than 70 per cent of a representative sample of South Africans between 18 and 35 years of age, male and female, defined adulthood as a state in which a person was able to look after and care for his or her children (Emmett, Richter & Makiwane, 2004).

Fathering behaviour

Infants tend to show a maternal preference in the early months of life, whether or not their fathers are engaged in childcare. In these early years, fathers are largely seen as mothers' helpers. Nonetheless, children show strong attachment to their fathers by the end of their first year of life (Cox, Owen & Henderson, 1992). Many studies have found that fathers play more with their toddlers and preschool children than do mothers, that children prefer to play with fathers, and that mothers' talk to and play with children is attenuated when fathers are present (Clarke-Stewart, 1978; Kazura, 2000).

Although there are reports that men in Southern Africa don't engage in intimate interaction with their young children and are surprised that they might be expected to do so (van Leer 1992, in Engle & Breaux, 1998), Wilson (Chapter 3, this volume) and the photographs assembled for the Human Sciences Research Council's Fatherhood Project attest to the fact that some African men do indeed spend time in caring engagement with younger and older children. I have argued elsewhere that notions of propriety in public behaviour and attempts to discern researchers' intentions and to respond in appropriate ways, may obscure aspects of African mother-child and, it seems, father-child interaction from observers (Richter, 1995).

As children grow older, paternal engagement with children declines, especially for girls (Lewis & Lamb, 2004), and other aspects of fathering come to the fore, particularly moral and ethical socialisation, and transitions to independence and autonomy. Another traditional role of fathers is to enforce rules and boundaries and administer discipline (Marsiglio & Day, 1997). Despite the harshness associated with the latter function, recent research indicates that positive child and adolescent outcomes are associated with paternal relationships characterised by closeness, mutuality and support (Baltes & Silverberg, 1994). Material from South African biographies, such as that of Malegapuru Makgoba (1997), is consistent with this empirical work.

Differential effects

There is some evidence that fathers affect children's behaviour and development through their effect on maternal behaviour, rather than directly, at least in the early years of life (Clarke-Stewart, 1978). Certainly, the interdependence between maternal and paternal behaviour makes it difficult to isolate effects that are directly or solely attributable to fathers. In addition, there are cultural differences in the amount of contact that residential and non-residential fathers have with their children. For example, it has been found that Latino and African-American fathers in the United States usually maintain contact with their non-residential children because of generally close family ties (Johnson, 1997). A similar situation might exist in South Africa amongst absent African fathers, who also have very close family ties. Nonetheless, there is a very substantial literature to indicate that:

- Father presence contributes to cognitive development, intellectual functioning and school achievement (Amato, 1998; Johnson, 1997). For example, in South Africa, Mboya & Nesengani (1999) found that boys who lived in father-present households had higher academic achievement than boys who lived in father-absent households. The paternal investment study of Anderson et al. (1999) showed that residential fathers, genetic and step-fathers were more likely to spend time with children helping with homework or talking English than non-resident genetic fathers.
- Father presence also contributes to emotional well-being (Johnson, 1997). Children in father-absent households are more likely to experience emotional disturbances and depression, although these effects may be confounded by socio-economic conditions and maternal stress. Father presence shows a strong relationship with higher self-esteem amongst girls (Hunt & Hunt, 1977), low levels of sexual risk behaviour, and fewer difficulties in forming and maintaining romantic relationships. Girls reared in single-mother homes are more likely to have an early pregnancy, a birth outside of marriage, early marriage, and an increased likelihood of divorce (McLanahan & Bumpass, 1988).
- Father absence or lack of contact with fathers appears to have its most dramatic effects on male children (Johnson, 1997; Mott, 1994), particularly on their social competence, behaviour control and school success. Although the literature is inconclusive, sons of resident fathers are more likely than sons of non-resident fathers to adopt masculine behaviours and attitudes, at least with respect to play and toy preferences. In contrast, sons of non-resident fathers are more likely to engage in stereotypically masculine behaviours, including aggression (Johnson, 1997). Father availability tends to have a modulating

effect on boys' aggressive tendencies by providing a model of culturally appropriate male behaviour. In the same way, boys in father-absent families engage in what has been called compensatory identification with hypermasculinity (Seltzer & Bianchi, 1988).

Recent research on fathering has moved beyond a family structure approach – residential versus non-residential fathers, fathers who have contact with their children and fathers who don't have contact with their children – to an emphasis on the quality of father care and relationships. This includes father behaviours and attitudes, parent relationships, and father-child interaction (Johnson, 1997; Lamb, 1987). This literature, on availability and involvement of fathers, is highly consistent with respect to showing benefits for children in school performance, reduced aggressive behaviours in boys and increased self-esteem in girls (Palkowitz, 2002). Some studies suggest that it is fathers' psychological care and 'emotional generosity' (expressiveness and intimacy) that has the greatest long-term implications for children's development (Grossman, Pollack & Golding, 1988).

What is unique about fathers or men?

Despite generally positive correlations between father involvement and child outcomes, it remains unclear whether these are father-specific effects or effects arising from socio-economic influences and/or multiple as opposed to single parenting. Decades of research on parenting has led to the conclusion that, at least in western cultures, 'authoritative' parenting (the appropriate combination of warmth and control) predicts higher levels of competence in children, including school achievement, self-esteem and social competence, and lower levels of emotional and behavioural problems (Baumrind, 1991). There is little in the research that indicates gender differences in the effects of this kind of parenting on children.

Frey (2003), a strong advocate of men's involvement with their children, argues that 'the contribution males can and should make to their children's development is precisely the same contribution that females make to their children's development, which is the daily ongoing care and nurturing of a human life' (p. 56). In his view, it isn't necessary to carve out a unique role for fathering, despite the empirical evidence of its benefits.

Although it is claimed that stepfathers, nonresidential fathers, kin and others can successfully fulfil the affective and regulatory roles of fathering in single-mother households, there is not very much evidence to support this view. This is not because the evidence is against this view, but rather because studies that have included non-residential fathers have tended to limit their analyses to issues such as maintenance payments and visitation schedules, and have not examined more detailed relation-ship qualities necessary to testing the claim (King, 1994). Some support for this assertion comes from studies that use a broad definition of fatherhood that allows children to nominate a father-figure. For example, Zimmerman et al. (1995) found that better quality relationships with, and emotional support from, fathers or father-figures predicted higher self-esteem, lower depression and anxiety, and lower rates of delinquent behaviour among poor black adolescent boys in the United States. Similar findings by Coley (1998) and others have led to the conclusion that policies should encourage divorced, never-married fathers and step-fathers to play significant roles in the lives of their children, particularly when fathers are absent, as non-parental men can have positive influences on children. What data is available in South Africa, for example the Anderson et al. paternal time and money investment study (1999), supports this recommendation.

What promotes father involvement in children's lives?

Does the biological fact of having sired a child prompt a father to involve himself in a child's life? Explanations with roots in evolutionary thinking account for biological fathers' investment in their children in terms of mating effort (Trivers, 1972). However, 'new family structures challenge the notion that biological relatedness fully explains fathers' investment of time and effort in children. Some biological fathers can be quite indifferent to their children, while some stepfathers, or other father figures, can be extremely involved' (Tamis-LeMonda & Cabrera, 1999, p. 7). While the interactions are very complex, co-residence is certainly a strong determinant of supportive fathering (Anderson, et al., 1999; Rangaranjan & Gleason, 1998). In addition, it is fathers' active participation in children's lives that makes a difference to child outcomes, rather than simply contact or amount of contact (Tamis-LeMonda & Cabrera, 1999). Nonetheless, biological connectedness, as well as the strength of the father archetype (see Chapter 10, this volume), make for strong motivations on the part of children and fathers to be involved with one another, provided all other supportive conditions are in place.

Specific factors that have been found to be associated with paternal involvement are:
*   Contextual factors, most specifically socio-economic status, which affects fathers' ability to provide adequate child support and may also affect men's relationships, and co-residence with their partners and their children (Tamis-LeMonda & Cabrera, 1999, and Chapter 18, this volume). In South Africa, socio-economic status has a significant overlap with race, and this gives rise to racial patterns of fathering behaviour. An additional contextual factor is age. Young fathers experience significant challenges in trying to support their children, and the fact that many of them don't live with their children is also a barrier to maintaining contact and increasing their involvement with their children (Cutrona, Hessling, Bacon & Russell, 1998). Young fatherhood is generally under-reported, but 10 per cent of South African men under 25 years of age in a national survey reported they had fathered a child (Emmett et al., 2004).

- Expectations about fatherhood, including whether a pregnancy was intended (Henshaw, 1998), affect paternal involvement. In general, though, little is known about how males develop a perception of fatherhood, their status as fathers, and the roles associated with being a father (Marsiglio, 1995a).
- Family of origin, including high levels of participation in his upbringing by a man's own father, encourages paternal engagement (Cowan & Cowan, 1987). While it is true that some men are motivated to emulate the behaviour of their fathers, others want to be better fathers than the ones they had (Daly, 1995).
- A healthy relationship with the child's mother has been found to increase involvement with children, as well as positive attitudes towards children and the role of parent (Furstenberg & Harris, 1993). Mothers' attitudes and views about father involvement strongly determine whether they encourage and support male caregiving, as well as men's satisfaction with the paternal role (DeLucci, 1995; Lewis & Lamb, 2004; Pleck, 1997).

On a personal level, the main reasons men become social fathers include the desire for the experience of caring for and raising children, opportunities to strengthen the bond with their romantic partner, to prevent loneliness or financial vulnerability in their older years, and to feel more connected to extended family and friends (Coney & Mackey, 1997). In addition to these factors, the lack of public policies, such as the exclusion of men from health care preparation for childbirth and childcare and education, as well as child support laws which are not linked to visitation rights, may be disincentives for men to be more involved in the care of their children (Daly, 1995; Parke & Brott, 1999).

Generative fathering

Erik Erikson (1963) proposed that three psychosocial strengths – hope, fidelity and care – must be achieved to become a healthy, functional person, and that these strengths correspond to the developmental challenges of the three major life phases – childhood, adolescence and adulthood. Trust and hope need to be acquired in childhood as a consequence of experiencing stable and caring childrearing; fidelity, or a sense of faith in oneself need to be acquired in adolescence with the forging of identity; and care, or generativity, needs to be acquired in adulthood. Generativity is defined as the desire to establish and nurture young people. Erikson believed that this was a fundamental motivation to make the world a better place in which the next generation can live. From this perspective, men's involvement in the care of children is not only important because it is good for children and in the interest of gender justice, it is also an important step in men's personal growth (Daly, 1995; Snarey, 1993).

A respondent in one study described the motivation to care in the following way: 'You feel like you are gifted by having a child, taking care of somebody and being responsible for their growth and development. It was just something I looked forward to…someone being dependent on me, someone to share life with, to take care of – that was my need, too (Gerson, 1993, quoted in Marsiglio, 1995b, p. 84).

This expanded conceptualisation of men's involvement with children moves away from deficit models of what men don't do at home and what goes wrong when they aren't present (Palkowitz, 1997). Men frequently report that fathering is good for them, and evidence supports this contention. Levine and Pitt (1995) cite an outreach programme for fathers, established in 1982 in Cleveland, that demonstrates that fostering the commitment of low-income fathers to their children is a strong incentive for men to develop themselves and to increase their community involvement (Marsiglio & Day, 1997). Young South Africans also define adulthood in terms of their capacity to care for and support children (Emmett et al., 2004).

Conclusion

Men's family roles have generally resisted change and, despite changes, fatherhood remains narrowly defined as providing, protecting and sometimes disciplining children (Brown & Barker 2004). Nonetheless, men are definitely more active in their children's lives than has previously been assumed and many men say they want to be more involved in the lives of their children. The experience of taking the HSRC's Fatherhood Project Photographic Exhibition around South Africa has brought to light the many organisations involved in changing men's behaviour and promoting positive fatherhood (see Chapter 22, this volume). We have also had conversations with, and received letters from, countless men who say that father-hood is important to them, who are very involved with their children, who missed the care and protection they wanted from their own fathers, and/or who are trying to be better fathers to their own children.

Many South African men are absent from the lives of their children. The reasons for this are complex. Migrant labour, restrictions on the movement and residence of people, disabling housing policies, poverty, lack of income, compensatory masculinities and survival strategies adopted by single mothers are among them. 'Desertion by fathers', says Mamphela Ramphele, 'is often prompted by their inability to bear the burden of being primary providers. The burden of failure becomes intolerable for those who lack the capacity to generate enough income as uneducated and unskilled labourers. Desertion is not always physical, it can also be emotional. Many men "die" as parents and husbands by indulging in alcohol, drugs or becoming unresponsive to their families' (2002, p. 158; see also Chapter 6, this volume). Despite widespread father absence and neglect, we should not make the mistake of underestimating the actual and potential contribution, interest, and impact of non-resident and low-income or unemployed fathers and, in doing so, marginalise them further (Brown & Barker, 2004; Tamis-LeMonda & Cabrera,

1999). Research is needed to understand men's perspectives, as well as those of women and children.

There is no doubt that, in South Africa, negative images of fathers, especially of black men, are pervasive (Richter, Manegold, Pather & Mason, 2004). As in the United States, stereotypes abound of 'hypermasculine males who are financially irresponsible and uninvolved in their children's lives' (Marsiglio, 1995a, p. 5). These images need to be countered while, simultaneously, responsible fatherhood and men's sensitivity to children's needs in both the public and the private realms needs to increase. The concept needs to be fostered that increasing men's exposure to children, and encouraging their involvement in the care of children, may facilitate their own growth, bring them happiness and gratification, and foster a more nurturing orientation in general (Marsiglio, 1995b). 'Ideas of what it means to be a father are formed long before men become parents' (Furstenberg, 1995, p. 128; see also Chapter 10, this volume). If we treat men as if they don't want to be, and aren't capable of being, good fathers, we will stumble on the first step of what is going to be a steep climb. We need to recognise that fathers and men in families represent one of the most important – yet in many cases untapped – resources for children's well-being. Children in difficult circumstances, including poverty and economic stress, may depend even more on good parenting, including good fathering, than those in more comfortable circumstances.

> Fathers make important contributions to child development, and in turn, the experience of fathering may make important contributions to adult development. (Roggman, Fitzgerald, Bradley & Raikes, 2002)

Biological fathers have particular bonds with their children that may come from biology, family culture and social norms. This relationship has the potential to be both supportive and destructive for children. However, a large number of South African children do not have a meaningful or constructive relationship with their biological fathers for the many reasons outlined in this book, for example in Chapters 3, 6, 8, 21 and others. For this reason, it is very important that men be encouraged and supported to be fathers to, as well as fathers of, children – that they develop caring relationships with young people wherever they encounter them. In recognising the needs of the child within themselves, men can be prompted to care for their own children as well as those of others.

Linda Richter is the Executive Director of the Child, Youth and Family Development Research Programme at the Human Sciences Research Council. She also holds honorary appointments at the Universities of KwaZulu-Natal, Witwatersrand, and Melbourne, Australia. Linda was trained as a clinical developmental psychologist but has worked in research environments for most of her career, investigating issues of risk and resilience in children, youth and families. She is co-author of *Mandela's Children: Growing up in Post-Apartheid South Africa* (New York: Routledge, 2001) and joint editor of *The Sexual Abuse of Young Children in Southern Africa* (Cape Town: HSRC Press, 2004).

References

Amato, P. (1998). More than money? Men's contributions to their children's lives. In A. Booth & A. Crouter (Eds.), *Men in families. When do they get involved? What difference do they make?* (pp. 241–277). Mahwah, NJ: Lawrence Erlbaum Associates.

Anderson, K., Kaplan, H., Lam, D., & Lancaster, J. (1999). Parental care by genetic fathers and stepfathers II: Reports by Xhosa high school students. *Evolution and Human Behavior, 20,* 433–451.

Bachrach, C., & Sonenstein, F. (1998). Male fertility and family formation: Research and data needs on the pathways to fatherhood. Chapter 3 of Nurturing Fatherhood: Improving data and research on male fertility, family formation and fatherhood. Report on the Conference on Fathering and Male Fertility. http://aspe.os.dhhs.gov/fathers/cfsforum/c3.htm (accessed 15 September 2004).

Baltes, M., & Silverberg, S. (1994). The dynamics between dependency and autonomy: Illustrations across the life span. In D. Featherman, R. Lerner, & M. Perlmutter (Eds.), *Life-span development and behavior* (*Vol. 12,* pp. 41–90). Hillsdale, NJ: Erlbaum.

Barry, H., & Paxson, L. (1971). Infancy and early childhood: Cross-cultural codes 2. *Ethnology, 10,* 466–508.

Baumrind, D. (1991). Parenting styles and adolescent development. In J. Brooks, R. Lerner & A. Peterson (Eds.), *The encyclopedia on adolescence* (pp. 758–772). New York: Garland.

Brown, J., & Barker, G. (2004). Global diversity and trends in patterns of fatherhood. In *Supporting fathers: Contributions from the International Fatherhood Summit 2003* (pp. 17–43). The Hague: Bernard van Leer Foundation.

Budlender, D. (1998). *Women and men in South Africa.* Pretoria: Central Statistical Services.

Budlender, D., Chobokoane, N., & Mpetsheni, Y. (2001). *A survey of time use: How South African women and men spend their time.* Pretoria: Statistics South Africa. http://www.statssa.gov.za (accessed April 2004).

Cabrera, N. (1999). Perspectives on father involvement: Research and policy. *Society for Research in Child Development Social Policy Report, 13,* 1–26.

Casper, L., & O'Connell, M. (1998). Work, income, the economy, and married fathers as childcare providers. *Demography, 35,* 243–250.

Clarke-Stewart, K. (1978). And daddy makes three: The father's impact on mother and young child. *Child Development, 49,* 466–478.

Cochran, M., Larner, M., Riley, D., Gunnarsson, L., & Henderson, C. (1990). *Extending families: The social networks of parents and their children.* New York: Cambridge University Press.

Coley, R. (1998). Children's socialization experiences and functioning in single-mother households: The importance of fathers and other men. *Child Development, 69,* 219–230.

Coney, N., & Mackey, W. (1997). Motivations towards fathering: Two minority profiles with the majority's context. *Journal of Men's Studies, 4,* 341–353.

Coontz, S. (2000). Historical perspectives on family studies. *Journal of Marriage and Family*, *62*, 283–297.

Cowan, C., & Cowan, P. (1987). Men's involvement in parenthood: Identifying the antecedents and understanding the barriers. In P. Berman, P. Pedersen & E. Pedersen (Eds.), *Men's transitions to parenthood: Longitudinal studies of early family experience* (pp. 145–174). Hillsdale, NJ: Erlbaum.

Cox, M., Owen, M., & Henderson, V. (1992). Prediction of infant–father and infant–mother attachment. *Developmental Psychology*, *28*, 474–483.

Cutrona, C., Hessling, P., Bacon, P., & Russell, D. (1998). Predictors and correlates of continuing involvement with the baby's father among adolescent mothers. *Journal of Family Psychology*, *12*, 369–387.

Daly, K. (1995). Reshaping fatherhood: Finding the models. In W. Marsiglio (Ed.), *Fatherhood: Contemporary theory, research, and social policy* (pp. 21–40). Thousand Oaks, CA: Sage.

Day, R. (1998). *Social fatherhood: Conceptualizations, compelling research and future directions*. Philadelphia, PA: National Center on Fathers and Families.

DeLuccie, M. (1995). Mothers as gatekeepers: A model of maternal mediators of father involvement. *Journal of Genetic Psychology*, *156*, 115–131.

Dubowitz, H. M., Black, M., Kerr, M. A., Starr, R. H., & Harrington, D. (2000). Fathers and child neglect. *Archives of Pediatrics and Adolescent Medicine*, *154*, 56–70.

Ehrenheich, B. (1983). *The hearts of men: American dreams and the flight from commitment*. New York: Anchor.

Emmett, T., Richter, L., Makiwane, M., et al. (2004). *The status of the youth report*. Johannesburg: Umsobomvu Youth Fund.

Engle, P., & Breaux, C. (1998). Fathers' involvement with children: Perspectives from developing countries. *Society for Research in Child Development Social Policy Report*, *12*, 1–23.

Erikson, E. (1963). *Childhood and society*. Toronto: Norton.

Frey, R. (2003). Fathers: Important, unique or uniquely important? In R. Sullivan (Ed.), *Focus on fathering*. Melbourne, Australia: ACER Press.

Furstenberg, F. (1995) Fathering in the inner city: Paternal participation and public policy. In W. Marsiglio (Ed.), *Fatherhood: Contemporary theory, research, and social policy* (pp. 119–147). Thousand Oaks, CA: Sage

Furstenberg, F., & Harris, K. (1993). When and why fathers matter: Impacts of father involvement in the children of adolescent mothers. In R. Lerman & T. Ooms (Eds.), *Young unwed fathers: Changing roles and emerging policies* (pp. 117–138). Philadelphia: Temple University Press.

Grossman, F., Pollack, W., & Golding, E. (1988). Fathers and children: Predicting the quality and quantity of fathering. *Developmental Psychology*, *24*, 82–91.

Guma, M., & Henda, N. (2004). The socio-cultural context of child abuse: A betrayal of trust. In L. Richter, A. Dawes & C. Higson-Smith (Eds.), *Sexual abuse of young children in southern Africa* (pp. 95–109). Cape Town: HSRC Press.

Heise, L., Pitanguy, J., & Germain, A. (1994). *Violence against women: The hidden health burden.* World Bank Discussion Paper 255. Washington, DC: World Bank.

Henshaw, S. (1998). Unintended pregnancy in the United States. *Family Planning Perspectives*, *30*, 24–29.

Hunt, L., & Hunt, J. (1977). Race, daughters and father loss: Does absence make the girl grow stronger? *Social Problems*, *25*, 90–102.

James, A., Jenks, C., & Prout, J. (1998). *Theorizing childhood.* Cambridge: Polity Press.

Jarrett, R. (1994). Living poor: Family life among single-parent, African-American women. *Social Problems*, *41*, 30–49.

Johnson D. J. (1997). Fathers' presence matters: A review of literature. NCOFF Review

http://fatherfamilylink.gse.upenn.edu/org/ncoff/litrev/fpmlr.htm (last accessed April 2004).

Kazura, K. (2000). Fathers' qualitative and quantitative involvement: An investigation of attachment, play, and social interactions. *Journal of Men's Studies*, *9*, 41–45.

Kennedy, E., & Peters, P. (1992). Influence of gender and head of household on food security, health and nutrition. *World Development*, *20*, 1077–1085.

King, V. (1994). Nonresident father involvement and child wellbeing: Can dads make a difference? *Journal of Family Issues*, *15*, 78–96.

Lamb, M. (1987) (Ed.), *The father's role: Cross-cultural perspectives.* New Jersey: Lawrence Erlbaum.

Lamb, M. (1997). Fathers and child development. In M. Lamb (Ed.), *The role of the father in child development* (3rd ed., pp. 1–18). New York: Wiley.

Lamb, M., Pleck, J., Charnov, E., & Levine, J. (1985). Paternal behavior in humans. *American Psychologist*, *25*, 883–894.

Levine, J., & Pitt, E. (1995). *New expectations: Community strategies for responsible fatherhood.* New York: Work and Families Institute.

Levine, J., & Pittinsky, T. (1997). *Working fathers: New strategies for balancing work and family.* Reading, MA: Addison-Wesley.

Lewis, C., & Lamb, M. (2004). Fathers: The research perspective. In *Supporting fathers: Contributions from the International Fatherhood Summit 2003* (pp. 44–77). The Hague: Bernard van Leer Foundation.

Lupton, D., & Barclay, L. (1997). *Constructing fatherhood: Discourses and experiences.* London: Sage.

Makgoba, M. (1997). *Mokoko: The Makgoba affair. A reflection on transformation.* Johannesburg: Vivlia.

Marsiglio, W. (1995a). Fatherhood scholarship: An overview and agenda for the future. In W. Marsiglio (Ed.), *Fatherhood: Contemporary theory, research, and social policy* (pp. 1–20). Thousand Oaks, CA: Sage.

Marsiglio, W. (1995b). Fathers' diverse life course patterns and roles: Theory and social interventions. In W. Marsiglio (Ed.), *Fatherhood: Contemporary theory, research, and social policy* (pp. 78–101). Thousand Oaks, CA: Sage.

Marsiglio, W., Amato, P., & Day, R. (2000). Scholarship on fatherhood in the 1990s and beyond. *Journal of Marriage and the Family, 62*, 1173–1191.

Marsiglio, W., & Day, R. (1997). Social fatherhood and paternal involvement: Conceptual, data and policymaking issues. *Report of the Working Group on Conceptualising Male Parenting. Report prepared and presented for the NICHD Conference on Fathering and Male Fertility: Improving Data and Research*, Bethesda, Maryland.

Mboya, M., & Nesengani, R. (1999). Migrant labor in South Africa: A comparative analysis of the academic achievement of father-present and father-absent adolescents. *Adolescence, 34*, 763–767.

McLanahan, S., & Bumpass, L. (1988). Intergenerational consequences of family disruption. *American Journal of Sociology, 94*, 130–152.

McLoyd, V., Jayarante, T., Ceballo, R., & Borquez, J. (1994). Unemployment and work interruption among African-American single mothers: Effects on parenting and adolescent socioemotional functioning. *Child Development, 65*, 562–589.

Mkhize, N. (2004). Who is a father? *ChildrenFIRST, 56, July/Aug*, 3–8.

Mott, F. (1994). Sons, daughters and fathers' absence: Differentials in father-leaving probabilities and in-home environments. *Journal of Family Issues, 15*, 97–128.

Nsamenang, B. (1987). A West African perspective. In M. Lamb (Ed.), *The father's role: Cross-cultural perspectives* (pp. 273–293). Hillsdale, NJ: Erlbaum.

Palkowitz, R. (1997). Reconstructing involvement: Expanding conceptualizations of men's caring in contemporary families. In A. Hawkins & D. Dollahite (Eds.), *Generative fathering: Beyond deficit perspectives* (pp. 200–216). Thousand Oaks, CA: Sage.

Palkowitz, R. (2002). Involved fathering and child development: Advancing our understanding of good fathering. In C. Tamis-LeMonda, & N. Cabrera (Eds.), *Handbook of father involvement: Multidisciplinary perspectives* (pp. 119–140). Mahwah, NJ: Erlbaum.

Parke, R., & Brott, A. (1999). *Throwaway dads: The myths and barriers that keep men from being the fathers they want to be*. New York: Houghton Mifflin.

Pleck, E. (1997). Paternal involvement: Levels, sources and consequences. In M. Lamb (Ed.), *The role of the father in child development* (3rd ed., pp. 66–103). New York: Wiley.

Population Council (2001). *The unfinished transition. Gender equity: Sharing the responsibilities of parenthood*. A Population Council Issues Paper. New York: Population Council.

Ramphele, M. (2002). *Steering by the stars: Being young in South Africa*. Cape Town: Tafelberg Publishers.

Rangaranjan, A., & Gleason, P. (1998). Young unwed fathers of AFDC children: Do they provide support? *Demography, 35*, 175–186.

Richter, L. (1995). Are early adult–infant interactions universal? A South African view. *South African Journal of Child and Adolescent Psychiatry, 7*, 2–18.

Richter, L., Manegold, J., Pather, R., & Mason, A. (2004). Harnessing our manpower. *ChildrenFirst, 8*, 16–20.

Roggman, L., Fitzgerald, H., Bradley, R., & Raikes, H. (2002). Methodological, measurement and design issues in studying fathers: An interdisciplinary perspective. In C. Tamis-LeMonda & N. Cabrera (Eds.), *Handbook of father involvement: Multidisciplinary perspectives* (pp. 1–30). Mahwah, NJ: Erlbaum.

Seltzer, J., & Bianchi, S. (1988). Children's contact with absent parents. *Journal of Marriage and the Family, 50*, 663–677.

Snarey, J. (1993). *How fathers care for the next generation.* Cambridge, MA: Harvard University Press.

Steinberg, L. (1987). Single parents, stepparents, and the susceptibility of adolescents to antisocial peer pressure. *Child Development, 58*, 269–275.

Tamis-LeMonda, C., & Cabrera, N. (1999). Perspectives on father involvement: Research and policy. *Society for Research in Child Development, Vol. XIII, No. 2.*

Townsend, N. (2002). Cultural contexts of father involvement. In C. Tamis-LeMonda & N. Cabrera (Eds.), *Handbook of father involvement: Multidisciplinary perspectives* (pp. 249–277). Mahwah, NJ: Erlbaum.

Trivers, R. (1972). Parental investment and sexual selection. In B. Campbell (Ed.), *Sexual selection and the descent of man 1871–1971* (pp. 136–179). Chicago: Aldine.

West, C., & Zimmerman, D. (1987). Doing gender. *Gender and Society, 1*, 125–151.

Zelizer, V. (1994). *Pricing the priceless child: The changing social value of children.* Princeton, NJ: Princeton University Press.

Zimmerman, M. A., Salem, D. A., & Maton, K. I. (1995). Family structure and psychosocial correlates among urban African-American adolescent males. *Child Development, 66*, 1598–1613.

Fatherhood in historical perspective

My grandfather and I by Sibonile Mkhize, aged 10, KZN

CHAPTER 6

Migrancy, family dissolution and fatherhood

Mamphela Ramphele and Linda Richter

In *Steering by the stars*, the lives of 16 young black people who grew up in New Crossroads in Cape Town are depicted through an analytical lens that focuses on the oppression under which their families were resettled, the fragmented social environment of artificial dormitory towns and the increasing disorder brought about through the gradual transformation of political violence into flagrant criminality. These teenagers participated in one part of a larger project, started in 1991, designed to understand the experiences of young people growing up in one of the contrived and physically arid environments created by apartheid. In order to create a milieu in which young people could talk about their lives – about their families, social networks, sexuality, violence and gangs – meetings, and then weekend trails, were held with the assistance of the Wilderness Leadership School. Some of the conversations, observations and reflections that emanated from the programme are captured in *Steering by the stars: Being young in South Africa*.[1] In telling us about the lives of this particular group of young people, the book is a powerful portrayal of how families were, in fact still are, affected by migrant labour and forced removals and, in particular, what was happening with men – disempowered, unemployed and uprooted – especially in relation to their families and their children. In each life story there is an account of a family, and a father, in one way or another – even if he is only a mental and emotional space that was never actually occupied. In this chapter, extracts are taken from the book to piece together the experiences of fathering among this group of young people, and what the significance of these experiences is in their journey to adulthood.

Setting the scene

New Crossroads – 'a harsher environment is hard to imagine' (p. 17) – was established in 1979, mainly to accommodate the growing number of illegal squatters in Cape Town. At the time of writing, the township comprised 2 000 residential sites with brick houses, from one- to three-bedrooms in size. While the area is lit by street lamps, and most homes have indoor water and sewerage, the construction of the houses is shoddy. Most of the inhabitants are women from the Eastern Cape, drawn to Cape Town to unite their families and to find work to support their children.

The challenge of the project was to find ways to encourage a group of adolescents to express themselves freely. They were unaccustomed to doing this. They lived in an area that was not recorded in the Planning Department, many of the young people had no personal records and the state census passed them by. What they tended to tell people about themselves was strategic – information was used to deflect attention from themselves, keep them out of trouble, and gain any glimpse of advantage in an environment where no, or only shoddy, services were resentfully provided to them. In contrast, the monthly wilderness trails over two years provided opportunities for friendships to develop and created safe spaces for the disclosure of painful memories and events, as well as tentative hopes and dreams.

Of the 16 young people whose stories are included in *Steering by the stars*, ten were reared mostly by their mothers, two by their grandmothers, and one by a sister. Only one adolescent had grown up with his mother and father. Only six of the sixteen families began with a marriage uncomplicated by the existence of prior children. One boy was killed in gang violence during the project. Two of the group, given the names Bulelwa and Bulelani, had achieved success in their careers by the time the book was published, and their journeys describe 'the ways in which young people survive – even flourish – within unbelievably harsh and deprived circumstances' (p. 31). However, even their success came with costs – primarily, alienation from the community. 'They had broken ranks with the group when solidarity meant survival' (p. 96).

Family life

The migrant labour system disrupted all aspects of family life. 'For eleven months of the year these women (rural wives left at home) were to lead celibate lives and focus on mothering the children. Little consideration went into the difficulty of re-establishing intimacy between husband and wife after such a long separation. Suspicions of adulterous activities poisoned many relationships. Often innocent women were physically and sexually abused by jealous husbands. Tension would flare up during the month's visit as the man tried to establish his authority in the household…Many men ended up with two families: an urban woman to satisfy immediate sexual needs; a rural wife to keep the home stable. Given low wages many men were trapped into neglecting their rural families. Consequently from the 1970s onwards, many women increasingly braved the threat of arrest under influx-control regulations to join their husbands in urban areas even if it meant leaving their children with relatives'. (p. 65)

Most of the children in the group experienced ongoing disruption. Their families moved from one place to another, as children they were sent to live with relatives, the partnerships of their parents were stormy and unstable, and they frequently changed schools. Relationships with mothers, although sometimes supportive and close, were complicated. Fewer than half of the chidren in the group had stayed with their mothers continuously into their late teens. Two had been abandoned shortly after birth, and five had been separated from their mothers in early childhood and their stable care had never been restored. 'Many children called their granny "mother" and their mother, "sisi" – sister' (p. 72). The truth – about fathers, money, partnerships, the future – was hard to come by, and many young people lived with silent confusion and resentment at the behaviour of their parents. 'How could they trust their parents, they asked? What other facts were being withheld?' (p. 69). That this was so demonstrates that young people had in their mind a picture of what a family, parent–child relationships, and fatherhood could and should be. They knew they had been dealt a raw hand, and it hurt them. For most of these young people, 'trusting and respectful relationships are an exception rather than the rule' (p. 154).

The images of stable, happy families and responsible caring fathers in the minds of young people were created, frequently, by grandparents. Some lived nearby or were in contact through visits and long-term stays. These idealised images were often associated with the rural areas, with its somewhat romanticised peace and quiet. Many young people could not have survived, or thrived, were it not for the care they received from grandparents and the way in which 'old-age pensions' were distributed through families to feed children, pay school fees and buy bus coupons so that people could get to work. Mothers, too, kept alive the image of family, caring, and of good men, even though they were few and far between. Most of the young people, though, 'grew up with little knowledge of their fathers as important figures in their lives. The dismantling of apartheid has not erased the patterns of behaviour entrenched by this system' (p. 154).

In addition to stresses brought about by the political system and by poverty, outmoded traditions create challenges for children and families. Children born before marriage are expected to stay with their mother's family, even when she later marries. This 'may have made sense in an era when the rate of births out of wedlock was low, and where such children could easily find loving care. But its difficult explaining this practice when 70 per cent of all births are "out of marriage"' (p. 68). The tradition is driven by fears that a child will be badly treated by an adoptive father, that there will be tension in the family about who belongs and who doesn't, and that the child might keep alive the relationship between the mother and father. However, some parents did not even disclose or acknowledge their children as they entered new relationships. 'Abandoning children in this way creates mistrust between adults and children. How can children trust adults who fail to disclose to them who their real biological parents and siblings are? It is not just the failure to disclose which is problematic. The discovery of the identity of your real mother, father and siblings later in life and through indirect sources adds to the sense of insecurity' (p. 155). 'People felt that the custom caused a lot of pain, but they felt bound by it' (p. 69). 'It is this gap between ideal and reality that is confusing to the young people who are trying to make sense of their community and society in general. How are young people to understand their own evolving roles in a community that insists on male dominance even when men are absent physically or emotionally?' (p. 71).

Kin, lodgers and neighbours, and even their families, were important sources of security to children whose lives were treacherously insecure. 'The meaning of family in this context was fluid' (p. 64). School teachers and principals, though sometimes callous and cruel, also provided help to many young people whose families were unstable and unhappy. Bulelani, a boy with physical impairments, developed a strong bond with his headmaster, a man who admitted Bulelani to his school, even though he had no uniform, or money for transport, lunch or school fees. Actions of this kind provide thin slivers of opportunity for children in very difficult circumstances.

Fathers

Young people in the group portrayed a complex and changing picture of men's roles in their lives. Some fathers are painfully missed, but absent, other fathers were cruel and depriving. Sometimes, as in the case of Mthetheleli, whose story is recounted below, a father's cruelty could simultaneously be a shield against the cruelty of outsiders. However, many young people described the care and protection they received from good men in their families and communities, and this was often a critical lifeline to them in their development.

Bulelwa's father left home and used his workman's compensation money from an occupation-related injury to buy another woman a beautiful house and a lifestyle of luxury for her children. He treated his own relatives to clothing and food and lauded his wealth over his first family. 'Lolo relied on Sisi Makoti (a lodger) and her elder sister to protect her from her alcoholic father with whom she shared a bedroom' (p. 64). Tomela's father 'always beats me even if I have not done anything wrong. I do not like that. Sometimes I sleep at the homes of friends to run away from him. He hardly buys clothes for me but he buys for other children in the family. He is never satisfied with anything I do' (p. 101).

Mthetheleli 'told me he had been severely beaten by his father at the behest of his mother. It was not the first time this had happened. He also showed me the scars on his back from a beating he had received a year before…(he) had a scarred face – testimony to other assaults…On one of our first weekend trips with him he burst into tears when we arrived at the beach cottage in Cape Point. When I asked him what the matter was he said he was so hungry that he could not wait for supper' (p. 75). This was despite the fact that Mthetheleli was the only child in the group who lived with his mother and father, and that both his parents were employed. His story describes a cycle of neglect and the absence of models of caring families. 'A combination of a strong shaming custom (of errant children) and an authoritarian-autocratic parenting style might well be perpetuated by the next generation' (p. 81). Yet Mthetheleli was protected from gang harassment by his father's reputation for violence, and this enabled the boy to ward off bullying in the street.

Lunga, in comparison, was well cared for by his kin, including the men in the family, even though he didn't know his father. 'The reason why I loved my grandmothers was because they were wonderful to me. The best part about being with my mother's mother was that my uncle was there and he looked after me very well. He bought me school uniforms and paid the school fees'…'It turned out that the "uncle" was actually his half-brother, born to his mother premaritally and left in the care of her parents. Lunga was only to learn of this much later' (p. 72). In fact, Lunga discovered who his 'uncle' was when he was nearly twenty years old. 'The discovery threw him into an identity crisis. What else did he not know about his origins and his real biological connections to those around him? How does he adjust to being a second-born with much reduced ritual status so late in his life? How does he continue to trust and respect the integrity of his parents under these circumstances?' (p. 156).

Dumo's mother's brother 'proclaimed himself Dumo's "parent"' (p. 66) and looked after and also assumed responsibility for the support of 'a household of thirteen people related in a complex manner defined as family' (p. 67). This caring man, though, was worn down by exploitation by his family members. '"It is very difficult for me to look after everyone", he said. "That is why I do not want to get married. No woman can take on the load of the family. I feel the pain. Even God will punish me for being too generous. My sisters just give birth and then leave their children with me without my knowing who their fathers are…" It is hardly surprising that Dumo's uncle eventually threw in the towel. He left without a word to his family and went to live in Khayelitsha with his girlfriend and their children' (p. 68).

Why fathers are important

New Crossroads history reflects the impact of the apartheid legacy. Many 'men and women in the township felt helpless to provide for their children and opted out in self-defence. This decision by many poor men to shed family responsibilities left little room for young men to model themselves on successful males. Conflict between the ideals of a patriarchal system which installs the male as provider, protector and decision-maker on one hand, and the harsh realities of lack of education and skills, compounded by high levels of unemployment and demoralisation on the other, leave young men confused. They lack the father model with the tools to assume the authority and responsibility of being male in a patriarchal society. To all intents and purposes many young people were abandoned by their fathers and left to find their own path into adulthood' (p. 103).

'The loss of his father (his father died shortly after his birth) weighed heavily on Bulelani and he maintained contact with his father's family in the Transkei. The loss of a father always complicates the lives of children, but it is a particular handicap in a community where the father is the key to entry into the world of men. For instance, it is the father who provides the name and introduces the boy to ancestors in a ritual called *imbeleko*' (p. 47). At the ceremony, an elder calls upon the ancestors of the clan 'to shower their blessings on the child, and to ensure that his/her future is under their protection. Those assembled add their voices. The child is welcomed as a joint responsibility by the nuclear and extended family as well as the neighbours'. What security for children! But, 'Failure to perform the *imbeleko* ritual is believed to make the child, and later adult, vulnerable to misfortune' (p. 48).

Bulelani went through the traditional Xhosa ritual of initiation. He was determined to be initiated into manhood because he felt it was 'about discipline, its about being respectful' (p. 57). His mother's brother stood in for his father and, with other men, gave the initiates support and encouragement in a process that promotes 'male bonding' (p. 58). Denuded of its social meaning, the 'ritual becomes a long, lonely process' for those disadvantaged young men, without 'fathers or responsible male relatives' (p. 60).

'By his own admission Bulelani had no role models to rely on. He was astute enough to take the best he could out of traditional life without being imprisoned by it...But he paid a heavy price...he was likely to continue into mature adulthood as a lonely man, because he did not identify with the popular notion of what it meant to be a man. Nor did he believe in violence or domination of others because they were smaller, weaker or less important. He failed to find someone to teach him how to be a man without the negative associations with the male dominance of a patriarchal system. He realised he would have to define manhood for himself' (pp. 152–153).

Conclusion

Households and families were harassed and torn apart by restrictions on people's movements, by migrant labour, by forced resettlement, and by the resulting poverty and disarray, in the most painful ways. One family had their shack burnt down three times and all their possessions destroyed. 'We stayed in that empty house with nothing. I was attacked by nerves (I fell into a depression) because I thought that everything I had was going wrong...We did not have a thing' (p. 112).

Political conflict and street violence, including the practices of 'forced sharing' and 'repossession' (when young activists took cars, food and other goods from people as a form of entitlement for their role in the struggle), together with gangs and their territoriality, led to a situation in which 'Lawlessness and helplessness are the order of the day' (p. 117). People took the law into their own hands and there was an 'underlying acceptance of mob justice as a legitimate response to the high level of criminal activity' (p. 118).

As youngsters, many of the young people saw battles between the 'fathers' (older, more conservative men) and the 'comrades' (the politically aware, activist youth), because the fathers were seen to be in cahoots with the police and, by extension, the apartheid state. They identified themselves by wearing white scarves on their heads (the *witdoeke*). In this abnormal environment, '"Comrade" became the catch phrase, the password into "manhood" – the social leveller between "men" and "boys"'. These youth took control, settled family disputes, flogged men who abused their wives, and presided over funerals. The power they wielded created a thin line between being a comrade in the struggle, and a *comtsotsi* member of a gang. 'Violence became, and remains, a means of enforcing compliance with the wishes of the powerful' (p. 113).

Basically, relationships between people were affected. The adolescents on the project had poor communication with their parents, with only a few exceptions (p. 114). Parents were perceived to be cruel, lacking in understanding and empathy, too busy and preoccupied to listen to their children. 'Most children in New Crossroads have lost respect for older people. They see adults as cruel. Some have become quite obstinate, rude and they swear at older people. Even those with disabilities and senior citizens are treated with disrespect. Unnecessary punishment tends to trigger this reaction because when children complain, they are threatened with even greater and more severe punishment' (p. 88). These difficult backgrounds are internalised by young people and 'Their anger from home goes straight onto the streets' (p. 121).

Schools are another source of support and connection for young people, and certainly some teachers were lodestones for children in trouble. However, many of the schools the young people attended compounded, rather than ameliorated, their problems. 'My meeting with the teachers confirmed my worst fears. They were a demoralised group of people. Many of the women teachers were grossly overweight. Some of the men had visible signs of heavy alcohol abuse. None of them could clearly express themselves in English in spite of the requirement that they should teach all content subjects in English' (p. 93).

'The damage done to the culture of people living on the edge of survival goes beyond material deprivation' (p. 142). 'Poverty adds to the burden of families. Desertion by fathers is often prompted by their inability to bear the burden of being primary providers. The burden of failure becomes intolerable for those who lack of the capacity to generate enough income as uneducated and unskilled labourers. Desertion is not always physical, it can also be emotional. Many men "die" as parents and husbands by indulging in alcohol, drugs or becoming unresponsive to their families. Women end up carrying a disproportionate load of responsibility in the nurturing of young people without the necessary authority to do so' (p. 158).

Bulelani's and Bulelwa's are success stories. 'There are countless examples of triumphs against the odds by children and young people around the world. But there are also and always casualties. The narratives of other members of the group showed a mixture of success and failure as they too steered by the stars into an uncertain future. Their personal resources were found wanting in many respects and they could not handle the pressures of their inadequate and unpredictable society' (p. 153).

Phato, who died in drug-related violence, paid the ultimate price. 'He was no longer steering by the stars as he had lost sight of them as he went deeper and deeper into a drug culture in which violence became the only language of power. He gave up on his parents who could not provide for his basic needs in the form of food and clothing. He also felt strongly that they neither trusted nor respected him. In fact, he gave up on all adults. The peer group he fell back on consisted of equally desperate young men who sought solace in drugs because they could not live with themselves in a society they saw as hostile and uncaring. The price of peer support is often high. Demands for conformity, loyalty and demonstrations of love are insatiable under such circumstances' (p. 159). Phato was not very different in his need for compassionate and involved parenting from the successful Bulelani, who in adulthood was a 'caring, responsible, mature young man wrestling with the child within' (p. 55).

The disruption of families and of parenting under colonisation and apartheid, by both men and women, has left its mark on children and on their children. In addition, the relationships between men and women have become deeply troubled. Men are 'disempowered by having to depend on the very women that a patriarchal culture designates as inferior to them. The dissonance between the cultural expectations of gender power relations on the one hand, and the reality of powerlessness on the other, sets off a vicious cycle of low self-esteem, resentment, anger and abuse of the very source of your support – the woman: mother, sister, wife, lover' (p. 160).

Children and youth recognise the disturbances and disruptions in their lives and understand how this affects their families. They are clearly aware that it is not normal for parents to care little for one another or for their children. Nor do they consider it normal for fathers to be absent. The youth long for and aspire to be better people and better parents than their parents were. What they need, desperately, is help and support to achieve their dreams. Yet it is not clear where this help is to come from. Perhaps with new insights into their own lives, these young people will be able to create happier families than the ones they had, and become the parents they longed to have. For those who were fortunate to have happy families and caring parents and parent-figures, the advantages are immeasurable.

Mamphela Ramphele is a medical doctor and anthropologist by training. She worked in the Southern African Labour and Development Research Unit (SALDRU) and the Department of Social Anthropology at the University of Cape Town before being elected, in 1996, as Vice-Chancellor. She was the first black person and woman to hold such a position at a South African university. In 2000, she joined the World Bank as Managing Director responsible for human development. She is the author of *A Bed Called Home: Life in the Migrant Labour Hostels of Cape Town; Bounds of Possibility: The Legacy of Steve Biko and the Black Consciousness Movement; Steering by the Stars: Being Young in South Africa*; an autobiography, *Mamphela Ramphele: A Life*; and (with Francis Wilson) *Uprooting Poverty: The South African Challenge*.

Linda Richter is the Executive Director of the Child, Youth and Family Development programme at the Human Sciences Research Council. She also holds honorary appointments at the Universities of KwaZulu-Natal, Witwatersrand, and Melbourne, Australia. Linda was trained as a clinical developmental psychologist but has worked in research environments for most of her career, investigating issues of risk and resilience in children, youth and families. She is co-author of *Mandela's Children: Growing up in Post-Apartheid South Africa* and joint editor of *The Sexual Abuse of Young Children in southern Africa.*

Note

1   Mamphela Ramphele agreed to Linda Richter using material from *Steering by the stars: Being young in South Africa.* (2002). Cape Town: Tafelberg Publishers, to construct a chapter so that this unique rendition of fathering, by a group of young South Africans, could be included in this book.

CHAPTER 7

The state as non-biological 'father': exploring the experience of fathering in a South African state institution in the period 1950 to 1970

Azeem Badroodien

Introduction

The state, via its institutions, plays an important 'fathering' role to children in state facilities. It fulfils this function in a number of ways, none more so than through mandating staff members in institutions to perform critical caring activities as part of their professional duty. In many such state institutions in the recent past, men executed the key 'fathering' functions, particularly in facilities that only provided for boys.[1] In such cases, this role was not given to all men equally. Under apartheid, a complex pattern of fathering in state institutions developed that, while reinforcing racial identities, also cut across these. The experiences that boys had of 'state fathers' profoundly influenced their adult lives, particularly in the realms of paid work and domestic responsibility.

In this chapter, I explore the experiences of two informants who grew up in a state institution for boys in Cape Town in the period 1950 to 1970, using narratives from interviews with the two men in 1999. More specifically, I analyse the various ways in which the state's discharge of its 'fathering' responsibility (through male employees) came to shape the institutional experience of the two coloured boys at the Ottery School of Industries. The chapter shows that in the harsh institutional world of a School of Industries, individual men performed fatherhood roles in a variety of ways. There was unexpected warmth and respect, but also firmness, fear and control. The way in which the boys who attended this institution experienced this fathering had a major influence on how they understood themselves as masculine, as workers and as coloured.

The narratives that are provided are reflections of men on their experiences of being fathered and fathering through their own life cycle. Moreover, they are intermittent observations held together here solely by my chosen focus on experiences of 'fathering and care' in a state institution. They are not responses to direct or focused questions on 'fathers' or care provided by men, but are contributions knitted together from the informants' numerous descriptions and narrations of life at the institution and their observations about life and family after they were released from state institutionalisation.[2]

Institutionalised in a state facility

The 'subjects' of this chapter are Pieter Botha and Lourens Marcus, whom I interviewed in 1999. Both live in Kraaifontein, Cape Town, and both have retired. They have never met each other nor have they any common acquaintances. Both men have been married for more than 20 years. Pieter was 51 years old in 1999, and has three teenage daughters. He was medically 'boarded' from the army in 1993, where he worked for 24 years as a chef. When I interviewed him in 1999, Pieter ran a daily soup kitchen funded by the local municipality in a nearby informal settlement in Bloekombos, Kraaifontein.

Lourens was 65 years old in 1999, and has three children and five grandchildren. He retired in 1996 after 35 years in state employment, having served in various capacities as a childcare minder, physical education instructor and old age home supervisor. Trained as a mechanic during his youth while at a state institution, Lourens still assists his mechanic son, who runs a workshop from his home, on a regular basis.

Both Lourens and Pieter were institutionalised as young boys at the Ottery School of Industries. Lourens spent five years at the institution[3] in the 1950s while Pieter was at the facility for eight months in the 1960s. Both Lourens and Pieter speak largely of hardship, pain, suffering, yearning and anger in relaying what it felt like to grow up as coloured boys in a males-only state institution under apartheid. However, they also relate the positive impact that various men had on their lives at the state facility, and the different levels and forms of 'fathering' that existed at the facility that shaped the ways in which they encountered institutionalisation.

To comprehend the impact of the Ottery facility on the lives of the two informants, it is first necessary to describe how and why state institutions evolved in South Africa, and to understand what they sought to achieve in 'fathering' individuals like Lourens and Pieter.

The state as 'saviour and protector'

During the twentieth century, the 'care' of children in public policy increasingly focused on the notion of 'protection' and on defining the ways in which the state should take responsibility for those children defined as having a special, vulnerable status. Over time, state public policy became invested with particular understandings of how best to control and 'protect' the behaviour and environment of children and/or their families (see Cameron, 1999).

The emphasis on protection emerged from the discourse of modernity and enlightenment that evolved at the turn of the twentieth century in South Africa. In this period, social reforms were initiated in institutions designed mostly for working-class children. These institutions were regarded as key sites where mechanisms of social control and 'saving' could be developed, and where the attitudes and morals of those who were institutionalised could best be 'moulded'. By 'observing', 'controlling' and 'transforming' the actions and movements of those deemed to live on the margins of the emerging modern society, it was widely believed that society as a whole could be 'regulated', 'looked after' and even 'cured'.

This form of social strategy, based on notions of rationality and scientific thought, was prevalent within many international debates on social reconstruction from the early twentieth century. Chisholm (1989), referring to comments made by a Union Education Department official in the 1920s, notes that during this period the ideals of 'moral salvation' and 'scientific intervention' were particularly pronounced.

> The sinner could be saved. The dishonest person could be made honest and morally whole. And the illiterate and mentally deficient could be trained in habits of decency and discipline if removed from conditions conducive to crime. On removal to environments where they could be cured of their crime, these persons, as in a hospital, could then be restored to social and individual health. (Chrisholm, 1989, p. 98)

From the 1930s, social policy with regard to vulnerable children in institutions asserted that, by providing working-class and poor children in state institutions with work skills and moral training, children would be instilled with the key attributes of productivity, peace, orderliness, and rationality. Adult men, as employees in state institutions, were deemed indispensable to the successful 'moulding' of children into dependable family members, state citizens and workers. Within the stable familial and social environments of state institutions, men represented conduits of love (care givers), traditional holders of respect (father figures), and proprietors of fear (Chisholm, 1989). In this regard, it is notable that a strict anti-egalitarianism existed in parental practice in this period that focused on teaching children to both respect and fear adults (and fathers).

The state institution as a site of 'racial salvation'

The Ottery School of Industries belongs to a set of institutions that has its origin in the industrial schools movement that evolved from the 1890s in South Africa. Chisholm refers to the first industrial schools as institutions meant to 'rescue' 'poor white' children from indigence and 'proneness to criminal activity' in a period wrought by the social disasters of drought, locusts and rinderpest. In South Africa after 1910, this 'salvation' was increasingly cast in terms of the removal of indigent white children from urban slums, where they were supposedly 'driven to immorality', begging, vagrancy and criminal activity by mixing with non-whites. In that regard, 'state fathering' through industrial schools was originally understood to entail the salvation of 'poor white' children, the stabilising of the racial category 'white', and the protection of the white colonial subject from any taint of backwardness and irrationality.

This conceptualisation of the purpose of industrial schools, of course, changed over time. With the accelerated urbanisation of non-whites from the 1930s, the state was increasingly confronted with non-white boys and girls waylaid by the vices of urban life. In seeking to provide institutions for such children, and influenced by advances in a number of scientific disciplines, the state redefined the original conceptualisation of its 'fathering' role (for poor whites) to focus more acutely on ways of 'treating' and 'resocialising' its institutional subjects to internalise the 'norms' and requirements of a modern industrialising society. In this endeavour, the state delineated 'its children' according to notions of nation and difference, and according to class status and differentiated access to the labour market.

It was within this context that the state facility, the Ottery School of Industries, to which Pieter and Lourens were confined in the period 1950 and 1970, needs to be understood. Established in 1948, the institution provided different kinds of programmes by which it sought to transform coloured boys, defined as 'in need of care' under the Children's Act of 1937, into 'healthy' future citizens and workers. These included:
- A residential programme that provided coloured boys with food, shelter, clothing, religious instruction, and a 'stable' living environment;
- Psychological counselling that focused on addressing the emotional needs and problems of individual boys;
- Academic education that sought to ensure that each boy attended school regularly. It was asserted that the knowledge attained at school and the regularity of schooling would induct boys into the routineness of the world of work;
- The provision of training in particular trades in which it was believed coloured males would find employment.

The running of each of the programmes at the Ottery facility lay in the hands of men. This meant that at every level, men not only determined how boys understood their lives and what was expected of them but, through institutional provision, imbued state subjects (coloured boys) with vital information on how to confront life outside institutional care and how to be fathers when they started their own families.

Indeed, if the state as 'non-biological father' is interpreted as a structure for 'firm and assured guidance', then the Ottery facility operated very effectively in first framing the race, class and gender aspects of the lives of institutionalised children at the macro level, and then shaping the everyday experiences of institutional subjects at the micro level through interaction with adult men who served both as intermediaries for the state and exemplars of 'good fathers'.

The Ottery institution as a site of 'fathering'

The notion of 'fathering' is normally associated with 'insemination' and biological intimacy. For this chapter, I draw on this 'association' in a more metaphorical sense to highlight the role of the state in 'inseminating' boys with 'a particular vision of life'. The key purpose of state institutions was to change the ways in which boys lived their lives, and reshape the manner in which they ate, slept, worked and understood who they were. Once a boy arrived at Ottery, the organisation of the institution was meant to structure every aspect of his life. Erving Goffman has described institutionalisation in the following way:

> First, all aspects of life are conducted in the same place and under the same single authority. Second, each phase of the member's daily activities is carried on in the immediate company of a large batch of others, all of whom are treated alike and required to do the same thing together. Third, all phases of the day's activities are tightly scheduled, with one activity leading at a prearranged time into the next, the whole sequence of activities being imposed from above by a system of explicit formal rulings and a body of officials. Finally, the various enforced activities are brought together into a single rational plan purportedly designed to fulfil the official aims of the institution. (1961, pp. 21 & 22)

The physical structure of the institution did not only inform the ways in which boys experienced life at Ottery but was used to construct every moment of each boy's life at the facility. In this regard, there exists significant documentation and evidence in the institution's archive that shows how the Ottery facility regulated and controlled the minute details of the lives of coloured boys during residential care.

The documents also testify to the complex processes that went into deciding how boys were fed, provided schooling and trade training, given religious instructions, taught personal hygiene, and shown how to work. Undoubtedly, life at an institution like the Ottery School of Industries was a terribly difficult and bitter experience for boys committed to the facility.

Importantly, caregivers and fellow 'inmates' were critical to the regulation of the goings-on within such an institution. Referring to 'total institutions', Goffman (1961) has described such agents in institutions as:

> A large number of like-situated individuals who, cut off from the larger society for an appreciable period of time, together lead an enclosed, formally administered round of life in places defined as either residence or work. These are social hybrids, living in part-residential communities, part-formal organisations, and are the forcing agents for changing people. (p. 17)

Having been separated from families and friends, institutionalised boys were confronted by two forms of strangers at Ottery, namely fellow inmates ('siblings') and institutional staff ('fathers'). These two groups differently informed the lessons that boys took away with them when released from institutionalisation, and the ways in which they experienced 'fathering' at the facility.

Leading by example

Like fathers shaping the ways in which their children related to each other, male staff members at the Ottery facility provided the parameters by which boys interacted with each other. Institutional boys were aware of this and used particular 'markers' not only to differentiate between themselves but also as portals through which to seek favour from 'fatherly' state officials. These markers included the ways whereby they came to be institutionalised (youths with delinquent tendencies, orphans that were too old to be in children's homes, impoverished children who were institutionalised because their parents were too poor to sustain them, boys committed to state care for having one 'native parent'), their trade/skill levels, educational standing, IQ levels, aspects of physical strength, and other communication and social skills and abilities. One informant noted in 1999 that the key lesson to be learnt at such an institution was what other boys were capable of, what they were prepared to do, and what adults at the institution subsequently allowed and disallowed. 'Only then', noted the informant, 'could you really formulate the way in which you approached life at the institution.'

> I was busy eating one day and talking to the boy next to me. I heard a prefect say 'quiet', but I was talking very softly. The next minute I looked up and just saw his boot. He kicked me full in the face, dragged me from the table and continued kicking me. The worse part – as I found out afterwards – was that he was from Alpha (hostel) and I always used to help him with his trade homework. That hurt, that. But he was showing off – you see – for the teachers and instructors that were sitting there. They wanted to see what he was prepared to do for them. What was worse though was that I was never going to leave it at that. I knew he used to run away at night to the shebeens on the 'outside'. So one night, I sat for almost four hours in the dark, there among the trees, and waited for him. Until today he still doesn't know who hit him, that's how dark it was. But *jong*, I used a *tamaaie* (huge) brick that night to hit a giant *gat* (hole) in that *ounooi's* head. Nobody gets away with hitting me you see, not adults or any *stinkgat laaitie* that is just looking to show off.[4]

There is little doubt that through the behaviour of their 'father figures' and through witnessing how power and violence came together to uphold order and stability, institutionalised boys were taught how institutional benefits were to be attained.

The institutional 'limits' to fathering

The Ottery institution was inhabited by a variety of 'fathers'. These included educators, instructors, caregivers and people in management structures who all resided on the grounds of the facility. All serving as *in loco parentis* caregivers according to Children's Act regulations, there were significant gradations between them based on race, qualification and professional focus.

First, there was the management team of well-qualified white Afrikaners. This team consisted of the principal, the deputy principals who each oversaw the academic, psychology, hostels and technical trade units, and administration staff.

Second, there was the professional team of white psychologists trained at Afrikaans-speaking universities such as Stellenbosch and Potchefstroom, who oversaw IQ tests, developed 'scientific' admission policies, provided psychological counselling, and managed the release and placement of children. This professional team often used their institutionalised charges at Ottery as 'scientific guinea pigs' to develop further research on coloured children in state care, that later served to inform the establishment of more state facilities for coloured children elsewhere.

Third, there were the trade instructors who were all white (mostly English-speaking but with Afrikaners in middle-skill trades such as upholstery and carpentry), followed by hostel wardens and kitchen and laundry heads who were white but who had a large coloured staff serving under them as caregivers, cooks, matrons and laundry workers. This largely unskilled group of coloured staff was divided into women who worked in traditionally female occupations in the laundry, kitchen and hospital, and coloured men who served as the chief caregivers and regulators in the boys' hostels. These men were all unqualified and served both as overseers of the boys' daily living needs and their principal disciplinarians.

Last, there existed a core staff component of qualified coloured male teachers and assistant trade instructors which was located just above the unskilled coloured component. This group was expected not only to educate the boys under their care but also to serve as key role models and 'fathers' to them. They were meant to earn the boys' respect and obedience by providing education and their portrayal of their class position and of 'civilised living'.

Race, gender and institutional imperative came together in complex ways at the Ottery facility to place particular limits on relationships and ensure that only coloured men could be like 'fathers' to institutionalised boys.[5] Every effort, for example, was made to limit the interaction between white male staff members and institutionalised boys, and white staff served mainly as 'living examples' to coloured staff on how to best fulfil their fathering responsibilities.[6] The only times that boys witnessed, interacted with, or heard white staff members speak were at official functions like assembly, or in overhearing coloured staff members being instructed on how to control or mould their charges. In this regard, institutionalised boys were constantly reminded about the race and class status of coloureds within society. Moreover, with the participation of emerging middle-class coloured males in ensuring the upliftment of the coloured working-class boys at the facility, the purpose of the Ottery institution was equally to develop and retain firm control of the 'coloured family' at the institution and regulate key class and gender differences amongst them.

Key 'father figures'

In the sections that follow, I provide biographical, historiographical and sociological detail about the lives of Pieter Botha and Lourens Marcus to throw some light on how their particular encounters with institutionalisation differentially informed their lives as well as their understandings of state 'fathering'.

I start by exploring the different sets of fathers that Lourens and Pieter encountered at the Ottery facility and then discuss how these 'fathering' experiences, combined with their individual histories and contexts, provided the core lessons that they took away with them about being fathers in later life.

Pieter Botha observed in 1999 that during his time at the Ottery institution he received 'fathering' from many people, despite policy that attempted to confine this within racial and functional parameters. This took many different forms and was delivered not by one 'father' but by a number of men. Indeed, Pieter noted that the variety of men that undertook a fatherhood role during his stay at Ottery were in different ways very important for his sense of himself and his later sense of family and fathering. In particular, Pieter singled out his personalised interaction with the white trade instructor, Mr Volksteun, who physically ensured that his life at Ottery turned out quite differently.

> Mr Volksteun was the closest I've ever come to having a father. At Ottery
> he was my carpentry trade instructor and the warden of Alpha A, where
> I slept at night. While I first spoke mostly to the coloured assistant,
> because I was fairly good at carpentry Mr Volksteun came to use me as
> his main helper in fixing things at the institution. We formed a bond. So
> much that when I planned to run away from Ottery, I always used to
> think about how I would disappoint Mr Volksteun and how he would
> hate me. Yes, it was he who showed me that someone cared. It was he
> who showed me how to be king of my trade. And it was him who used
> to get me out of Ottery over weekends to work with him so that I would
> not get into fights with other boys. Mr Volksteun may have been an
> Afrikaner, but he was not like the rest of them, like Oubaas Hoepel (the
> principal). No, Mr Volksteun taught me so much. (Interview 6 with
> Pieter Botha, 27 July 1999, Transcript 6 (2), p. 19)

> But it was also his fault that I wanted to run away so much. By being
> part of his family over weekends – okay, I was still his *boytjie* and had to

do all the main chores – I wanted to find my own parents. I knew my mother and father were out there somewhere – the nuns used to tell me especially about my mother from the letters she wrote in my first few years at the children's home in George. And because I worked a lot on outside jobs with Mr Volksteun, I always knew that I would have enough money to survive once I got away. (Interview 6 with Pieter Botha, 27 July 1999, Transcript 6 (2), p. 19)

In noting the impact of Mr Volksteun on his life, Pieter also pointed out that coloured teachers and caregivers were very important to improving his stay at Ottery, but that often they had 'issues of their own to deal with'.

They had no power you see. They taught us, they laughed a little with us, they helped us in everyday life. But if you wanted to get something done, like get out of there for a while, you had to hook up with someone who had some say, like Mr Volksteun. Hey, I must tell you that while I loved the man, he always treated me like a coloured. I was his *gardtjie* who always listened and obeyed him, and was maybe also there because I was a fairly good carpenter. (Interview 6 with Pieter Botha, 27 July 1999, Transcript 6 (2), p. 20)[7]

Lourens Marcus similarly spoke of the enormous impact that the white principal of the Ottery facility, Dr FA Bester, had on his life, and also how a coloured instructor, through his provision of care and trade instruction, served to instil communal notions of love for family and respect for work.

When I left Ottery in 1955, I used to write a lot to Principal Bester just to tell him where I was, how I was, and how I missed Ottery. I had no-one else to write to, no-one that cared about me. I had developed a sort of bond with Oubaas when he used to use me as a prefect to punish the boys. We thought similarly, much like with a father and son. Oubaas used to write back too, just saying things like 'it's nice to know I'm alright and that I must look after myself and not drink and take drugs'. That helped a lot, you know, knowing someone cared enough to write back. I used to read those letters over and over. Oubaas Hoepel was a *watse* disciplinarian, a real hard ass, but I really liked him. Anyway, Oubaas Hoepel came through for me later on when he offered me to come stay and work at Ottery in 1961. After that, I spent my life working for the state, being a 'father' to the boys much like Oubaas was to me in the early 1950s. (Interview with Lourens Marcus, 25 August, Transcript 2 (2), p. 14)

Lourens noted that Mr Moses, a coloured instructor in the boat machinery workshop, had taught him that, if as an adult he did not transfer what he was taught to his community and family, then he would have failed as a man and a father.

> I used to help out this one coloured instructor in the late afternoons. He lived on Ottery and used to fix cars for extra money. He taught me lots of things, like changing spark plugs, points, even fix sumps. I loved helping him. He made me laugh and I looked forward to every afternoon. If there is one thing he taught me is how to mess around with things until they worked. 'Don't ever give up, and always respect what you do, for then others will respect you', those were his words. More importantly, Mr Moses reminded me that I needed to share what I learnt with other coloureds if I was to become a good person and future father. (Interview with Lourens Marcus, 25 August, Transcript 2 (2), p. 5)

Certainly, Pieter and Lourens's encounters with 'fathering' differentially informed the ways in which they negotiated their lives after leaving the Ottery institution and the ways in which they fulfilled their fathering roles in later life. Lourens's experiences at the Ottery facility, for example, later came to inform, in distinct ways, not only how he performed his job as physical-training instructor at Delta Hostel (punishment hostel) from 1961, but also his understanding of himself as a 'father'. These understandings were firmly embedded in his own experiences of control, shame, fear and discipline at the Ottery facility.

> When you leave a place like Ottery, you know a bit about life. When I returned to Ottery in 1961 I still had the instincts of the place. You know, the boys, they would think 'this man's an idiot and will not know if we do certain things'. They got the fright of their lives when they found out that I understood them. With those kinds of boys you just had to be strict in the right way at the right time and place. Speak clearly and make the boy understand what you want. At the end of the day all the boys wanted was attention and love. I was their father and mother. I taught them the manly things of how to be disciplined, how to protect yourself, how not to take nonsense, but also the girly things like how to wash themselves cleanly, to brush their teeth and shine with cleanliness. You know, if you put a boy like that in a place like Ottery, with just a little encouragement you will definitely get a better type of child. I stayed in the Delta Hostel for eight years because those boys needed me most. (Interview with Lourens Marcus, 25 August, Transcript 2 (2), p. 20)

Lessons learnt for becoming 'respectable fathers'

Indeed, for whatever period boys were committed to the Ottery School of Industries, their experiences of life there, and encounters with various kinds of 'fathers', left indelible marks on their understandings of what a father was, how important a father could and should be, and they took this with them into their adult lives. In this regard, their understandings of fatherhood were shaped by two aspects of their institutional experience, namely (a) the role of poverty in their initial committal to state care, and (b) the link between work and the 'virtues of discipline and diligence' deemed necessary for making them 'decent' men and prospective fathers.

Poverty, institutionalisation and state care

If anything, the reasons provided in state documents for the institutionalisation of Pieter Botha and Lourens Marcus at the Ottery School of Industries emphasise the impact of being poor and coloured in the period 1950 and 1970.[8]

Pieter Botha had been removed from his mother's care in 1950 (when he was two years old) because it was illegal under apartheid for a child to reside with his mother at her place of domestic employment.[9] Given that his mother had no other family in Cape Town to 'take him in', Pieter was raised in a children's home in George[10] until 1965, when he was transferred to the Ottery School of Industries (in Cape Town) as a seventeen-year-old. The initial decision to institutionalise Pieter was based on the 'unsuitable nature of his mother's employment for the adequate care of children' and the belief that, as a single mother, she was 'incapable of providing a family environment for his appropriate upbringing'.[11] Pieter never saw his mother again and state institutional staff became his 'parental figures' for the rest of his life.

Lourens Marcus grew up in Johannesburg and was institutionalised as a thirteen-year-old in 1947 because his stepfather constantly beat him, causing him to run away and 'roam the streets'. Social workers in the Johannesburg municipality believed that his persistent return to night shelters and mission stations would eventually lead to a life of crime and recommended committal to a children's home.[12] Importantly, they suggested that he be sent to a children's home in the Cape 'where he would be able to better interact with other coloured children away from the "native kids" of Johannesburg'.[13] Lourens subsequently spent three years at the Lawrentia State Institution in Kraaifontein, Cape Town, and five years at the Ottery School of Industries. He was released from state care on his twenty-first birthday in 1955. While Lourens did reconnect with his mother in 1965, he was by that time a mature adult, living in Cape Town. By then, his impressions of what he wanted and needed to be in adulthood had been firmly shaped by his institutional life experiences.

In interviews with Pieter and Marcus in 1999, both spoke of how they had had to come to terms with being coloured 'orphans' in a large institution and how they had struggled initially to survive. Slowly, however, they came to understand their predicament and embrace the institutional staff as their 'fathers' or 'father figures'. In recounting his institutional experience at Ottery, Pieter noted in 1999 that:

> You must remember. I was an orphan that spent most of my life in a children's home before I was transferred to Ottery. When I first got there at Ottery, I was scared stiff. I knew no one, I had had some bad

experiences with other adult men at St Joseph's Trade School in Aliwal-North, and the Ottery institution in Cape Town was huge. There were more than a thousand boys at Ottery at that time and hundreds of staff members. Then there were the family members of staff who stayed on the institution. It was a town, man. Only after a while did I begin to cope. (Interview 6 with Pieter Botha, 20 July 1999, Transcript 6 (1), p. 3.)

Where could I have gone anyway? Who was going to take care of me, look after me, feed me, and teach me how to be a man? With me, it was like, you know, I was an orphan boy, so what was the use of crying about my life. Anyway, where would I be today if I wasn't sent to Ottery? A vagrant? There at Ottery we at least got food, care and shelter. We were also taught how to work so that one day when we were fathers we could provide for our children. I was just grateful for what I got at that time. So I did my time at the institution and waited until I could get on with my life. Ottery did teach me though that I didn't want to ever be in places like that again. I used to tell my girls all the time as they grew up: You don't want to be poor or without a father or mother to protect you [sic]. (Interview 6 with Pieter Botha, 20 July 1999, Transcript 6 (1), p. 10)

Both Lourens and Pieter spoke of poverty as an experience that emphasised the need to work, and to retain dignity, discipline, diligence and control in the face of adversity. In fact, attaining these virtues were key reasons for both their transfers to the Ottery School of Industries. Lourens was transferred to the Ottery School of Industries in 1950 because caregivers at the Lawrentia institution felt that he would benefit from the 'adult world of trade instruction' provided at the Ottery facility, while Pieter was sent to the Ottery facility in 1965 because until then he had been raised solely by females. Caregivers at the children's home in George felt that he needed 'firm' male supervision and disciplined interaction if he was going to succeed in adult life.[14]

The father as 'decent', disciplined and diligent provider

In transferring Pieter and Lourens to the Ottery institution, social workers firmly believed that the facility would provide them with vital skills that would secure them employment and ensure their 'survival' once released. In that respect, they argued that the state institution would 'guide' the boys and help them acquire the two key attributes of what was thought to a 'good father', namely how to be the provider for one's family and how to uphold firm discipline and control within one's family. Educators and caregivers at Ottery repeatedly reminded boys that learning to work, being disciplined, and securing an income were the main yardsticks by which they would be judged as human beings and later as 'fathers'.

Pieter noted in 1999 that:

> Mr Volksteun always said that if I wanted a good living so that I could feed a family and be able to teach them good values and habits, I needed to work all the time. This is a lesson I always carried with me, and I always remind myself when I am in trouble and mixed up in my head, that if I do not work hard to bring food home, then it would be the same as my children not having a father at all [sic]. (Interview 6 with Pieter Botha, 20 July 1999, Transcript 6 (1), p. 22)

The notion of provider was not, however, about learning to work in simply 'any job'. Rather, the job had to be 'decent' work, as well as what was thought of as 'man's work'. Coupled with learning discipline, respect, and how to work, the notion of 'the father as provider' was also very much about being a 'real man'.

Lourens noted in 1999 that the key mechanism or conduit for becoming a 'real man' at the Ottery institution was through the prefect system. This system was used to reward loyal boys at the Ottery institution, and was instrumental in embedding within institutionalised boys the virtue of acceptance and 'control'. These virtues were deemed critical in helping boys withstand the various challenges that life would throw at them.

Lourens noted in 1999 that becoming a prefect demonstrated 'the coming of age' and signified a rite of passage from being a poor, neglected and incapacitated 'child' to the mature adult male who displayed loyalty, discipline, diligence and control.

> You must remember that becoming a prefect was not just about 'getting respect' or feeling proud that teachers and instructors had 'faith in you', it was also about getting access to privileges and being recognised as dependable. You may not know, but when you got to Ottery, you got just one jersey for the whole winter and one pair of shorts. Only prefects were allowed to wear long pants and boots. At that time, it was just gravel roads, so you can imagine how wet, sore and blue your feet became in the winter. *Ja*, you can imagine why we all wanted to become prefects. When you became prefect, you knew that you had it made because not only did the staff trust you, the other boys treated you like 'the real *manne*'. They worshipped you and were also *vrek* scared of you. It was something we learnt at the Ottery institution, how to take control and uphold control and discipline at all times. (Interview with Lourens Marcus, 14 July 1999, Transcript 2 (1), p. 17)

The notion of discipline also operated at a further level. Institutionalised boys were constantly reminded that being 'good fathers' meant being diligent and accepting. This was most evident in the way in which Lourens embraced the search for employment once released from the Ottery institution. Lourens noted that in sweating 'blood and tears' looking for a job, he always knew that to be accepted in 'normal society' he had to appreciate each and every job opportunity he got and always 'do the best' that he could.

> I walked every day for months before I got a job. I used to have to get up at four or five in the morning so that I could jump train (and then walk between stations and then jump train again) as I had no money to get to places like Maitland. The only job that I could get that time was as a cleaner at *Southern Life Insurance* in town. Funny, I was told that I was overqualified for the cleaner job. So I said, man, I'm willing to do anything. So I scrubbed floors. After a few months they asked me to fix something and when they saw that I knew what I was doing, they made me a handyman. That was what you had to do, show them what you can do and be patient. That was the mark of a real man [sic]. (Interview with Lourens Marcus, 14 July 1999, Transcript 2 (1), p. 18)

Conclusion

Over the last 150 years, whether as liberal philosophers, colonial policy makers or nationalist thinkers, adults have undoubtedly been overwhelmingly concerned with children, their upbringing and the malleability of their minds. All have attended in some way to the importance of breeding self-disciplined children and virtually all have warned about the dangers of racial and class mixing to the well functioning home. For each, in varying ways, the family has been where a child's sense of personhood, citizenship, and sexuality is subverted, perverted or well formed (Aries, 1962; Davin, 1978; Stoler, 1995; Yazawa, 1985).

In South Africa, the notions of 'familial reconstruction' and the reinforcement of the role of the father therein, were taken up by the state in very particular ways at various moments of social upheaval. At such times, it invariably turned to state institutions to provide vulnerable and maladjusted children with the guidance required to succeed in a modernising world (Chisholm, 1989).

Institutions were test sites (from the 1950s onward) where the uncomfortable fits between class, race, gender and notions of respectability were confronted, where notions of 'fathering' were tried and tested, and where attempts to 'rebuild' the coloured family were initiated. In that respect, the Ottery School of Industries was formative for Pieter Botha and Lourens Marcus not only in shaping how they as individuals engaged with life after institutionalisation, but also in harnessing their individual pasts, foibles and needs in ways that sought to 'mould' them into decent and respectable 'future fathers', and in so doing reconstitute their (coloured) families.

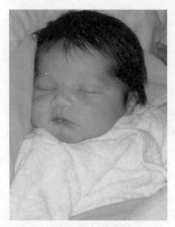

Azeem Badroodien is a Chief Research Specialist with the Human Sciences Research Council. He holds a PhD from the University of the Western Cape. A key focus of his work at the HSRC to date has been on the links between further education and training and the workplace, both at the empirical data level and within the underpinning theoretical discourse of education and work. His other interests include exploring how apartheid and geographical/social/identity issues impacted on the ways in which the lives of institutional (reformatory) boys were shaped and the role of correctional institutions and the attached discourse in shaping their life perspectives. Azeem's new work at the HSRC will focus on the meshing of youth socialisation, masculinity and deviance.

Three-week old Imaad
Badroodien, born July 2005

Notes

1   State institutions have tended to be characterised by gender divisions. Women generally have administered and populated institutions (children's homes and church-run schools) that served young children (boys and girls) under the age of 14 years. Men, on the other hand, have served as heads and managers at facilities for youths (males only) older than 14 years.

2   In my doctoral thesis I compiled 'life histories' for each of my informants. These 'life stories' are based not only on extensive interviews with the informants but also on institutional and other official documents located at the institution in question, and triangulated with viewpoints from interviews with old staff and instititional members. See Badroodien (2001).

3   Lourens also later spent eight years at the Ottery facility as a childcare minder/supervisor in the punishment hostel. After he left Ottery in 1969, Lourens worked for a further 27 years in the state's employ as a physical trainer at the Coloured Cadet Camp at Faure, Cape Town, chief childcare supervisor at Faure Reformatory for Boys, supervisor at the De Nova Rehabilitation Centre for Coloured Alcoholics, and chief supervisor/minder at a coloured old age home, Huis Rosenthal. Pieter Botha similarly spent 24 years in the state's employ (the army) after leaving the Ottery institution.

4   Interview 6 with Pieter Botha, 20 July 1999, Transcript 6 (1), pp. 12–14.

5   The Secretary for Education asserted in 1938 that 'the non-European races need to be provided with opportunities to participate in the work of upliftment of their own people. The Europeans have initiated educational and social welfare work on behalf of non-Europeans, and at present they are still responsible for the major part of such activities, but we should make increasing use of the services of non-Europeans and provide them with the means of apprenticeship, as it were, in the task of serving their own people' (Union of South Africa, 1938, p. 36).

6   An Afrikaner educationalist, W. K. H. Du Plessis, argued in his doctoral thesis on schools of industries in the 1950s that 'the inability of the coloured teachers to keep order and control

made it necessary that "white" trade instructors sometimes guide them. The Cape *skollie* doesn't seem to want to follow instructions from fellow coloureds. The situation should improve once the coloured personnel gain some experience, once they start improving their qualifications, and once they learn how to control and discipline their "own" boys [sic]' (see Du Plessis, 1958, p. 296).

7   The word '*gardtjie*' is an original reference to the person who collected tickets and money on the train. On the Cape Flats because these individuals were seen as 'law-enforcers' against poor, non-ticket-carrying, people, the word took on a more aggressive character. This was later further reinforced in taxis on the flats who often had someone in the back (who might even be carrying a gun) who collected the money and ensured everything ran smoothly. On the flats, given the fluidity of language, in different contexts *gardtjie* became *boytjie* with a bodyguard aspect or trusted right-hand man. In the context of this quote, *gardtjie* essentially translates as 'right-hand man'.

8   These documents are part of the Ottery School of Industries Archive (OSIA) that was initially accessed at the institution and is now housed at the Institute for Historical Studies at the University of the Western Cape. The archive includes numerous kinds of documents, the most important being individual institutional files for the more than 15 000 boys that resided at the Ottery School of Industries between 1948 and 1998. Two such files provide information about the early lives of Lourens and Pieter. See OSIA, File F and File B.

9   Sandra Burman notes that in the 1950s it was illegal for domestic employees to have their children live with them at their place of employment. While it seems unlikely that this apartheid law would have been 'operational' as early as 1950, the existence of the law (which the employer probably found out about via word of mouth) may have afforded the employer with the opportunity to 'release herself' from the burden of caring for the child (Burman & Van der Spuy, 1998, p. 241).

10   See OSIA, File F, 'Report on progress of pupil dated December 1964, St Joseph's School' and '*Report on pupil and application to transfer to another institution in terms of the Children's Act of 1960*, ref: KW 3148, dated 19/1/1965'.

11   OSIA, File F, 'Probation Officer's Report of 3/11/1950', p. 2.

12   OSIA, File B, '*Social Worker Report dated 14/11/1946*'.

13   OSIA, File B, '*Social Worker Report dated 14/11/1946*'.

14   See OSIA, File F, '*Report on progress of pupil dated December 1964, St Joseph's School*' and '*Report on pupil and application to transfer to another institution in terms of the Children's Act of 1960*, ref: KW 3148, dated 19/1/1965'.

References

Aries, P. (1962). *Centuries of childhood: A social history of family life*. New York: Vintage.

Badroodien, A. (2001). A History of the Ottery School of Industries in Cape Town: Issues of race, welfare and social order in the period 1937 to 1968. Unpublished doctoral thesis, University of Western Cape, Cape Town.

Bester, F. (1961). Die etiologiese agtergrond van die gedragafwykende Kleurlingkind en die implikasies daarvan vir sy heropvoeding. Unpublished doctoral thesis, Potchefstroomse Universiteit vir Christelike Hoër Onderwys, Potchefstroom.

Brannen, J., & Moss, P. (Eds.). (2003). *Rethinking children's care.* Buckingham, UK: Open University Press.

Brannen, J., Heptinstall, E., & Bhopal, K. (2000). *Connecting children: Care and family life in later childhood.* London: Routledge Falmer.

Burman, S., & Van der Spuy, P. (1998). Communities, 'caring' and institutions. Apartheid and childcare in Cape Town since 1948. In P. Horden & R. Smith (Eds.), *The locus of care: Families, communities, institutions and the provision of welfare since antiquity* (pp. 239–258). London: Routledge.

Cameron, C. (1999). Child Protection and independent day care services: Examining the interface of policy and practice. Unpublished doctoral thesis, University of London, Institute of Education, London.

Chisholm, L. (1989). Reformatories and industrial schools in South Africa: A study in class, colour and gender in the period 1882 to 1939. Unpublished doctoral thesis, University of the Witwatersrand, Johannesburg.

Davin, A. (1978). Imperialism and motherhood. *History Workshop Journal, 5,* 9–65.

Du Plessis, W. (1958). Die nywerheidskool as onderwys- en opvoedingsinrigting in Suid-Afrika. Unpublished doctoral thesis, Potchefstroomse Universiteit vir Christelike Hoër Onderwys, Potchefstroom.

Foucault, M. (1978). *Discipline and punish: The birth of the prison.* Aylesbury, UK: Hazell Watson & Vinney.

Goffman, E. (1961). *Asylums: Essays on the social situation of mental patients and other inmates.* Harmondsworth: Penguin Books.

Ottery School of Industries Archive (OSIA). File F and File B. University of the Western Cape, Cape Town.

Stoler, A. (1995). *Race and the education of desire. Foucault´s history of sexuality and the colonial order of things.* Durham, USA: Duke University Press.

Union of South Africa (1938). *Annual report of the Union Education Department for 1937 (UG51/1938).* Pretoria: Government Printer.

Yazawa, M. (1985). *From colonies to commonwealth: Familial ideology and the beginnings of the American Republic.* Baltimore, USA: John Hopkins University Press.

Interviews

1. Interview with Lourens Marcus, 14 July 1999, Transcript 2 (1).

2. Interview with Lourens Marcus, 25 August, Transcript 2 (2).

3. Interview 6 with Pieter Botha, 20 July 1999, Transcript 6 (1).

4. Interview 6 with Pieter Botha, 27 July 1999, Transcript 6 (2).

CHAPTER 8
Fathers without *amandla*:
Zulu-speaking men and fatherhood

Mark Hunter

The phrase *anginawo amandla* (I don't have power) expresses many forms of weakness among isiZulu speakers in KwaZulu-Natal. Sometimes it denotes physical frailty, for instance if a person is tired or ill. More relevant for the purposes of this chapter is its use as an indicator of social weakness including – perhaps most pointedly – a man's inability to pay *ilobolo* (bridewealth). A man who doesn't marry can be seen as 'failing' *ukwakha umuzi* (to build a home/homestead). In this chapter I explore how high unemployment and low marriage rates shape contemporary meanings surrounding fathering and fatherhood. I argue that a disjuncture exists today between many men's relative ease at *fathering* children (in a biological sense) and their inability to fulfil the social roles of *fatherhood*. This fissure, I try to show, provides an important entry point for understanding the contradictory contours of male power in post-apartheid South Africa.

That African men impregnate women and then deny paternity is a prominent media stereotype that plays into longstanding racialised tropes of 'promiscuous' Africans (on which, see McClintock, 1995; Vaughan, 1991). Yet the notion that men in Africa today have absolute power has been decisively challenged by Silberschmidt's work in Kenya and Tanzania. Showing how exertions of male power, such as violence, emerge partially out of male disempowerment, she says: 'Precisely because of patriarchal structures working to the detriment of women, hardly any attempts have been made to investigate and analyse the impact of socioeconomic change on men's lives, and how men are dealing with the situation' (Silberschmidt, 2001, p. 658). Such an analysis can be usefully applied to South Africa.

Given the relative lack of literature on the subject of fathers in South Africa, what follows is tentative and exploratory. Fathering, or paternity, is taken to be the biological act whereby a man's sperm results in the birth of a child. Fatherhood is the social role associated with the care of children (see Chapter 1 of this volume for further discussion of these definitions). I will argue that central to a historically rooted understanding of both fathering and fatherhood among isiZulu speakers is recognition of its embroilment with the project of 'building a home'. In the pre-colonial and early colonial era, the building of a successful home required men to control a large amount of agricultural labour. Men who fathered the most children tended to become the most respected household heads. Although the social value attached to fathering remained strong over the twentieth century, a number of social dynamics helped to reduce the importance of fertility: the gradual replacement of rural agriculture with migrant men's wages as a source of livelihood; the rising dominance of Christian models of smaller nuclear families; and the movement of men and women into smaller urban houses. Meanings around fatherhood also shifted as migrant labour detached men from the homestead and their children for very long periods. Men were now geographically distant 'providers', although fatherhood remained intertwined with the long term process of 'building of a home'.

The rest of this chapter considers changes in relationships and notions of fatherhood that have accompanied the rise of chronic unemployment. I argue that men's abandonment of their social role of fatherhood through the denial of paternity emerges not simply from men's power but from men's disempowerment in certain spheres, including the economic. By contextualising men's actions within the political and economic realities of early twenty-first century South Africa, I dispute the stereotype that young African men are irresponsible, abandoning fathers and, more broadly, that male power is a fixed and unified structure.

The following arguments emanate from ethnographic data carried out in KwaZulu-Natal between 2000 and 2004 as well as from archival and secondary sources. The interviews were conducted as part of an ongoing PhD project to examine the changing political economy of relationships in the last 50 years. Since 2000, I have lived in Isithebe Informal Settlement in Mandeni for approximately 18 months in total. I also stayed in rural Hlabisa for a month. Further background to the Mandeni area and my PhD project can be found in Hunter (2002; 2004).[1] The following sections sketch out briefly the changing contexts of fatherhood in the twentieth century before exploring, in more detail, fathering and fatherhood over a period of chronic unemployment.

Men becoming fathers in twentieth-century KwaZulu-Natal

Fathering and fatherhood were inextricably linked to building a home among isiZulu speakers in the nineteenth century. Each *umuzi* (homestead) was headed by an *umnumzana* who could, resources permitting, marry polygamously. The sons of an *umnumzana* would, in time, marry and break from their father's *umuzi* to build their own. Women moved from their father's lineage to their husband's through the giving of *ilobolo*, usually cattle. In an agrarian, labour-intensive economy, the command of labour was paramount and it was women and children who engaged in the crucial task of agricultural labour while animal husbandry was the domain of men. As a consequence of the centrality of childbirth, *ilobolo* was less 'bride price', as it was commonly called, and rather 'child-price' – an exchange for a woman's reproductive capacity rather than the sale of a woman (see Jeffreys, 1951; Guy, 1987). If a bride was barren, her father could be forced to return his daughter's *ilobolo* or assign another daughter to raise seed. The institution of *ukugana* – often too neatly translated as 'marriage' – was centred on the building of an *umuzi*, a task that itself necessitated childbirth.

In the pre-colonial and early colonial era then, *fathering*, that is spawning children, was central to the continued existence of the homestead and the continuation of the male lineage through a male heir. *Fatherhood*, however, was intertwined with the social role of *umnumzana* (head of household) as leader and protector of his *umuzi*. The social role of the *umnumzana* included providing *ilobolo* for his sons and overseeing his daughters' marriage. A father could also be required to provide *inhlawulo* (a fine or damages) should his son impregnate another woman out of marriage. The father clearly provided a role model for his sons, but the day-to-day socialisation of young men appears to have taken place through peer groups or elder brothers and relatives as well as through the biological father. Certainly, fatherhood was a fluid category, with a boy's uncles referred to as *ubaba omkhulu* (bigger/elder father) or *ubaba omncane* (smaller/younger father).

In the early twentieth century, colonial seizure of land, the introduction of government taxes, and the extraordinary hunger for labour of the diamond and gold mines pulled African men rapidly into the colonial labour market. As the agrarian economy slumped throughout the twentieth century, agricultural production, largely the responsibility of wives and children, began to play a lesser role in rural society. Men were forced to seek employment for longer and longer periods away from home. The stretching of men's lives between rural and urban areas was symbolised by the shift in payment of *ilobolo* from cattle, secured from a man's father, to cash gained from wage labour.

Fathering and fatherhood were reworked in this new milieu. The social value of *fathering* diminished. With declining rural production and new requirements for school fees, children were apparently no longer the asset they once were. Christianity also promoted more modest nuclear families. In addition, *fatherhood* was transformed by men's absence for long periods. In 1936, the ratio of 35-year-old KwaZulu men at home compared to those at work was 2 to 1; but by 1970 nearly half the men aged 50 to 54 years were still absent from home (Nattrass, 1977). Wage labour gave men new powers, but it also imparted on them fresh expectations. In assuming the position of 'breadwinners', men took on primary responsibility for supporting the *umuzi* (Silberschmidt, 2001). A good father was now one who provided reliable support for the *umuzi*.

It is difficult to reconstruct the emotional role of fathers in the pre-colonial and early colonial period. Elderly informants I spoke with tended to remember fathers and grandfathers as authoritarian figures who persistently demanded *inhlonipho* (respect). Eileen Krige said that 'In Zulu society the father, called *baba*, is respected and feared and his command obeyed. A man does not talk when his father is present unless he is addressed' (1936, p. 24). Even if these were accurate accounts of the early twentieth century, how much they reflect the 'traditional' role of fathers and how much they had been shaped by colonialism, migrant labour, and a system of customary law that shored up African men's power as the head of the household, is a moot point. However, it is clear that migrant labour meant that whatever intimacy and emotional support fathers had provided became increasingly impossible. When a man could return only at Christmas, the social role of fatherhood became increasingly attached to a man's position as 'provider'.

Nevertheless, an increasing number of men and women moved to towns and were not therefore part of the migrant labour system. The mass construction of four-roomed township houses in the 1950s and 1960s attempted to channel families into a western-type nuclear model. We need to be sensitive to teleological accounts of social 'individualism' or 'modernisation' and yet Brandel's (1958) study of urban *ilobolo*, like many of the time, posits quite dramatic changes in expectations and norms found in urban areas. Brandel suggests that urban marriage was being organised around individuals and not the family and that there was therefore a 'changing emphasis from cultural or social fatherhood and motherhood to biological parenthood' (Brandel, 1958, p. 39). Rather than the biological father being one among many, such changes potentially fostered a more direct relationship between biological father and son.

The centrality of *umuzi* to the identity of men (and men to the identity of *umuzi*) is well demonstrated by the close symbolical attachment between a man and his *umuzi*, despite his often long absences. This can be illustrated through common saying, prevalent even today. An often used term in isiZulu is '*Ubaba walayikhaya*' (the father of the house) locating the father as head of the household, even if he is absent. Moreover, most *imizi* (homesteads/houses) have an *isihlalo sikababa* (father's chair) from which mischievous children can be seen to scamper when *ubaba* is spotted entering the *umuzi*. Such terms demonstrate well the enduring association between *ubaba* and the long-term processual project of *ukwakha umuzi* (building of a home) despite the exigencies of the labour migrant system that undoubtedly threatened the stability of relationships (see, for instance, Murray, 1981).

The social context of fatherhood in the era of unemployment

It is possible, I believe, to suggest that in the last three decades fathering and fatherhood have been shaped by a set of relatively new, interlinked, social dynamics. Of course, social change of the complexity discussed here is never easy to pin down to particular moments or periods of change. The literature on the family in South Africa is replete with claims of there being unprecedented 'crises' at varying points in history.[2] At the same time, it is imperative to probe discontinuities in relationship patterns and possible causes of such transformations. Three important changes are briefly noted here. First, from the mid-1970s, unemployment began to rise dramatically to its current rate of over 40 per cent nationally. Whereas male informants remember the 1960s as a time when work was unstable and men were constantly harassed by influx controls, there was still a strong demand for male labour. By the 1980s, however, an increasingly large group of men were finding employment difficult to secure.

Second, and linked, marital rates slumped significantly. Population census data suggest that marital rates began to drop from the 1960s. This was probably as a response to increased cohabitation in urban areas, more educated women gaining new work opportunities, and migrant labour biting deeper into the ability of men and women to form long-term relationships. By the 1980s, however, an important reason for reduced marital rates was men's inability to pay *ilobolo* and to fulfil their 'provider' role. Marriage has always been a process and not an event; despite this, the task of setting up an independent household, *ukwakha umuzi* is not achievable for many South Africans today in an era of chronic unemployment. According to the most recent population census, less than 30 per cent of African men and women over 15 years of age were in marital relations.[3] Thus we are witnessing today an accelerated undermining of the joint but contested project of 'building a home'. Closely linked, the present era is one characterised by a sharp reworking of the obligations that men hold towards their biological children.

Third, from the mid-1970s, bio-medical interventions to control African fertility expanded considerably. Thrust forward with the racist aims of stemming black population growth (see Brown, 1987), contraception, particularly Depo Provera, became widely used in South Africa. Already in decline, fertility rates reduced at a quickening pace, following the onset of the government's family planning programme in the mid-1970s. African women now bear on average three children as compared to six in 1970 (Potts & Marks, 2001). In the post-apartheid period, another reproductive intervention, termination of pregnancy, became available through the state and, as described below, this sparked great controversy in townships and rural areas.

Social divisions have widened quite dramatically in post-apartheid South Africa (see Seekings & Nattrass, 2002). I have argued elsewhere that the climate of chronic unemployment and deepening social differentiation has significantly affected relationship patterns. Compared to a generation ago (and being wary of the great variety in relationships), a number of changes can be hypothesised: men and women are much less likely to be able to marry and build *umuzi*; monetary gifts play a greater role in fuelling relationships, including among multiple partners; and manhood is expressed less in building a home and acting as a 'provider' and more in terms of men's success with women (see Hunter, 2002; 2004). The fathering of children and the social role of fatherhood are profoundly altered by these changing relationship patterns.

Ambiguous fatherhood, irresponsible men?

Children might not represent the economic value today that they were in the past, but men still place a high value on fathering children and on the social roles of fatherhood. Fathering a child symbolises sexual virility and propels forward the status of a young man. The social values attached to fatherhood, including acting as a 'provider', also remain highly valued. But while biological *fathering* is relatively easy to achieve, requiring only sexual intercourse, fulfilling the social role of *fatherhood* is much more challenging. In order to satisfy his girlfriend's family, it is still frequently necessary for a man to pay *inhlawulo* (damages for impregnation). These expectations tend to be strongest in rural areas. Of course, the biological father is not always clearly identified or in acceptance of his position. Yet even when a man accepts paternity, he is unlikely to be able to afford to pay *inhlawulo* and almost certainly not *ilobolo* (bridewealth). Still more unlikely is that a young, unemployed, man will be able to fulfil a 'provider' role and support his child. Abandonment – usually seen as an inherently male, particularly African, phenomenon – has to be seen in this context. Certainly, men draw upon gendered discourses to blame 'promiscuous' women for unexpected pregnancies, and yet there is more than a twinge of culpability when deserting men are labelled as unmanly. Many discussions that I have had with young men suggest that they would like to support their children, or at least to pay *inhlawulo* (damages). The problem is their lack of *amandla*. Sipho, in his early twenties, from Sundumbili Township, Mandeni, describes this contradiction: 'having children makes me like a man but it would be better to pay *inhlawulo* and support'.

Below is Mdu's explanation of why men deny paternity. Like many men in South Africa and elsewhere, he does not see the prevention of pregnancy as a man's responsibility. And yet we can glimpse from his testimony, the insecurity of many relationships and the connection between the denial of paternity and economic difficulties:

> [denial of paternity] is caused by different things. Maybe you are in love with someone you don't trust, may be you met her at a bash [street party] or at bad places like that, maybe you become lovers when she already had someone else. When you slept with her maybe she is already pregnant…and then when you count the date that she slept with you if you are clever you will see that it's not yours especially if you don't trust her. Sometimes the reason [for denial] is because you are scared of your family. What are they going to say or do about a child? Maybe you are still in school so you have to leave school to work in order to support the baby. Sometimes you don't deny your baby because you want to but because of the situation.

Denial of paternity is not therefore a form of innate pathology, but has to be seen in the context of the mismatch between men's ability to father children and their ability to act out the social role of fatherhood. While, as argued, this situation results in part from men's lack of *amandla*, men justify their actions through utilising their social power to position single mothers as 'loose'.

A woman's family will tend to take the clearest moral position in such circumstances, often dismissing the father of the child as 'useless'. The fact that so many men are not able to pay *inhlawulo* or *ilobolo*, and also that many daughters do not live with parents, can, to some extent, quieten such views. In some cases, men's active involvement in their children's lives even without *inhlawulo* or *ilobolo* can partially take the place of marriage as a sign of love, commitment, and permanence. Certainly, being *ubaba wengane* (father of the child), catapults men into notionally permanent relationships with their girlfriends. Again, *inhlawulo* or *ilobolo* validates this relationship, but even without these payments the mother of the child will usually wish to have a continuing relationship with the father of her child. Taking this commitment seriously, some men father children with only one women, although many father children with different mothers. Philani and Sandile offer insights into how the high value of being an *isoka* (man with many girlfriends) is balanced against the disadvantages of having children with several women:

> MH: Are you more of a man if you have three children with one woman or one child with three women?

> Philani: We do not have the same views, I don't think I can have three children from the same person. I wish to have children from different women. If I have done that then I can call myself a man.

> Sandile: I want to have ten children from the same person so that when the children have grown to our age now they will not hate each other due to them having different mothers. So that is why I want to have children from the same person.

Women's right to contraception and abortion also fundamentally shapes relationships and struggles over paternity today. Opposition towards condoms by some men is well recorded but less so are men's attempts to prevent women from *jova*-ing (being injected, meaning taking Depo Provera). Depo Provera is often chosen by women because it is clandestine, a form of contraception easily hidden from men. Even so, a number of men oppose their girlfriends' use of Depo Provera because they say that it makes their body 'wet'. The termination of a pregnancy can also be violently opposed by men. One informant recalled how a friend was badly beaten up after her boyfriend found out that she had aborted his child without telling him. In this instance, the boyfriend's manliness was challenged by his girlfriend taking control of her body and ending his fathering of a child.

Conclusion

The violence and coercion that characterises many relationships in South Africa can lead to representations of gender as a zero-sum phenomenon. If men have power, women have none; if women are empowered, men must be disempowered. This chapter has argued that men's power in certain spheres, including their ability to abandon pregnant women, is linked to men's disempowerment in other spheres, notably economic participation. Many men are extremely frustrated at not being able to meet the accepted social roles of fatherhood, including paying *inhlawulo*, *ilobolo*, and acting as a 'provider'. These contractions lead to an 'ambiguous fatherhood' whereby manliness is partially boosted by *fathering* children, at the same time as which, men who are unable to fulfil roles associated with *fatherhood* are branded as unmanly. The continued racialised stereotypes of African men as holding unmitigated power and being irresponsible and 'promiscuous' need to be replaced by conceptions of sexuality as embedded within social change and South Africa's racialised history.

Mark Hunter is a Research Associate at the School of Development Studies, University of KwaZulu-Natal. He has written journal articles on the social context of HIV/AIDS in South Africa for *African Studies, Transformation*, and *Culture, Health and Sexuality*. He will shortly submit his PhD to the Department of Geography at the University of California at Berkeley.

Notes

1   I would like to thank the Busane and Thabede families with whom I have stayed; Philisiwe Mabunda for invaluable research assistance; the many informants with whom I spoke; the Africa Centre, Mtubatuba, for facilitating my stay in Hlabisa; and Rob Morrell for detailed criticisms of an earlier draft of this chapter.

2   Of the recent historical literature on sexuality in southern Africa, Delius and Glaser (2002) provide a good summary of changing sexual socialisation in the twentieth century, while Ann Mager (1999) links increased sexual violence to men's disempowerment in 1950s Ciskei. Classic ethnographies that chart the changing context of fatherhood in the early twentieth century include Hunter [Wilson] (1936) and Schapera (1947).

3   According to census figures, the number of married people older than 15 years was as follows: 1936 (56%); 1951 (54%); 1960 (57%); 1970 (49%); 1980 (42%); 1991 (38%); 2001 (30%) (author's calculation from various census reports, Statistics South Africa, Pretoria).

References

Brandel, M. (1958). Urban *lobolo* attitudes: A preliminary report. *African Studies, 17*, 34–51.

Brown, B. (1987). Facing the 'Black Peril': The politics of population control in South Africa. *Journal of Southern African Studies, 13*, 256–273.

Delius, P., & Glaser, C. (2002). Sexual socialisation in South Africa: A historical perspective. *African Studies, 61,* 27–54.

Guy, J. (1987). Analysing pre-capitalist societies in southern Africa. *Journal of Southern African Studies, 14,* 18–37.

Hunter, M. (2002). The materiality of everyday sex: Thinking beyond 'prostitution'. *African Studies, 61,* 99–120.

Hunter, M. (2004). Masculinities, multiple-sexual-partners, and AIDS: The making and unmaking of *Isoka* in KwaZulu-Natal. *Transformation, 54,* 123–153.

Hunter (Wilson), M. (1936). *Reaction to conquest: Effects of contact with Europeans on the Pondo of South Africa.* Oxford: Oxford University Press.

Jeffreys, M. (1951). *Lobolo* is child-price. *African Studies, 10,* 145–83.

Krige, E. (1936). *The social system of the Zulus.* Pietermaritzburg: Shuter & Shooter.

Mager, A. (1999). *Gender and the making of a South African Bantustan: A social history of the Ciskei, 1945–1959.* Oxford: James Currey.

McClintock, A. (1995). *Imperial leather: Race, gender, and sexuality in the colonial conquest.* New York; London: Routledge.

Murray, C. (1981). *Families divided: The impact of migrant labour in Lesotho.* Cambridge: Cambridge University Press.

Nattrass, J. (1977). *Migrant Labour and underdevelopment: the case of KwaZulu. Black/white income gap project.* Interim research report No. 3. Durban: Department of Economics, University of Natal, Durban.

Potts, D., & Marks, S. (2001). Fertility in southern Africa: The quiet revolution. *Journal of Southern African Studies, 27,* 189–205.

Schapera, I. (1947). *Migrant labour and tribal life: A study of conditions in the Bechuanalad Protectorate.* Oxford: Oxford University Press.

Seekings, J., & Nattrass, N. (2002). Class, distribution and redistribution in post-apartheid South Africa. *Transformation, 50,* 1–30.

Silberschmidt, M. (2001). Disempowerment of men in rural and urban East Africa: Implications for male identity and sexual behavior. *World Development, 29,* 657–671.

Vaughan, M. (1991). *Curing their ills: Colonial power and African illness.* London: Polity Press.

CHAPTER 9

Men and children: changing constructions of fatherhood in *Drum* magazine, 1951 to 1960

Lindsay Clowes

Introduction

Images of fatherhood have differed over time. The wide variety of ways in which fathers have been presented in differing media and at different times serve to remind us that the content of fatherhood is contested rather than fixed. In the last couple of decades, for example, there have been significant shifts in the understandings of fathers, with 'new dads' becoming a popular subject of magazines. The rise of the 'new dad', represented as a hands-on father who looks after the kids, changes nappies and takes his share of domestic responsibility in private and public, can be contrasted with a time not so long ago when such activities were considered to be the domain largely, or exclusively, of women in general, and mothers in particular. In this chapter, I show that this historical comparison is not altogether accurate. Representations in the 1950s of African men in *Drum*, a magazine with a huge, continent-wide readership, often portrayed men as fathers happily ensconced in domestic situations.

This chapter examines changes in the ways in which African fathers were portrayed in the South African version of *Drum*. I show that in the early 1950s black men were regularly portrayed as fathers in domestic situations. But this changed over the course of the decade as both verbal and visual images of men in *Drum* increasingly portrayed them either in work contexts devoid of wives and children or in the process of leaving wives and children behind on their way out of the home. These kinds of images were much more typical of the ways in which white men had, for decades, been represented in magazines aimed at white audiences. The period thus sees the images of black men produced by *Drum* converge with those produced for white audiences, showing parenting as women's work. The involved and nurturing father was, in other words, written out of *Drum*'s discourse on manhood over the 1950s.

Twentieth-century discourses around fatherhood

In the west, twentieth-century hegemonic discourses around fatherhood have seen a privileging of the role of 'mother' at the expense of that of 'father'. Played out on an international as well as a domestic stage, these discourses helped shape the South African law that narrowly defined the rights of, and limited the possibilities for fathers while at the same time entrenching the rights and duties of mothers. It was (and remains) widely believed to be only 'natural' that as well as bearing children, it was also women's work to raise them, and that all women are born with an innate ability to nurture – or to mother. In early modern Europe, however, fatherhood – and motherhood – were constructed differently. '[I]t was the father who was considered to shape the child, to be the "natural parent"' (Lupton & Barclay 1997, p. 37). The changing role of the father has often been contested. In early nineteenth-century South Africa, male slaves in the Western Cape were denied any legal or social rights to their children. This became a source of friction and at least one slave rebellion was inspired by conflict between a slave owner and a slave man over the treatment of the latter's child (Van der Spuy, 1996). It was the legal and social recognition of 'fatherhood' that gave important content to 'freedom', following the emancipation of slaves in South Africa in 1834 (Scully, 1997).

Drum magazine

What has come to be known simply as *Drum* first appeared as *The African Drum* in March 1951. Funded, owned and edited by white men, the post-World War II society into which the magazine was born was one in which industrialisation and urbanisation had seen significant change in South Africa's racial demography. Census records indicate that there were more than two million black South Africans living in urban areas in 1951, compared to just one million in 1936 (Department of Statistics, 1980; 1.17, 1.13). Thus by 1951, the rural migrant labour workforce upon which white industrialists had previously relied had been supplemented by an urban black working class, a working class that was both 'settled' and 'permanent' according to the government commission of 1948 chaired by J.H. Fagan (SAIRR, n.d., p. 7). It was this ethnically mixed, urbanised and urbanising black population that was to become *Drum*'s main audience in the 1950s (Clowes, 2002).

Although it remained under the ownership and editorship of white men, the magazine's content and layout were produced almost entirely by black men, photographers such as Peter Magubane and Bob Gosani, and journalists who, through their writing, were to become household names in South Africa. In the early 1950s, Henry Khumalo – Mr *Drum* himself – was joined by Todd Matshikiza, Arthur Maimane, Can Themba, Casey Motsisi, Bloke Modisane, Ezekiel Mpahlele and Nat Nakasa, as well as many others. Together these men produced an enormously influential magazine that had, by the early 1960s, developed into five separate editions produced in five different locations around Africa. It was to become, according to one analyst, 'one of the most popular magazines in Anglophone Africa' (Mutongi, 2000, p. 1; Clowes, 2002).

The political context into which the magazine was born was one in which the Nationalist Party was beginning to implement its plans for separate development or apartheid after winning the election of 1948. The times were characterised by the growth of authoritarianism and political repression alongside rapid economic growth. These racially charged conditions touched the lives of both producers and consumers of *Drum*, helping to infuse both black and white notions of sex and gender and informing the particular images of manhood and masculinity produced by the magazine over the next few decades. This chapter, however, focuses on the early period of *Drum*'s history, in which I suggest that black males were initially portrayed through their relationships with other people – through parents, grandparents, wives, siblings and – most importantly – children. How and why this changed over the course of the 1950s is the focus of the discussion that follows.

Fatherhood in the early *Drum*

In marked contrast to images elsewhere (Lupton & Barclay, 1997; Chopra, 2001; Davidoff & Hall, 1987), the 'nurturing father' was a crucial component of the adulthood portrayed by the early volumes of *Drum* magazine. In contrast to magazines such as *Outspan* and *Femina*, aimed at white South African audiences, *Drum* represented fatherhood as central to manhood, privileging men's relationships with children, particularly their sons, in a variety of ways. Articles about important men foregrounded their role as fathers, photographs emphasised the proximity of fathers and children, and even advertisements accentuated fathers' concerns for their offspring. The early *Drum* emphasised male identities in which being both father and son were important. But over the course of the 1950s images emphasising these kinds of identities slowly disappeared. By 1960 such images were scarce and texts, advertisements and photographs that featured children located them alongside 'mothers' rather than 'fathers'. As the 1950s wore on, the images in *Drum* grew to resemble more closely those in *Outspan* and *Femina*, with 'father' increasingly narrowly constructed to embody the primarily financial obligations of the stereotypical western middle-class nuclear family.

In the early to mid-1950s interactions between fathers and children were presented by *Drum* as an unremarkable part of a man's daily life. The members of a man's family were, for example, very clearly foregrounded in an article about retired black cricketer Oom Piet Gwele, which began:

> We found the Gwele family cuddled around a glowing fire on a chilly evening: parents, children and grandchildren. Mama Nancy Gwele had a bad 'flu, and eldest daughter Edna Mnguni had left her boxing promoter husband in Germiston to nurse her – and contracted the 'flu too. (November 1954)

The *first* mention of Oom Piet, the supposed subject of the article, only occurred in the *second* paragraph. In other words Oom Piet, the man, was constructed *through* his children and his children's achievements. And in framing the text with photographs of Oom Piet's children and grandchildren, *Drum* surrounded him, both metaphorically and literally, with evidence of his fatherhood and grandfatherhood. Fatherhood, in other words, was central to *Drum*'s representations of Oom Piet, the man.

This kind of reporting was commonplace in the early *Drum*, with articles regularly conflating the notions of 'father' and 'man'. Stories about men frequently saw their children claim centre stage. Israel Alexander, for instance, hailed by *Drum* as 'South Africa's richest African' was photographed with his daughter, Joy, at work, and with his family at home (December 1954). It was Jake Tuli's children who were foregrounded in *Drum*'s coverage of the boxer's fights. After losing the Empire flyweight title in 1954, *Drum*'s headline declared that 'Jake loses crown, kids comfort him', while two of the three pictures published alongside the text featured his children (December 1954). In an article in which his mother loomed large, King Edward Masinga (the first black radio broadcaster to be employed by the South African Broadcasting Corporation), was portrayed with his two daughters and a niece (April 1955). Even political and traditional leaders – as the coverage of future Botswanan president, Seretse Khama, his wife and children made clear – were portrayed against the backdrop of their families. At the other end of the social scale, it was 'husbands' and 'fathers' rather than 'men' who were the victims of homicide attacks (July 1955; June 1955).

Articles in magazines produced for white audiences tended, in contrast, to downplay white men's identities as fathers, constructing children as the responsibility of housebound white mothers. Even on those rare occasions when white readers were promised something more than a simple account of a man's public life, they were disappointed. Despite promising that it would 'tell you about the man very few people really know', *Outspan* focused almost exclusively on the professional career of national cricket captain Dudley Nourse, effectively eliding his identities as both father and son (May 1951).

Advertisements in *Drum* in the early 1950s also clearly conflated the identities of father and man, in contrast to advertisements aimed at white audiences. Perhaps constructing the black male breadwinner as guardian of the family purse, advertisements (usually placed by white-owned firms) tapped into notions of black fathers' pride in their sons. A variety of advertisements featuring black men and babies, but not mothers, clearly privileged the role of father, suggesting that at least some advertisers believed the route to a man's pocket lay through his male offspring. 'Your baby is a fine healthy son', declared a female nurse to a solitary man in an advertisement for the antiseptic liquid, Dettol™. 'How happy a father feels when he hears those words', commented the text (September 1952), while another advertisement for Dettol™ erased both the female nurse and the mother who had given birth, portraying one man congratulating another on 'a healthy childbirth – and such a fine baby' (October 1952).

While advertisements for baby foods in both *Outspan* and *Femina* portrayed only white women with babies, those in *Drum* often employed images of fathers and sons. It was father, rather than mother, for example, who appeared to be holding the baby in an advertisement for Incumbe™ baby food in April 1952. The manufacturers of Nutrine™, another baby food, employed the racialised hierarchies so familiar to South African audiences to tap into local working-class aspirations of upward mobility. In one of these advertisements, Stanley Msomi, a skilled mechanic is confronted by his white male boss. 'You used to be a good worker Stanley, now you stand around doing nothing. What's wrong?' Msomi explains that 'I'm worried about my little boy. He's thin and weak and always crying.' The supervisor's response is also to identify with him as a father: 'My son was thin and weak too till Nutrine made him strong. *You* should try Nutrine.' The next frame shows Stanley telling his wife Rose that 'we must get it', followed by the penultimate frame in which Rose informs us that '*Nutrine* certainly is nourishing. It has made baby fat and strong in only three months.' The final frame presents the reader with a smiling Stanley Msomi who 'works better than ever now' (November 1952).

These kinds of images were not to last, however, and as the 1950s drew to a close advertisements tended increasingly to depict babies and children with housebound mothers. Likewise articles and features about important men contained fewer details and photographs of their offspring. Although men were often acknowledged as husbands, they were seldom recognised as fathers, let alone as sons or grandfathers. And even if these kinds of biographical details were revealed, the chances of pictures or texts exposing the ways in which men shared their lives with children and parents diminished. It was increasingly the office – rather than the home – that was the place for a man to be seen in the pages of *Drum*.

The late 1950s

Emblematic of these changes was *Drum*'s three-part biography of black South African cricketer, Basil D'Oliveira, in 1960. Apart from one brief mention of D'Oliveira's father (in his capacity as his son's first cricketing coach), not a word was said about other members of D'Oliveira's family and both the text and the images more closely resembled that of *Outspan*'s article about Dudley Nourse in 1951 than they did *Drum*'s article about Oom Piet in 1954 (June 1960; July 1960; August 1960). Coverage of politicians, too, now frequently separated them from their families. Where much had been made of Sir Seretse Khama's children in 1955, not a word was written about the family of Hastings Banda, future president of Malawi, in an account of Banda's achievements in March 1959. And in terms of more ordinary men, anonymous children and unnamed wives might be the justification for the demand for higher wages which 'would bring immense benefits to a majority of below breadline workers' and let 'the black man…stand on his own two feet'. But this was a construction that, like those in magazines aimed at white audiences, emphasised an identity built around purely financial commitments (July 1960, p. 33). Similar trends were evident in advertisements. By the mid-1950s, black fathers had disappeared from advertisements for Dettol™ and baby foods, even as the range of baby foods advertised increased. Instead, like advertisements placed in white magazines, it tended to be black women (presented as mothers) or white males (presented as experts) who exhorted mothers, rather than fathers, to purchase such products.

Explaining change

While pictures and texts elided the identities of father and son, images of adult males continued to appear in the magazine in the late 1950s. These images, however, increasingly located black men outside a home that contained women and children. In other words, the magazine increasingly located black men as solitary bread-winners for the archetypal middle-class nuclear family. But if this was the image, the reality was a little different. Although the first half of the twentieth century had seen rapid urbanisation of both men and women, with some urban couples 'remarkably western in form', and 'living "in family circumstances"' by 1950, these were primarily working-class families (Bozzoli, 1991; Bonner, 1988). Few black wives and mothers could choose to stay at home. But the growth of nuclear, let alone middle-class, households was curtailed over the 1950s and 1960s. The period saw the 'number of men living with their wives and children in urban areas…drastically reduced,' according to one commentator (Wollheim, n.d., pp. 6,8). The consolidation of influx control, pass laws, forced removals, job reservation, the Group Areas Act and so on, after the election of 1948, both limited the opportunities for black men, women and children to live together in towns, and saw increasing numbers of children raised by grandparents in the rural areas. The images produced in *Drum* could not, therefore, be a simple reflection of socio-economic change, and explana-tions need to be sought elsewhere. Such explanations also need to take into account that the advertisements featured in the magazine were generally drawn up and placed by white men, while articles, stories, investigative journalism and photo-graphs were written, produced and edited primarily by black men.

Changes in advertisements could be attributable to changes in the South African advertising industry. In the 1950s, the industry was beginning to recognise the growing significance of the urban black market, and to professionalise. These elements were combined in research projects exploring the relationships between black consumers and the advertising industry and reinforced through the recruitment of black men into white-owned advertising firms. Thus the late 1950s saw Nimrod Mkele hired as head of the newly created African market division of

J. Walter Thompson, while a year or so later, ex-*Drum* staffer Dan Chochco, was appointed first as adviser and then as manager for the new African Research Division of another local agency (*Selling Age*, March 1960). Overall, attempts to tap into the black market over the 1950s seem to have produced a consensus amongst advertisers that advertisements aimed at black customers would be more successful if they reflected the values, structures and relationships portrayed in advertisements typically aimed at middle-class white consumers (Burke, 1996).

Explaining change in the material produced by *Drum* itself is more challenging. To begin with, as de Kanter (1987) notes, there are multiple meanings to the term 'father'. A 'father' might be an individual whose role was simply to provide the biological material that generated a child. On the other hand, there may be no biological relationship between a father and those who are perceived to be his children. In some societies, kinship and blood relationships play a role in signifying fatherhood. The brothers of a biological father are also understood to be 'fathers' to their sibling's child in some southern African societies, for example. While not constructed as 'father', the brother of a mother also has a particular and significant role to play in a child's life in these societies. These kinds of relationships tend to be unrecognised and/or misunderstood in the west, where the praxis around child-raising has, during the twentieth century, increasingly marginalised the role of male parents.

Since the beginning of the twentieth century, western baby and childcare manuals have increasingly addressed women with advice about how to raise their offspring. This coverage has generally been located in women's magazines or in the women's pages of other media. The assumption that children were women's business also underpinned global policy documents. Just three years before the first edition of *Drum* was published in 1951, the *Universal Declaration of Human Rights* had not a word to say about fathers and fathering. Despite constructing the autonomous human subject as male, and despite stating that 'the family is the natural and fundamental group unit of society', the *Declaration* makes absolutely no mention of 'fatherhood'. In privileging the role of 'mothering', in reflecting and establishing 'nurturing' as something of which only women – and all women – are capable, the *Declaration* concurrently denied such roles to fathers. In South Africa, as van der Spuy has noted (with the exception of Clingman's 1998 study of Bram Fischer), 'any form of domestic relationship is profoundly silenced' in twentieth-century biographies of local male political leaders (Van der Spuy, 2002, p. 9). It is, I suggest below, these understandings of the role of 'father' (which has only recently begun to break down) that shaped the twentieth-century discourse which lay as a backdrop to the changing images portrayed in *Drum* in the 1950s.

With the exception of Henry Khumalo (and later on Ezekiel Mphahlele), none of the black men hired by *Drum* had any experience of writing or publishing. And yet, in the struggle to establish the magazine in the early 1950s, these writers were apparently given a great deal of leeway in constructing their stories. Anthony Sampson, the white editor imported from England in 1951, recalls allowing his writers to write what they liked. My 'ignorance' he recalls, 'had its advantages. I had to let the black journalists tell their own stories with a vigour and freshness that broke all the rules, but that expressed the true spirit of the townships' (Sampson, 2001, p. 13). So it is possible that the black producers of *Drum* were relatively unfamiliar with these western discourses. Indeed it is more than likely that they drew on constructions of manhood that were closely tied to African understandings of masculinity in which, for men, full adulthood was tied to marriage and fatherhood, and where 'fatherhood' meant a great deal more than a simple biological connection. If this is indeed the case, then why did these representations change? Perhaps it is no more than a coincidence that the first signs of change corresponded with Sampson's departure and his replacement as editor by a series of highly experienced white South African and immigrant English journalists who may have adopted a far more hands-on approach (Clowes, 2002).

It is more likely that black journalists themselves subtly adapted their writing to embrace the 'modern' (i.e. western) narratives of individualism that, even within the nuclear family, treated men as isolated, autonomous and independent of both women and children. Stuart Hall is one of those who have argued that the very idea of modernity and its celebration of 'civilisation', 'progress' and 'rationality' is predicated on difference (Hall, 1992). At the same time, scholars have argued that discourses of colonialism are characterised by these sorts of notions of difference, and have highlighted the common patterns by which colonised countries and colonised peoples were regarded as 'feminine' and 'childlike' in opposition to colonisers who were set up as masculine and adult (Markowitz, 2001; Moane, 1999; Sinha, 1997). Take into account the idea that '[t]he more pronounced degree of differentiation between white men and women is offered as one factor separating whites from other races and signaling their superiority' (Ferber, 1999; p. 77), and it becomes clearer that western discourses around manhood have been inextricably tied to those of race as well as gender, and that what makes a man is both his whiteness as well as the ways in which he is distanced from women and children.

Given this, it could well be argued that portraying black men inside the home surrounded by children and wives inadvertently played *into* the apartheid project of racist unmanning. Representing black males as men through the proximity of children, wives and other family members, was a discourse typical of African rather than western societies. In the minds of white audiences and the apartheid regime, far from demonstrating successful manhood, the proximity of children and women actually helped feminise black men. With this in mind, *Drum*'s shift towards displaying males as men through the proximity specifically of other men can be understood as a process by which black writers elected to adopt and adapt from the overarching hegemonic framework in ways that reclaimed agency. Rather than a simple evolutionary process in which black writers slowly learned the 'proper' discourse, writing fatherhood out of manhood can thus be understood as an implicit challenge to the apartheid project of racist unmanning.

Conclusion

In the early editions of *Drum* magazine, black males were represented as men in both articles and advertisements through the foregrounding of their relationships with children generally and sons in particular. But by the beginning of the 1960s, images of children were confined to the flanks of women presented as home-bound mothers, women portrayed as married to breadwinning men whose significant others were increasingly presented as other non-kin men such as employers and colleagues. Changes in advertisements can be attributed to changes in the advertising industry which encouraged the production of images of black families in ways that resembled the structures and relationships typical of middle-class white families. Changes in the articles that appeared in *Drum*, on the other hand, have more complex causes. In the early *Drum*, images of black men with children owed a great deal to understandings of what it meant to be a man that emerged out of African rather than western traditions. That these images changed could be read as the simple consequence of black writers' increasing familiarity with and uncritical emulation of the western discourses that established children as women's business. Alternatively, given the context of white supremacist and colonial discourses that endeavoured to establish adult black males as effeminate/boys, the shift towards creating distance between black fathers and their children can be read as the product of agency, representing an implicit challenge to the racist construction of a subordinate black masculinity. With this in mind, changes in *Drum*'s later representations of men can be read as a declaration that – *just* like white men – black males were indeed men and not boys.

Lindsay Clowes is a Lecturer in Women's and Gender Studies at the University of the Western Cape, following her training in Historical Studies at the University of Cape Town. Her recent research explores media representatives of identities with particular focus on masculinities and sexualities in South Africa's *Drum* magazine.

References

Bonner, P. (1988). Family, crime and political consciousness on the East Rand, 1939–1955. *Journal of Southern African Studies, 14*, 393–420.

Bozzoli, B. (with Nkotsoe, M.). (1991). *Women of Phokeng: Consciousness, life strategy, and migrancy in South Africa, 1900–1983*. Johannesburg: Ravan Press.

Burke, T. (1996). *Lifebuoy men, Lux women: Commodification, consumption and cleanliness in modern Zimbabwe*. London: Leicester University Press.

Cape Times, 4 April 2003.

Chopra, R. (2001). Retrieving the father: Gender studies, 'father love' and the discourse of mothering. *Women's Studies International Forum, 24*, 445–455.

Clingman, S. (1998). *Bram Fischer: Afrikaner revolutionary*. Cape Town: David Philip & Mayibuye Books.

Clowes, L. (2002). *A modernised man? Changing constructions of masculinity in* Drum *magazine, 1951–1984*. Unpublished PhD thesis, University of Cape Town, Cape Town.

Davidoff, L., & Hall, C. (1987). *Family fortunes: Men and women of the English middle class 1780–1850*. London: Hutchinson.

de Kanter, R. (1987). A father is a bag full of money: The person, the position and the symbol of the father. In T. Knijn, & A. Mulder (Eds.). *Unravelling fatherhood* (pp. 6–26). Dordrecht: Foris.

Drum. March 1951–April 1965.

Femina. January 1951–December 1951, January 1954–June 1954.

Femina & Woman's Life. January 1958–June 1958, January 1960–June 1960.

Ferber, A. (1999). *White man falling*. New York: St. Martin's Press.

Hall, S. (1992). *Modernity and its futures*. Cambridge: Polity.

Lupton, D., & Barclay, L. (1997). *Constructing fatherhood: Discourses and experiences*. London: Sage.

Markowitz, S. (2001). Pelvic politics: Sexual dimorphism and racial difference. *Signs, 26,* 389–414

Mkele, N. (1959). Advertising to the African. *Selling Age*, November, 22–25.

Moane, G. (1999). *Gender and colonialism*. Basingstoke: Macmillan.

Mutongi, K. (2000). 'Dear Dolly's Advice': Representations of youth, courtship and sexualities in Africa, 1960–1980, *International Journal of African Historical Studies, 33,* 1–23.

Outspan. January 1951–June 1951, January 1955–June 1955, January 1957–May 1957.

Sampson, A. (2001). *Sunday Independent*. 1 April.

Scully, P. (1997). *Liberating the family? Gender and British slave emancipation in the rural Western Cape, South Africa, 1823 1853*. Cape Town: David Philip.

Sinha, M. (1997). *Colonial masculinity: The 'manly Englishman' and the 'effeminate Bengali' in the late nineteenth century*. New Delhi: Kali for Women.

South African Department of Statistics (n.d.) *South African Statistics 1980*. Pretoria: Government Printer.

SAIRR (South African Institute of Race Relations) (n.d.) *A Digest of the Fagan Report*. Johannesburg: SAIRR.

van der Spuy, P. (2002). *Not only 'the younger daughter of Dr Abdurahman': A feminist exploration of early influences on the political development of Cissie Gool*. Unpublished PhD thesis, University of Cape Town, Cape Town.

van der Spuy, P. (1996) 'Making himself master': Galant's rebellion revisited. *South African Historical Journal, 34,* 1–28.

Wollheim, O. (n.d.). *The new townsmen: The legal position of the African in the white areas today*. Cape Town: Civil Rights League.

Representations
and roles

Bongani Ngwenya and his daughter Sibonisile by Val Adamson, professional photographer

CHAPTER 10
The father in the mind

Graham Lindegger

Introduction

Both in South Africa and internationally there has been a growing concern with fathers and fathering, characterised by attempts to increase the involvement of fathers with their children and to enhance the experience of fathering for men. Why is it that some fathers are involved and committed, whilst others are distant and disinterested? What facilitates or inhibits the involvement of fathers with their children? What can be done to increase the involvement of fathers with their children? These questions have been asked from both theoretical and practical perspectives, and various social and psychological theories have been used in attempts to answer them. There are many and varied ways of understanding the process and experience of fathering, its source and its impact on family and children.[1]

Psychoanalysis, an interdisciplinary field of study of psychological experience, has also been used to investigate these questions. The work of Carl Jung, a scholar within the broad paradigm of psychoanalysis, is one particular theoretical approach which has been widely used, and has found particular support in South Africa. Jung argued that the fathering experience, involving both giving and receiving fathering, is based on innate psychological dispositions that he termed archetypes. According to Jung, archetypes determine many different aspects of life experience and behaviour, of which fathering is only one example, albeit an important one. This chapter will introduce and explain the notion of the archetype, and of the father archetype in particular. It will then go on to critically examine various aspects of Jung's ideas – their implications for understanding fathering, and how they might apply to South Africa.

What is an archetype?

The notion of archetype comes from Jung's theory of the collective unconscious. Jung, like all psychoanalysts, saw the unconscious as the core of psychological functioning. However, unlike his predecessor Sigmund Freud, Jung introduced the notion of a 'collective unconscious' alongside the personal unconscious of each individual. According to Jung, all members of the human species shared the same unconscious experiences and predispositions, regardless of their situation in history or geographical location, and he argued that there was empirical evidence for these universal aspects of the collective unconscious, especially as manifested in symbols. Archetypes can be seen as predispositions which shape one's experience of the world. Knox (1999, p. 522) describes archetypes as 'simple orienting structures'.

The function of archetypes is to facilitate adaptation to the environment. Jung believed that the archetypes were rooted in the unconscious, where 'there resided the collective wisdom of our species, the basic programme enabling us to meet all the exigent demands of life' (Stevens, 1982, p. 34). For Jung the archetype was a biological entity, having the 'capacity to initiate, control and mediate the common behavioural characteristics and typical experiences' of humankind, and Stevens sees a close parallel between Jung's idea of archetypes and Chomsky's idea of innate capacity for speech in 'deep structures' (Stevens, p. 39). As applied to the experience of fathering, this suggests that all humans have an innate capacity to father, although the exact form of fathering would be culturally determined.

But Jung is also at pains to point out that archetypes are forms without content. Much as archetypes represent predispositions, or pre-existing possibilities for behaviour, they remain broad predispositions. The exact quality and shape of the archetype depends on the life experience and cultural context of the person. While archetypes are expressed in images and symbols, Jung believed that they provide a broad predisposition rather than an inherited image, and that the specific image of the archetype is derived from the socio-cultural environment by learning; so, the specific image is a particular representation of the underlying archetype.

What is the father archetype?

Given their adaptive function, Jung argued that there are as many archetypes as there are life experiences. However, certain archetypes are more dominant and familiar in the lives of most people. Typical examples of these are the archetypes of father and of mother.

The father archetype may show itself in many forms, often including the elder, lawmaker, king, and father-in-heaven. The father is the embodiment of the logos principle, that is, the principle of thought and wisdom. 'His attributes are activity and penetration, differentiation and judgement, fecundity and destruction' (Stevens, 1982, p. 105). If the father (archetype) has a good and caring side, it is also true that it has a potentially destructive side, such as a preoccupation with power and control.

In most societies, largely because of the gendered organisation of labour, fathers have an instrumental role acting as the bridge between family life and the life of society at large, in contrast with the mother's more expressive and caring role, concerned with the home and family. '[T]he father is concerned with events occurring in the tangible world in the context of space and time – events which are approached, controlled and modified through consciousness and the use of the will … he constellates for them the whole extroverted potential of the world as place-to-be-known-and-lived-in' (Stevens, 1982, p. 107). In this position, fathers can model and foster the development of skills necessary for successful adult adaptation to the external, social and physical world, including the world of social relationships, work, money, politics and power. The father archetype may be seen as the predisposition to developing the skills to deal with this 'external' world.

The particular flavour of the attributes developed on the basis of the father archetype is contributed by the developing boy's own father or father-figure, and the father images available in particular socio-cultural settings. Early in his work, Jung was of the view that father-related behaviour was entirely the result of the experience of the personal father. Towards the end of his life, however, he gave far greater weight to the role of the father archetype in the development of these attributes. From the point of view of Jungian psychology, the father archetype plays a major role in the development of these attitudes and attributes for dealing with the external world, in so far as it provides the predispositions from which these qualities are fashioned.

Functions of the father archetype

Stevens suggests that father and mother represent two quite different modes of being and loving, with mother loving in an unconditional way, whereas father's love is conditional upon performance. This is linked with the father's function of facilitating connection with and adjustment to the demands of the external world.

Samuels (2001) claims that too much has been made of the law-enforcing and rule-setting role of fathers, and too little has been made of paternal warmth. He says that 'warmth and erotic playback' (p. 108) between fathers and their sons and daughters is developmentally very important. It is important for daughters because it recognises and affirms them as people in their own right, rather than only as potential mothers, enabling them to break out of the trap of seeing womanhood as synonymous with motherhood. But it is also important for sons for the development of what Samuels calls 'homosociality', which leads to forms of social and political organisation in society. At present, though, there is a pervasive fear that warm fathers will be effeminate and stir the development of homosexuality in their sons. Samuels suggests that the notion of fatherly warmth helps to break the split between the idea of the male body as abusive and damaging, and the female body as comforting and reassuring, and that mothers may serve a particular function in this regard, insofar as they may model a pattern of paternal warmth.

One of the commonly recognised and important functions of the father is the establishment of gender identity or gender-consciousness. The boy child grows to the realisation that 'I and father are one' taking on the gender characteristics of the father, whereas the girl child realises the inherent otherness of father and males in general (Stevens, 1982). Samuels (1989) suggests that this is as much about 'gender certainty and uncertainty' (p. 74) as it is about gender identity. He uses the concept of gender-certainty/confusion to refer to the extent to which people are identified with normative patterns of gender. While such identifications may serve adaptive purposes if they have a moderate degree of 'certainty', there is also the risk of restrictive psychological function if they are too 'certain'. Samuels suggests that 'unhelpful gender certainty in the unconscious' (p. 72) has the effect of denying the child of either sex a full richness of experience, and the challenge is one of 'not being too gender certain or too gender confused' (p. 75). It is here that Samuels sees a critical role for the father, in helping the child to find a satisfactory balance between gender certainty and gender confusion.

For Samuels, fathers should have 'an optimal erotic relationship', or 'playback' with their daughters (p. 82). This playback allows the daughter to break out of the narrow equation of women = mother, and the erotic relationship with father allows the daughter to explore a 'plurality of other, non-uterine female paths'. This erotic playback has a significant role in challenging and discarding a constricting feminine psychology. It is important to note that this erotic relationship with the father is not in any way the same as an actual sexual relationship – on the contrary, the relationship forms in psychological space and in such a way that the girl's development is safe and protected.

Alongside the role fathers play in the establishment of gender identity, another important function of fathers is to teach children, to transform antisocial sadistic aggression into socially useful aggression. The channelling of aggression into constructive uses is a key developmental achievement. Traditionally, the father mediates between the family and the world, and shows how it is possible to engage actively and assertively with the world without being destructive.

Psychoanalysis claims that one of the functions of fathers is to redeem children from being permanently psychologically merged with their mothers. In psychoanalytic terms, this merger is called a 'psychotic symbiosis'. Margaret Mahler, in particular, described this process of separation, which might be seen as the awakening of children from their sleep (meaning symbiosis with mother), and turning towards the world (Mahler & Gosliner, 1955). Partly resonating with this idea, Stevens suggests that from a Jungian perspective, the absence of the father or masculine insufficiency of the father, could mean 'a failure to activate the father archetype within the boy's psyche, (so that)...uninitiated into the masculine world, (he is) doomed irredeemably to languish under the dominance of his mother complex' (p. 117).

While the functions of fathers in relation to their developing children is well described, the question may be raised whether the notion of the father-archetype is in any way necessary for this description, or whether it can adequately be accounted for by the presence of the father per se, or even the mother. This issue will be returned to later in this chapter.

Failure to activate/realise the father archetype

Given the importance of all archetypes for adaptation, Jungians assert that a failure to activate or actualise the archetype (for personal or broader social reasons) could lead to complications for the individual and, ultimately, for society. Stevens (1982) argues that archetypes have developed on the basis of natural selection, and cannot be ignored or repressed, because these archetypal predispositions will find an alternate, and often more complicated, route for realisation. He claims that there are signs of a contemporary anti-authoritarian *Zeitgeist*, that represents the rejection of the father archetype, showing itself in a blanket opposition to traditional patriarchal values. In South Africa we have seen a political process whereby old forms of authority have been rejected, part of which has been a move away from automatic respect for elders and for fathers in particular. But new forms of male authority have emerged through gang identification, high rates of violence amongst young men, and sexual violence against women.

While Stevens claims that the father archetype provides 'a dependable paternalistic tradition' (1982, p. 124), there is the risk of such archetypal patterns being used as a sanction for oppressive patriarchal domination. From a Jungian perspective, what is needed is to rediscover the balance of continuity to which the father archetype may contribute, as new forms of non-oppressive masculinity emerge and are developed.

Father archetypes and the external father

Jung and his followers operated from the assumption that archetypes are forms without content, and that the content of archetypes is filled in by life experience and socio-cultural influence. The extent to which archetypal predispositions are developed or expressed depends on personal circumstances and the psychosocial and cultural environments of individuals. Exposure to life experience gives archetypes their solid form in images available to consciousness. However, Jung still saw the personal, including the personal father, as 'an active, pre-programmed participant in the developmental process' (Stevens, 1982, p. 44). This suggests that the external or real father derives his power only from the fact that he resonates with the archetypal dispositions within the individual. The archetypes operate as the 'author-director or actor-manager' in the behaviour and experience of the person (Stevens, 1982, p. 52). The innate capacity for the perception and experience of fathering, including responding to father-figures, or the capacity to act in a fatherly way to others, is *triggered* by the presence of external father-figures, and develops and matures in relation to these figures, but under the 'organising influence' of the father archetype within the developing individual (Stevens, 1982, p. 64).

Despite his strong archetypal assumptions, Jung was quite clear about the need for the presence of an external father for the healthy development and wellbeing of the individual, and for the actualisation of the father archetype. But Jung also believed that children saw their parents as external personifications of their father (or mother) archetypes, 'thus imparting to them a magic power and significance far transcending…their personal qualities as people' (Stevens, 1982, p. 66). Jung says that 'The personal father inevitably embodies the archetype, which is what endows this figure with fascinating power' (Stevens, 1982, p. 104). In fact, one may argue from a Jungian perspective that it is this very projection or personification which enables non-biological father figures to take on these strong psychological fathering properties, as effectively or sometimes more effectively than biological fathers.

While the archetype provides the unconscious root of fathering, various figures may serve as embodiments of the father archetype at a personal and collective level. These might include the biological father, non-biological father-figures, other family members, or other people in the community or society. This is important to recognise especially where actual fathers are not present, for a range of reasons, as is commonly the case in South Africa. In fact, one may suggest that in the South African context historically important political leaders, such as Nelson Mandela, have served as typical examples of such embodiments of the archetypal father, facilitating the transitional development of a new nation-child.

The risk of certain brands of Jungian thought may lie in the implicit assumption that because of the archetype of father present in all people, the critical role of real fathers or father-figures may be underestimated. This type of thought may suggest that it is 'the father within' that plays the most critical role. Nowhere is this more apparent than in some manifestations of the contemporary men's movement, which will be discussed later.

Playing the role of father

If the father archetype may be activated and even embodied by people other than the biological father, the contemporary preoccupation with the detrimental effects on children of growing up in fatherless families is puzzling. In fact, Samuels goes further to suggest that anatomy should not determine paternal destiny, and that it is rather the importance of 'a good enough father of either sex' (2001, p. 105). There is ample evidence of mothers performing the instrumental tasks of fathering, described above, as effectively as fathers, and even evidence of women teaching this role effectively to men (see Chapter 12 of this volume for example). Samuels goes on to suggest that this has been the case especially with single mothers, with the rapidly emerging flexibility of gender roles. He adds that 'men too only *play* the father's role' (2001, p. 106), in the same way that men looking after small infants may play the mother role, and that there is nothing inherent in men that makes them better equipped to play the role of father than women. '…[I]t is not the actual maleness of the person from whom the child obtains fathering that is important. What matters is whether or not the relationship between the father of whatever sex and her or his children is good enough' (2001, p. 107). It is possible for women to act in the role of men and fathers effectively, even if this is not the role for which they are constitutionally best equipped.

One of the problems with archetypal notions of fathers and fathering is that they tend to cast the role of fathers in stone. Considering the possibilities of mothers (or other women) acting as 'fathers' raises the question of whether there are fixed patterns of fathering, associated with masculinity in particular, that are appropriate for positive effects to be exerted on children. Samuels (2001, p. 115) points out that there are many people who are opposed to the idea of diverse patterns of fathering or to the idea that fathers can change, implicitly suggesting that there is only one inherent type of fathering. But he goes on to argue that there is considerable evidence for enormous cross-cultural variation in patterns of fathering, all of which may be valid expressions of the fathering archetype.

According to Samuels (1987), some of the important changes that we are seeing in fathering are towards greater physical involvement of fathers in families, away from being just the agent that separates mother and child and makes the link between family and society. It could be argued that rigid social and cultural stereotypes of fatherhood enacted by patriarchal men may have reinforced the idea that particular styles of fathering are necessary, if not inevitable and, further, that these patterns derive from inherent archetypes. But it is also clear that there is a wide range of fathering roles available and that it is a mistake to see particular patterns as inevitable, as the next section illustrates.

The father archetype and the men's movement

One of the most powerful manifestations of the use and application of the father archetype is seen in some forms of the contemporary 'men's movement', especially in the USA. The men's movement has played an important role in the renegotiation of forms of masculinity in many countries, including South Africa. This is seen in organisations in South Africa such as 'The South African Men's Forum' and 'Men as Partners' (see Chapter 22, this volume).

In the face of father-loss, or the inadequate experience of fathering, some parts of this movement, especially in the USA, have suggested that this situation can be rectified by finding the 'father-within', referring to the archetypal version of the father – seen as the solution to the father absence. Tacey has described the 'ideal, all nurturing, all loving Father to be found within ourselves' and the 'near ecstasy and personal relief of connecting with patriarchal archetypes' (1997, p. 54) in this version of the men's movement.

This may be seen as a manifestation of exactly what Jung thought was the primary function of the archetypes, that is, the activation of internal psychological potential.

However, these ideas and practices also reflect a deeply conservative leaning, in that the return to the archetypal represents a return to destructive, patriarchal power in society, rather than a real transformation of the masculine. The risk is that Jungian archetypes are viewed, quite wrongly, as rigid manifestations of immutable unconscious predispositions. But these so-called archetypal blueprints are often no more than stereotypes about fathering and masculinity, which are used to justify a return to rigid, patriarchal notions of masculinity. 'With the power of archetypes, reality can be refashioned, reshaped, to suit the desires of any fantasy agenda' (Tacey, 1997, p. 5).

The Jungian men's movement, seen in the work of people such as Robert Bly (*Iron John*), often presents a picture of the ideal, all nurturing, all loving Father to be found within ourselves, based on the father archetype. This is a kind of 'omnipotent Father', who provides a solution to all the ills of society. While such movements, founded in the Jungian notion of archetypes and the father archetype in particular, are presented as a solution to much of the contemporary crisis of masculinity, they are seen to be rooted in father absence.

The risk of this approach is that the appeal to the ideal internal father archetype becomes a kind of 'new age fantasy system' in which everything that is lacking in society (for example, present fathers) can be found in the hard-wiring of the unconscious. The challenge, according to this view, is to find all the resources (for example, fathers) that are lacking in the external world, within oneself.

Tacey (1997) argues that a great deal of what is portrayed as Jung's work is, in fact, a particular conservative interpretation of Jung, in which archetypes are idealised as 'all knowing parental and ancestral figures'. He describes much of the contemporary men's movement as 'romantic' and an 'infantilisation of Jungian theory'. According to Tacey, Jung believed that these primal ancestral figures should be defeated rather than blindly acceded to and identified with.

Clearly the men's movement, which is gaining increasing ground in South Africa as well, needs to be examined more closely. On the one hand these emerging movements play a critical role in providing new, positive, transformative roles for men, enabling men to have more engaged and more affectionate relationships with their children.

On the other hand, the American, so-called mythopoetic, men's movement highlights the risk of such endeavours in reproducing old and unhelpful stereotyping; often reinforcing patriarchal, oppressive practices by men. But the core issue, the recognition of the importance of attending to fathering and masculinity, cannot be overlooked. It is important to seek a balance between rediscovering the importance of fathering, and unhelpfully idealising the father role, especially in certain rigid and stereotyped ways.

Critique of the notion of the father archetype

Samuels (2001, p. 102) suggests that there is a 'damaging and misleading idealisation of fathers and the roles men play in families' that can result in the stigmatisation of women-headed households or single mothers (again, see Chapter 12). For example, female-headed households are frequently discussed as if they were a form of social pathology. In this idealisation, the father is seen as 'a source of stability, discipline and order in the family and, by some kind of magic, in society as well' (p. 103). The father is also seen as 'a public school fagmaster, the older boy who is assigned younger boys as servants and in return helps to form their characters' (p. 103). Such views of fatherhood are part of a universal pattern of male domination.

There is also the particular risk of seeing this idealisation as deriving from the inherent nature of the father archetype, and the consequent risk of absolutising a socially or culturally derived notion of fatherhood, leading to what Samuels describes as the denial of the possibility of other styles and models of fathering.

What, then, is helpful about the notion of archetype and what is unhelpful, especially regarding the emerging concern with fathers in South Africa? Does the assumption about archetypes add anything useful to the debate about fathering? Most of what is described as a function of the archetype could equally be seen to be a function of external good-enough father figures (which might include mothers) in the social environment.

We might argue that the value of the differentiation of father and father archetype is the very notion that the archetypal function may be triggered and represented by various people, not only the father, and that many other people may perform the function as well as or better than the biological father. This is consonant with the emphasis on social fatherhood in, for example, the Human Sciences Research Council's Fatherhood Project, and it also acknowledges the role that men other than the biological father can play in the lives of children in the context of high male mortality as a result of violence and HIV/AIDS (see Chapters 18 and 19, this volume). For example, it is estimated that, of the 13 per cent of children in South Africa who are estimated to have lost a parent in 2003, the majority of them had lost their father (UNAIDS, UNICEF, USAID, 2004).

Stevens identifies strongly with a biological view of archetypes, including the father archetype, going so far as to suggest that it 'is planned for in the genome of all primate males, (although) it depends on the exigencies of the environment whether or not it is activated and expressed' (1982, p. 109). By contrast, we can argue that many of the characteristics of the father seen by Jung and Jungians in the father archetype are actually images of the father formed from the values of a particular historical and social period in western culture (Samuels, 2001, p. 119). In fact, even Stevens himself seems to suggest that the characteristics of the father archetype are really those most typical of 'the traditional patriarchal values enshrined in Judeo-Christian civilisation for millenia' (p. 121).

Samuels (2001) states that Jung ignores the important role of culture in the many features that he described in the father archetype. Further, he argues that fathering (like mothering), is 'not as natural, biological, innate, ahistorical, universal and "given" as we used to think' (p. 120); rather 'the father is a culturally constructed feature'. He suggests that the depiction of the benevolent aspects of fathering have been largely ignored and undeveloped in favour of controlling and malevolent features. Finally, he asserts that too much attention has been given to the power of the father, especially in the family, at the expense of other important roles such as fathers as carers.

Conclusion: the dilemma and the challenge of new approaches to fathering

The book in which this chapter appears, and, indeed, the project of which it forms a part, is designed to explore ways in which we can reconnect South Africans with positive and supportive images of masculinity and fatherhood. Jungian psychology provides a helpful way of viewing collective unconscious structures of fatherhood, and a way of differentiating psychic structures of fathering from the roles of particular individuals. However, it may also be the case that the Jungian approach may allow for the overvaluation of particular cultural (and conservative) ideas about fathering which, instead of being presented as the cultural constructions they are, are seen as biologically and phylogenetically inevitable.

There is clearly something of a dilemma in how we see the importance of fatherhood, and of men in caring roles in our society. On the one hand, the widespread absence of men from such roles is rightly recognised as a source of concern, and the effects of their absence are very clear. On the other hand, insisting on the importance of men's roles may recall patterns of the past in which men were assumed to be 'naturally' dominant, and may link with conservatism about gender roles in our society. The dilemma is not one that can be easily resolved, but is rather one which needs to be borne in mind as work on positive masculinity and fatherhood continues.

Graham Lindegger is Professor of Psychology at the University of KwaZulu-Natal, Pietermaritzburg, and Director of the Programme in Professional Psychology. He is also Principal Investigator of the HIV/AIDS Vaccine Ethics Group, which is part of the South African AIDS Vaccine Initiative. He has a particular interest in the psychology of masculinity, and has a number of research projects in this area.

Note

1   Grateful thanks to Prof. Leslie Swartz for helpful comments on this chapter.

References

Bly, J. (1990). *Iron John: A book about men*. New York: Addison-Wesley

Jung, C. (1981). *The concept of the collective unconscious. Collected Works. Vol. 9.1*. London, Routledge and Kegan Paul.

Knox, J. (1999). The relevance of attachment theory to a contemporary Jungian view of the internal world: Internal working models, implicit memory and internal objects. *Journal of Analytical Psychology, 44*, 511–530.

Mahler, M., & Gosliner, B. (1955). On symbiotic child psychosis. *Psychoanalytic Study of the Child, 10*, 195–212.

McDowell, M (2004). *The landscape of possibility: A dynamic systems perspective on archetype and change*. http://home.erthlink.net/maxmcdowell/jap94web.html (accessed 25 March 2004).

Samuels, A. (2001). *Politics on the couch: Citizenship and the internal life*. London: Karnac.

Samuels, A. (1989). *The plural psyche: Personality, morality and the father*. London: Tavistock/Routledge.

Singleton, W. (2003). *The father archetype and the myth of the fatherless son*. Doctoral dissertation, Pacifica Graduate Institute (http://www.online.pacifica.edu/dissertations/stories/storyReader$183 (accessed 23 February 2004).

Stevens, A. (1982). *Archetype: A natural history of the self*. London: Routledge.

Stolorow, R., & Atwood, G. (1992). *Contexts of being: The intersubjective foundations of psychological life*. Hillsdale, NJ: The Analytic Press.

Tacey, D. (1997). *Remaking men: Jung, spirituality and social change*. London: Routledge.

UNAIDS, UNICEF, USAID (2004). *Children on the brink 2004: A joint report on new orphan estimates and a framework for action*. New York: United Nations Children's Fund

CHAPTER 11

Where have all the fathers gone?
Media(ted) representations of fatherhood

Jeanne Prinsloo

> It is in the mundane world that media operate most significantly. They
> filter and frame everyday realities, through their singular and multiple
> representations, providing touchstones, references, for the conduct of
> everyday life, for the production and maintenance of common-sense.
> (Silverstone, 1999, p. 6)

While it is broadly accepted that the media do not reflect society, they do provide us
with a repertoire of roles and images which we encounter and with which we engage.
As the opening quote suggests, the media play a vital role in the circulation and
mediation of ideas, attitudes and actions and their significance is commented on
frequently. It is noteworthy that such commentary in South Africa identifies that men
are infrequently depicted in parental roles. This is in comparison to the other roles
men inhabit and in contrast to the role of women as mother. It is also suggested that
the macho masculine identities that the media offer serve as proxy father roles (Nair,
1999). Consider the following pair of critiques of the media in relation to fathering.

Farid Esack grew up in the Western Cape and comments that he did not 'have' a father
because his biological father abandoned the family when he was a few weeks old. In
pondering why many men do not embrace the role of fatherhood in a responsible way,
Esack, at the time a member of the Commission on Gender Equity, implicates the
media, albeit more by the omission than the representations of fathers:

> Our most common source of information, the media, also has little to
> offer. Articles, radio stories or television programmes on fatherhood are
> rare. (Esack, 1999, p. 3)

Yet, if the media fail to foreground fatherhood, they also stand accused of providing
violent masculine role models. Roshila Nair proposes that a celluloid version of
fathering is effected through the media and argues that the aggressive film character
of Rambo served as a father figure with particular allure for underage combatants
in the Midlands of KwaZulu-Natal in the early 1990s (Nair, 1999). She writes about
these boys, who were between nine and sixteen years of age, as living under violent
circumstances where their fathers were mostly emasculated by extreme poverty.
Caught up in the conflict, she argues, they had to make sense of their new role as
participants in violence. This they did 'by adopting the hero Rambo as father' (Nair,
1999, p. 18). Nair's concerns lie with the reverberations such macho masculine

identities hold for the women these men encounter, and the destructive fathers they might become. She reminds us of the relative lack of representations of men as fathers in the media.

Clearly both these responses share a concern with the nature of representations of fathers and men in the media and their societal role. If media representations can be considered as moments within the 'circuit of culture' (Hall, 1997) that relate to other contextual issues in a complex manner, they are linked to issues of identity, of gendered identities and various constructions of parenting. This chapter acknowledges that fathers are not common media fare. Rather than dismissing that which is omitted, it proposes that such relative absences are significant and must be seen in relation to the repertoire of masculine roles that are foregrounded. It sets out, using very broad brush strokes, to reflect on the representations of fatherhood in both non-fictional and fictional forms of media primarily by considering the scholarly literature in the field.

Literature on 'dads' in the media

That serious, sustained scholarly interest in media portrayal of fathers or fatherhood is rare, particularly in contrast to motherhood, seems at first to be surprising. After all, patriarchy, or the law of the father, still substantially underpins the assumptions of contemporary societal institutions and their workings and one might be forgiven for imagining that men would be foregrounded in the role of father. However, I think this can be accounted for in a couple of ways.

Interest in gendered representations in the media emerged historically as feminist critiques of the patriarchal nature of the media. If women are subordinate within patriarchal power relations, the initial task was to identify how the media represented women. The nature and scale of representations of men were examined primarily as a foil against which to understand the positioning of women and were secondary to the feminist project. Thus, to start with, there is far less literature concerned with men than with women in the media.

More recently, an expanding body of literature has been emerging around representations of men and masculinity. It addresses the common repertoire of roles in which men are portrayed – a range of roles more numerous and varied than those allowed women, but perhaps surprisingly one that, quite simply, does not foreground fatherhood. Media narratives, whether fictive or non-fictive, tend to replay particular masculine scenarios, ones that assume the normality of heterosexuality and fatherhood but do not foreground the latter (see, for example, Chapters 2, 8, 14 and 15 in this volume, all of which discuss the separation of fatherhood from masculinity).

Gender theory and media constructs

Media and gender theorists have considered this repetitive enactment of predictable but limited scenarios and argue that it plays a significant social role in relation to gendered identity. Rather than accept an essentialist explanation for this compulsive repetitiveness, post-structuralist approaches enable us to view gender as socially constructed. Connell (1987) describes patriarchal power relations in terms of a gender order that depends on creating categories of inclusion or exclusion. It constitutes masculine and feminine identities as distinct. In this, masculinity is constructed as powerful, physical, rational and located in the public sphere, and femininity as passive, dependent, emotional and inhabiting the domestic sphere. This conceptualisation of the gender order also allows for a particularly powerful, or hegemonic, masculinity which, while dominant, is in continual contestation with other forms of masculinity.

In this way, a binary distinction between the private and public spheres is put in play whereby the private becomes associated and conflated with the domestic, the natural, the family, personal life and intimacy, caring, reproduction and unwaged labour. The public becomes the (privileged) domain of the marketplace, production, waged labour, rationality, citizenship, critical public discourse and the state. This dichotomy is argued to be gendered and deployed to preserve 'traditional patriarchal and heterosexist practices' (Duncan 1996, p. 128). The patriarch (and not the *pater*[1]) holds sway in the public domain; the private domain is identified with the feminine and women are therefore allocated the caring parental role (or the *mater*). Locating men and masculinity within the privileged public sphere effectively excludes the private sphere from significance. Within this discourse, the primary role of fatherhood is constrained to bringing home the bacon (but not cooking it).

Both feminist and media scholars have considered how the media privilege the discourse of hegemonic masculinity (for example, Mulvey, 1989; Weedon, 1987; Van Zoonen, 1988). Through their selection of representations, of narratives, of the gendered actors within such narratives and the recurrent themes and genres, the media generally work to maintain the naturalisation of hegemonic gendered relations of power. While hegemonic masculinity presumes familial patriarchy as 'normal' (Hanke, 1992), it is generally enacted in the public sphere and so works to disallow a role for the patriarch in the private domain in intimate and caring relationships.

This hegemonic frame tends to constitute a 'good' father as the responsible breadwinner/provider and the protector. While these roles are not foregrounded, they are assumed. Media representations locate the father in the public spheres of the workplace or in contexts of physical endurance and challenge. He may be judged as inadequate when he fails in these roles. In contrast, the 'good' mother is defined by her ability to care for and nurture her family and sustain intimate relationships with them. Her engagement in economic labour is subordinate to these roles, in spite of the fact that women are increasingly the heads of households, particularly in places like South Africa. Yet, beyond this frame, discourses of social and gender justice challenge such binary distinctions in terms of parental functions. They foreground caring, nurturing and intimacy in conjunction with providing and protecting children for both parents.

Fathers in the media

With this preamble to account for why fathers do not appear frequently in the media, whether international or South African, I turn to the literature that does take account of how men are represented as fathers.

While a survey of the literature identifies an emerging body of writing that examines the mediations of masculinities in the media, few dedicated studies on fathers are evident and reference to fathers in South African media is negligible. Because the literature tends to emerge from northern contexts, more specifically from the USA and, to a lesser extent from Britain, writers tend to discuss American media and television principally.

Common to the literature I examine is the position that the media provide a wide variety of images of masculinity which validate particular ways of living, attitudes and actions as positive or desirable, and propose others as negative facets, deploying them as cautionary messages. As Kimmel states in the introduction to Craig's volume *Men, masculinity and the media*, 'Media messages tell us who we are, who we should be, and who we should avoid' (1992, p. xii). While Craig's edited volume marks a significant stage in considering men in the media, few of the articles deal directly with fathers. Macho roles, on the other hand, receive extensive discussion. They include comic-book superheroes, heavy metal subculture, buddy/male bonding, Hollywood war films, newsmakers, athletes, and beer commercials with their active outdoor lifestyle marked by challenges, risk and mastery – all scenarios distant from intimacy and caring for the family. It reinforces the point that while patriarchy speaks the law of the father, the father is not highly visible in the private domain.

Fejes (in Craig, 1992) examines quantitative studies on representations of men in the media. His account of sex roles has some relevance in relation to fatherhood for he discusses 'adult television' (what is generally referred to as prime-time television) and advertising. One of the consistent findings in relation to 'adult television' is that men are more frequently portrayed than women, but are less likely to inhabit situation comedies (sitcoms) and soap opera genres that are located in the domestic realm and consequently to recount family relationships. While men are more likely to be shown as employed in higher-status, traditionally male occupations (doctors, lawyers, ministers), studies suggest that men are less likely to be represented as married.

Men are powerful and successful, occupy high status positions, initiate action and act from the basis of the rational mind as opposed to emotions, are found more in the world of things as opposed to family and relationships, and organise their lives around problem solving. (Fejes, 1992, p. 12)

Family sitcoms and fathers

While prime-time television represents men in the roles discussed above, one exception, where men are consistently represented primarily as fathers, is in the popular situation comedy (sitcom) genre. According to a study by Cantor and Cantor (1992), family sitcoms seldom show stereotypical macho men.[2]

The generic formula of the sitcom calls for a particular conflict to set in motion the narrative of a particular episode that relates to an issue within the family, and this is resolved by the end of the programme. The consequent reinstatement of the status quo tends to inscribe conservative family values. While the heterosexual nuclear family is the predominant form, alternative family forms do exist. Consider *My Two Dads*, also screened on South African television, where two men care for and nurture the orphaned daughter of a woman who had been involved with both men. In these instances, the fathers are constructed as loving, thoughtful and centrally concerned with their families, even if at times they seem a bit ridiculous.

While some popular sitcoms portray families of different race, and in spite of very popular series that centre on black families, the white nuclear family predominates as the ideal in these American programmes. Where the sitcom is located in a working-class scenario, these fathers and husbands are likely to be depicted as clumsy, awkward and inept, and slightly ridiculous, while the wife dominates as the primary decision-maker. Discussing *The Honeymooners*, an early TV sitcom, Cantor and Cantor note that 'in each episode, the more practical and wiser Alice reprimands and scolds Ralph for his foolishness. Ralph is always the incompetent fool, Alice is always right' (1992, p. 28). In contrast, the middle-class father and husband has tended to be represented as kind, sensitive, caring and domesticated – a kind of comical superdad.

Academic interest has also been directed at whether family sitcoms are progressive in terms of their representations of family power relations and whether media representations of hegemonic masculinity are in transition. Representations of the 1980s 'sensitive man' have been discussed in relation to the family melodrama *thirtysomething*. One study claimed that this series 'broke new ground in portraying the conflicts and feelings of its male characters…where sensitive nurturing men, aware of themselves and their feelings, take the spotlight' (Lehrer, 1989 in Hanke, 1992, p. 192). In contrast, a further critique of *thirtysomething* makes the point that while this series appears to incorporate critiques of patriarchy with the provider constructed as sensitive, supportive and concerned with the emotional needs of his nuclear family, the series is centrally concerned with male heterosexuality (Torres, 1989). In spite of the occasional 'soft man', Hanke argues that 'unreconstructed' male figures still abound on prime-time television and that series such as *thirtysomething* perpetuate the myth that middle-class professional men are less sexist than their working-class counterparts or Third World men. This argument is premised on the frequencies of representations. However, as it is the exceptional rather than the humdrum that arouses attention. I would be reluctant to dismiss the significance of the 'soft man' and would argue that such diversity of roles and representations enables more complex negotiations of identities and expectations, in this instance, around fathering.

Moving from issues of representation to reception, Berry considers how the fathers in two prime-time sitcoms depicting black American families were perceived. This audience study probed the responses of a group of black youth participating in a 1987 summer program in Austin, Texas. *The Cosby Show* and *Good Times* present contrasting representations of black family life. *The Cosby Show* has been hailed as inventing new definitions of the black male and black family for American television. In the chosen episode, Heathcliff Huxtable, described as a 'loving, caring, responsible, perceptive, and good-humoured' father, responds to a family crisis (a joint of dagga found in elder son Theo's book). Together with his wife Claire he confronts his son verbally. In contrast, in the episode of *Good Times* with its more stereotypical family, the less tolerant and stereotypically punitive James Evans responds to his son's failure to complete a test with physical punishment, while his wife attempts to restrain him. Most of the research participants judged James Evans as more manly and stronger because of his dominance over his family and his harsh disciplinary approach. In contrast, half the group identified Heathcliffe Huxtable's sensitivity and soft-hearted nature as weak and unmanly. Berry concludes that, 'Television as a mirror of changing and contrasting definitions of black manhood remains a significant yet limited component of black male gender image and style' (1992, p. 123).

Advertising genres

Another media form, advertising, has consistently been critiqued for its stereotypical gendered representations (see Bertelsen, 1998). Studies undertaken in the 1970s found that a highly predictable set of gender roles tend to be invoked in advertising. If women were foregrounded in their domestic roles as housewives and mothers in the private realm of the home, in advertisements for products to do with the home men were portrayed as more autonomous (that is outside of relationships), in a range of occupations, in outdoor or business settings (i.e. public spaces), and in advertisements for alcohol, vehicles or business products. Their physical absence from the family space need not be interpreted as their not being fathers, however. Bread-winning is what fathers do, and this in a public arena.

More recently, Barthel suggests a changed role mode in the 1980s New Man: 'He is one of capitalism's most successful products: a consumer and a gentleman' (1992, p. 139). She describes the various aspects of the new male role model: 'the young man on the make' in the corporate game, at leisure in nature, powerful and in control. While these are all aspects of the patriarchal world, she also identifies a changing trend in advertisements that portray the New Man as able to invest himself emotionally in relationships. Interestingly, the men's magazines in which he appears depict him with his father, while the mother is absent: 'almost always absent, out of sight, outgrown'. She also notes that the New Father 'wants to spend "quality time" with his children' (1992, p. 146) and appears in advertisements for products ranging from watches, to underpants, shoes, and Calvin Klein's fragrance, Eternity™. He is able to express his affection and love for his children and is constructed as seeking quality time with them; he is a super-dad. She concludes her description of the New Man in advertisements as follows: 'Men of the nineties continue to feel they have the right to self-expression and self-indulgence, to love and be loved, or, at least fool around a bit. Advertisements suggest ways to facilitate the process' (1992, p. 148).

Studies undertaken to investigate changes in gendered roles in British magazines indicate a small and gradual movement toward the non-sexist portrayal of men over the twenty-year period. At the same time they note that representations of men still tend to 'themes of sex appeal' and these portray men 'as career-oriented', and involved 'in *activities and life outside the home*' (Fejes, 1992, p. 15 – my emphasis). Yet a more recent volume on British men's magazines makes no reference to fathers or fatherhood at all because, I would argue, men are not represented in the father role (Jackson, 2001).

Dads that make the news

There is very little research that examines non-fiction genres and non-fiction representations of men, more particularly fathers, and most of it focuses on representations produced in northern countries. News media operate within the public sphere, the public realm which Habermas proposed as a desirable space in which citizens meet to debate issues of public concern. However, the public sphere, with its promise of universal access, excludes the domestic or private sphere and is argued by feminist media scholars to have been constructed through the exclusion of women, the proletariat and popular culture (McLaughlin, 1993). It is then un-surprising that fathers and fatherhood get short shrift in the news media, appearing infrequently in defined parental roles.

If the masculinist trajectory of the heroic successful patriarch provides the natural-ised discourse for society and other media narratives, then what exceeds the threshold of the ordinary is the deviance from, or amplification of, such roles. Where men are identified in the news as fathers they are more likely to be there either as 'elite' people with considerable social status (Galtung & Ruge, 1981) or as deviant fathers. Consalvo (2003) argues that when fathers are portrayed as deviant in some way, the causes for their actions are deflected.

This relegation of violent behaviour, validated by so many media genres, to the monstrous is commented on by Wykes who examined the British media coverage surrounding 'the house of horror' murders. In these, Fred and Rose West were implicated in several murders, including the murder of Fred's own daughter. In discussing such family murders and abuse by fathers of children and family members she concludes that:

> Instead of analysing the dangerousness of families, journalists tend to
> adopt a strategy of deflection. This shifts discussion of family problems
> into discourses where all but the actual causes are addressed...If men are
> explored as 'dangerous' this is done through personalisation,
> pathologisation or 'Faustianism'. Such men are unique, damaged, in
> league with the devil; they are thus excluded from masculinity per se
> and often rendered as beasts, monsters...or evil. (1998, p. 236)

By reporting such events as deviant, the press fails to explore the very processes of masculinity and patriarchy, and ignores the '*masculinism at the heart of its project*' (Wykes, 1998, p. 245).

When do dads make the media in South Africa?

Arguably, the literature that has been discussed above in relation to media produced in northern countries is relevant within a South African context as South Africans (and people globally) receive and negotiate these television programmes daily. Consider that South African broadcasters are only obliged by their licence conditions to meet a minimum quota of local content. Consequently, most South African TV is sourced from northern countries, notably the USA.

As British theorists Hearn and Melechi argue, 'Processes of imaging are nowadays characteristically international' (1992, p. 217). The United States, they argue, has a particular significance in the international arena of imaging.

Two things are apparent from the studies mentioned. Fathers are significantly invisible in most media forms and are more likely to appear in family sitcoms than in other media forms. This applies equally to those under-researched South African popular soaps such as *Generations* or *Isidingo*, and *Madam and Eve*-type sitcoms.

South African media remains a rich field for research with its own particularities and historical shifts. In the section that follows, I consider media studies that relate to fathers in South African media and make reference to dads in advertising, before focusing on news media.

Dads in South African advertisements

A recent content analysis exercise undertook a 'snapshot' of the gendered lives of children in advertising in popular South African magazines by looking at a single edition of the most popular South African magazines (Prinsloo, 2003). While the findings tend to present a snapshot of hegemonic masculinity at work (at play?), it is worth noting that children were frequently portrayed with their parents. Relevant to the topic here – when they were portrayed with a single parent, in all instances they were shown with their mothers. Where a father was included in the advertisement, he was depicted with the wife/mother in the predictably tight nuclear family. The father stands there larger than his wife and protectively hovers over the group. In some of the men's magazines, including magazines such as *Kick-Off* which assumes a working-class black male readership, there was a total absence of representations of children in the first instance, let alone of children with parents.

Dads in the South African news

News conventions have emerged historically and taken different forms at different historical moments in relation to social contexts. Shifts in the representations of black fatherhood and manhood can be discerned, for example, in *Drum* magazine between the 1950s and those of a decade later (see Chapter 9, this volume). In *Drum's* early years, manhood was constituted through a range of familial relationships including those of grandfathers, fathers and sons. Certainly *Drum* conformed to those news conventions that tended to foreground sporting figures, entertainment celebrities and community leaders, but the articles simultaneously acknowledged these men as husbands, fathers and sons, portrayed in domestic and affectionate roles. This tendency was echoed in the advertisements which depicted fathers feeding babies and playing with their children. Subsequently, from the late 1950s, a shift in the representations of men in *Drum* in editorial copy and advertisements began to disregard the role of black men within their families in line with the trends of the white publications of the time. The 'modern man' of the 1960s became constructed as self-made, without the nexus of family relationships of a decade earlier (Clowes, 2004).

This trend continues. A recent southern African study of news content, The Gender Media Baseline Study (2003) conducted in ten southern African countries, quantitatively assessed news coverage along gender lines. It found that men were represented in a much wider range of activities than were women, but that they were rarely identified in terms of their relationships, as father or husband, for example, in contrast to women who were more likely to have such relationships ascribed to them.

If the above discussion has tended to more abstract reflection, a brief examination of the representations of fathers in contemporary newspapers is presented to provide a concrete illustration of the ways in which fathers are commonly depicted in the news. I chose a single South African Sunday newspaper, the *Sunday Times*. Using the electronic archive (www.IOL.co.za), I extracted every report for the year 2003 that included the word 'father'. This search produced a selection of news reports, features and obituaries, but I disregarded movie and book reviews and regular columns. Even so, the results were very lean.

Thirty-six reports or articles contained the word 'father', but only two features, eighteen news reports, and one obituary had a significant focus on the father. It is these that are the subject of discussion here. The feature articles both covered topical gender issues. One describes the increasing role men play in the domestic space, the other addresses fathers who renege on their maintenance payments. Interestingly, both features foreground the importance of the father's engagement in the domestic space both in terms of finances and housework. However, it is characteristic of features to identify and discuss topical social issues and thus they are markedly different from news reports.

What is more interesting for this discussion is the circumstances under which fathers actually make the news. Bearing in mind the nature of the news industry, it is important to recognise that what makes 'news' is that which is outside the ordinary or abnormal. News is news because it exceeds the threshold of the normal. No matter how much particular interest groups desire news stories that provide good father role models, Mr Average Good Dad does not easily cut it with the reporters, their editors or their financial managers. He is quite simply not considered newsworthy.

In the sample identified in the *Sunday Times*, a small number of the fathers are constructed as caring and engaged with their children and families. It is unsurprising that these fathers hold celebrity status, thereby meeting the news criterion as 'elite people' (Galtung & Ruge, 1981). Two of the fathers are referred to in articles about celebrities in the entertainment section. In one, a woman TV presenter, describes her estranged husband as a 'wonderful father' who cared for the children during her extended absence abroad ('Khanyi's 10-year marriage is over', 26 January 2003). Then, a male news presenter's relationship with his son is described similarly as warm and caring ('TV news reader's two-year-old son is star of the show', 30 March 2003). Third, former president Nelson Mandela attends the funeral of his daughter-in-law prior to his eighty-fifth birthday celebrations (20 July 2003). The article comments on his support for his son and the affection he demonstrates to his grandchildren. Fourth, in an article in the Company News section, ('In the name of the father'), Ross Perot junior is interviewed and speaks of the good relationship he shares with his father (14 December 2003).

Then there are obituaries. As obituaries mark the status of the deceased person as a public figure, in the first instance it is characteristic of this genre to discuss the dead with respect. In an obituary entitled 'Family man' (11 May 2003), Walter Sisulu is acknowledged as a responsible and loving father, although, in spite of this, he is described largely in terms of his public persona.

Such representations of fathers are important in their inscription of the discourse of the caring father but tend to be located in the 'soft' news pages. More numerous are reports that fulfil the news criterion of negative news (Galtung & Ruge, 1981), and that are foregrounded as 'important' by their placement on the front pages. These relate misfortune or asocial deeds and these fathers are neither 'elite' nor celebrities. Misfortune occurs in 'A family's agony of wondering and waiting', where a father has gone missing and is missed by his daughter (22 June 2003). Bad news is also the criterion for the report on a man who has been forced to beg in order to support his family after a bureaucratic bungle denied him his employment ('"Dead" school cleaner forced to beg to stay alive', 2 March 2003). In both reports, the father's role as breadwinner is important. Then, two examples of contested property rights arise in the sample of news reports, with one reporting a family dispute over the inheritance left by a deceased father ('Mystery of millionaire's faked will', 1 June 2003), and another a contestation between father and son over money ('Brothers, fathers in bitter legal battle over house', 9 February 2003).

If those news reports locate fathers within the patriarchal frame of breadwinners or in relation to property, four others introduce fathers as linked to an assortment of murders. A report on an accused murderer makes mention of the fact that his father had murdered his mother ('I didn't kill them, the Nigerians did it', 26 October 2003). In 'Mourners praise priest held for murder' (16 February 2003), a community sides with the father charged for his son's murder as the son was considered a thug and troublemaker. An Oedipal conflict involves a son who has killed the father over money ('Murder rap teen tells how he hit dad with trophy', 7 September 2003). In contrast, another father is accused of lying to shield a son accused of murder, here constructed as a protecting (if dishonest) parent ('Young killers shed a tear in court', 17 August 2003).

Another negative but predictable role filled by fathers in the media is their abuse of children (three in this small sample). One report, 'Please save me from my father' (14 December 2003), describes how a young Eastern Cape boy walked a long distance to the police station to request protection from abuse by his father. In the follow-up report, 'Father of battered child is finally behind bars' (21 December 2003), the father has been arrested. Then, Michael Jackson's father is reported to be supportive of his son during his trial for child molestation, but the report goes on to describe Jackson's father as having treated his son roughly and having beaten him as a child ('Jackson parents stand by disgraced pop star', 28 December 2003).

If dads tend to make hard news as celebrity or monster dads, it is interesting to compare this with how mothers are represented. To serve merely as a contrast, news reports that related to mothers were similarly identified for three of the 12 months (February to April 2003). In this smaller sample, there were 20 hard news reports that foregrounded women as mothers, approximately as many as for men over a full year. Of these, one presented an article about 'bad' mothers – who are described as drawing the child maintenance grant and abandoning their children with their fathers. In a further two articles, women were identified in relation to their biological roles of giving birth and breast feeding. The remaining 17 articles portray strong bonds between (non-elite) mothers and children. These 'mums' are presented as 'emotional experts' (Van Zoonen, 1988, p. 38), supportive of their offspring. They give interviews about conflicts at school; one woman attends the court case of a murderous son; another attends the court case of the man who allegedly murdered her mother; one mother forgives the murderer of her child. They offer commentary about their sick children and are identified as their sons' role models or the objects of their affection. They are constructed within the private realm of care and nurture, and appear in the news media far more frequently than fathers.

There are some striking aspects to this news reporting. First, it is significant that hard news reports include fathers far less frequently than mothers. Second, it is the contrast in the nature of the representations themselves that is more the issue. While women are mostly portrayed as emotionally invested in their families, among men the role of being a caring, responsible father is generally reserved for 'elite' figures and more frequently features in soft news. Murder, abuse, Oedipal wrangles and disputes over money and property mark much of the father/family relationships in hard news reporting. That certain themes recur, here paternal violence and/or struggles over property (eight of 14 hard news stories), signals that these issues generate social concern. Fathers do inhabit a range of different roles in news reporting, albeit unequally. This diversity of news representations indicates that within the changing context of South African society, the discourses around fatherhood contest each other.

Concluding comments

This literature overview and discussion has identified two issues, namely the limited representation of fathers quantitatively, and then the limited repertoire of roles for dads. Fiction media often present men in macho roles in which force and violence frequently feature and are enacted in the public space. When men are represented as 'dads' they are frequently the butt of jokes. Continuing the trend of the portrayal of men as engaged in assertive, often violent fictional scenarios, the news media brings us few fathers, but many of these are presented as dysfunctional. When I first started thinking about how fathers are constructed in the media, it seemed contradictory to me that patriarchy (as the law of the father) should be bolstered by so few images of fathers. It becomes self-evident, of course, that this must be so if dominant patriarchal power relations are dependent on the dichotomy between the private and the public. It is a discourse that relegates fathering and care-giving to the private realm, the realm of nurturing and intimacy.

If there is a tendency to largely erase caring fathers in the media, then we need to be aware of the implications of this erasure. As Silverstone notes in the opening quotation, the media 'filter and frame everyday realities' and provide 'touchstones, references, for the conduct of everyday life'. What we have noted is that the filters and frames for fatherhood are confined, they tend to include the ridiculous or the nasty and brutish. Clearly these must be judged inadequate as touchstones and references for the everyday lives of men and their children, their partners and society in general. The media touchstones for everyday life can work in different ways. They could enable creative engagement with a broader repertoire of images. They could expand how we imagine the world, how we envisage relating and caring, and how we expect fathers to be 'good' fathers.

Jeanne Prinsloo is an Associate Professor in the Department of Journalism and Media Studies at Rhodes University in Grahamstown. She pursued her post-graduate studies in the fields of Cultural and Media Studies at the Universities of Natal, London and the Witwatersrand. She teaches and researches issues in the broad fields of media, gender and education for critical literacy, and within these areas of interest, texts and textuality remain a particular focus.

Notes

1   The distinction I am making here, to put it fairly crudely, is that patriarchy refers to a system of power relations enacted by male subjects in the public sphere, while *pater* signals the relationship or connectedness of men within the family.

2   Their study on American sitcoms up until the 1980s does not focus on fathers specifically, who tend to be mentioned in the same breath as mothers.

References

Barthel, D. (1992). Men, media and the gender order when men put on appearances. Advertising and the social construction of masculinity. In S. Craig, *Men, masculinity, and the media. Research on men and masculinities* (pp. 137–153). London: Sage

Berry, V. T. (1992). From *Good Times* to the *Cosby Show*: perceptions of changing televised images among black fathers and sons. In S. Craig (Ed.), *Men, masculinity and the media* (pp. 111–123). London: Sage.

Bertelsen, E. (1998). Ads and amnesia: Black advertising in the new South Africa. In S. Nuttall & C-A. Coetzee (Eds.). *Negotiating the past: The making of memory in South Africa* (pp. 221–241). Cape Town: Oxford University Press.

Cantor, M., & Cantor, J. (1992). *Prime-time television. Content and control.* London: Sage.

Clowes, L. (2004). To be a man: Changing constructions of manhood in *Drum* magazine. In L. Ouzgane and R. Morrell (Eds.). *African masculinities: Men in Africa from the late 19th century to the present.* (pp. 89–108) New York: Palgrave.

Connell, R. (1987). *Gender and power.* Cambridge: Polity Press.

Connell, R. (1995). *Masculinities.* Cambridge: Polity Press.

Consalvo, M. (2003). The monsters next door: Media constructions of boys and masculinity. *Feminist Media Studies, 3*, 27–45.

Craig, S. (1992). Considering men and the media. In S. Craig (Ed.). *Men, masculinity and the media* (pp. 1–8). London: Sage.

Duncan, N. (Ed.). (1996). *Body space: destabilizing geographies of gender and sexuality*. London, Routledge.

Esack, F. (1999). Foreword: Of fools and bravehearts. *Track Two*, December, 1–4.

Fejes, F. (1992). Masculinity as fact: A review of empirical mass communication. Research on masculinity. In S. Craig (Ed.). *Men, masculinity and the media* (pp. 9–22). London: Sage.

Gallagher, M. (1981). *Unequal opportunities: The case of women and the media*. Paris: UNESCO.

Galtung, J., & Ruge, M. (1981). Structuring and selecting the news. The manufacture of news. In S. Cohen and J. Young (Eds.). *Deviance, problems and the mass media* (pp. 62–73). London: Sage.

Hall, S. (1977). Culture, the media and the ideological effect. In J. Curran, M. Gurevitch, & J. Woollacott (Eds.). *Mass communication and society* (pp. 315–348). London: Edward Arnold.

Hall, S. (Ed.) (1997). *Representation: cultural representations and signifying practices*. London: Sage.

Hanke, R. (1992). Redesigning men: Hegemonic masculinity in transition. In S. Craig (Ed.). *Men, masculinity and the media* (pp. 185–198). London: Sage.

Hearn, J., & Melechi, A. (1992). The transatlantic gaze: Masculinities, youth and the American imaginary. In S. Craig (Ed.). *Men, masculinity and the media* (pp. 215–232). London: Sage.

Jackson, P., Stevenson, N., & Brooks, K. (2001). *Making sense of men's magazines*. Cambridge: Polity.

Kimmel, M. Introduction to S. Craig (Ed.). *Men, masculinity and the media* (pp. xi-xii). London: Sage.

Kuhn, A. (1982). *Women's pictures: Feminism and cinema*. London: Routledge.

McLaughlin, L. (1993). Feminism, the public sphere, media and democracy. *Media, Culture and Society, 15*, 599–601.

McLaughlin, L. (1998). Gender, privacy and publicity in 'Media event space'. In C. Carter, G. Branston, & S. Allan (Eds.). *News, gender and power* (pp. 71–90). London: Routledge.

Metz, C. (1981). History/discourse: A note on two voyeurisms. In J. Caughie (Ed.). *Theories of Authorship* (pp. 225–231). London: Routledge.

MISA & Gender Links. (2003). *Gender and media baseline study: South African regional overview*. Johannesburg: MISA & Gender Links.

Mulvey, L. (1989). *Visual and other pleasures*. London: Macmillan.

Nair, R. (1999). Rambo's boys: The lure of the violent father. *Track Two, December*, 17–20.

Prinsloo, J. (1992). Beyond Propp and Oedipus: Towards expanding narrative theory. *Literator, 13*, 65–81.

Prinsloo, J. (2003). Childish images. The gendered depiction of childhood in popular South African magazines. *Agenda, 56*, 26–36.

Silverstone, R. (1999). *Why study the media?* London: Sage.

Torres, S. (1989). Melodrama, masculinity and the family: *thirtysomething* as therapy. *Camera Obscura, 19*, 86–106.

van Zoonen, L. (1988). Rethinking women and the news. *European Journal of Communication, 3*, 35–53.

Weedon, C. (1987). *Feminist practice and poststructuralist theory*. Oxford: Blackwells.

Wykes, M. (1998). A family affair. The British press, sex and the Wests. In C. Carter, G. Branston and S. Allan (Eds.). *News, gender and power* (pp. 233–247). London: Routledge.

News articles

All news articles were retrieved on 28 April 2004: http://www.iol.co.za

Baker, M. 14 December 2003. In the name of the father. *Sunday Times*.

Davids, N. 17 August 2003. Young killers shed a tear in court. *Sunday Times*.

Govender, S. 7 September 2003. Murder rap teen tells how he hit dad with trophy. *Sunday Times*.

Govender, S. 9 February 2003. Brothers, fathers in bitter legal battle over house. *Sunday Times*.

Lehihi, M. 22 June 2003. A family's agony of wondering and waiting. *Sunday Times*.

Mlangeni, B. 16 February 2003. Mourners praise priest held for murder. *Sunday Times*.

Mlangeni, B. 11 May 2003. Family man. *Sunday Times*.

Mofokeng, L. 26 January 2003. Khanyi's 10-year marriage is over. *Sunday Times*.

Mofokeng, L. 30 March 2003. TV news reader's two-year old son is star of the show. *Sunday Times*.

Mofokeng, L. 28 December 2003. Jackson parents stand by disgraced pop star. *Sunday Times*.

Naidu, B. 2 March 2003. 'Dead' school cleaner forced to beg to stay alive. *Sunday Times*.

Padayachee, N. 14 December 2003. Please save me from my father. *Sunday Times*.

Schoonakker, B. 26 October 2003. I didn't kill them the Nigerians did it. *Sunday Times*.

Sukhraj, P., Naidu, B., & Mofokeng, L. 20 July 2003. A week of celebration, a week of pain. *Sunday Times*.

Sunday Times. 20 April 2003. Anglophile oil heir Paul Getty dies at 70.

Sunday Times. 21 December 2003. Father of battered child is finally behind bars.

Trench, A. 1 June 2003. Mystery of millionaire's faked will. *Sunday Times*.

CHAPTER 12

Representations of fatherhood in black US film and how this relates to parenting in South Africa

Solani Ngobeni

Introduction

John Singleton's movie *Boyz 'n the Hood*[1] was released in 1991, the year popularly known as the year of the African-American film, the year of the black movie boom (1992). According to Wallace (1992), virtually every newspaper in America has re-minded us that in 1991 more black-directed films were commercially released than in any previous year. Other noteworthy films that were released that year include *A Rage in Harlem*, *New Jack City* and the re-release of *Chameleon Street*. The public response to the release of *Boyz 'n the Hood* was overwhelmingly positive and it made handsome profits. It cost a modest $6 million to make and so far has earned over $60 million (Wallace, 1992). The film paved the way for the proliferation of films directed by African-Americans that starred or had significant roles for black actors, while at the same time dealing with 'hood sensibilities'. Examples of subsequent films include *Menace II Society* and *Jason's Rylic*.

At the centre of *Boyz 'n the Hood* is a consideration of the father–son relationship. A major theme is that of paternal abandonment. The film explores the coming of age of three black adolescents, Tre Styles (played by Cuba Gooding Jr), Ricky (Morris Chestnut) and Doughboy (Ice Cube). It is a story about a triangular relationship between: the three boys whose lives we track to mature adolescence; the relationship between one of the boys (Tre) and his father (Furious); and the relationship between the other two boys (Doughboy and Ricky) and their mother (Brenda). The film follows the three boys as they struggle to survive into adulthood and examines their attempts to escape the constraints of the tight socio-economic space to which they have been relegated. The film's narrative tries to show the differences in their upbringing and how that upbringing impacts on their eventual predicament.

Tre Styles grows up under the care of his father Furious (played by Laurence Fishburne), and he eventually ends up in college. In contrast, Doughboy and Ricky grow up under the care of their mother and both end up as victims of the violence that is endemic to the neighbourhood. The film presents Tre as a foil to Doughboy. This is shown in terms of the stability and instability of their family backgrounds, the importance they attach to education and the different ways in which they respond to the demands of masculinity.

Singleton's conception of positive masculinity is inextricably bound up with the traditional patriarchal belief that the man is the provider in a family. The absence of the father, therefore, is equated with the poor upbringing of the children. On the one hand, the presence of Furious is rewarded by the eventual success of his son. On the other hand, the inability of Mrs Baker to raise her children is bemoaned through the way in which the two (Doughboy and Ricky) end up as victims of the violence in the neighbourhood.

My contention in this chapter is that, although we should celebrate positive fatherhood, we should not romanticise it as we might end up denigrating mother-hood. In black South African communities, because of the migrant labour system under the policy of apartheid and compounded by patriarchy, fathers have to all intents and purposes been absent in the lives of black children. Because of the movement of men from the rural areas to the cities in search of work, most black children have been brought up by their mothers. In most cases, fathers only return home at certain times of the year and therefore mothers are the ones left with the burden of raising the children. In the absence of fathers, it is the mothers who have been the pillars of strength, not only in the family but in the community as well.

It must be noted that as much as the film raises pertinent issues about fatherhood and its impact on the development of children, the preoccupation with the 'crisis of black men' mystifies the plight of black women. Critical responses to the film have indicated that it relegates the female characters to the periphery of the narrative, as this is a story about fathers and sons. Wallace (1992) commented that the film essentially projects the fact that boys who don't have fathers fail. The boys who do have fathers succeed. This raises questions about where women locate their experiences in this narrative.

There is a pervasive silence about the predicament of black women in the narrative. The central message of the film is that black men must raise black boys if they are to become socially stable and responsible men. Thus Tre, his father Furious, Ricky and Doughboy, the four black men whose lives form the fabric of Singleton's narrative guilt, are the film's interpretative centre.

While the women in the film – Reva (played by Angela Basset), Brenda Baker (Tyra Ferrel) and Brandi (Nia Long) – the mothers of Tre, of Ricky and Doughboy, and Tre's girlfriend respectively, occupy the film's distant periphery. They can be seen as adjuncts to the male protagonists of the film. Not only are their experiences distorted and trivialised, but their portrayal as being inadequate is used to vindicate the redemptive nature of the presence of the father.

Singleton's contention that as the fate of the black man goes, so goes the fate of the black family, is problematic. It uncritically affirms hegemonic family values and denies the importance of single-parent households headed by women. It suggests that in all cases the absence of the father is catastrophic for the emotional and psychological development of the child. Singleton defines healthy masculinity as being formed primarily in the relationship between father and son. In this way, he denies the influence of other important people in the lives of young men, not least their mothers.

The absentee father

> 'The boys who don't have fathers fail. The boys who do have fathers succeed'. (Wallace, 1992, p.121)

> 'You know my father never left home. He's still at home. And I think that's the reason that I'm the way I am. Because, you know, a woman can raise a boy to be respectable. But a woman can't raise a boy to be a man. You need a man there'. (Icc Cube, in hooks, 1994, p. 141)

Singleton's film investigates the ways in which the breakdown of black family life compounds the crisis of the relationship between fathers and their sons. In the opening credits of the film we are told that black men are more likely to be killed in their own communities than black soldiers were at the height of the Vietnam War. We are also told that one out of four black men in the US will end up in the hands of a prison warder. Similar claims could easily and credibly be made about black men in South Africa (Morrell, 2001, pp. 20–22).

The film's discourse, which presents black men as an 'endangered species', is based on the assumption that black men must raise black boys if they are to become socially stable black men. Thus Tre is a shining example of the positive impact that the presence of the father figure can have on a young black man. Unlike his peers, he survives the violence that is endemic in the neighbourhood and eventually goes to college.

It is this analysis with which I profoundly disagree. As I have suggested before, black fathers have been conspicuous by their absence in most South African black families. Therefore, the assertion that black men need their fathers in order to escape delinquency is far from the truth. There are a lot of successful black men who were not raised by their fathers.

Be that as it may, I need to state categorically that I am not saying that the presence of fathers is immaterial. I am saying that we should not necessarily view it as the be-all and end-all in the lives of both sons and daughters. Of course, the positive presence of both the father and the mother can have a tremendous effect on the children. There can be no doubt that the presence of both the father and mother can bring emotional as well as financial stability, especially in cases where both are economically viable.

Building binaries: fathers, mothers and sons

Boyz 'n the Hood conveys its message about good fathers and marginal mothers by using what Stratton (1995) refers to as psychological-doubling. In this process, Singleton juxtaposes two characters, the one representing the socially acceptable or conventional personality (in this instance, Tre Styles) and the other externalising the free, uninhibited often criminal self (in this instance, Doughboy). Through this aesthetic feature of the film, the essentialisation of the father-figure in the lives of the black men is foregrounded. It tells us that fathers are imperative in the lives of their children.

In an interview with bell hooks, Ice Cube, who portrays Doughboy in the film, asserts that Doughboy could have turned out to be a good boy like Tre if he had had the right guidance, essentially if he had had a father (hooks, 1994). In a sense this assertion suggests that the right guidance can only emanate from a father. It also essentialises the father figure, with the conclusion that boys without fathers are not socially stable.

The use of binary opposites is not confined to the male characters and is also enacted through the female characters. Although Reva (Tre's mother) is presented as a careerwoman, and the antithesis of Doughboy's mother who relies on social welfare, she is also presented as being quite incapable of raising her son. The film tends to deliver its message in terms of simple binary oppositions. It juxtaposes the image of the 'good' single-parent father with a number of images of 'bad' single-parent mothers.

Feminist critics, such as Jacquie Jones, have noted that women in the film occupy only two flattened-out categories, 'bitches' and 'ho's'. Therefore, Furious's brilliant presence as a redemptive and unswerving North Star and Brenda's uncertain orbit as a dim satellite are the telling contrasts in Singleton's cinematic world (Jones in Wallace, 1992). It is a celebration of fathers which ends up chastising women for bad parenting.

Singleton does not castigate only professional women (such as Reva) as being incapable of good parenting, but poor working-class women as well. Doughboy's mother is presented as an irresponsible mother who is not concerned with the well-being of her children. She is like the other nameless woman who is a dope addict and leaves her children to run amok in the streets.

It is in these streets that they are vulnerable and Singleton makes this point by having Tre rescue one of her children from the path of an oncoming speeding car. The two women are compelling examples of Singleton's castigation of black single mothers as negligent and incapable of good parenting.

Changing relationships and changing roles

The family has never been a stable social unit in South Africa. In the late nineteenth and twentieth centuries, the African family was invariably a fluid structure, affected by colonial and apartheid labour processes, by urbanisation and industrialisation, and shaped by gendered forces that pressed more heavily upon women than men. In the last two decades, a new trend has emerged with the rise in single-parent households headed by women. This means that the majority of black children are born out of wedlock and a minority of black children live in two-parent households (Posel & Casale, 2002). Therefore the nuclear family cannot be assumed as the norm.

Despite the changing nature of family structures and lives, scholars still readily draw an analogy between single-parent households headed by women and the notion of the 'dysfunctional family'. Hacker (1992) notes that it has yet to be shown that the absence of a father is directly responsible for any of the supposed deficiencies of broken homes. Singleton's film suggests that the absence of the father in Doughboy's family results in them leading directionless lives because they don't have a father like Furious who can advise them or who they can look up to.

Boyz 'n the Hood can be seen as suggesting that boys like Doughboy don't succeed in life because they come from families that are 'dysfunctional' as a result of the absence of a male breadwinner. On the other hand, Tre grows up to be a responsible black male precisely because of the financial viability of his father. This kind of analysis draws on the patriarchal assumption of men as the sole breadwinners. With changes in the labour market, such assumptions no longer bear scrutiny and, at the very least, need major qualification. In fact, the South African labour market has, in the last decade or so, been feminised with many women entering the world of work and becoming economically independent (Posel & Casale, 2002).

Failure to document healthy productive households that do not conform to prevailing notions of the nuclear family helps to further the erroneous assumption that any household that deviates from the accepted pattern is destructive. Singleton's *Boyz 'n the Hood* seems to suggest that the stability of the family results from the presence of the father. Therefore, the absence of the father, both economic and physical, facilitates the instability of the family. The salvation of that family can only be brought about by the presence of the father, which not only means his physical presence but also his gainful employment and economic viability. The non-availability of this option will mean that the family will have to rely on welfare.

Boyz 'n the Hood fails to capture the way in which the structure of families has changed and how this change has impacted on family dynamics. Black women who are economically viable and are in positions to raise their children without the presence of the father are not foregrounded. Had the film elected to show Reva as Tre's main caregiver, it would have gone a long way towards debunking this myth. But the film portrays her as a professional woman and thus does not give her the opportunity to raise Tre on her own. *Boyz 'n the Hood* is trapped in the old conception of women as dependent on husbands for their livelihood. Thus Doughboy's mother suffers because she does not have a husband who can provide for her and her children.

Feminist critics such as Jacquie Jones argue that black mothers in *Boyz 'n the Hood* are shown to be neglectful at best and as bearing responsibility for their sons' problems and suffering at worst (Jones, in hooks, 1994). There is a concerted casti-gation of black single mothers as being incapable of good parenting. The central protagonist, Tre Styles, rises above the conditions of his peers because he alone has a strong, present and neo-nationalist black father.

Although *Boyz 'n the Hood* is a story about the father–son relationship, this is no reason to vindicate the film's treatment of women. Jones bemoans the conspicuous absence of women in the film's narrative: 'the boys, of course, are in the forefront, but always behind them, just inside the frame, is the corps of silent girls, standing on the curb or sitting on the couch. Somehow these girls seemed to me to exist in the space of the accused. After all, it was those teenage, female-headed households that produced these boys' (Jones, in hooks, 1994, p. 96).

The inadequate characterisation of women can be discerned from Singleton's portrayal of single-parent households headed by women. Thus, the portrayal of Mrs Brenda Baker (Doughboy's mother) can be read as a compelling example of the inadequate depiction of black single mothers. Little is revealed about Mrs Baker. The film's narrative does not tell us what she does for a living, or whether she is on welfare. Neither are we told whether she has ever been married. This is the woman whose children get mowed down in the streets. Brenda belongs to a much-maligned group, whose members are vilified with charges of promiscuity, judged to be the source of all that is evil in the lives of black children or, at best, stereotyped as helpless beneficiaries of the state. In Singleton's cinematic worldview, both Ricky and Doughboy seem doomed to violent deaths because, unlike Tre, they have no male role models to guide them. This premise embodies one of the film's central limitations. This is precisely because even as he assigns black men a pivotal role of responsibility for the fate of black boys, Singleton uncritically elevates the impact of black men over the efforts of present and loyal black women who more often prove to be at the helm of strong black families (Dyson, 1995).

Conclusion

> I really want to respect the black women single parents who have raised
> their kids through the hardships of poverty in this country and
> aloneness, and although I believe that every child needs men and
> women in their life, we can't focus too much on saying we need the
> father because a lot of kids are never gonna have contact with the father.
> (hooks,1994, pp. 141–142)

Boyz 'n the Hood essentialises the father figure in the lives of young black men. The film seems to suggest that the father's absence as a large-scale social problem results in social instability among young black men. In the psychological theories of Freud and Jung, the father is the towering figure in the psychological development of the child. Therefore, the criminal inclinations that Doughboy espouses can be seen as the result of paternal abandonment. The film reinforces the symbolic death of the father in discourses about the black family. Analyses that focus exclusively on the presence or absence of the father trivialise and distort the positive contribution that the presence of the mother can have on the development of the child. *Boyz 'n the Hood* uses psychological doubling to project how the father's absence or presence impacts on the lives of young black men.

Singleton's depiction of black single mothers in *Boyz 'n the Hood* can be seen as a concerted castigation of such women as incapable of good parenting. If Singleton is saying that it is difficult for a black single mother to raise a black male into a respectable and responsible black man, then he fails to tell us why is it possible for black men who come from middle- and upper-middle-class families with little or no material discomfort and with both the father and mother present, to turn out to be socially unstable. '[N]ow you have a kid that comes from a broken home who turns out to be the best kid. Then you have a kid with a mother and father that boom, boom just wild' (hooks, 1994, p. 133).

Recent changes in the structure of the family and of work are laying the foundation for new attitudes towards parenting roles. There are women in society who are economically affluent and are in a position to raise their children despite the conspicuous absence of the fathers. It is the experience of these strong black single mothers that *Boyz 'n the Hood* fails to document. At the same time, there are black single mothers who are poor but who nonetheless are doing their utmost to raise their children into respectable and responsible adults in society. The perseverance and resourcefulness of these mothers must be celebrated, not trivialised.

Solani and his son Neo in 2004

Solani Ngobeni is the Managing Director of Juta Learning, a division of Juta & Co. He obtained a Masters degree in Publishing Studies from the University of the Witwatersrand, Johannesburg. Before assuming his current position, he was a Higher Education Publisher specialising in psychology, political sciences, education as well as public administration. He is interested in issues around publishing management, book reading and buying as the Achilles heel of African publishing, as well as the impact of the dominance of knowledge produced in the developed countries on viable publishing in the developing countries of the south.

Note

1   Singleton, J. (1991). *Boyz 'n the Hood*. Columbia Tristar Home Video.

References

Brod, H. (Ed.). (1987). *The making of masculinities: The new men's studies.* Boston: Allen & Unwin.

Dyson, M. (1993). *Reflecting black: African-American cultural criticism*. Minneapolis, MN: University of Minnesota Press.

Dyson, M. (1995). *Making Malcolm: The myth and meaning of Malcolm X*. New York: Oxford University Press.

Fanon, F. (1963). *The wretched of the earth*. Harmondsworth, UK: Penguin Books.

Guerrero, E. (1993). *Framing blackness: The Afro-American image in film.* Philadelphia: Temple University Press.

Hacker, A. (1992). *Two nations: Black and white, separate, hostile and unequal.* Oxford: Maxwell Macmillan.

Harris, E. (1996). *African-American screen writers now*. Los Angeles: Silman-James Press.

Hearn, J., & Morgan, D. (Eds.). (1990). *Men, masculinities and social theory*. London: Unwin Hyman.

hooks, b. (1994). *Outlaw culture: Resisting representations*. New York: Routledge.

hooks, b. (1990). *Yearning: Race, gender and cultural politics*. Boston: South End Press.

Jones, J. (1992). The accusatory space. In G. Dent (Ed.). *Black popular culture. A project by Michele Wallace* (pp. 95–98). Seattle, WA: Bay Press.

Morrell, R. (Ed.). (2001). *Changing men in Southern Africa*. Natal, Pietermaritzburg: University of Natal Press.

Posel, D., & Casale, D. (2002). The continued feminisation of the labour force in South Africa: An analysis of recent data and trends. *South African Journal of Economics, 70,* 156–184.

Poussaint, A. (1987). Black men must organize. *Black Scholar, 18,* 12–15.

Reid, M. (1993). *Redefining black film.* Los Angeles: University of California Press.

Smith, V. (1992). The documentary impulse in contemporary US African-American film. In G. Dent (Ed.). *Black popular culture: A project by Michele Wallace* (pp. 56–64). Seattle, WA: Bay Press.

Snead, J. (1994). *White screens black image: Hollywood from the dark side.* New York: Routledge.

Staples, R. (1987). Black male genocide: A final solution to the race problem in America. *Black Scholar, 18,* 2–11.

Staples, R. (1982). *Black masculinity.* Washington: The Black Scholar Press.

Thumim, J., & Kirkham, P. (Eds.). (1995). *Me Jane: Masculinities, movies and women.* London: Lawrence and Wishart.

Thumim, J., & Kirkham, P. (1995). *You Tarzan: Masculinities, movies and men.* London: Lawrence and Wishart.

Wallace, M. (1992). *Boyz 'n the Hood* and *Jungle Fever*. In G. Dent (Ed.). *Black Popular Culture. A Project by Michele Wallace* (pp. 123–131). Seattle, WA: Bay Press.

CHAPTER 13
Children's views of fathers

Linda Richter and Wendy Smith

There is nothing that I want, besides love [to] me.

I would like to have a husband who is always there for our children, who helps around the house and helps with taking the children to school. If we have a son or a girl he would take them to there sports matches and cheer them on, a father who never brakes his promise and a father who is always there when our children need him most. A father who doesn't fight with me when our children are near. I know this kind of father sounds impossible but this would be my perfect father.

Introduction

These two poignant extracts from essays and responses to open-ended questionnaires are written by children, 10 to 12 years of age, and express the longing for and idealisation of a father that many children experience. These, and other aspects of children's relationships with men, are reflected in the large body of narrative pieces we have collected from children about how they view their fathers and what fatherhood means to them. Not only is it a right children have under the Convention on the Rights of the Child to express their views on issues affecting them (Howard, Curtin, & Hardy, 2003), but we believe that children envisage fatherhood in ways that are affirming to men, even when their fathers are unemployed, living apart from their children or neglectful. Children, quite simply, invite one or more men into their lives to be their fathers. In return, children offer men extraordinary honesty, validation and affection.

Historically and traditionally, fathers have fulfilled numerous roles, including those of 'breadwinner' and 'protector' of women and children. In this guise, men typically control domestic decisions and discipline and control their children. In the main, men have tended to be distant and detached from family affairs to do with children (Tanfer & Mott, 1997). Media reports frequently cast men as dangerous perpetrators of violence, oppressors of women and children, uninvolved in children's lives, externally focused and generally uncaring and unemotional (Richter, 2003; see also Chapters 9, 11, 12 and 14, this volume). In a new view of fathering that has emerged largely in the northern hemisphere over the last three decades, men welcome their role as fathers (Henwood & Procter, 2003). This changed role of fathers from the 'traditional stereotypical father' to the contemporary 'new father', involves intimate engagement with and caring for children (Richter, 2003).

In writings about old- and new-style fathering and changes in conceptions of masculinity, 'what is largely missing are the voices of children themselves. It is one thing for present-day adults to reflect back on what things were like when they were children, but to understand father–child relationships today, we need to also hear the view of those who are now children themselves' (Sullivan, 2000, p. 6). There is a conspicuous lack of information, both internationally and locally, about children's constructions of fatherhood and their views of the men who father them (Howard et al., 2003; Tanfer & Mott, 1997). A lack of research in South Africa on children's perceptions of fathers motivated the study described in this chapter, which actively sought children's constructions of fatherhood and examined accounts given by children from a selection of schools in KwaZulu-Natal and Soweto-Johannesburg.

Recent research on fatherhood has focused on a range of issues, including symbolic representations of fatherhood, men's perceptions of their fatherhood roles, and the nature and extent of father involvement with their children. Psychological and anthropological studies of children reveal that they have an intense hunger for a secure, abiding and constant father-figure. There is strong evidence, claims Pruett (2001), of children's 'father need' for safety, respect, companionship and guidance provided by men. With increasing external and internal pressures, families are changing, including breaking up and reconstituting with new step-members. In these situations, many children have significant relationships with men who are not their biological fathers and who fulfil the role of father for longer or shorter periods of time. In the same vein, fathers themselves may have to re-think their positions as fathers several times in their lives and in relation to different children. They may begin as biological fathers out of the home of the mother, then later become in-home fathers, out-of-home distant fathers, and even stepfathers to other children while remaining in contact with their own biological children (Mkhize, 2004, p. 5). This range of relationships between men and children means that while some children live with their biological fathers, many children have 'other men' who fulfil a father role. The concept of 'social fatherhood' includes all the child-rearing roles, activities, duties and responsibilities that fathers are expected to perform and fulfil (Bachrach & Sonenstein, 1998, in Sullivan, 2000).

New sociological approaches to the study of childhood entail attempts to study 'real children' and their experiences of being children. 'Precisely because the social space of childhood has been determined for so long through the model of the developing child, questions are now being asked about what children can say and what status children's words can have' (James, Jenks, & Prout, 1998, p. 177). In this approach, the child is conceived of as a social actor, a new subject rather than 'object' of research, who can be understood in his/her own right, with recognition for the varied socio-cultural contexts in which children grow up and live. Children's presence and their rights are important issues, and there is strong support for the view that their voices and viewpoints about issues directly affecting them need to be heard (James et al., 1998). It is acknowledged, however, that interpreting the words and ideas of children and finding their 'authentic world' (Ritala-Koskinen cited in Davis, 1998) is a difficult task, and that what children have to say may be very different from 'normal' (adult) conceptions. Hearing children's voices adds a deeply relevant dimension to research on fatherhood and specifically in South Africa, we believe their portrayals of fatherhood open up rewarding opportunities for men's conceptions of themselves as fathers.

Studying children's views of fathers

The rationale behind the study described in this chapter is to complement and contribute to a growing body of literature internationally and in South Africa on children's voices generally, and on fatherhood more specifically. Three recent studies in Australia and New Zealand have sought to capture the views of children as they relate to fatherhood. In the first Australian study, Russell and colleagues used children's drawings to determine how fathers are constructed by children in order to obtain a better picture of the 'basic social arrangements' of families. In the New Zealand study, the *Children's Views on Fathering* project, the researchers used a range of methods including drawings, semi-structured interviews, story-writing and focus groups to determine how children of different ages see father roles and responsibilities. Some children identified 'okay' and 'not okay' characteristics of fathers and most displayed an awareness of potential influences on father's behaviours, such as work, alcohol, and the father's relationship with the child's mother. Lastly, The Children's Commission of Queensland sought to facilitate the publication of the views of children, working with all schools in the State to explore children's perceptions of their fathers. Through a state-wide Father's Day competition, children were encouraged to share their ideas in words or pictures (Sullivan, 2000).

In this South African study, an open, exploratory qualitative approach was used to elicit children's views. Participants were children ranging in age from 10 to 12 years, at four different schools in KwaZulu-Natal, as well as children participating in the Birth to Twenty (Bt20) study in Soweto-Johannesburg (Richter, Norris, & de Wet, 2004). The schools varied by the socio-economic status of the school's catchment community, and Bt20 includes children from the full spectrum of society in the metropolitan area.

This study was conducted as part of the Human Sciences Research Council's Fatherhood Project which involves, amongst other things, an attempt to encourage responsive fatherhood through visual and narrative public presentations of positive images of fatherhood in order to create a conceptual space in which fatherhood interventions can be fostered and promoted.

Children were required to either write a short essay on 'my father' (40 were selected from a rural school in KwaZulu-Natal and 33 from Bt20) or to respond to a simply structured open-ended questionnaire on aspects of fatherhood, including what fathers do that makes their children happy or unhappy, what they do that make mothers happy or unhappy, what fathers do to help around the house, and lastly, what kind of character is the 'perfect father'? From the large number of question-naires returned, 120 were randomly selected to render a sample of questionnaires of 40 boys and 40 girls from each of three schools. The data are extensive and cannot be covered adequately in this chapter.

The Fathering Indicators Framework identifies a number of categories by which fathering can be defined. A father's significance and involvement can be classified in terms of a father's presence and availability; care-giving and nurturing roles; active engagement with children to develop their social competence and academic achievement; supportive and co-operative parenting with other caregivers; provid-ing a role model through healthy living; material and financial support to children and the existence of a healthy relationship with the mother of the child (Gadsden, Fagan, Ray & Davis, 2004). Father involvement, therefore, extends far beyond the traditional roles of provider and breadwinner.

Here we focus on some of these issues to reveal aspects of fatherhood that are either not dealt with adequately in the fatherhood literature or are not dealt with from the particular perspective of a child. These issues are: the wide range of men who fulfil father roles in children's lives; children's longing for a secure, constant and loving father-figure; idealisation of fathers; children's observations and appreciation of fathers' involvement in domestic work and childcare; the co-existence of men's household work with traditional notions of father provision and protection; how children manage the contradictions between idealisations of fathers and the reality of their imperfections and inadequacies; and lastly, the hurt and anguish children experience in the face of father absence, neglect and/or cruelty. As far as possible, we draw on the words of children to express their views on this selection of issues.[1]

The men who fulfil father roles in children's lives

The fathers or father figures referred to by the children and young people partici-pating in the study included biological and non-biological fathers – grandfathers, uncles, brothers, stepfathers, mothers' boyfriends, foster fathers, and 'big' or 'little' fathers (relatives of the child's father who adopt a fatherly role towards the child). Although many men did not live with their children, every child identified someone as a father. Some men took on the father role as part of traditional custom, through adoption, by virtue of a relationship with the child's mother, and through the child's residential care in an institution. The child's biological father was merely absent, was deceased, socially problematic, or in jail. The majority of relationships with social fathers were characterised by affection and security. Although the sadness of children at the loss of their fathers can be discerned, most children adapt to their situation and appear to be happy with the men who have become their fathers.

> My father caused trouble in the family, so now my grandfather is my father.

> My father is died but my brother is a good man and I need him in my life.

> Me and my brother (and the rest of the family besides my mother) call him *Ntata omdala*, which means older father. He is the head of the family therefore he sees to everyone's problems

> My father is a man who took me in to his life when my mom was ill and took care of me when my mom died he and my gran adoped my sister and I and now I live with them.

> I like my big father [my father's older brother] because he buy for me thing that I want's because my really father is in jail.

> I met my dad when I was 4 years old. He came to all the fathers days even when he wasn't married to my mom (I did ask him to come). My dad loves being around people. He shouts but isn't always angry he play sometimes when he shouts. He has always called me his daughter since my mom and dad have been married.

> I love my stepdad he is like my real dad. He cares for me as if I was his own child. Some children would feel a bit neglected but I don't. when ever my mom goes on abut things he's always there to stand up for me. He's realy cool. He has three girls but the oldest lives with her aunt. The other two are like my best friends. Whenever I'm sad I can always [talk] to my stepdad about anything and he always has the right answer. He is a very loving person and I'm glad that he is my stepdad. Also when I'm feeling down he always has a compliment to make me laugh. My stepdad and I are like best mates.

> My father good step father but is not riyel [real] father if is like my father. I live that place that live children that [don't] have Mothe and fathe [an orphanage]. I happy for that I have clothe I have school that make my life and mond riter. And this father that is not riyel father is halpy me about the school work and about clother. I so happy for that Lord give me step father that live that one I have now. But my riyel fathe I a one I have 5 years tha time that I see my riye father.

> I live with my uncle. His name is uncle Simphiwe. He is like a father to me. He is the only one who is working at home. When my uncle finds that there is no bread or potatoes, he goes to the shop and buy these

things for us at home. He care for his home. One day my uncle came from work he came with a door frame, he noticed that home needs a door frame. He fixed it himself we were very much happy about that. He is a loving person…I wish he was my father.

Well my father has died. He died from a bus when a bus crashed on top of his car but unfortunately I was not there and now I live with with my grandparents and sometimes we miss him a lot and my granny has these dreams of him sometimes and the most sad thing is that when my father died my mother was stil pregnant she had a baby in her tummy after my father died and now my baby brother was born without seeing his own flesh and blood and that breaks my heart and that is really sad and he doen't ever know my baby brother, that his father has died and so we always ask God for his help. But even though my father has died I know that I have a father and he will always be my father and that *I love him* and happy fathers day to him and my grandpa.

What does patently sadden children are the difficulties surrounding separation, divorce, and hostilities between their parents. Living apart from a parent was very disturbing to some children, and less so to others, depending on the frequency and quality of their contact with their father. The greatest problems seem to arise for children in this situation from conflicts between parents around access frequency and arrangements.

My father make me fell unhappy if I say I want to visit you and he say no.

My father make me feel unhappy if he does not visit my.

My father he is nice and buys me stuff even though I see him Monday, Tuesday, Wednesday, Thursday, Friday, Saterday I am happy. I don't mind if I don't live with him. He is still my father.

I love him and he is always there for me to talk to. He lives in Cape Town but when I need someone to talk to I phone him. H is always willing to talk or sms me when I need help. He is funny and when I go see him he will do anythink to make me happy and enjoy my time with him. I only see him about 4–7 times a year.

My father makes me unhappy when he asks me a lot of questions about my mom. He also makes me unhappy when he doesn't see me for a long time, and doesn't phone me.

My parents are divorced and I live with my mom so I see my dad every 2nd weekend and twice a week. My dad has got remarried and has just had another child this week. My parents don't talk to each other and when they do they have a big arrgument and my dad doesn't pick my brother and I up. My dad is often busy working on the weekends that I go and see him on. I can understand all this since he is a doctor and he works in a practice, but sometimes I just wish we could go see a movie together or go to the beach. He probably doesn't go to the beach and stuff anymore because he says he isn't as young as he used to be.

My father stays with a girlfriend. He doesn't like splitting me and my [step] brother – when he buys thins for us he doesn't buy for one person he buys for tow of us. He is very nice – he comes every month to see us…my mom and dad hate each other sometimes they fight on the phone – well I can't really do anything so I just keep quiet. My mom always wants my father to be unhappy. And sometimes my mother doesn't let us see him – that's when she's angry at him. Some-times when my father comes with his girlfriends children & they come to take us to sleep in a hotel my mom sometimes say No! so then my father just wants cry.

Children's longing for a secure, constant and loving father-figure

Most children expressed the desire for their father to spend time with them. Of course, some children wished that their fathers would buy them sweets, clothes, a new bicycle or a cell phone, but the strongest, most consistent yearning children expressed was for their father to be with them. Correspondingly, apart from abuse and violence, not having time with their father or not having their father's attention was one of the things that most disappointed and distressed children.

He makes me happy when he is around. That is the thing that makes me happy.

He makes me happy when I can play with him and spend time with him. He also makes me happy when he says 'I love you'.

My father doe's not have to do anything to make me happy…just knowing he is there makes me happy because…When a think of many children who do not have a father it makes me appreciate my dad.

Sometimes I se other boys playing football with their fathers and wish that I could also play with my grandfather, but I can't because he is old.

My father just ly's down in his bed and watches T.V. and never spend a nough time with his family he never takes us out and never plays with us. all I want is my dad to spend more time with his family. Every night I go to bed cryind because he always picks on me for no reason. All I want to him to do is just let me talk.

My father does not spend a lot of time with me. My dad is always busy with his work. Sometimes he is on call and this really makes me sad. My father is sometimes tired when he comes home from work and I understand this, but when he is not tired he is always busy. When he does this, it really makes me sad. Sometimes my dad takes a day off, but all he does on that day off is sleep, sleep and sleep zzz. Then the next he's back to work again. It's just not fair.

Idealisation of fathers and ideal fathers

Children idealise fathers in a number of ways. They idealise the men who are their fathers by describing them as perfect, omniscient and superhuman, and they create images of ideal fathers they would like to have, to be, or be with, one day. While the father as provider, protector and disciplinarian is in the background of many children's descriptions of their fathers, what comes to the fore is the new contemporary father – a person who is involved and caring, who enjoys being with his children and doing things with and for them.

My father is a king to me.

There can be no father more perfect than my dad I have already. In no way would I change my dad.

Maybe he has made me unhappy once or twice but I have forgotten.

When I grow up and have children, I would not mind being my dad. For one, he is very clever. You can practically ask him anything and he will always be able to tell you something about it. He is the smartest man I know and ever will know.

My father is the best father to me and my brother. He loves us too much. He loves his wife my mom. He is a very honest person and very protective. My dad I think is one of the strongest men in the world. Just to tell you my best friend in the world is my dad. I love my dad the best in the world. My dad is really really fun…And to me and our family he's the best father in the world.

My father is great. He's out going he's fun to be with and is realy funny. My father is a great roll model to my life…My dad always has a smile on his face he's never sad or worrid about anything I love my dad a lot and he is always there for me…I can talk to him about anything…I can always relie on my dad he's always at my hocky match and my netball matches. If he had to clime the highest mountain to get to my match he would and thats what I like about him.

The ideal fathers children would like to have and/or one day be are, by and large, men who are affectionate and caring, who do not abuse drugs or alcohol or punish their children severely or unreasonably, who balance work and family time, and who are interested in their children.

> I would like to have a caring person who doesn't smack my children for nothing or abuse them. He must also be trusting and not take drugs or smoke. He musn't loose his temper easily. The perfect father will always love and care for you.

> I would like to help my children in their school work and sport. I would like to have an equil balince of work and play. I would help my wife with the house work and sometimes watch the news.

> The father I would like to have for my children one day is a father who works hard, loves his family (including me and the children obviously) never argues but has his bad days and good days so I can learn what he does and doesn't like – he would be very much like my own father but also different (if you know what I mean). Thank you for reading and I really hope your servey works out!!!

> The perfect father wouldn't go to work on weekends and his job wouldn't take over everything. He would be kind and friendly. He would look after his children and cook and ply with them. He would talke his children to beaches, parks and to camp. He would be funny, friendly, responsible and go to church. He would hlp people and his wife and always be kind. He wouldn't shout at his children unless they were naughty. He would sometimes give the children surprises when he came home from a trip or take them to a park or something as a surprise and he must be at all the children's birthday parties.

> I would like to have a father that is kind and gentle. I would like to walk in the house and the children yell daddy's here and they come and hug me. I would like to spend alot of time with my family and know them inside out. I would like to play with them and cheer them on at every single sport game they play. I would be proud of them and take them on holidays. I would give them treats, but not so that they become greedy. I would love them and help them and take them to school and clean theis school shoes say hot choc date's ready! Watch movies with them and take them to party's and not let my wive pay one cent on fees and bill's.

Children's observations and appreciation of men's domestic work and childcare

There is a public and media portrayal of men as uninvolved in domestic work and childcare. However, when children speak, the overwhelming sense is that there is widespread participation by men in household chores and childcare. The household work men do is not limited to washing cars or doing the garden, traditionally construed as men's chores about the house, but extend also to washing and ironing clothes, making beds, doing the dishes, shopping for groceries, bathing and dressing children, and cooking. Only a handful of children said their fathers did little or nothing around the house, and this was characterised as slothful, problematic, and especially unhelpful for their mother. The portrait of the ideal father, advanced by both boys and girls, was a man who did his share of the housework, helped his wife and performed childcare duties. Children approved of their father's involvement in the home and many saw him doing these tasks well. In addition, men's household and child work was interpreted by children to be an expression of love and affection towards their mother and towards themselves.

> He clean the house. He helps her by cooking food. He clean the garden waterint it. He wash the clothes and iron it. If my mother is sick he cooks the food.

> He cooks and makes beds and sweeps and cleans and helps with homework and projects and tidy the house and many other things.

> My father works as a trucker. But he helps in the house with the dishes, beds, sweeping etc, and he looks after us.

> My fathers name is Thulani. He is a kind man because everyday where he comes from work he help my mother with dishes and cooking food if my mom is not well. He earns not much but he can do everything at home for us.

> My dad helps my mother to do anything that my mom need help with. He cook, vacuums the house, does the ironing and (only when he has to) fold the washing. My dad takes time off work when my mom goes to Bloemfoentein to do her studying. He picks us up from school when mom can't.

> We are four children at home. Our father loves us at home. We always see a smile on his face when he watching us playing. He teaches us games to play with him. He is a good cook. He help my mother by cooking food when we are hungry. After super e washes the dishes to give us a chance to do homeworks.

My father's name is Mlungwane. He is not working. It is only my mother who is working. My father stays at home and he does house chores every day. He cleans the house. He cooks the food and washes clothes My mother doesn't have to come back from work and do the house. He is a caring father when we come back from school he checks our excise books and he helps us with our homework. At school we were asked to collect kiwi polish tins. He helped me to collect kiwi polish tins. I remember when my mother was sick she was admitted in the hospital. My father used to wake up in the morning and prepare our lunch boxes and he checked if we were clean. When we go to school he helps us combing our hair.

Fathers in their traditional guise

Co-existing with their appreciation of fathers who are loving and affectionate, involved in their children's lives, and who do their share of household work, children value very highly the traditional roles of fathers as providers, protectors, and guides into the social and moral worlds of their communities. In this role, fathers were perceived to be teachers and custodians of the past, transferring knowledge and skills. Additionally, fathers also conveyed social norms through their behaviour, which is closely observed by children. Attitudes of respect towards others, being an upright, generous and kind person, and not drinking and smoking, were all behaviours that made a big impression on children and which they admired and wished to emulate. Children also perceive that caring fathers work very hard, and often make significant sacrifices to please their families and live up to their children's expectations.

> He works hard for us at home and that makes me very happy.

> My father works very hard to give our family money. He tries his best to make me and my family safe.

> My father [who lives away] sends money and presents, and manternents for my mother. I would like him to send more money, but he is also batterling.

> My grandfather…is a nice, polite and funny gentleman that takes care of me like himself. He gives us shelter, food and other things that make me a happy child…He teaches me things in life.

> Is that he always makes us comfortable with him and he always tells us what good and what bad for us and he always tells us what to do to keep our self safety and he always teach us about hand work and he always tells us about my life of growing.

He is a good listener, he listen carefully when someone is talking to him. He is responsible man because he cook for us when my mother is not at home. He protect us as a family. He doesn't want outside the house at night. He is a good father. He loves us.

I think my father is a wounder full man and he likes every thing which is right. If he think to do something he thinks first that this thing is wrong and this thing is right and if it is right I must tell my children if you think some thing you must think before you do that thing if it is right. My father wants his children to know about good things and bad things.

My father is my teacher and my advisor. He teaches me some good things in life. He teaches me to respect old people to greet people when I meet with them. He advises me not to go out with boys. My father does not drink alcohol. He doesn't want any chirld to drink. He is my hero and the one I can trust he never hurts me. He gives me all the love I need. My father is everything to me if I have any problem he is there for me. He helps me to cross the road every morning when I got to school. When I am busy with something else he washes my uniform. I love my father very much.

Idealisations of fathers versus the reality of their imperfections and inadequacies

While the majority of fathers were described by children in ways that constructed them as 'good fathers', by no means were all fathers seen in this way. Children's observations of their fathers' behaviour is detailed and acute, and they are especially disturbed by deceit, either towards themselves or towards their mothers. Children perceive and accept that they live in a not-ideal world with not-ideal people, and their essays indicate that they accept this and can adapt to it. Even when they found fault with their fathers, many such descriptions began with 'I love my father, but …'. Indeed, some of the most touching and insightful descriptions of fathers by children entail the simultaneous expression of love and affection for a man who they perceive as all-too-human, and sometimes with serious faults and difficulties.

What he does do that makes my mom unhappy is when he farts.

My dad isn't the tidiest man that fell upon this earth, he doesn't know what a washing basket is used for, his clothes are forever lying on the bathroom floor. My mom could go mad.

I would want to be just like my father but without the smoking, drinking and having a short temper and my father to me is all ready the perfect father.

I love him…He makes promicis but he douse not for full them and he let us down when he dose that.

My father is a professor…he is generous and fair in all that he does. He drinks beer, doesn't really cooperate with my mother, sleeps around and lies a lot.

I don't lie it when my dad smokes, sleeps, watches T.V., or doesn't want to go anywhere…and when he is lazy and doesn't want to do any work, and also when he goes places that my mom doesn't know about.

Something I know about him…every Monday he does'nt come home. I don't know or he sleep with his girlfriend he come in the midnight to home. He said in his night he fix his car. My mom knows him now…about when he doesn't comes home.

The things I don't like about my dad is when he goes to the bar while I'm at a friends house. And when he fetches me he's drunk and I don't like that because it embarrasses me and I don't like it. And whenever I ask him why he's drunk he just tells me that he's not and makes an excuse saying that he's tired and has had a long day and I don't like it when he lies to me.

I would like him to keep his cool for a bit longer. I know that that can be a little difficult at times but I would like him to be able to. He sometimes makes promises and then breaks them. Sometimes he will even lie to me to keep me happy. I find it hard to respect someone like that, so I would like him to keep his promises and not tell lies. He is at times a bit over-protective. I would like him not to be so overprotective.

My father is careless with everything he does. He has a big stomach. His name is Revson. He doesn't want to buy a house and we live in a garage, we pay R300 every month for rent. And I do not like it when he drinks alcohol. When he comes back he smells alcohol and he snors and when he snors you will think there is a tiger in the garage. And when I grow up I want to be like him but I will not drink.

He leaves his clothes on the floor. He demands back scratches or foot massages. He switches all the lights off when he goes to bed. He turns the T.V up really loudly. He always wants big dinner and never wants pasta. He complains if there are no chocolates in the chocolate bin. He complains if theres no pudding. He never fixes things. He moans that her work and marking (she's a teacher) takes up to much time. He's forgetfull. He's always asking her to buy things for him. He cuts his toenails with the scissors. He moans about the mess in our house. He makes the whole bathroom wet when he has shower and he always jumps in the shower before her even nough she's got to be at work much earlier than him.

How children feel in the face of father absence, neglect and/or cruelty

Some fathers put their own interests before those of their children and families; are unfair and selfish; shout, swear and behave in vulgar and embarrassing ways; gamble, drink and smoke away needed family income; and beat their children and their wives. Children are sensitive to and extremely pained by these events, especially when they are interpreted as manifestations of generalised lack of respect and love.

> My dad sits on the cellphone all the time when he is in South Africa it is always interfering while playing golf or any other sort of sport. I would like his to loose the cellphone…

> My father works too much and goes to to much meetings and hardly spends time with us he is never available. I would like him to stop putting work before us and start spending time together.

> He gave me money I still say that and he buy food if get money. But he buy clothers four he self and drink alcohol. job and what makes my unjhappy is to go in the moning go to drink go in anthe house smoking staying in the shops drinking with auther peopls in the shops.

> He always go not with him to town for shopping dress and my mother become sad and beggin crying. My mother always stick on ironing for my father but my father just say mmm not saying thank you my wife. And mother become sad and go to her room crying beause he did any thing to make my father happy but he a just our smilling by not saying thanks to my Mom. And that how he spoil the mood of his family easily as that. But I don't see the problem because he doesn't drink alcoholic.

> When we walk around in shops you can see his *belly* hanging out of his T-shirt. He never has patience. He is always self senterd. He cares more about his girlfriend than about me and my brother. He is always trying to make arrangements with me instead of my mom. He always embarresis me while I am in a match or anything like that. He is trying to loose weight and he keeps on asking us do we think he has lost weight well he has actually gaind he is always barking at people or growling.

> And me I don't like my father drunk because when he drunk my father become write bad things and I don't like it like to heart my mother and my mother hear my father and my father say to mother Im sorry for that thing to hear you and my mother say you disappoint me and my mother say but it okay and my father say it fine but I don't like those things and I become cry when my father heart my mother.

> My father thing do that makes me unhappy is when is drunk he hit my mother and I fill unhappy and he disturb my family and my family

gonna dissapoipted him and it get said and other thing my father does to my family he take the food and give some family to eat and we don't have good to eat.

He beats my momy a lot, when he beats momy I feel sad when he is too angry no one can stop him from beating. He doesn't do a lot of things that make me unhappy. So I don't have to write more there is nothing more than love.

My father hurt me in the back and I feel unhappy and he eat meat but we don't eat meat every day. He don't want me to hurt someone when he do hurt me and I feel so very very very worried of him and he do not want us to visit other place and I don't want to do wrong thing and my father hurt us and we feel unhappy and we started to stay away from him and I feel so very very said and I started to cry and I play quietly every day and I go to sleep. And he do not buy toiys fo me.

Conclusions

In short sentences, a few lines and page-long essays, children describe the multiplicity of their aspirations, feelings, observations and disappointments about their fathers. At this age, in the pre-teen years, children seem able to balance both their longing for a close loving relationship with their father and their acceptance of him as an ordinary person with shortcomings. Although there are some obvious social and economic differences between children's needs and their views of fathers, there were, in the main, few differences in what children valued about fathers across gender and socio-economic status

What is most striking about the materials we have in hand, some 250 pages of children's text, is that children are less concerned about receiving status and possessions from their father than they are to be the recipient of his attention and affection. Of course, there is a bottom line of provision and children are extremely distressed when this is not met as a result of their father's selfishness or anti-social behaviour. However, children were accepting of unemployment as a reason for a father's inability to provide for his family, and sympathetic about the ways in which this affected their father's self-image. These messages are important for men to hear, especially for the many men who are not able to provide materially for their children as a result of unemployment or disability. While they may feel they have little to offer their children, there is a great deal that they can give that their children want from them.

> What I like most about my father is that I look so much like him than my mother. I have got rickets like him and even walk like him. His deep voice makes me laugh sometimes and he craks jokes, I think he does that

every second. He can gets crossed with me when I laugh very loud or fighting with my sisters. He like to tell wonderfull stories every knight especially on weekend. I suspect he took them from his great great grand mother and father. My father stopped working when I was only three years old and he always reminds me of that. He started drinking alcohol and become a real problem in my family for about two to three years after that he realised that he was wrong, then he started to look for a job and he couldn't find it by then, one day he found a peace job but it did not last. At home we have a coal stove so in winter when it gets very cold my father always go out and look for wood and coals and come back to make fire so that we can all be warn in the house. Even though he does not have a job he cares about us a lot than anyone could ever imagine. Everyday I pray and thank god for giving me such a loving father who adores me and appreciate the way I am and was I do things. I am so glad to have someone like him.

Linda Richter is the Executive Director of the Child, Youth and Family Development programme at the Human Sciences Research Council. She also holds honorary appointments at the Universities of KwaZulu-Natal, Witwatersrand, and Melbourne, Australia. Linda was trained as a clinical developmental psychologist but has worked in research environments for most of her career, investigating issues of risk and resilience in children, youth and families. She is co-author of *Mandela's Children: Growing up in Post-Apartheid South Africa* and joint editor of *The Sexual Abuse of Young Children in Southern Africa*.

Wendy Smith is an intern Research Psychologist. Prior to enrolling for a Master's degree in Psychology, she worked in fundraising, materials development, and training and development for a number of NGOs, particularly in the field of Adult Basic Education. She has filled a number of positions including Training Facilitator and Marketing Co-ordinator for World Vision, Fundraiser and Office Manager for the Natal ABE Support Agency, and has co-ordinated an International Conference on Adult Basic and Literacy Education (ABLE) in 2002 for all SADC member states. Her current research interests include socio-behavioural aspects of HIV infection, women and HIV/AIDS, and the changing nature of families due to HIV/AIDS.

Note

1   We have stayed faithful to children's actual writing, and added a word in brackets to clarify meaning only when it seemed that the child's words could not be understood without an explanation.

References

BBC Online (2004). Fathers are 'ignored' says study. BBC Online (Announcement posted on the World Wide Web: http://news.bbc.co.uk/1/hi/england/tyne3540695.stm (accessed 3 August 2004).

Davis, J. M. (1998). Understanding the meanings of children: A reflexive process. *Children and Society, 12,* 325–335.

Gadsden, V., Fagan, J., Ray, A., & Davis, J. (2004). Fathering indicators for practice and evaluation: The fathering indicators framework. In R. Day & M. Lamb (Eds.) *Conceptualising and measuring father involvement* (pp. 385–415). Mahwah, NJ: Erlbaum.

Hendricks, A. (1999). *Fathers who care: Partners in parenting. Children's views on fathering.* New Zealand: Officer of the Commissioner for Children, and Save the Children. Queensland, New Zealand.

Henwood, K., & Proctor, J. (2003). The 'good father': Reading men's accounts of parental involvement during the transition to first-time fatherhood. *British Journal of Social Psychology, 42,* 337–356.

Hickman, D. (2003). The role of fathers in the care and protection of children. *National Child Protection Clearinghouse Newsletter, 11,* 14–16.

Howard, S. D., Curtin, P., & Hardy, F. (2003). Fathers: Exploring the voices of children and young people. In R. Sullivan (Ed.). *Focus on fathering* (pp. 35–54). Melbourne: ACER Press.

James, A., Jenks, C., & Prout, A. (1998). *Theorising childhood.* Cornwall: TJ International.

McBride, B. A., Schoppe, S. J., & Rane, T. R. (2002). Child characteristics, parenting stress, and parental involvement: fathers versus mothers. *Journal of Marriage and the Family, 64,* 998–1012.

Mkhize, N. (2004). Who is a father? *ChildrenFIRST, 56,* 3–8.

Pruett, K. D. (1997). How men and children affect each other's development. *Zero to Three, 18.* http://www.zerotothree.org/fathers.html (accessed 4 December 2003).

Pruett, K. D. (2001). *Fatherneed: Why father care is as essential as mother care for your child.* New York: Broadway Books.

Richter, L. M. (2003). *Development and evaluation of a media intervention to promote responsive fatherhood.* Durban: Child, Youth and Family Development, Human Sciences Research Council.

Richter, L., Pather, R., Manegold, J., & Mason, A. (2004). Fatherhood: promoting men's care and protection of children. *Child & Youth Care, 22,* 4–5

Richter, L., Norris, S., & de Wet, T. (2004). Transition from Birth to Ten to Birth to Twenty: The South African cohort reaches 12 years of age. *Paediatric and Perinatal Epidemiology, 18*, 572–579.

Rohner, R. (1998). Father love and child development: History and current evidence. *Current Directions in Psychological Science, 7*, 157–161.

Shikwambi, S-J. (2001). When everyone wins. *ChildrenFIRST, August/September*, 14–17.

Silverman, D. (2003). *Doing qualitative research*. London: Sage

Smit, R. (2002). The changing role of the husband/father in the dual-earner family in South Africa. *Journal of Comparative Family Studies, 33*, 401–415.

Sullivan, R. (2000, July). Fathering and children – the contemporary context. Paper presented at the Focus on Fathering Symposium at 7th AIFS Conference, Sydney.

Tanfer, K., & Mott, F. (1997). The meaning of fatherhood for men. Report to the NICHD workshop on Improving Data on Male Fertility and Family Formation, the Urban Institute, Washington, D.C, 16–17 January.

CHAPTER 14

Fatherhood from an African cultural perspective

Desmond Lesejane

Introduction

The father as patriarch has long been a respected figure in southern African society. Over the years, socio-cultural and, later, political changes have undermined the authority of African men and their status within the family. This change has, in recent times, posited different perceptions of what it means to be a father, resulting in increased conflicts between men and women, older and younger men, rural and urban authority systems, and between children and their fathers. This chapter argues, however, that traditional culture in southern Africa has an image of fatherhood which can be restorative, and which offers a model for the redefinition of fatherhood.[1]

Clearly African culture is not homogeneous, but there are sufficient commonalities to enable us to draw a common picture of what fatherhood meant within this broad value system over a given time. I have focused on the Sotho cultural groups, especially the Sepedi and the Setswana groups, to support my views. The choice of this cultural system was primarily influenced by the fact that the writer, as a Motswana, is familiar with developments in this social group.

The notion of 'fatherhood' in the southern African context has been undergoing fundamental change over the years. Fathers were providers and protectors in precolonial times. In the context of the hierarchical and patriarchal authority systems of the day, the father sat at the pinnacle of the pecking order followed by the eldest son, other male relatives, with women and children coming in last. In effect, the father was the patriarch, the symbol and custodian of ultimate power and responsibility in the family and in the community.

The respected father, the patriarch, is an image that no longer even has national resonance. Once respected in African culture(s) as a man of wisdom, good judgement, care and consideration, the father today is an object of suspicion. Indicted in cases of violence and sexual abuse of women and young children, his reputation is in tatters. And with the disruption of the family, both nuclear and extended, his authority has also declined. Yet the dawn of a democratic dispensation in South Africa in 1994, with its commitment to equality, human dignity and freedom, coupled with a commitment to the affirmation of the experiences of all people, has created an intellectual climate for debate that takes into consideration the socio-cultural realities of the diverse population. 'The call of the African renaissance has, therefore, found fertile ground…(it gives) philosophical shape and direction to a way of life that was struggling for recognition' (Pityana, 1999, p. 138).

The challenge of promoting fatherhood, which forms the immediate backdrop of this chapter, is essentially a moral challenge and a nation-building initiative that seeks to promote men's involvement in the care and protection of children. The creation of strategies and the development of a framework for such an engagement can therefore not be pursued or concluded without tapping into the wealth and wisdom of local African cultural value systems. This does not imply a wholesale acceptance of these systems. It is generally accepted that not all that was part of African heritage was perfect. There is, in fact, a growing acknowledgement that all cultures are by nature dynamic and susceptible to abuse and misuse.[2]

This chapter seeks to identify lessons and experiences of fatherhood in an African context that may be useful in the promotion of fatherhood among men, especially African men, who still have an allegiance to an African cultural value system. Holding this system together is the notion of '*botho/ubuntu*', a concept that emphasises a spirit of communalism among members of a community. *Botho/ubuntu* is characterised by caring and compassion for others, especially the most vulnerable; connectedness to and ongoing fellowship with the ancestors; and commitment to the common good. It is within this broader framework of values that the chapter seeks to reflect critically on the role of men in society, focusing on the relationship they have with women and children, and the responsibilities associated with these relationships.

The concept of a father as the one with ultimate authority and responsibility was central to the determination of the role of men in the family and society. This resulted in patriarchy becoming the norm. From many perspectives, the system which became ingrained in African culture through patriarchy can be regarded as sexist as it discriminates against women (Masenya, 2004). This chapter does not offer a blanket endorsement of patriarchy nor does it issue a clarion call for a return to some romanticised ideal of a traditional past when women and children knew their place.[3] What this chapter seeks to do is to offer a redefinition of fatherhood that is rooted in an African cultural value system.

I begin by outlining my understanding of the father as a patriarch in my culture. This is followed by a reflection on the changing patterns of the system as a result of a changing social, political, cultural and economic milieu. A comparative analysis of the traditional view of fatherhood and the demands of 'modern' society then follows. Lastly, I consider some suggestions as to how men can better protect and care for children.

In the limited space available it is not possible to do justice to the complexity of the debates about patriarchy and gender inequality. This chapter does not adequately analyse the way in which the system shapes the socialisation of both males and females in society.[4] Nor can it fully cover the debates about fatherhood within the context of patriarchy (Tanfer & Mott, 1997). Discussion hitherto has been constrained by the nature of research data, which has often been sourced from mothers who speak about their experiences of fathers' attitudes to, and relationships with, their children.

Men and fathers have generally been silent in public discourse. In an attempt at redress, this chapter is based on the views of an informal group of men with whom the issues were debated, although the writer takes sole responsibility for the conclusions drawn. The intention is simply to introduce the views of some men into the discourse, hopefully resulting in less biased perceptions of the challenges of parenting.

Images of a father in African culture: father and child

Traditionally, fatherhood was an ascribed status rather than an achieved one. In a crude sense, one did not become a father only by virtue of having biologically fathered a child. Various idioms attest to this. In Sepedi they say '*ngwana ga se wa shete, ke wa kgoro*', literally meaning a sperm does not beget a child, but also asserting that a child belongs to the broader family. Or in Setswana, '*ngwana ke wa dikgomo*' or '*o e gapa le namane*', which means that marrying someone also means marrying his/her children. It should be noted that marriage in the traditional sense included more than the husband and the wife; whole families were married and became relatives.

In instances where children were born out of wedlock and there was no intention on the part of the biological parents to marry, provision was made for the maternal family to approach the paternal family and the two families would work out an arrangement as to how the child would be raised. Generally this involved the paternal family acknowledging the child and compensating the maternal family in some way, as well as performing initiation rituals, including naming the child.

As I will show, such a child 'acquired' through marriage or 'acceptance of responsibility' also received the benefits of fatherhood provided for in the system.

The status and position of the father

Those who achieved the status of fathers were invariably married. They were seen as the heads of their families and, often, this would include being head of the extended family. This extended family could include unmarried sisters and brothers and their children, widowed elders, and any orphans in the family. The most senior male in the extended family would become the family patriarch. By its nature, it was never *just* a nuclear family as we know it today. The patriarch was also a community leader, being part of the *kgotla* and *kgoro* (village or tribal councils).

The position of the father carried a number of responsibilities. The father was:

- The custodian of moral authority within his family and with other patriarchs in the broader community;
- A leader who had final responsibility in the affairs of the family;
- A primary provider of the material needs of the family, from shelter to food;
- A protector of the family against threatening forces of whatever nature, and
- A role model to young men in particular.

It follows then that a good father was one who could provide for the family, maintain the unity of the family, and assert his moral authority on the family. Correspondingly, a man who was abusive, irresponsible, a drunkard and a general social misfit, would be regarded as a bad father and would, over time, be stripped of his responsibilities and stature.

The roles of a father

Fathers had to be available. This meant a father had to literally spend time with his children in order to exercise his moral authority, maintain family customs and laws, and be a leader. Availability was also a prerequisite for being a role model.[5]

Fathers had to be responsible. This included providing for, guiding, organising and generally overseeing the management of their children's lives. They would be key participants in deciding, for instance, when a child went to initiation school and to whom they got married.

It was important for fathers to interact with their families. While they had the final say on all things, it was a sign of a good father to listen to members of the family, consult with other members of the *kgoro*[6] and revert to established systems and values upheld by the *kgotla*.[7] Rarely would a major decision be made on behalf of children and the wife without such consultations taking place.

Support systems for the father

In African culture, a number of processes and practices were designed to sustain fatherhood. These are briefly outlined below.

Bogwera

Firstly, boys were prepared for fatherhood. They had to go through an initiation process, (*bogwera*)[8] that prepared them for manhood and fatherhood. Someone who did not go through this school would forever remain a boy, barred from the responsibilities and privileges of manhood, regardless of his age. Further counselling sessions (*go laiwa*) were held with men before they married.[9]

Mophato

Men who went to an initiation school together would form a regiment (*mophato*). These regiments, 'besides promoting group solidarity amongst the various graduates of the ceremonies,…instilled key common values amongst the participants, and within society' (Embassy of Botswana, n.d.). The regiment also formed an immediate peer group that served as the first referral and advisory point for its members throughout their lives. Whenever a man needed support or was in trouble, he would go to his regiment for support, advice and counselling.

Kgoro

While a man inherited some assets from his father upon marriage, it was the broader clan (*kgoro*) that apportioned him a piece of land to plough and farm so that he could take care of his family. In instances of economic hardship, members of the clan would club together to assist the besieged family. A typical example is the provision of *kgomo ya mafias*, literally a breeding cattle loaned to the family by a better-off relative until it has bred enough cattle to make the family self-sufficient again. It is almost like interest-free start-up capital!

It was also through the *kgoro* that 'illegitimate'[10] children and orphans would be taken care of. Either a maternal uncle would assume the fathering responsibilities described above, effectively raising such children as his own (surrogate fatherhood), or a male relative would be appointed to take care of a family upon the death of a father (levirate fatherhood). The system's intention was to retain the household wealth, take care of the children and sustain the paternal family lineage, which could be lost if the woman remarried.

Kgotla

This body served as the final arbiter of community disputes and also sat as a law enforcement court. While only men sat in the council, women who had complaints, even against their husbands, were allowed to make representations. It was not uncommon to have men sanctioned, especially when they were considered to have brought the image of the community into disrepute.

The naming of children

Sotho culture regarded children as gifts from the ancestors and, at times, as the same ancestors having come back to life. This worldview resulted in children being revered. It was common, for instance, to name a child after an admired older or deceased person, such as a grandparent or even a parent. Once a child had been so named, they would be treated as if they were that person. From the time of naming, the child would have the same authority as the person after whom he or she had been named. If not named after a specific person, a child could be named after a totem, a revered symbol in the clan, or could be given a descriptive name relating to events surrounding the birth or expressing feelings and gratitude for the birth. Children thus named would be treated with the utmost respect and were accorded the best protection. No upstanding man would, for instance, abuse a child named after his mother because that child was, in essence, an embodiment of his mother. The mother lived in the child and the relationship with ancestors was thus enriched.

The changing times

The notion and practice of fatherhood in South Africa has gone through a number of changes as a result of the historic changes in the country.

Colonisation and missionary endeavours undermined, and declared as heathen, cultural practices such as initiation schools. This resulted in the disruption of what were stable cultural preparatory and support systems. While in many communities efforts were made to sustain these systems, operating from the underground as it were, improvisations and adaptations were not always successful. For instance, the practice of initiation schools has become little more than traditional circumcision and the practice of *lobola* has become synonymous with men buying women.

The advent of the mining economy and the resultant migrant labour system literally took men away from their families, making it impossible for fathers to be available to care for and nurture their children. The absence of men sharpened the household division of labour. Women were ascribed the role of caregivers and nurturers while fatherhood increasingly became equated with material provision to the exclusion of other forms of parenting such as guiding and being a role model.

The establishment of urban townships for Africans did not help the situation even though it allowed some men to stay with their families. The harsh realities of the apartheid system humiliated many men, effectively undermining their ability to lead and be role models in their families and in society. The economic and land dispossession of the African majority made it difficult for fathers to provide for their families. Over time, fathers came to be judged only on their ability to provide, and this rested exclusively on their economic muscle. Only men with economic means were seen as good fathers.

The rise of political resistance in the 1940s and 1950s did not restore the status of fathers or support the importance of fatherhood. This started with the African National Congress Youth League (ANCYL) of the 1950s asserting its influence over the broader movement and it reached its climax with the 1976 revolution, which saw the youth (mostly young men) taking over political and community leadership from their fathers. Thus the stature of a father as patriarch of the family and community was further eroded.

The advances of the struggle for the liberation of women further challenged the notion of men as heads of families, especially when women began to have the economic means to provide for children. For instance, the custom of a male relative marrying the widow of a close male relative or of uncles becoming social fathers could not be sustained because these practices were seen to condemn women to perpetual adolescence. Furthermore, the displacement of the extended family by nuclear families has undermined the practice of surrogate fatherhood further, rendering the *kgoro* solution irrelevant.

Whereas in the past a child could not be fatherless or parentless, the erosion of the traditional African family and community systems has effectively spawned a generation of 'parentless' children – children who are social outcasts with little prospect of meaningful development. At its worst, this situation is seen in the phenomenon of street children. In some areas of the country, though, there are still pockets of traditional communities where no child is left without parents and the traditional *kgoro* system is still in place.

Lessons for fatherhood today

We should note that the system of patriarchy was part of a broader cultural system. In this broader African cultural system, values were embedded in a patriarchal system that accommodated children while insisting on respect for women as much as for patriarchs. Patriarchs in this system had authority, but they also had obligations and the position of patriarch was not for life. True, the system seldom permitted women to ascend to positions of authority, but it imposed duties on men that allowed it to work to the benefit of children. If the system was imperfect, it nevertheless provided some stability and protection for children and women from the absolute power of men. This system was disrupted by colonialism, although some of its values remain in the hearts of Africans.

The current problem is that 'African patriarchy' has become distorted and a new patriarchy without obligations or reciprocity has emerged. It gives men power but imposes few duties. The constraints on men, as well as the support and censure systems, have disappeared.

In our quest for improved and increased male involvement in the care and protection of children, we can still learn from the systems and values outlined above. The image of a father as a patriarch, somebody who cares for, nurtures, leads, guides, and is a role model in the family and community, can be restored. To overcome attendant distortions and abuses, it is proposed that such a restoration process should be in harmony with the core values of equality, respect, human dignity and freedom such as those enshrined in South Africa's Constitution.

Recommendations for the restoration of fatherhood

The concept of *kgotla,* entrenched in southern African culture, offers a model of management and communication within the family. A *kgotla* is a forum for discussion where all participants are equal, as symbolised by circular seating arrangements. Decisions are made by consensus after everybody has had an opportunity to air their views. Reappropriating this concept will facilitate better interaction between fathers, children, mothers and other members of the family. A prerequisite for the concept to work today would be to open up the *kgotla* to women, and even children, as equal participants.

Men have to be prepared for fatherhood (and boys have to be taught to be men). To date, society has not come up with an alternative to the traditional initiation schools, resulting in transmission of wrong values and glorification of poor practices, sometimes in the name of culture. There is a need to initiate and run co-ordinated fatherhood formation processes that embrace the ideals of gender equality. This process could be included in the school curriculum, within the broader life orientation learning area. It is essential that such initiatives should operate within a gender equality framework.

Much has been said about the influence that men have over one another and the time they spend with each other in men's clubs. It is suggested that possibilities exist to re-orientate these clubs into peer support networks in the mould of *mephato* (regiments) referred to above. Once rid of gender stereotyping, sexism and discrimination, these '*mephato*' would become spaces and platforms for men to counsel and advise each other. Responsible fatherhood and role-modelling could be encouraged, with irresponsible fathers being censured by their peers.

As the numbers of orphans increase (because of AIDS-related deaths), South Africa faces a challenge of parenting (see also Chapters 18 and 19, this volume). We can learn from the concept of a child belonging to the *kgoro* and, by implication, to the family. If more men could become fathers beyond their biological and marital obligations, there would be fewer parentless children in our midst.

Desmond Lesejane, the father of two children, began his career as a parish pastor in Alexandra and Thembisa. Subsequently, he has filled the positions of Programme Director of Faith and Mission & Poverty Eradication for the South African Council of Churches (SACC), Chief Executive Officer of the Civil Society Secretariat of the World Summit on Sustainable Development and, more recently, Programme Co-ordinator of the Moral Regeneration Movement. He is currently the Director of the Ecumenical Service for Socio-economic Transformation (ESSET).

Notes

1 This chapter was written in collaboration with Bafana Khumalo and William Mashakoe.

2 Culture by definition is never static. Any culture that seeks to become so renders itself irrelevant and ineffective in informing how people live and coexist. Cultures by their very nature borrow from each other.

3 Some sections of South Africa's religious and traditional authorities consistently insist that the provision of children's and women's rights in the Constitution has prevented men from exercising their traditional and God-given roles of maintaining law and order, hence the breakdown in the moral fibre of society.

4 The point is not being raised to question leadership of women in the struggle for gender equality. Women should continue to lead because they remain the primary (though not helpless) victims of patriarchy and other forms gender discrimination. It simply seeks to promote men's involvement in the debate.

5 An interesting feature of African culture was that good role models (including women) would go on to become 'badimo', ancestors. This meant that role-modelling extended beyond death.

6 The 'kgoro' is a collective of relatives that provided the immediate social and economic support base for families.

7 A 'kgotla' was the highest governing body of a given community, tasked with, among other things, settling disputes and maintaining community values.

8 A parallel initiation process for women, called 'bojale', was also practised

9 It is often alleged that only women received this counselling. This is not true. What is at issue is that over the years the counsel given promoted men's control and ownership of women. For instance, women would be counselled to accept that men will have extramarital affairs.

10 I have put the term in quotation marks as this notion does not exist in the cultures I have explored. The nearest term is 'letlaleanya' meaning a child who came already breastfeeding. There was no stigma attached to this status and such children could even inherit the kingship.

References

Embassy of Botswana, (n.d.). Traditional government and social order. www.botswanaembassy.or.jp/culture/body2_1.html (accessed April 2004).

Masenya, M.J. (ngwana' Mphahlele) (2004). *How worthy is the woman of worth? Rereading Proverbs 31:10–31 in African-South Africa*. New York: Peter Lang Publishing.

Ngobese, N. (2002). *One goat is enough. Taking a fresh look at women's issues at the dawn of the African Renaissance*. Pietermaritzburg: Women Stuff Series.

Pityana, N. (1999). The renewal of African moral values. In W. Makgoba (Ed.). *African Renaissance: The new struggle*. (pp. 137–148). Johannesburg/Cape Town: Mafube/Tafelberg.

Tanfer, K. & Mott, F. (1997). The meaning of fatherhood for men. Report to the NICHD workshop on Improving Data on Male Fertility and Family Formation, the Urban Institute, Washington, DC., 16–17 January.

Interviews

Oral Interview with M. Pataki. (22 June 2004). Polokwane, Limpopo, South Africa.

Oral Interview with S. Phogole. (26 July 2004). Alexandra, Gauteng, South Africa.

CHAPTER 15

African traditions and the social, economic and moral dimensions of fatherhood

Nhlanhla Mkhize

Introduction

This chapter analyses fatherhood from a socio-cultural position. It notes the existence of many negative masculine identities, but it also notes that such identities can be changed. Images of fathers as caring and loving people already exist but economic marginalisation, especially among township males and other poor groups, has undermined the capacity of these men to accept or believe in this role. This chapter argues that in order to promote fatherhood it may be useful to revisit traditional African understandings that define fatherhood as a collective social responsibility of the family. This allows for the acknowledgement of the role played by uncles, aunts and grandparents in raising children. It also offers a fatherhood role to all men, irrespective of whether they are biological fathers or not, on the understanding that children belong to everybody.

Poverty and the decline of fatherhood

Fathers are an essential component of the family which, in turn, has been recognised as one of the most important units of society. The family is critical for the wellbeing of children (Nsamenang, 2000). However, the family seems to be in crisis worldwide. The UNESCO report of 1991 stated that 'in the family system of every human society, incomplete families emerge due to various reasons – demographic, economic or social: such as the death or divorce of a spouse, partition of the family, or migration' (p. 11). A dramatic increase in the number of non-intact families and female-headed households has been reported. This phenomenon is associated with an increase in the number of children living in poverty. In the United States, Mintz (1998) notes that poverty tends to be more pronounced among single-headed African-American households. The association of poverty with single-parent households also exists in South Africa (Barbarin & Richter, 2001).

In South Africa, unemployment and poverty are most pronounced among the African population. Wilson (2004) notes that in 1995, close to two-thirds (61%) of the black population was classified as poor, followed by the coloured community at

38 per cent. Yet, only one per cent of the white population was so classified (see Chapters 3 and 18, this volume). Although the first ten years of democracy have seen an improvement in the lives of the poor (for example, the expanded provision of electricity and clean drinking water), unemployment figures remain very high in the previously disadvantaged communities. Wilson (2004) further notes that in March 2003, 43 per cent of the black African population who were willing and able to work could not find employment.

The high rate of unemployment means that many African males are unable to assume the social responsibility associated with fatherhood. Hunter (2004 and Chapter 8, this volume) has written about the disempowerment of economically marginalised African men. Unemployed men (and even young employed couples, see Bennie, 2004) struggle to raise *ilobolo*[1] and to perform cultural marriage ceremonies, without which the marriage is not fully recognised by the family and the community. Ramphele (2002) reflects on this situation by noting that 'desertion by fathers is often prompted by their inability to bear the burden of being primary providers. The burden of failure becomes intolerable for those who lack the capacity to generate enough income as uneducated and unskilled labourers' (p. 158, also see Chaper 6, this volume). It should be noted that it is not always the case that fathers desert their children. In some cases, class differences between the boy's and the girl's families rule out the possibility of the boy's involvement in the upbringing of his child, even if he is prepared to play the fatherly role (see Box below). Unemployment and poverty, coupled with the social and cultural tendency to define manhood and fatherhood primarily in terms of ability to provide economically for one's family, rob many men of the opportunity to play the fatherly role in the raising of their children.

Fatherhood and class differences

The following extract, taken from the author's ongoing research on moral and ethical reasoning, indicates that class differences can be an obstacle for some men who are otherwise prepared to assume their responsibilities as fathers. The extract also shows that for this man, ability to father a child was an important part of his identity (manhood) and self-definition.

Author: What is the most difficult moral dilemma you have ever faced?

Interviewee: I was in love with this girl. I loved her very much but then she became pregnant. Both of us were still at school. So, her parents did not accept me because I was still at school and my family was of low standing in the community. So,…the pregnancy continued…When the time to deliver came, the child was already dead when she was delivered…You see, these people were 'very good' in hurting me, they really hurt me! When my parents enquired how we could assist with the burial of the child, they refused to allow us to take any part or to have anything to do with our family. 'We will bury the child ourselves, thank you very much! We do not need your help', they said…

Author: Why was it important for you or your family to take part in burying the child?

Interviewee: I wanted the child to be buried by my family because I believed she was my child. I was even prepared to pay all the penalties according to Zulu traditions, but their actions prevented me from doing so. They even registered the child in their own surname. They said it was their child: it had nothing to do with me. They said nothing connects me to the child.

Author: You would have been happy if the child was registered in your surname?

Interviewee: It was my first child; a sign that I am a man and capable of getting children.

That would have been very good to me, to have the child registered in my name. Though she died, she should have had my surname. I wanted the child to belong, but since they wanted the child to belong to them, it is OK.

Author: Why do you think this family acted this way?

Interviewee: The problem was that I had fallen in love with the wrong person at the wrong time...I found love in the wrong place because I do not work. That was the major issue against me. The men going out with the girls from that family were all professionals. Me? I was nothing! I did not have the economic muscle! This was the worst experience of my life; it hurt me a lot.

When the father or both parents are unemployed, this has negative economic and psychological consequences for the family as a whole. Unemployment impacts negatively on people's quality of life. In a study conducted in Mossel Bay and surrounding areas (cited in Wilson, 2004), a significant relationship was reported between parents' self-reports of depression and children missing meals due to lack of money. This was true for both men and women. Another study investigating long-term effects of unemployment in the Mpophomeni area in KwaZulu-Natal reported parental depression and disruption of families (Radford, 1993[2]). The men, however, were the most affected. This is what some of the men said in interviews:

Extract 1: *If you are not working you are not a genuine father. You are a father because you work.* My children do not love me as they used to. I sometimes get angry with my wife when she asks me whether I am searching for a job. *I have lost my status as man of the house.* (emphasis added)

Extract 2: *If you are not working, you are as good as dead. I have lost my dignity as a human being. I sometimes think people see me as kind of a fool*. I am now staying in someone's house because mine was taken away [repossessed]. My children are all over the place. I would like us to be together as a family. *I cry a lot. Even today I was crying.* I have lost my manhood [*ngilahlekelwe ubudoda bami*]. A man is a man because he can provide for his family. (emphasis added)

Extract 3: [Being unemployed] is a big problem. I am now doing my wife's work [house chores], and she is gone to work [as a domestic]. It should not be so. I have lost the respect of my children. My children used to come and greet me when I returned from work but they do not do so anymore. I can't provide them with anything. I am just like a child. Now I am thinking so much I think I will go crazy.

These extracts highlight the centrality of work to these men's identities as fathers. They also indicate the psychological and economic consequences of unemployment to the family as a whole. Further, children are affected because their parents are unlikely to be able to buy them school uniforms and other school necessities. Duncan and Brooks-Gunn (1997) have shown that economic resources are important for children's cognitive development, especially in early and middle childhood. Day (1998) also argues that the educational performance of children from low-income groups where the father is absent, tends to be poor.[3] It is therefore important to investigate how fatherhood can be promoted, particularly among fathers who are unemployed and live in impoverished communities.

Fatherhood and the identity project

This chapter conceives of fatherhood as an identity project immersed in social, cultural, historical and economic contexts. Fatherhood is intertwined with the process by means of which men come to an understanding of who they are – their sense of identity and place – in society. Fatherhood does not occur in a vacuum; it is a socio-moral process informed by the dominant discourses of what it means to be a man in one's society. In this chapter, it is argued that traditional understandings of identity formation in terms of intra-psychic processes – as a progressive unfolding of psychological processes from within a person – hinder the recognition of fatherhood as a social, moral and relational process. Nor is the tendency to understand fatherhood in biological terms sufficient. The sociocultural-psychological tradition, which conceptualises identity formation in social, historical, political and ideological terms, provides better tools for understanding fatherhood. This is particularly the case in contexts characterised by rapid social change. The socio-cultural approach is in line with Hearn's (1989, 1992, 1994) position. Hearn has called for debates about fatherhood to be more explicitly gendered and to focus more on power. A gendered approach understands fatherhood as social rather than natural; fatherhood is interconnected with the social production and reproduction of masculinities and men's practices.

African societies and collective child-rearing

Before discussing the processes whereby notions of fatherhood are produced, it is important to briefly revisit child-rearing practices in traditional African societies. This is because the social and cultural approach to fatherhood adopted here is in line with the communal view of the self and the family, characteristic of African societies, which contrasts sharply with the dominant view of the self and the family in western thought.

Traditional African thinking is informed by communal life. Psychological development is not an individual journey; a person realises his or her place and responsibilities within a community of other people (Mkhize, 2004). Sayings such as *umuntu ngumuntu ngabantu* (Nguni) and *Motho ke motho ka batho babang*[4] (Sotho/Tswana) capture this relational dimension of being. The term 'community' refers to an organic relationship between individuals. People are morally obliged to be responsive to others' needs. This collective mode of existence explains why many people are treated as members of one's family – being addressed as father, mother, and brother irrespective of the genetic relationship. The extension of such terms to a number of people pledges these people to parental responsibilities. The family is of utmost significance: a child is born into a family community, which includes members of the extended family, the living and the deceased.

Child-rearing is the collective responsibility of the extended family as a whole. For example, when I was growing up in Ndwedwe, north of Durban, my father's brothers, my aunts and my grandfather all played an important role in raising us children. They would counsel me and my cousins – all of us living within a single household and considering ourselves members of a single family unit – about the importance of family cohesion and the like. *Ubab'omncane* ('small father'), meaning my father's younger brother, would return from work in the early hours of the evening and head straight to my mother's house to enquire about our health and wellbeing. My own (biological) father would reinforce these values upon his arrival from his place of work. He was particularly fond of telling stories about how his mother (my granny, who was then deceased) had instructed him and his three brothers never ever to quarrel among themselves because the day they did so, 'one of you would die'. He would then instruct me never to lay a hand on my sisters or my mother, no matter what they might have done and no matter how angry I might be. 'Just go away and come back when you have cooled down', he would say. This advise played an important role in shaping my identity as a man. To this day I remember his words as a guide for action.

On many occasions the family would gather together – including those not living within our household – for a ceremony or joint prayer meeting to strengthen relationships between immediate members of our clan. The family became an important part of our social identity, apart from which full personhood was (and continues to be) almost inconceivable. Collective fatherhood, discussed below, should be understood in this context.

Self-understanding in western thought: individualism and the nuclear family

The view of the self described above contrasts sharply with self-understanding and child-rearing practices in modern western societies. In these societies, self-understanding – the process by means of which we come to develop a sense of who we are – is individualistic. Child-rearing practices are geared towards fostering individual autonomy. Self-understanding is characterised by an increasing differentiation of the self from the social and cultural world. Identity formation involves the discovery of one's inner essence. This includes, among other things, leaving home and establishing a separate identity. Psychological development tends towards separation (known as *individuation*) rather than connection. The same applies to ethical decision making, which is abstracted from people's lived experiences – the concrete reality of their everyday lives. For example, principles such as justice and fairness are thought to be the principles that would be discovered by any rational moral agent, independent of history and time. Thus, we would expect a man who has reached the necessary stages of moral and ethical maturity to refrain from abandoning his child. The logic is that any rational moral agent understands that abandoning a child is unfair to the mother and the child. The social and cultural context of fatherhood plays a less important role.

The focus on the individual: implications for fatherhood

The individualistic paradigm is concerned with individual differences. A person has reached moral maturity (in terms of individual development) when he is deemed capable of discerning the rights and wrongs of being a father. Failure to assume one's responsibilities as a father is reducible to what is inside the person. The deficit resides in the individual. Cultural, historical and class differences are not taken into account. Essentialist accounts of fatherhood are in line with the paradigm of the individual. Essentialism focuses on biological sex differences between men and women. These differences are thought to have a bearing on the parenting process. Fatherhood is a biological fact; there is no room for collective or social forms of fatherhood discussed below.

Problems with the individualistic paradigm

There are four main problems with the individualistic tradition of the self and the moral: (a) the tendency to draw sharp distinctions between our 'inner' and 'outer' lives, (b) failure to account for contradictions in self-understanding and changing family patterns, (c) inability to account for culturally varied understandings of fatherhood, and (d) the tendency to discount the relationship between history, colonisation and masculinity.

Individualism and the distinction between our 'inner' and 'outer' lives

Individualism draws sharp distinctions between what is 'inside' the person (for example, thoughts and emotions) and the social world. The individual and society are mutually exclusive; they cannot coexist. This makes it difficult to understand the influence of social, economic and cultural factors on fatherhood. For example, in traditional African societies, parenthood was not considered a bio-psychological given. That is, one does not become a parent because one has sired children. Social parenthood is established through the *imbeleko*[5] sacrifice. This is a ritual by which the new-born is introduced to his or her family community and *abaphansi* (the community of the departed) (Ramose, 2002). Prior to this, the new-born has no socially designated status and parenthood has not been established. Focusing on the biological or the psychological aspects of fatherhood ignores this social dimension.

It is conceivable that, among other factors, unwillingness to assume fatherly responsibilities can be attributed to the breakdown of the social and communal structures that gave meaning to personhood and parenthood. For example, according to African thought, being a person (*umuntu/motho*) includes an idea of excellence. In the course of growing up, a person undergoes a process of social and ritual transformation culminating in the attainment of the full complement of excellencies seen as definitive of being a true person. Not only did these rites endow the growing person with a sense of identity and meaning in life, they also played an essential role in inculcating the value of *ubuntu*, thought to be essential for the harmonious functioning of society. Among the values cherished were family unity and, most importantly, being responsible to one's kin, including prevention of family disunity of any kind. In the case of a man who did not look after his children, the family as a whole would take corrective action because, as the saying goes, 'our children cannot cry in the wilderness, uncatered for' (*izingane zakithi azikwazi ukukhala endle, zinganakiwe*).

Tensions and contradictions in self-understanding

Fatherhood is not a single, unchanging concept. It needs to be understood in context and time. For example, how do we explain the fact that someone can be a good father for the first five years of his child's life, and then abandon fatherly responsibilities later? Does it mean that the person no longer understands the principles by means of which we make sense of right and wrong? How is such a regression possible, given the forward-directed, progressive nature of psychological development envisaged in the individualistic moral paradigm? Social and historical constructions of fatherhood can explain these changes.

Further, biological or purely psychological accounts of fatherhood cannot account for the structural changes that are taking place in our families. Bianchi (1995) and Mintz (1998) point out that it is not uncommon for a child growing up these days to have a stepfather living with him or her on a regular basis. Also, many children will experience irregular contact with their biological father and/or stepfather as the boundaries of the family change, sometimes frequently, during the course of a child's time at home.

Fathers themselves are being called upon to re-think their positions several times in their lives: they may begin as biological fathers, then later become in-home fathers, or out-of-home distant fathers, only later to become stepfathers to children while remaining in contact with their own biological children.

Likewise, children will have to define and re-define their relationships with their parents as these men move in and out of their lives. The question is: what form does or should fatherhood take in such circumstances? An essentialist account of fatherhood cannot help us to deal with the question of fatherhood in the context of change.

Fatherhood in different cultural contexts

Biological or purely psychological accounts of fatherhood cannot explain historical changes to the traditional African conception of the family, nor can they help us to come to terms with changes to what it means to be a man. I refer here to changes to conceptions of masculinity, resulting mainly from colonisation, urbanisation and forced migrant labour (Morrell, 1998).

While the nuclear family is the dominant family pattern in most western cultures, sub-Saharan societies tend towards collectivism. People become members of extensive social networks through birth and marriage ties. Kin and supportive friends attempt to promote a sense of belonging through these social networks. In the extended family system, the responsibility to raise and support children does not fall exclusively on the biological parents. Members of the extended family are expected to take an active responsibility for the wellbeing of their relatives' children. Collective fatherhood is practised; one's father's brother is also one's father, he is addressed as such, and is expected to behave in a manner deserving of a father (see page 191). The advantages of collective fatherhood are not only economical – collective fatherhood also enhances the child's social capital. Social capital, in this context, refers to the number of interactions the child is exposed to within the family. These interactions contribute to the child's emotional, cognitive, educational and social development (Day, 1998).

Collective fatherhood

Mowetsi's case, cited by Anderson (1997), is a good example of collective fatherhood. The citation illustrates the complex and fluid nature of the concept of fatherhood.

> Mowetsi has seven children, engendered between 1954 and 1975. Throughout these decades he lived most of every year in South African mining camps which prohibited families, while his wife lived with their children in her parents' village. As a result of this economically necessary separation, Mowetsi's fatherly activities during this time consisted primarily of sending money to his inlaws that was used to raise his own, his in-laws' and his wife's siblings' children. He travelled home for important occasions in his children's lives, but obviously could not tend and guide them day-to-day. These functions were discharged by his father-in-law, whom his own children called 'father'. Mowetsi had almost no contact with his children until he retired, upon which he returned to his village community to take over his parent's household. He continues to raise his grandchildren, in the same way that his father-in-law raised his own kids.

A fatherly career such as the one above is not unusual to many African migrant workers in southern Africa. It shows that alternative models of fatherhood can, and do, work.

It should be noted that although the extended family continues to exert influence, particularly in rural contexts, it is fast losing control over individual welfare and family security (Nsamenang, 2000).

Collective fatherhood is still practised in some settings, where maternal uncles, aunts and grandparents play a significant fatherly role in the upbringing of children. However, there is a rapid decline in this practice due to urbanisation and HIV/AIDS-related poverty. The economic injustices of the apartheid era also continue to make their presence felt in African communities. In South Africa, a further breakdown of family ties and support systems occurred during the violence that preceded political emancipation.

All these factors make it difficult to meaningfully enforce the concept of fatherhood as a collective responsibility of male members of the family. Nevertheless, where it is still feasible, collective fatherhood can be, and is being, used to complement the traditional biological/ essentialist model of fatherhood.

The historical role of the father

Essentialist accounts of fatherhood do not take into consideration the historical role of the father within the family in many traditional societies (Nsamenang, 2000). Historically, the father assumed a critical role in decision-making and enforcing standards of behaviour among children. He was also expected to be the first person informed or consulted in the event of a child getting sick, or the like. The father was an important social figure, an esteemed member of the community. In most African societies, the father conferred a social identity on the child by giving him or her or his name (Nsamenang, 2000). He carried considerable authority, even after his death, as prescribed by the tradition of respect for departed elders. The father's position in the community determined the social status and lifestyle of his family. His success accorded status and prestige to his wife and children.

We should never lose sight of the fact that fathers derived their position and power from cultural prescriptions of manhood. These prescriptions determined the roles and responsibilities of family members in general. Following these prescriptions, men did not take an active role in childcare, which was delegated primarily to the mother and other female relatives. There were positive aspects to fatherhood and manhood built into the cultural system, however, and these should not be lost. Being a man and a father meant having the ability to exercise self-restraint. For example, this entailed not resorting to violence, especially against women. Abusing women was considered a cowardly act. Men who engaged in such practices were socially excluded by their peers. Ability to provide economically and otherwise for one's children was also a defining feature of being a man. If a man failed to provide for his children, his family was supposed to take over the responsibility or share the blame in the eyes of the community.

For African males, the esteemed position of the father (male) came under severe challenge during colonisation, as discussed below. The upward social and economic mobility of women continues to challenge men. Fatherhood should be seen not in essentialist terms but with reference to these challenges. The question is: how do men define and re-define themselves in response to this?

African masculinities and industrialisation

From the late nineteenth century onward, there was a mass movement of African men to the cities to find poorly paid work, often as unskilled workers on the gold and diamond mines. These men were uprooted from the support system that had been provided by their families. This led to the emergence of a new form of male identification, known as *indlavini* (Beinart, 1991). *Indlavini* is an *Nguni* term indicating a masculine identification characterised by violent behaviour, recklessness, and disrespect, especially towards the elders and the traditions they stood for.

Later, this was to be followed by the emergence of *utsotsi* – a street-wise petty criminal characterised by oppositional thinking. Alienated from his traditional roots and faced by the harsh realities of life in the cities, *utsotsi* had no option but to resort to violence to assert his masculinity (see box below). Intergenerational differences emerged between the urbanised young and the rural old as the former sought to assert their independence from the latter. It is conceivable that *utsotsi* would also avoid fatherly responsibilities, which were a sign of virtue in the old order. Today, we are witnessing something similar, with the emergence of the gangster as a hero in marginalised communities. *Utsotsi, indlavini* and the gangster are all manifestations of an identity alienated from traditional community.

Marginalisation and the emergence of gangsterism

The following extract from an article by Jonny Steinberg (2004) illustrates how industrialisation marginalised African males in South Africa, leading to the emergence of gangsterism.

> From four books written between 1975 and 1983 it emerged that the 26s, 27s and 28s [the numbers denote prison gangs] all originated from bands of outlaws that had plagued Johannesburg in the late-nineteenth and early-twentieth centuries. The most memorable of these gangs was called the Ninevites; its rank and file were lumpen proletarians – young black men who had left their ancestral land in the countryside but had refused to take up wage employment for white bosses in the early mining town.
>
> The Ninevites were led by a charismatic young Zulu migrant, 'Nongoloza' Mathebula. Imbued with a crisp and feisty imagination, which had been instilled by the injustices that lay in his own past, Nongoloza shaped his crew of outlaws into a paramilitary hierarchy. It borrowed its rank and structure and its imaginary uniforms from the Natal Colony's judiciary and the Transvaal Republic's military.
>
> Perhaps most interesting of all, Nongoloza imbued his bandit army with a political purpose. 'I reorganised my gang of robbers,' he reported to his white captors in 1912. 'I laid them under what has since become known as Nineveh law. I read in the Bible about the great state Nineveh which rebelled against the Lord, and I selected that name for my gang as rebels against the government's laws.'
>
> The Ninevites lasted nearly two decades. At their height, in the early 1900s, they had absorbed scores of the vagrants and drifters of early Johannesburg into their ranks. They had also infiltrated the labour compounds where Johannesburg's gold mine workers lived, and they had taken control of the inmate population at many of the Transvaal's prisons…

→

Among their favourite pastimes was to rob black labourers as they made their way home on pay day. And so early Johannesburg's black proletariat remembered Nongoloza with a mixture of fear and awe. It was said that he and his bandits established an underground world in a disused mine shaft, complete with shops, *beautiful white women and a Scottish bookkeeper.* (Steinberg, 2004, pp. 33–34, emphasis added)

Apart from the gang's name, which connotes rebellion against the established order, the masculinity theme is evident throughout the extract. The reference to living underground with 'beautiful white women' is further evidence of the gang's masculine conquests.

The socio-cultural tradition

The individualistic or biological paradigm of fatherhood cannot explain the above-mentioned changes in narratives of male identity. These changes pose a challenge to long-held understandings of family life, including conceptions of what it means to be a man. Although most of the examples have been drawn from African communities, similar challenges to traditional masculinities could be cited from other population groups.

Critics have argued that the contemporary period requires a re-thinking of taken-for-granted cultural understandings of the masculine, in what has been called a *crisis of masculinity*. The central feature of the masculinity crisis involves a fatherless generation of children, the loss of jobs for men and the increase in the number of women doing traditionally-male jobs (Figlio, 2001). This has necessitated a re-definition of what it means to be a man. This chapter argues that the socio-cultural psychological tradition offers a helpful way for men to engage both with the challenges of fatherhood and the contemporary changes in understandings of masculinity, and introduces two concepts of the socio-cultural paradigm in relation to the fatherhood project: (a) identity as the selective appropriation of cultural symbols and (b) fatherhood as human action.

Identity as the selective appropriation of cultural symbols

In the socio-cultural tradition, there is no radical break between individuals and society; the two exist in a dynamic, irresistible tension. We come to understand who we are by virtue of cultural scripts, symbols, stories, images, sayings and ways of doing things that surround us (Penuel & Wertsch, 1995). I have referred to the role played by such cultural practices (for example, story-telling) throughout this chapter. Moral identity formation is the selective appropriation of the symbols that surround us. It is a process by means of which we come to 'own' these symbols.

Further, moral identity is not about sameness or continuity over time. It is concerned with how men and women struggle with dominant cultural scripts to come to terms with their membership in societies and with their own sense of who they are. In the past, this struggle took place predominantly within the family. The division of labour between men and women ensured that women's activities were relegated to the private sphere (for example, the family), while government and other national formations (for example, the police, the military, and the industrial complex) were powerful centres of men's activities. Men's powers in these organisations were maintained partly through adoption of hegemonic forms of masculinities (for example, the father as breadwinner) (Hearn, 1992, 1994). But the gender order in South Africa has been changing. Women are increasingly occupying professional positions and they have the economic independence to break away from abusive or exploitative relationships. The advances of women in business, politics and the economy necessitate a rethinking of the roles of men and women in society. If the father historically has been the provider, what is his role going to be when provision is secured by mothers or other parties? Exploring this question, in my view, is the task of the fatherhood project.

Fatherhood as human action

The socio-cultural tradition emphasises *meaningful human action*, and not the abstract, theoretical understanding of what is the right thing to do. We should pay attention to actual human action or what people do, for it is action that is the best indicator of how we have grasped right and wrong. Fatherhood is not the mere knowledge that one has sired a child, or the knowledge that one ought to be a responsible father. Rather, it is the practical implementation of this knowledge. This has been referred to as the enactment approach towards fatherhood (Lamb, 1997). Enactment suggests the *dynamic* and *interactive* quality of fatherhood. We need to study fathers as they engage in activities such as caring and making provision for their children. In so doing, our evaluation can be informed by the African notion of collective fatherhood outlined above. When men act in their capacity as fathers, their engagement with children and other family members needs to be understood holistically rather than simply as the actions of one individual relating to another individual.

Conclusion

Fatherhood is a socio-moral process. It is intertwined with a person's position and role in society. It cannot be understood independently of social, political, cultural and other changes. This chapter has contrasted essentialist and collectivist (social) approaches to fatherhood, arguing that there is room for both. In traditional societies, fatherhood (*ubu-baba*) is performed by anyone available to guide and counsel young boys as they grow into manhood. This form of counselling is captured by the term '*imfundiso*' (education about one's roles and responsibilities in life, as opposed to education as mastery of the subject matter).

Despite the existence of negative masculinities as described in this chapter, the socio-cultural tradition is optimistic because social identity is not fixed. It is possible to engage dynamically with negative masculine identities with a view to changing them. Periods of social transformation provide us with opportunities to study and re-shape conceptions of manhood. Television shows, newspapers, the radio, the family and even the workplace and other media all offer us *positions* or ways of understanding ourselves as fathers and mothers. These media play a role similar to the one previously played by practices such as initiation to manhood and family values through story-telling, albeit indirectly. It is therefore important to ensure that the positive images of fatherhood that continue to exist even under harsh social and economic circumstances are portrayed, and not only the negative ones.

Nhlanhla Mkhize is an Associate Professor of Psychology. He currently lectures in Psychology at the University of KwaZulu-Natal, after having studied at the Universities of Natal and Iowa (USA), where he was a Fulbright Scholar. He has been a Moody Visiting Scholar (University of Michigan, 1998) and a Bram Fischer Scholar (Oxford University, 2001). His main interests are indigenous psychologies, narrative psychological approaches, and gender and moral-ethical decision-making. He is one of the editors of *Critical Psychology* (UCT Press, 2004), in which he contributed particularly to African approaches to psychology.

Notes

1 It is, perhaps, the commercialisation of *ilobolo* that is the cause of this problem. Previously, the amount of ilobolo was not fixed; it was rarely paid in full before marriage could take place.

2 These extracts are from interviews conducted in isiZulu by the author in Mpophomeni as part of Radford's (1993) study. Some of these quotes were not included in Radford's final report.

3 These conditions are also associated with early pregnancy.

4 Literally, the sayings mean 'a human being is a human being because of other human beings'. They point to the understanding that to attain the virtues associated with personhood, one has to partake in a community of similarly constituted selves – a community characterised by caring, justice, love, and mutual interdependence.

5 A ritual sacrifice conducted by some Nguni groups in South Africa to introduce a new-born baby into the family of the living and the deceased. The sacrifice established a link between the baby and the deceased ancestors. Prior to this sacrifice, the baby has no socially-designated status.

References

Anderson, D. (1997). *Men, reproduction and fatherhood*. Policy Research paper no 2: International Union for the Scientific Study of Population. Retrieved March 2004, from http://www.iussp.org/Publications_on_site/PRP/prp12.php

Barbarin, O., & Richter, L. (2001). *Mandela's children: Child development in post-apartheid South Africa*. New York: Routledge.

Beinart, W. (1991). The origin of the *indlavini*. Male associations and migrant labour in the Transkei. In A. D. Spiegel (Ed.). *Tradition and transition in southern Africa. African Studies, 50*, Special Issue, 102–128.

Bennie, T. (2004). Why I married my husband twice. *ChildrenFirst, 58*, 49–50.

Bianchi, S. M. (1995). The changing demographic and socioeconomic characteristics of single parent families. In S. M. H. Hanson, M. L. Heims, D. J. Julian & M. B. Sussman (Eds.), *Single parent families: Diversity, myths, and realities* (pp. 71–97). New York: The Haworth Press.

Day, R. D. (1988). *Social fatherhood: Conceptualisations, compelling research, and future directions*. National Center on Fathers and Families. Philadelphia, PA: University of Pennsylvania Graduate School of Education. Retrieved March 2004, from: http://www.ncoff.gse.upenn/edu/wrkppr/day.pdf

Duncan, G., & Brooks-Gunn, J. (1997). (Eds.). *The consequences of growing up poor*. New York: Russell Sage Press.

Figlio, K. (2001). *Psychoanalysis, science and masculinity*. Philadelphia, PA: Brunner-Routledge.

Hearn, J. (1989). Reviewing men and masculinities, or mostly boys' own papers. *Theory, Culture and Society, 6*, 665–689.

Hearn, J. (1992). Changing men and changing managements: a review of issues and actions. *Women in Management Review, 7*, 3–8.

Hearn, J. (1994). Making sense of men and men's violence. *Clinical Psychology Forum, 64*, 13–17.

Hunter, M. (2004). Fathers without *amandla*? *ChildrenFirst, 58*, 16–20.

Lamb, M. E. (1997). *The role of the father in child development*. New York: John Wiley & Sons.

Magnani, R. J., Bertrand, J, T., Mahani, B., & Macdonald, S. W. (1995). Men, marriage and fatherhood in Kinshasa, Zaïre. *International Family Planning Perspective, 21*, 19–25 & 47.

Mintz, S. (1998). From patriarchy to androgyny and other myths: Placing men's family roles in historical perspective. In A. Booth and N. Crouter (Eds.), *Men in families: When do they get involved? What difference does it make?* (pp. 3–30). Mahwah, NJ: Lawrence Erlbaum Associates.

Mkhize, N. (2000). Gender and moral decision-making. Unpublished raw data.

Mkhize, N. (2004). Socio-cultural approaches to psychology: Dialogism and African conceptions of the self. In D. Hook, N. Mkhize, P. Kuguwa & A. Collins (Eds.), *Critical psychology* (pp. 53–83). Cape Town: UCT Press.

Morrell, R. (1998). Of boys and men: Masculinity and gender in southern African studies. *Journal of Southern African Studies, 24*, 605–630.

Nsamenang, A. B. (2000). *Fathers, families and well-being in Cameroon: A review of the literature.* National Center on Fathers and Families. Philadelphia, PA: University of Pennsylvania Graduate School of Education. Retrieved March 2004, from http://www.ncoff.gse.upenn/edu/wrkppr/BamePaper.pdf

Penuel, W. R., & Wertsch, J. V. (1995). Vygotsky and identity formation: A sociocultural approach. *Educational Psychologist, 30*, 83–92.

Radford, E. J. (1993). The psychological effects of mass dismissal. Unpublished Doctoral Dissertation. University of Natal, Pietermaritzburg.

Ramose, M. B. (2002). *African philosophy through ubuntu.* Harare: Mond Book Publishers.

Ramphele, M. (2002). *Steering by the stars: Being young in South Africa.* Cape Town: Tafelberg.

Steinberg, J. (2004, August 7). The long arm of the gangs. *Sunday Times*, pp. 33–34.

UNESCO (1991). *Broken families and the issue of child socialisation.* Report of Informal Meeting of Experts, 5–7 February 1991. Bangkok: UNESCO.

Wilson, F. (2004). Ideal of manhood beyond many men. *ChildrenFirst, 8*, 39–43.

Being a father in South Africa today

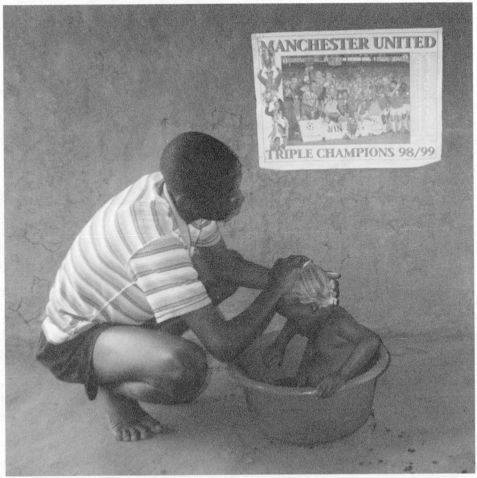

Mboneni Luthuli taking care of his baby brother, Sthembiso by Thabani Luthuli, aged 10, KZN

CHAPTER 16

Legal aspects of fatherhood in South Africa

Jacqui Gallinetti

In South Africa, the legal aspects of fatherhood fall in the domain of family law. Family law is divided into two main sections – the law of husband and wife, and the law of parent and child. Apart from the legal aspects of fatherhood, the concept also has certain philosophical aspects. These include care, support, guidance, love and affection. Fathers are seen as being an integral part of a family that consists of a mother, a father and children. However, in a world ravaged by poverty and HIV/AIDS, this idealised nuclear-type family is constantly being eroded, and children often find themselves either orphaned or being raised in a single-parent family. Where children are raised by a single mother, however, there are certain legal constraints still placed on the absent father – whether such absence is caused by death or divorce or abandonment – namely, inheritance and maintenance.

The advent of same-sex relationships has also impacted upon the notion of family, and South African law has recently dealt with the issue of whether same-sex partners can adopt in *Du Toit and Another* v. *Minister of Welfare and Population Development and Others.*[1] In this matter the applicants, who were partners in a long-standing lesbian relationship, wanted to jointly adopt two children. They could not do so, however, because the current legislation, namely the Child Care Act[2] and the Guardianship Act[3], confined the right to adopt children jointly to married couples. Consequently, the second applicant alone became the adoptive parent. A couple of years later, the couple brought an application in the Pretoria High Court challenging the constitutional validity of sections 17(a), 17(c) and 20(1) of the Child Care Act and section 1(2) of the Guardianship Act which provide for the joint adoption and guardianship of children by married persons only.

In the High Court, the relevant provisions of the Child Care Act were challenged on the grounds that they violated the applicant's right to equality[4] and dignity[5] and do not give primacy to the best interests of the child as required by section 28(2) of the Constitution. In the High Court, Judge Kgomo found that these provisions of the Child Care Act and the Guardianship Act violated the Constitution. Judge Kgomo ordered the reading in of certain words to the impugned provisions to allow for joint adoption and guardianship of children by same-sex life partners. The applicants then applied to the Constitutional Court for confirmation of the High Court order concerning the invalidity of the relevant provisions of the Child Care Act and the Guardianship Act in terms of section 172(2)(a) of the Constitution.[6]

Family law in South Africa is historically grounded in Roman–Dutch common law, but has undergone some changes through the enactment of various statutes over the years, such as the Marriage Act 25 of 1961, the Divorce Act 70 of 1979 and the Matrimonial Property Act 88 of 1984. However, developments in medical technology have also resulted in situations such as surrogate parenthood and artificial fertilisation. No law has yet been enacted to regulate this, despite a Draft Bill on Surrogate Motherhood being proposed by the South African Law Commission.[7] When this Bill was not adopted, the Law Commission placed the issues in the draft Children's Bill where the provisions not only apply to children, but also seek to regulate agreements between the parents and parties contracting the surrogacy.[8]

The fact that a law specifically aimed at the welfare and care of children also deals with contractual relations between adults in relation to this issue is somewhat incongruous. It seems to indicate that the Law Commission was attempting to 'fit' the issue into a statute in order to ensure that law was eventually enacted to deal with it.

This chapter examines the legal consequences of fatherhood – and, as such, looks at the duties, rights and responsibilities of fathers of children born from a marriage and those of children born out of wedlock.[9] In addition, family law has evolved over the years through numerous court judgments, and some of the more seminal decisions will be discussed. The chapter is not intended to be an intensive critique but rather an overview of law relating to fathers.

Parental power

Parental power is the sum total of the rights and duties of parents in relation to their minor children (Cronje & Heaton, 1999) and it is acquired by:
- The birth of a child by a valid marriage;[10]
- The birth of an extra-marital child;
- The legitimation of an extra-marital child; and
- Adoption.

For fathers, acquisition of parental power over an extra-marital child is not possible unless such a birth is subsequently legitimised. Such birth is legitimised through the provisions of the Children's Status Act, which states that a child is legitimised when his or her parents enter into a valid marriage at any time after the birth.[11] The father will then acquire parental power over the child as from the date of the marriage.

The main controversy in this area of the law is in relation to the rights of fathers of children who are not born from a valid marriage and whose births are not subsequently legitimised. In addition, there has been considerable development in the law in relation to which parent acquires custody over a child on divorce.

Consequences for fathers

A child born from a marriage is subject to the parental power of both parents and only the High Court, which is the upper guardian of all children, can interfere with this power.[12] When a child is adopted, the parental power over the child, which vests in his or her parent/s immediately prior to the adoption, is terminated and vested in the child's adoptive parent or parents.

There are various important aspects of parental power and the parent–child relationship, and these are discussed in the sections that follow.

Guardianship

Guardianship is often confused with custody over a child. Although one of the aspects of guardianship is custody over the child, the guardian of a child need not necessarily have custody. Rather, guardianship relates to the legal duties that a parent has in respect of his or her child, particularly in relation to the child's contractual capacity and the management of the child's estate and property. It also relates to matters such as application for a passport or consent for a medical procedure.

In terms of the Guardianship Act, both parents of a child born from a valid marriage have guardianship over their child.[13] An adoptive parent also acquires guardianship over an adopted child.

On the death of one parent, the surviving parent will be the sole guardian of the child. On divorce, guardianship remains vested in both parents, unless the court orders otherwise. It is custody, on divorce, that often becomes an issue in relation to the children born of the marriage.

Custody

Custody is an aspect of guardianship and, ordinarily, both parents have custody over their child. Custody entails the day-to-day care of and control over a child, and therefore entails the child living with the custodian parent/s. If the parents are separated and not yet divorced, custody can be awarded to one parent by order of court.[14]

The determination of custody of children upon divorce is regulated by section 6 of the Divorce Act.[15] This legislation requires that a court hearing a divorce matter, *inter alia*:

• Ensures that the arrangements relating to the welfare of the child are satisfactory or the best possible arrangements in the circumstances, and must consider a Family Advocate's report, if an inquiry in terms of the Mediation in Certain Divorce Matters Act has been instituted; and[16]

- Makes any order it deems fit in relation to the access, custody, maintenance and guardianship of the child, including an order awarding sole guardianship or custody to a parent, in terms of section 6(3).[17]

There is no provision in the Divorce Act requiring the court to act in the best interests of the child, the principle contained in section 28(2) of the Constitution of South Africa Act 108 of 1996; however, the wording of section 6(1) of the Act is such that it is implied that this principle is inherent.

In making custody orders, there have been a number of court judgments that clarify how courts award custody in divorce matters. Historically, custody orders followed the principle that the mother is the most suitable parent to care for the child on a daily basis and generally custody awards were made in accordance with this, giving the mother preference in relation to custody. This approach has been eroded over a number of years and has essentially been replaced with the best interests of the child principle. This began with the Appeal Court decision in *Fletcher* v. *Fletcher*, which placed 'the paramount or best interests principle' at the fore.[18] However, one must distinguish the development of this principle through case law from the entrenchment of the principle in the Constitution.[19] The Constitution is now the supreme law of South Africa and courts are therefore bound to apply it. Before its adoption, the principle was alluded to in court decisions, but with the enactment of the Constitution the 'best interests of the child' has now become a constitutional principle.

The best interests approach has been criticised on the grounds that the apparent impartiality of the test in fact relies on the decision of a presiding officer to determine which factors are relevant to the interests of the child and then to assess the relative weight of these factors as being either 'good' or 'bad'. (Bonthuys, 1997, p. 623) This means that the determination of what is in the best interests of the child ultimately lies within the discretion of the court, which is a subjective and not an objective determination.

In *Van der Linde* v. *Van der Linde* the court held that mothers are not necessarily the better parent to be the daily caregiver of the child.[20] Furthermore in *Madiehe (born Ratlogo)* v. *Madiehe* the court stated as follows:[21]

> [c]ustody of a young child is a responsibility as well as a privilege and it has to be earned. It is not a gender privilege or a right.

In making the shift from the maternal preference rule to the best interests of the child principle, there has been an articulation of the factors that courts should consider in awarding custody. In *McCall* v. *McCall* the father applied for the variation of a divorce order that had granted custody of the minor children born of the marriage to their mother, requesting that custody of their minor son be awarded to him.[22] The court in this matter set out a comprehensive list of criteria that courts should apply in determining what the best interests of a child are in a custody dispute between the parents. The court held that in determining what the best interests of a child would be, it must decide which of the parents is better suited to promote and ensure the physical, emotional, moral and spiritual welfare of the child.[23] The factors that the court enumerated to assist it in making this determination are:[24]

- The love, affection and emotional ties that exist between parent and child and the parent's compatibility with the child;
- The capabilities, character and temperament of the parent and the impact thereof on the child's needs and desires;
- The ability of the parent to communicate with the child and the parent's insight into, understanding of and sensitivity to the child's feelings;
- The capacity and disposition of the parent to give the child the guidance which he/she requires;
- The ability of the parent to provide for the basic physical needs of the child, the so-called 'creature comforts', such as food, clothing, housing and the other material needs – generally speaking, the provision of economic security;
- The ability of the parent to provide for the educational well-being and security, both religious and secular, of the child;
- The ability of the parent to provide for the child's emotional, psychological, cultural and environmental development;
- The mental and physical health and moral fitness of the parent;
- The stability or otherwise of the child's existing environment, having regard to the desirability of maintaining the *status quo;*
- The desirability or otherwise of keeping siblings together;
- The child's preference, if the court is satisfied that in the particular circumstances the child's preference should be taken into consideration;
- The desirability or otherwise of applying the doctrine of same-sex matching;
- Any other factor which is relevant to the particular case with which the court is concerned.

What is important to note is that this decision was handed down prior to the promulgation of the South African Constitution or Interim Constitution, which definitively set out the principle regarding the best interests of the child. Subsequent to the adoption of the final Constitution, there have been a number of court decisions that have expressly used this constitutional principle in determining custody orders.

One such decision is the case of *V* v. *V*.[25] In this matter the parties had been separated for two years, and had exercised joint custody over the two minor children born of the marriage in terms of a separation agreement. However, in the divorce proceedings, the father sought custody over the children, with very limited access rights reserved for the mother. His reasons for seeking this order related to the fact that the mother was conducting a same-sex relationship and that she suffered from a psychiatric condition.

The mother argued against this and maintained that she had recovered from her illness, and that the parties had exercised joint custody for two years and so the *status quo* should be allowed to continue.

In making its determination, the court stated as follows:

> The old position where fathers were almost always left with guardianship on divorce while the custody of young children was invariably granted to mothers has changed. As far as young children are concerned, the pendulum has swung to accommodate the possibility of a father being a suitable custodian parent to young children.

In looking at the case before it, the court went on to confirm that in custody matters the children's rights are paramount and need to be protected. Despite the fact that the court referred to the right of equality in the Constitution, in relation to the allegations that the mother's lesbian relationship precluded her from obtaining joint custody of the children, it nevertheless held that the difficulty in custody cases is that the court only indirectly deals with the parents' rights. Therefore, the matter is 'not merely one of a mother's right of access to her children per se, but the extent of the children's right of access and right to parental care'. (see Chapter 23, this volume). Accordingly, the court, after a thorough examination of the facts and circumstances of the matter, found that joint custody would be in the best interests of the children, and made such an order.

Within this framework, it has been argued that the 'best interests' principle is fluid, value-laden and caters to changing priorities, such as the focus on biological links between fathers and children as opposed to whether the father is able to satisfactorily nurture and care for the child (Bonthuys, 1997, p. 636).

Maintenance

During marriage, both parents have an equal duty of support toward minor children, a duty that does not terminate on divorce. Both parents must continue to maintain their children in proportion to their respective means(Cronje & Heaton, 1999, p. 197). This means that the custodian parent is not entitled to claim maintenance for the minor children if the non-custodian parent is not in a financial position to pay such maintenance. However, the onus is on the non-custodian parent to prove that he or she is not wilfully failing to pay, but that his or her circumstances are such that he or she simply does not have the means to pay.[26] Once the non-custodian parent is in a position to pay maintenance, he or she must do so. The importance of providing a child with maintenance has been emphasised by the recent decision of *Petersen* v. *Maintenance Officer and Others*, where the Cape High Court ordered that paternal grandparents have a duty to maintain a child to the same extent to which the maternal grandparents are liable to maintain the child.[27] Up until this decision, the common law had stated that a paternal grandparent had no duty of support in relation to an extra-marital child, while maternal grandparents did. The Court held that the common law rule and, in particular, the differentiation between the duty of support of grandparents towards children born in and out of wedlock and constituted unfair discrimination on the grounds of birth, and amounted to an infringement of the dignity of such children.[28] The court held further that the common law rule was also contrary to the best interests of extra-marital children.[29]

A maintenance order usually provides for maintenance to be paid until the child reaches a particular age, and when the child reaches that age the order lapses automatically.[30] It is uncertain whether a maintenance order will automatically lapse if the child becomes self-supporting prior to reaching the specified age; there are court decisions that assert that it does and others that say that it doesn't lapse (Cronje & Heaton, 1999, p. 191). The way to avoid this uncertainty is for a court to make an order for maintenance until the child reaches a particular age or becomes self-supporting , whichever occurs soonest.

In order to calculate the amount of maintenance that a non-custodian parent should pay, a court normally takes, *inter alia*, the following factors into consideration:
• The child's needs from time to time;
• The age, state of health and educational needs of the child;
• The respective income of each parent;
• The social status of the parties; and
• The fact that the custodian parent is already burdened with custody of the child.[31]

Failure to pay maintenance in terms of a court order is regarded as contempt of court. The offending party becomes subject to a criminal charge if the custodian parent lays a complaint against him or her. Where a maintenance order has been issued on divorce, the custodian parent can approach the maintenance court in that district in relation to increase of maintenance payments or failure to pay maintenance.

Fatherhood and extra-marital children

The fathers of extra-marital children have received a great deal of attention in the law over the last few years. In the late 1990s there were numerous court challenges, and new legislation enacted around this issue and the new Children's Act will also move to address the matter in its provisions.[32] This section will examine guardianship and custody, followed by developments in the law and case law relating to these, before moving on to the issue of maintenance.

Maintenance

Both parents of an extra-marital child are obliged to support the child according to their respective means even though the father has no inherent rights to guardianship, custody and access to the extra-marital child.[33]

Guardianship and custody

In Roman Dutch law, an illegitimate child fell under the parental power, and therefore under the custody and guardianship, of the mother; the father had no such authority (Van Leeuwen, 1.7.4; Van der Linden, 1.4.2). This forms the basis of our common law, in which fathers have no inherent right to guardianship and custody of a child born out of wedlock. It was only during the 1990s that this aspect of our law was challenged in the courts. The challenge began in relation to a father's right of access to his illegitimate child, as access is also an aspect of parental power and, as such, was denied to fathers of children born out of wedlock.

Case law relating to fathers of illegitimate children

Courts have cited different arguments to create an inroad into the position of fathers of extra-marital children established in terms of the common law.

In *Van Erk* v. *Holmer*, one of the reasons given by the court in granting a father an inherent right of access was that he was obliged to maintain the child because of his biological relationship with the child, but this relationship did not allow him access to the child.[34] This type of reasoning could border on being dangerous, as the mere fact that a father contributes financially to the upbringing of the child does not necessarily make him suitable to exercise parental power, including custody and access, over the child.

This point was illustrated quite clearly by the case of *Jooste* v. *Botha*.[35] In this case the applicant was an 11-year-old minor who sued his biological father in deficit for damages caused by his father's refusal to acknowledge that the boy was his son, to communicate with him, and to show any love or interest towards him. The father had paid maintenance for the child. The court in this case stated that there are two aspects to a parent–child relationship: the economic aspect of providing for the child's physical needs, and the intangible aspect of providing for the child's psychological, emotional and developmental needs. The court went on to confirm that the best interests of the child demand an environment of love, affection and consideration, in addition to economic support. The court in *Jooste* eventually decided that the Constitution does not state that parents are obliged to love and cherish their children nor to give them attention and interest, and that the law will not enforce the impossible and cannot create love and affection where there is none.

However, in *Van Erk* the court went on to decide that the father's application for access to the minor child was:

> [n]ot simply a plea for a *quid pro quo* but a proper recognition of a biological father's need to bind and form a relationship with his own child and the child's interest that he or she should have an unfettered opportunity to develop as normal and happy a relationship as possible

with both parents. This is not only in the best interest of the child but it is in fact a right which should not be denied unless it is clearly not in the best interests of the child.[36]

This move to determine the matter in accordance with the best interests of the child mirrors the development in custody and access disputes between married parents, which began to focus on the best interests of the child as opposed to the maternal preference rule. At this stage, the principle regarding the best interests of the child is not yet that envisaged by the Constitution, but a common law concept.

Another case that decided an application for access by the father of an extra-marital child, on the basis of the common-law best interests of the child principle, was the matter of B v. S,[37] where the court stated:

> [c]urrent South African law does not accord a father an inherent right of access to his illegitimate child. It recognises that the child's welfare is central to the matter of such access and that access is therefore always available to the father if that is the child's best interests.

It has been noted that this best-interest principle has been developed on the basis of the biological link between the father and child (Bonthuys, 1997, p. 629). Current thinking does not seek to assert the rights of parents with regard to their children, but seeks to ensure that a child is suitably cared for and is safe. Therefore, merely because the father has no inherent rights over a child because of his failure to enter into marriage with the mother, he is not precluded from being a custodian parent if the best interests of the child dictate that custody should be awarded to him.

Parliament enacting new law in relation to fathers of extra-marital children

In 1997 the Natural Fathers of Children Born Out of Wedlock Act was passed.[38] In terms of this legislation, fathers of extra-marital children are granted guardianship, custody and access rights to such children. However, these are not automatic rights and, in order to assert these rights, the father must apply to court. The order can only be granted if it is in the best interests of the child, and after the application has been investigated by the Family Advocate.[39]

In the case of I v. S,[40] the court confirmed that, in applying the Act, the best interests of the child had to be the focus of the inquiry. In addition, the court accepted that it was generally to the advantage of a child to have communication with both parents, unless there were particular factors that demanded that the welfare of the child be protected by depriving him or her of the opportunity of maintaining contact with one parent.

A highly publicised case that brought the issue of fathers of children born out of wedlock to the fore was that of Lawrie Fraser.[41] Fraser, an unmarried father, tried to adopt his biological child and was denied this opportunity through the provisions of the Child Care Act. Other parties who had applied for adoption, adopted his child.

Fraser first applied to the High Court to overturn the adoption order. The High Court did so and referred the matter back to the Children's Court. However, instead of going back to the Children's Court, Fraser brought another application claiming that the provisions of the Child Care Act were unconstitutional as they discriminated against fathers of extra-marital children.

In deciding the matter, the Constitutional Court stated that consent to adoption of such children is not necessarily required of all fathers – various factors should be considered, including the duration of the relationship between the parents of the extra-marital child, the age of the child, the bond between the child and the father, and the best interests of the child. The Court declared section 18(2) of the Child Care Act unconstitutional and gave Parliament an opportunity to correct the section within two years of the order.

It has been argued that the Constitutional Court took the approach that an emotional and material involvement between the father and child would result in the father obtaining rights towards his child, rather than using the biological bond as the reason for this (Bonthuys, 1997, p. 628).

Amendments to the Child Care Act have been effected, but, at the time of writing, a Children's Bill was before Parliament and some of the provisions contained in the Bill will affect the present law relating to fathers of children born out of wedlock. The Children's Bill represents a complete overhaul of welfare legislation aimed at children and aims to address the current fragmentation of child-welfare law in South Africa.

However, while it was initially intended to comprise an holistic and comprehensive approach to children and basically result in the codification of most laws pertaining to children, it has been changed substantially since the first draft was released by the South African Law Reform Commission. It has also undergone severe excisions by the various state departments mandated to examine the draft.

Clause 21 of Children's Bill 70 of 2003 deals with the parental rights of unmarried fathers. The issue of granting automatic parental responsibilities and rights to unmarried fathers has proven to be controversial, and this clause purports to address the controversy and provide a solution that suits both the father's rights and takes the child's best interests into account.

The section provides that an unmarried father acquires parental rights and responsibilities in certain circumstances, for example, by living with the mother in a long-term relationship or where he has contributed, or attempted in good faith to contribute, to expenses related to the maintenance of a child for a reasonable period of time. The wording of the section is very broad and open to interpretation and so the practical application of this section is a matter that will need to be tested.

The parental right of chastisement?

To date, South Africa has abolished the imposition of corporal punishment as a sentence by the court[42] and in schools.[43] The Constitutional Court has also ruled that corporal punishment of children infringes on their rights to dignity and their right to be protected from cruel, inhuman and degrading treatment or punishment.

While there is an international move towards abolishing all forms of corporal punishment of children, including that which is imposed in the home or by parents, in South Africa, this practice (the imposition of corporal punishment by parents) still remains.[44] This might be attributed to the fact that parents have a (common law) right to reasonably and moderately chastise their children and this includes the imposition of corporal punishment.

Despite the existence of common law crimes in South Africa, such as assault, assault with the intention of causing grievous bodily harm, and attempted murder, parents charged with these crimes against their children can raise the defence of reasonable chastisement and avoid being held liable for physically punishing their children. Thus, while parents can be criminally charged for physically punishing their children, they can potentially escape being held responsible for their actions by raising the defence of reasonable chastisement as a ground of justification for their actions. The court will then decide whether it is a valid defence in the circumstances. This situation denies children the equal protection of the law and provides parents with the potential to violate their child bodily as well as harm her or his physical integrity and dignity.

It is recognised that the debate on this topic is a deeply personal one as it involves issues of parenting, and most parents feel that they have the right to bring up their children as they see fit. This conviction often stems from very strong religious and moral beliefs and various other arguments in favour of the practice.[45] However, the common law rules permitting reasonable chastisement do not protect children from assault. This is because parents have discretion as to the nature of the punishment they wish to impose, and the courts will not lightly interfere with this discretion unless it is exercised improperly. When a parent charged with assault raises the ground of justification of reasonable chastisement, the onus then shifts to the prosecutor to prove that the punishment was excessive or unjustified.

The United Nations Committee on the Rights of the Child has interpreted article 19 of the Convention to extend to protection of children while in the care of their parents, and has emphasised that corporal punishment in the family is incompatible with the provisions of the Convention.[46] It has further expressed concern at laws that, while protecting children against serious physical assaults defined as child abuse, allow for parents or other caregivers to use physical forms of punishment on children provided they are reasonable and moderate. The Committee has therefore recommended and called for a clear prohibition of all corporal punishment, including that which is imposed by parents. In addition, it has proposed that legal reforms be coupled with education campaigns in positive discipline to support parents, teachers and others.

The South African Law Reform Commission originally dealt with this issue in their investigation into the Child Care Act,[47] and recommended a repeal of the defence of reasonable chastisement. However, the present Children's Bill 70 of 2003 neglects to deal with the issue, thereby, in effect, maintaining the status quo.

Conclusion

There is a tension between the best interests of children, a principle that is not a right but rather an interpretative guide, and the rights of equality and non-discrimination. South African law has undergone a number of developments in this regard as shown above – from the maternal preference rule, to the common law best-interests principle, to the constitutional best-interests principle, and to various pieces of legislation trying to give effect to the Constitution. It is within this framework that fathers and children coexist and their relationship, or lack thereof, is regulated through legal principles.

Jacqui Gallinetti is an admitted attorney of the High Court of South Africa and the Senior Researcher and Project Co-ordinator of the Children's Rights Project, Community Law Centre, University of the Western Cape. She practised law for six years, focusing on criminal law, family law and the representation of children. She now researches children's rights, particularly child justice and legal processes concerning children. She is editor of *Article 40*, a quarterly child justice publication and co-editor (with Julia Sloth-Nielsen) of *Child Justice in Africa: A Guide to Good Practice* (Community Law Centre, 2004).

Notes

1   *Du Toit and Another* v. *Minister of Welfare and Population Development and Others* 2001 (12) BCLR 1225 (T).

2   Act 74 (1983).

3   Act 192 (1993).

4   Section 9 of Act 108 (1996).

5   Section 10 of Act 108 (1996).

6   Section 172(2) (a) provides that: 'The Supreme Court of Appeal, a High Court or a Court of similar status may make an order concerning the constitutional validity of an Act of Parliament, a provincial Act or any conduct of the President, but an order of constitutional invalidity has no force unless it is confirmed by the Constitutional Court.'

7   Government Gazette No. 16479 (1995).

BEING A FATHER IN SOUTH AFRICA TODAY

8   B70 of 2003.

9   This chapter will proceed on the basis that paternity is accepted in the case of a child born out of wedlock. However, often paternity is rejected by the putative father and then legal rules and procedures regarding paternity and proof thereof come into play. Section 1 of the Children's Status Act 82 of 1987 provides that if, in any legal proceedings where it has been placed in issue whether any particular person is the father of an extra-marital child, it is proved by way of a judicial admission or otherwise, that he had sexual intercourse with the mother of the child at any time when the child could have been conceived, he is presumed to be the father of the child unless the contrary is proved. The alleged father can then also raise a defence that at the same time another man or men also had intercourse with the woman, but he must be able to prove this. The final option of proving paternity is by way of blood tests, which is the manner most commonly used, since medical science has developed to the stage that such tests can show paternity quite accurately.

10   Cronje (1990) notes that marriage is defined as the legally recognised life-long voluntary union between one man and one woman to the exclusion of all other persons (p. 179).

11   Act 82 (1987).

12   There can be other statutory interventions, for example in terms of the Child Care Act 74 (1983), where children in need of care can be removed from one or both of their parents.

13   Section 1 of Act 192 (1993). If the parents disagree over an aspect of guardianship, then the issue can be referred to the High Court, which, by operation of law is the Upper Guardian of a child.

14   The Matrimonial Affairs Act 37 (1953).

15   Act 70 (1979).

16   The Mediation in Certain Divorce Matters Act 24 (1987) provides that Family Advocates may be appointed to institute an inquiry, if requested by a party or the court, in order to make a recommendation regarding custody, guardianship and access. This procedure can be instituted not only in relation to the granting of a divorce order but also in relation to applications for the variation, rescission or suspension of an order made in terms of the Divorce Act. According to Act 24 (1987), the Family Advocate's central function is to institute an inquiry to enable him or her to furnish the Court with a report and recommendations on any matter concerning the welfare of a minor or dependant child of the marriage concerned. The role of the Family Advocate has been described as threefold: namely to monitor, mediate and evaluate (Glasser cited in Burman, 2003, p. 110).

17   Section 6(4).

18   *Fletcher* v. *Fletcher* 1948 1 SA 130 (A).

19   Section 28(2) of Act 108 (1996).

20   *Van der Linde* v. *Van der Linde* 1996 3 SA 509 (O).

21   *Madiehe (born Ratlogo)* v. *Madiehe* 1997 2 All SA 153 (B).

22   *McCall* v. *McCall* 1994 3 SA 201 (C).

23   *McCall* v. *McCall* 1994 3 SA 201 (C) At 204 I-J.

24   *McCall* v. *McCall* 1994 3 SA 201 (C) At 204 J-205G.

25   *V* v. *V* 1998 4 SA 169 (C).

26   The Maintenance Act 9 of 1998.

27   *Petersen* v. *Maintenance Officer and Others.* 2004 (2) BCLR 205 (C).

28   *Petersen* v. *Maintenance Officer and Others.* At p. 213 G-H.

29   *Petersen* v. *Maintenance Officer and Others.* At p. 213 H-I.

30   While the statutory age of majority is 21 years and therefore parents are obliged to maintain children until such time, some orders have made use of the age of 18 years (Cronje & Heaton, 1999, p. 191).

31   A maintenance order can be varied and terminated by another court order. Examples of the variation of a court order relate to increases of the amount of maintenance or for maintenance payments to continue after the child reaches the stipulated age if the child remains in need of support. The duty to support a child is terminated by the child's death but not by the death of the parent as the child then has a claim against the deceased parent's estate (Cronje & Heaton, 1999, p. 189).

32   The section 75 version of Children's Bill 70 of 2003 was passed by the National Assembly on 22 June 2005. This version deals with all issues that require national competencies from the relevant government departments. The section 76 version of the Bill, which still has to be tabled, deals with the provisions that are provincial competencies. It is envisaged the section 76 Bill will only be tabled in 2006 as the section 75 version still has to be approved by the National Council of Provinces.

33   Section 15(3)(a) of the Maintenance Act 99 of 1998.

34   *Van Erk* v. *Holmer* 1992 2 SA 636 (W).

35   *Jooste* v. *Botha* 2000 2 SA 199 (T).

36   *Van Erk* v. *Holmer* 1992 2 SA 636 (W), per Van Zyl, J. At p. 650

37   *B* v. *S* 1995 3 SA 571 (A).

38   *I* v. *s* 2000 2 SA 993 (C)

39   Act 86 of 1997, section 2.

40   Act 86 of 1997, 2000 2 SA 993 (C).

41   *Fraser* v. *Children's Court Pretoria North and Others* 1997 2 BCLR 153 (CC).

42   *S* v. *Williams* 1995 (3) SA 632 (CC).

43   Section 10 of the South African Schools Act of 1996

44   To date, 11 countries have abolished all forms of corporal punishment of children including the imposition of corporal punishment in the home or by parents. These countries include Austria, Croatia, Cyprus, Denmark, Finland, Latvia, Norway, Sweden (the first country to abolish this form of corporal punishment as early as 1979), Germany, Italy and Israel (see Nilsson, 2002).

45 Some of these arguments include that children learn from smacking to respect their elders; that physical punishment is a necessary part of their upbringing; 'it never did us harm', and so on.

46 See Hodgkin & Newell (1998). In particular, see the Committee's response to Spain's (Spain, IRCO, Add.28, par 10 and 18) and the United Kingdom's (UK IRCO Add 34, paras 16 and 31) Initial Report.

47 Project 110.

References

Bonthuys, E. (1997). Of biological bonds, new fathers and the best interests of children. *South African Journal on Human Rights, 13,* 4.

Cronje, D. S. P. (1990). *The South African law of persons and family law.* Durban: Butterworths.

Cronje, D. S. P., & Heaton, J. (1999). *South African family law.* Durban: Butterworths.

Glasser, N. (2003).Custody on divorce: Assessing the role of the family advocates. In S. Burman (Ed.), *The fate of the child.* Cape Town: Juta Law.

Hodgkin, R., & Newell, P. (1998). *Implementation Handbook for the Convention on the Rights of the Child.* Geneva: UNICEF.

Nilsson, M. (2002). *Corporal punishment from an international perspective.* Paper delivered at a National Workshop on Corporal Punishment in South Africa, 20–21 February 2002.

Van der Linden, *Koopmans Handboek 1.4.2* .

Van Leeuwen, *Het Roomsch Hollands Recht 1.7.4.*

CHAPTER 17
Men, work and parenting

Alan Hosking

Globally, a major difficulty for parents is to negotiate the tension between work and the care of children (Castelain-Meunier, 2002; McNaughton & O'Brien, 1999). However, in most societies, men vest more of their energy and identity in their work than in their children (Stancanelli, 2003). This chapter examines the dilemmas involved in balancing work and parenting; the available international research on the issue; and new policy directions that enable men to better navigate between their commitments to and investments in work and childcare.

Introduction

Never before has the role of fathers been more under the spotlight (McNaughton & O'Brien, 1999), and with this new-found focus has come an examination of the role of men as 'working fathers' (Appolis, 1998). While much has been written about working mothers, the same cannot be said about working fathers. In one sense, though, fathers have been wrestling with their dual responsibilities regarding the home and the workplace for longer than women have, simply because men have been in the workplace, outside of the home, for longer (Berry, 1997).

The workplace which men have inhabited over the past half-century has not been at all sympathetic to the responsibilities of working fathers. Home and childcare have been constructed as female activities and the notion of father has been largely limited to economic provision for the family. Men have therefore been expected to be somewhat stoical about their parental instincts and ambitions in the interests of their careers. Mothers, though, have been entitled to various benefits such as maternity leave, benefits that are only now slowly being extended to men. Fathers have therefore been a neglected group, so to speak, with regard to being given the opportunity and support necessary for building and sustaining happy and healthy families without compromising their careers.

It can be argued that two external factors have played a significant role in determining the roles of men at work and in the family. Both agricultural livelihoods and industrialisation require the majority of men to engage in physically demanding jobs outside of the home. This results in the development of two different worlds for men – one, the world of work where the majority apply themselves to physical tasks during the course of their working day, and the other, the home to which they return at night in order to rest from the day's work and prepare for the challenges of the next day's labours. This results in mothers being regarded as the primary caregivers of their children. Nothing much more is demanded from fathers than to be a good provider and protector for their families.

For most men in the western world, First and Second World Wars further reinforced this traditional model. During these periods, women again stayed at home to look after the children while every able-bodied man was expected to answer the call to arms to defend the way of life he enjoyed. After the Second World War, those in control of the workplace – mostly men who had probably served as military officers during hostilities – resorted to a model of business which they knew very well. This was a military model, where everybody had a particular function, took orders from their superiors, and carried out those orders to the best of their ability with very little thought for their own interests. This is at least one of the reasons why workplace cultures, management techniques and business models over the next half-century came to be based largely on military models. Further evidence of this can be found in the terminology still used in the business world, where phrases such as 'strategy', 'attack a market', 'defend a customer base' and 'management ranks' describe normal business practices. Even the words 'recruit', 'company' and 'division', all integral to business vocabulary, have strong roots in the military.

With this military mindset, it is no wonder that the workplace has long been considered a place where men are expected to attend to the responsibilities at hand without a thought for their roles as parents. This military approach to business has also played a significant role in socialising men to seek their identities more in their work responsibilities than in their domestic roles. Ask any man what he does, and he will most likely tell you which company he works for, give his job designation and/or a description of what he does in the company. However, he is less likely to tell you that he is a father or to describe his children. For men have come to understand that the military model adopted by business frowns upon men having children as their focal point or on any activities beyond the workplace; family and children in this context are considered as distractions and are thought to be detrimental to the optimal performance of tasks.

The dilemma of fathers

However, over the past three decades there have been a number of increasingly rapid changes in the workplace (Casper & O'Connell, 1998). These changes have been fuelled by the unstoppable pressures of globalisation. In addition, globalisation has confronted a younger generation of workers who were not raised during these wars, with the need to conform to the military workplace organisation which was imposed on their parents. Such changes have triggered a move away from an overly militaristic approach to managing people in the workplace toward a more humanistic management philosophy, as business leaders have come to understand that it is the people who work in their companies that are the real assets of the business and that the value of a company does not lie in its buildings, infrastructure and machinery (Noe, Hollenbeck, Gerhart & Wright, 2002).

The slow disintegration of the rigid structures, philosophies and practices of the military business model has resulted in a growing dilemma for men: the need to redefine their identities to include not only their activities in the workplace but also their roles as nurturers and caregivers in their families. This latter role has previously been almost exclusively occupied by mothers, a state of affairs generally endorsed by child psychologists (Backett, 1982).

Working fathers who have successfully embraced their role as involved parents are therefore torn between their desire to participate in the lives of their children and their commitment to their career activities, and this has become a source of stress in the lives of many men.

Whereas the 50-something-year-old fathers at the head of many companies believe that work commitments come before family, younger generations of fathers do not share the same view (Coles, 2002). Younger men saw their fathers give years of unquestioning, dedicated service to their companies, often depriving their families of their presence and involvement, and themselves of the joys of parenthood and family life, because of long working hours that often flowed over to weekends. Just as these older, dedicated men reached their early fifties and started to relax in their careers, thinking they had finally 'made it', they fell victim to ruthless retrenchment exercises undertaken to effect cost savings in companies struggling to sustain themselves. The younger generation of workers made a note that they would not make the same mistakes as their fathers who were put out to pasture at a time when they were probably at their most vulnerable. Many of the men who were retrenched had little in the way of a cultivated private family life.

The younger workers and fathers have therefore sought to redefine their employee role, to the extent that the loyalty of previous generations of fathers who belonged to the one-career-for-life generation no longer exists. Companies have been forced to recognise that employees' greatest loyalties no longer lie with their employers, but rather with their own careers and their private lives (Greenhaus & Beutell, 1985, Quick & Tetrick, 2003).

This, together with the increasing global shortage of talent, has caused a shift in bargaining power away from the employer into the hands of employees with 'the smart talent'. Now, employers who want to acquire the services of top-rate talent have to look for ways to attract and retain these people (Mazengwa, 2004a). This has started to play into the hands of fathers who want more from life than a career that takes them away from their families (Hofferth, 2003).

Aside from changes in the workplace, the past three decades have seen unprecedented changes in the home, resulting in a reversal of the traditional roles of fathers and mothers. In addition, the combined stresses of work and parenthood have increased for a growing number of single parents who have to cope with the demands of single-handedly looking after their children, as well as coping with issues of joint custody and other challenges that are a consequence of the breakup of the traditional family unit. But until these changes are embraced in the workplace on a significant scale, working fathers will continue to be torn between their parental ambitions and responsibilities on the one hand, and their professional ambitions and responsibilities on the other.

Previous generations lived in a society that operated according to the agricultural day, where men spent their daylight hours at work and returned home at night. But economic pressures, an increase in job opportunities for women, and the desire of many women to seek fulfilment in their own careers, coupled with many companies' need to operate on a 24/7 (24 hours a day, 7 days a week) basis, have eroded the fairly simple traditional model of parenthood to the point where women's and men's roles have become blurred. The work day now runs throughout the day and night, crisscrossing the routines of children and families. Many of the childcare tasks traditionally undertaken by mothers are now performed by fathers, and vice versa in terms of income generation.

This has bred a generation of 30-something fathers who have come to silently resent the demands their companies make on them. The 50-something men who grew up in homes where fathers went to work and mothers remained at home manage these companies. And the 50-something men are struggling to come to terms with the fact that the new generation of fathers do not regard their jobs as the most important part of their lives, but seek a greater balance between work and their personal lives (Greenhaus & Beutell, 1985). Younger fathers do not have a live-to-work philosophy but a work-to-live one, and this has changed the dynamics of the workplace and of the family (Coles, 2002).

The desire for such a work–life balance is found not only at the managerial level of the company, or in one population group. There are involved and caring fathers who sit around boardroom tables controlling the purse strings and direction of the companies they work for, and there are caring fathers who sweep factory floors and stand in employment queues. In both scenarios, fathers may find their jobs take them away from their homes for long hours, although it may be for different reasons. The company director may be required to work long hours because of the need to ensure an attractive return for the company's shareholders, while the sweeper may be away from home from early until late because of the time it takes to commute between his home and his place of work, and the job-seeker may migrate over considerable distances to find work. This means that managers, floor sweepers and unemployed fathers probably leave for work before their children have woken up in the morning and arrive back home after their younger children have gone to sleep.

Two other factors contribute to the dilemma of fathers. First, some fathers have to work night shifts, which removes them from their homes at times when family members usually interact with one another, when family ties and relationships are built and strengthened. Second, certain fathers work as contract workers rather than as employees, a trend that is increasing as companies attempt to shed costs. This means that any leave these men take is unpaid; this has a major impact on both the financial wellbeing of the father and his dependants, as well as on his capacity to participate in and foster healthy family relationships.

International trends

Despite the need to be realistic about the fact that the workplace won't change overnight into an environment that accommodates all the needs of working fathers, there is still hope. There is a growing trend across the globe toward employers seeking ways to create what is known as a 'father-friendly' or 'family-friendly' workplace (Fine-Davis, 2004). The governments of certain countries are also propelling this initiative. For example, OECD (Organisation for Economic Co-operation and Development) countries have introduced paternity leave policies targeting parental leave for fathers (EU Commission, 1998, in Stancanelli, 2003, p. 11). However the uptake varies from country to country. In Scandinavian countries, the uptake by men reaches nearly 100 per cent among men employed in the public sector (Brandth & Kvande, 2001; Stancanelli, 2003).

Initiatives to create family-friendly workplaces include the following (Levine & Pittinsky, 1997):

- Support for fathers from top management: this includes senior managers acting as role models in supporting family-friendly activities. Nike™ nearly compromised its brand when it was accused of poor labour standards affecting mainly males in Asia. In order to save its brand image, Nike™ responded by introducing 'father-friendly' work policies that were openly supported by top management.
- Flexible work hours: companies are now offering certain employees the opportunity to start and finish work within a window period not dictated by daylight hours. Such schemes allow employees to commence work at, say, 05h00 in the morning and finish at 14h00 in the afternoon; or at, say, 10h00 and finish at 19h00 in the evening. This is a win-win situation for companies with 24-hour business, as they are able to have staff working a longer day and at times that overlap with other time-zones in the world. At the same time, fathers who wish to start work late or finish work early (they may want to take children to school or day care in the morning, or watch a child's sporting activity in the afternoon) have the flexibility to do so. The ability to control their working hours (by, for instance, telecommuting) is considered to be one of the most important benefits for working fathers. James Levine, director of The Fatherhood Project at the Families and Work Institute in the United

States, points out that most fathers want flexible scheduling and that more companies are starting to give consideration to this benefit for fathers.

- Pay for performance and not time: in certain professional job activities, employers are rewarding employees according to the work that is completed and not for the time they are at work. This means employment contracts are negotiated on an outcomes basis. Employees are then able to complete the work they are assigned as and how they wish, as long as they meet their deadlines.
- Time off for fathers to stay with an ill child: in families where both parents are employed, it is not necessarily convenient for the mother to remain with an ill child. In such a case, fathers who are able to take time off with the knowledge and support of their employer (so-called family responsibility leave) are not exposed to the levels of guilt and stress experienced by a father not granted such a benefit. This plays a major role in the retention of highly-skilled talent.
- Father and/or family enhancement education programmes: such programmes enable fathers to cope better with work–life imbalances by interacting with other fathers and by acquiring coping skills and insights. This assists working fathers to cope in appropriate ways with accommodating work and family demands.
- Paid or unpaid paternity leave: while some companies grant unpaid paternity leave, men generally do not utilise this benefit. When paternity leave is granted on a paid basis, however, more men are likely to take it. While paid paternity leave is one of the more obvious benefits offered in father-friendly companies, there is still reluctance on the part of many men to make use of the benefit for fear of their absence from work, and the motivations driving their absence, negatively affecting their career progress.

A look at international developments regarding paternity leave is instructive. The US, the UK, Sweden, Norway, Denmark, France, Germany, Luxembourg, Belgium and Australia are some of the countries that have taken steps to create father-friendly workplaces, in many cases supported by government and/or legislation. The most common first step towards this has been the granting of paternity, family or parental leave.

In the US, the federal Family and Medical Leave Act of 1993 stipulates that any company with 50 or more workers who live in a 75-mile radius should be given upto 12 weeks of unpaid leave during any 12-month period for four specific reasons, two of which refer to children. One of these is for the birth and care of a newborn child of the employee, and the other is in order to care for an immediate member of the family (spouse, child or parent).

Research shows that American fathers are extremely concerned about their parental responsibilities. According to a 1998 national survey conducted for the National Partnership for Women & Families, by Lake Sosin Snell Perry and Associates, 29 per cent of men and women expressed concern about getting time off to care for a new baby or sick family member. The report found that 90 per cent of those polled wanted employers to do more to help working families.

From April 2003, the UK Government introduced paid paternity leave of one to two consecutive weeks, based on certain terms and conditions. Employers are able to claim back 92 per cent of the Statutory Paternity Pay (SPP). There is now talk of this paternity leave being lengthened. In addition, eligible employees who are parents of children under six years of age, or parents of a disabled child under 18 years of age, have the right to apply to work flexibly – and their employers have a duty to consider such requests seriously. When UK Prime Minister Tony Blair's youngest child, Leo, was born, Blair initially indicated to the media that he was not going to take time off, but subsequently did take a few days off to be with his family. By contrast, Blair's contemporary, the Finnish Prime Minister, Paavo Lipponen, took a few months off by way of parental leave.

In Australia, the Federal Government's Workplace Relations Act of 1996 makes provision for companies to introduce family-friendly policies and practices that include flexible working hours and paid paternity leave. The aim of this is to help both men and women balance their work and personal lives.

In a public address in 2003, the Australian Minister for Employment and Workplace Relations, Kevin Andrews, pointed out to delegates that it was important for parents to be given flexibility and choice in their family and work arrangements. He went on to say that, with children being critical to Australia's future, support for families was a national issue and not simply a work issue (Melbourne Institute and the Australian Economic and Social Outlook Conference, 2003).

Paternity leave in European countries is becoming common practice. France introduced paternity leave on 1 January 2002, stipulating that a father may take up to 11 days of paternity leave for the birth (or adoption) of a single child and 18 days for a multiple birth or adoption. A French government survey revealed that 94 per cent of fathers took leave for the maximum time. In addition, there was no indication that the attitude of French employers deterred men from taking paternity leave. What did serve as a deterrent, though, was the fact that the Social Security allowance provided for this leave was often less than what the father earned. Despite this, however, 12 per cent of fathers were prepared to incur a drop in earnings in order to be with their new babies.

In the Far East, Japan's Health, Labour and Welfare Ministry introduced an initiative to promote paternity leave in April 2003. This provides financial incentives for companies granting paternity leave, but it doesn't seem to have had the desired effect. Holland, Spain and Luxembourg all provide for two days of paid paternity leave, while Sweden, which has been offering paternity leave for about 30 years now, gives up to 450 days of paid parental leave.

South African fathers are permitted by law to claim three days of family responsibility leave, while the granting of paternity leave in Namibia hardly occurs at all. The Namibian press has, however, been debating paternity leave in light of a submission by the Legal Assistance Centre (LAC) to the National Council Standing Committee on Constitutional and Legal Affairs about the country's new Labour Bill. The LAC is proposing that the Committee consider whether there is a need for paternity leave in the Namibian workplace (*The Namibian*, 25 June 2004; 2 July 2004; 16 July 2004).

Best practice

Certain progressive companies are outspoken in their support for fathers in the workplace, and use father-friendly policies as a marketing tool to attract and retain the most talented employees. Benefits such as paternity leave are therefore designed to ensure that staff who have had much invested in them by way of training and development, remain with the company.

There is a sound business reason for this in that companies estimate the cost of replacing an employee to be about two-and-a-half times the employee's annual salary (Noe et al., 2002). In addition, there is a demonstrable and inseparable link between fatherhood policies and corporate social responsibility (Mazengwa, 2004b). What companies do for working fathers has a direct bearing on the communities to which the business sells and attempts to serve.

Certain companies go beyond their countries' legislated minimum requirements. The New Zealand bank Westpac Trust, which estimated staff turnover costs related to parenting to be equivelant to about R6 million per year, was so convinced of the business benefits of ensuring that their employees are supported in their roles as parents that they took a decision before paid parental leave became law in July 2002 to top up the New Zealand government's 12-week paid parental leave scheme to ensure that their staff continued to receive 100 per cent of their salaries when taking parental leave. The bank believes this plays a crucial role in retaining highly-skilled staff, citing its experience in Australia which indicated that the provision of paid parental leave increased the return-to-work rate by over 50 per cent.

Companies around the globe are offering fathers incentives. The North Carolina-based software company SAS Institute offers parenting classes and workshops. Nike™ Australia grants employees with more than 12 months' continuous service two weeks' paid, or 50 weeks' unpaid, paternity or adoption leave. Nike™ is exploring telecommuting and already has several employees partially working from home. Where a Nike™ employee is required to be away from home for an extended time, the company covers the costs of the family joining the employee. National Rail in Australia is undertaking a study of work and family issues to align the company's policies with its business needs and with family responsibilities (Australian Government, 2004).

Conclusion

As the stresses caused by the conflicts and challenges that working fathers face in finding and maintaining a balance between building a successful career and rearing well-adjusted and secure children start to impact on fathers' performance in the workplace, businesses will begin to count the cost of lost productivity and lost talent. On-the-job absenteeism on the part of fathers who cannot concentrate on the task at hand because of worry related to their families, has not yet been quantified. This information is essential as it will clearly establish the benefits of supporting fathers through the implementation of certain best practices, in some cases helped by legislation and in others, prompted by market forces (Stancanelli, 2003).

It would seem that the time is coming when all responsible (and astute) employers will develop and implement comprehensive and effective policies to support the fathers they employ to benefit both employer and employee. Unfortunately, to date, the workplace has been dominated and driven by men with extremely well-developed financial skills and business acumen, but poorly developed interpersonal and emotional skills. If fatherhood policies are to be implemented with any success, it will require courageous men to implement them, men who have high levels of emotional intelligence and maturity, in addition to their excellent business skills.

It is encouraging to note that as younger generations of fathers move into decision-making positions in the boardrooms of the corporate world, policies that allow fathers to embrace both their careers and their children have a much better chance of succeeding.

Alan Hosking is the publisher of the award-winning human resource magazine *HR Future* and has been a contributing editor for the UK human resource magazines *HR World* and *Global HR*. He is also the author of *What nobody tells a new father: The new dad's guide to pregnancy and parenthood*, and he has been a regular speaker at antenatal and parenting groups for the past ten years, as well as at human resource seminars and conferences. Alan graduated with a degree in English and Psychology and worked in the education and financial services sectors before launching his own media company, Osgard Media, eight years ago. Alan has been married to Jenny for 25 years and they have three daughters, Courtney, 19, Kelsey, 15 and Brittany, seven.

References

Appolis, P. (1998). Workers as fathers. *Agenda, 37*, 78–81.

Australian Government (2004). *Father friendly workplaces* available at www.workplace.gov.au/workplace (accessed 2 June 2004).

Backett, K. C. (1982). *Mothers and fathers: a study of development and negotiation of parental behaviour*. London: Macmillan Press.

Berry, J. (1997). Balancing employment and fatherhood. *Journal of Family Studies, 18*, 386–403.

Bond, J., Galinsky, E., & Swanberg, J. E. (1998). *The 1997 National Study of the Changing Workforce*. New York: Families and Work Institute.

Brandth, B., & Kvande, K. (2001). Flexible work and flexible fathers. *Work, Employment and Society, 15*, 251–267.

Casper, L., & O'Connell, M. (1998). Work, income, the economy, and married fathers as childcare providers. *Demography, 35*, 243–250.

Castelain-Meunier, C. (2002). The place of fatherhood and the parental role: Tensions, ambivalence and contradictions. *Current Sociology, 50,* 185–201.

Coles, R. (2002). Black single fathers: Choosing to parent full-time. *Journal of Contemporary Ethnography, 31*, 411–439.

Fine-Davis, M. (2004). *Fathers and mothers: Dilemmas of the work–life balance: A comparative study in four European countries*. Dordrecht/Boston/London: Kluwer Academic Publishers.

Greenhaus, J., & Beutell, N. (1985). Sources of conflict between work and family roles. *Academy of Management Review, 10*, 76–88.

Hofferth, S. (2003). Measuring father involvement and social fathering: An overview. Paper presented in session on Father Involvement and Social Fathering, at a conference on Measurement Issues in Family Demography, November 13–14 2003.

Hill, E., Hawkins, A., & Miller, B. (1996). Work and family in the virtual office: Perceived influences of mobile telework. *Family Relations, 45*, 293–301.

Levine, J. A., & Pittinsky, T. L. (1997). *Working fathers: New strategies for balancing work and family*. Reading, MA: Addison-Wesley.

Mazengwa, P. (2004a). Fatherhood in the workplace: Innovative human resource development strategy. *HR Future, June*, 10–13.

Mazengwa, P. (2004b). Corporate social responsibility and fatherhood. *HR Future, 10*, 14–15.

McNaughton, T., & O'Brien, J. (1999). Perspectives on fathering. In S. Birks, & P. Callister (Eds.), *Perspectives on fathering* (pp. 18–29). Palmerston North, New Zealand: Centre for Public Policy Evaluation, Issues Paper No. 6.

Melbourne Institute and the Australian Economic and Social Outlook Conference. (2003). 'Pursuing Opportunity and Prosperity', session entitled 'Living and Working in Australia'.

Miller, S. (1994). Conference proceedings: The role of men in children's lives. www.menweb.org/throop/nofather/confproc.html (accessed 2 May 2004).

National Partnership for Women & Families. (1998). National survey conducted by Lake Sosin Snell Perry and Associates, available online at www.nationalpartnership.org (accessed April 2004).

Noe, R., Hollenbeck, J., Gerhart, B., & Wright, P. (2002). *Human resource management: Gaining competitive strategy*. (2nd Ed.). Burr Ridge, Illinois: Irwin McGraw Hill.

Quick, J. C., & Tetrick, L. E. (Eds.). (2003). *Handbook of occupational health psychology*. Washington, DC: American Psychological Association (APA).

Stancanelli, E. (2003). *Do fathers care?* Paris: Observatoire Français de Conjonctures Economiques.

CHAPTER 18
HIV/AIDS and the crisis of care for children

Chris Desmond and Cos Desmond

Introduction

The HIV/AIDS epidemic poses a number of new challenges, while magnifying a number of existing ones. This chapter examines issues relating to the provision of care for children in the context of HIV/AIDS. The provision of care, and men's involvement – or lack of involvement – in childcare, is by no means a new challenge, but it is one that is being made more and more difficult as the epidemic progresses. As Francis Wilson, Philippe Denis, Radikobo Ntsimane and others in this volume have noted, there are numerous factors, particularly poverty, unemployment and more than a century of enforced migrant labour, that have had a negative impact on men's ability to fulfil their responsibilities as fathers. Further, the forced removal policy also destroyed many of the support structures that used to exist in families and communities, including those for the care of children.

As HIV in South Africa is primarily transmitted through heterosexual sex, infections are concentrated in the sexually active population – that is, in the 15–49 year age group, peaking at around 30 years of age. The majority of people in this age group are parents. Many mothers and fathers will, or have already, become infected, are progressing to illness and will eventually die as a result of HIV/AIDS if they don't receive antiretroviral (ARV) treatment. Already, it is estimated that deaths resulting from HIV/AIDS almost equal deaths from all other causes combined (Actuarial Society of South Africa (ASSA), 2002). As a consequence of these trends, the epidemic has serious implications for the care of children.

An often-discussed impact of HIV is the associated increase in the number of orphans. This impact is, however, only one aspect of a myriad of implications for children associated with their parents' illness and death. Prior to becoming orphans, children living with their parents may well endure long periods of suffering as their parents' health progressively deteriorates. As Sister Miriam Duggan, a missionary, medical doctor, and member of the AIDS Commission in Uganda, wrote:

> Maybe one of the lessons I learned during my ten years of caring for
> families affected by AIDS, was the amount of hidden pain and tragedy
> the disease was causing, not only to the person sick and dying, but
> especially to the children who went through the agony of watching, and
> often caring for, their sick parents as they died. Many of these children

became psychologically disturbed or rebellious, because nobody had helped them through their pain and bereavement. We discovered that there is a great need to counsel the children during the time of their parents' illness and also afterwards. It took time to discover that not only the sick person needed help. (Duggan, 2000)

A focus only on orphaning can lead to the neglect of other important problems faced by children in the context of HIV/AIDS. 'Orphanhood in itself is a process that begins long before the death of a child's caregiver with differently compounded vulnerabilities at different points along this continuum. Research repeatedly demonstrates that the period of a caregiver's terminal illness is one during which children are prone to exacerbated vulnerability – in which caregivers typically face increased struggles to support their children as they become less able to work to earn money and as cash is diverted to health care and treatment.'[1]

A common thread to impacts on children associated with their parents' illness and death is the need for additional care and support as their parents' ability to provide these is diminished. At the same time as children are in need of care, ill parents also need support. This support is sometimes only available from the children, and there are cases of children dropping out of school to help at home. Just as household budgets shrink through breadwinners' inability to work, subsistence activities in rural areas decrease or even cease altogether while the expenses associated with treatment increase. This means that the demand for care of children increases as the ability to provide it is reduced.

Examining the estimated trend in orphaning highlights the scale of the problem. As mentioned already, orphaning is only one aspect of the difficulties children face. However, orphans have also probably experienced other difficulties, thus monitoring orphan rates helps in understanding the magnitude of all the impacts of the epidemic on children. Figure 3 shows an estimate of the number of children whose mother has died. It shows total maternal orphans as well as those relating to causes other than AIDS.

Figure 3 Estimated number of children under 15 whose mother has died

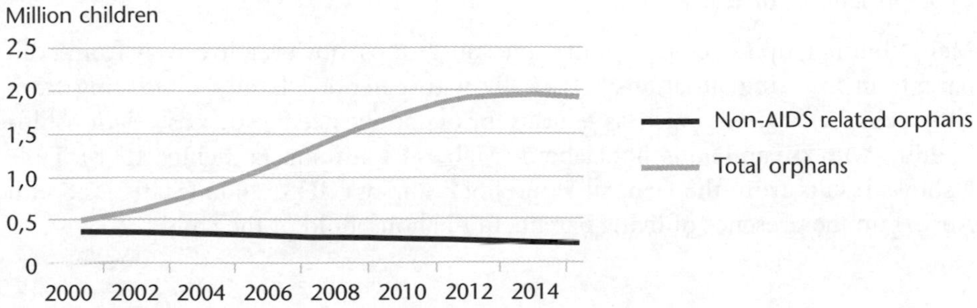

Source: ASSA, 2000.

227

The graph suggests that in 2004 there were already a significant number of children under the age of 15 who had lost their mothers. A large proportion of these deaths would have occurred even in the absence of HIV/AIDS. The impact of HIV/AIDS, however, can be seen in the projections to 2015. As the epidemic progresses, the number of children living without their mothers looks set to rise sharply, dwarfing existing numbers. What is important to note from this graph is that the impact of the epidemic on children is still in its infancy and its full magnitude has yet to be felt. For the next ten years there will be a steady increase in the number of orphans requiring care, while at the same time more and more carers will be dying. These figures consider only children under 15, but older children will also require care and support.

It is important to note that orphaning resulting from HIV/AIDS lags behind the other waves of the epidemic. New infections peak long before prevalence, and prevalence long before deaths, and orphaning long after that. Thus, while there may be signs that HIV prevalence is levelling off, we are still a long way from the peak numbers of orphans. Although this means conditions will worsen for children, it also indicates that there is still time to organise a comprehensive response.

Given the resource constraints and the poverty-stricken environment in which the epidemic is playing itself out, there is a need to use as effectively as possible the resources that are currently available in the community to respond to the needs of children. One group of resources, which is available but not drawn upon as much as they could be, is men in general and fathers in particular. This chapter examines, very broadly, what role fathers, and more generally men, are currently playing in the care and support of children, particularly in the context of high parental mortality.

Who's there?

Although not a direct measure of care, the presence of parents in the household is a minimal proxy for who carries the responsibility for children's care and protection. From the data[2] it would appear that fathers are absent from their children's home more often than they are present. Mothers, however, are far more likely than fathers to be present in the household.

Many children, up to 20 per cent in some sub-groups, however, live away from both parents in fostering situations – typically with extended family – resulting from either children's needs, such as education, or family needs, such as relationship-building with kin and household labour (Maharaj, Kaufman, & Richter, 1998). Table 7 shows results from the General Household Survey (GHS) 2002 (Statistics South Africa) on the presence of living parents in the household of the child.

Table 7 Parental presence in the household for children under 18[3]

Present	Father	Mother
Yes	48%	80%
No	52%	20%

Source: Own estimates (based on GHS, 2002).

According to the data, living fathers were present in the same household as their child in only 48 per cent of cases, compared to mothers who were resident in 80 per cent of the cases. As discussed in Chapter 4 of this collection, there are a number of reasons why the level of father absence is so high and each may have different implications for the care of children. For example, some absence may relate to the migrant labour system with fathers possibly returning during leave periods and supporting their families through remittances. A father's absence does not necessarily denote a lack of involvement in the care of his children. Some fathers may well not be resident yet still be very involved and supportive, while other fathers may reside with their children but not be involved. Despite the limitations of the data, they do suggest that the burden of care and responsibility for children falls largely on women. This, however, is an observation and not a judgment. There is no data available on the reasons for absence and, in many cases, it is likely that circumstance rather than choice has led to the separation of men from their children.

As demonstrated in Chapter 22 of this volume, there are a number of initiatives being taken both nationally and internationally 'to involve men in promoting gender equality, ending violence against women and playing a more active role in reducing the spread and impact of HIV/AIDS'. They argue that 'there is a growing recognition that men's full and active support is needed to achieve' this aim. But it is likely to take a long time, without specific intervention to address father absence, before there are sufficient men able and willing to play a meaningful part in providing care for children affected by AIDS, including those children whose mothers have died.

Addressing the Microbiocides 2004 Conference in London, Stephen Lewis, UN Special Envoy on HIV/AIDS in Africa, warned:

> It's entirely possible that we will make more progress over the next five years than we have made in the past twenty. But I cannot emphasise strongly enough that the inertia and sexism which plague our response are incredibly, almost indelibly ingrained, and in this desperate race against time we will continue to lose vast numbers of women. That is not to suggest for a moment that we shouldn't make every conceivable effort to turn the tide; it is only to acknowledge the terrible reality of what we're up against... We have to work with the men. Of course we do. But please recognise that it's going to take generations to change predatory male sexual behaviour and the women of Africa don't have generations.

Dumisane Nqina, a man who has 'seen the light' and now runs a men's organisation that deals with domestic violence against women, children and men, agrees. He believes that there are many men who are 'desperate to be fathers, yearning to be liberated from their macho image of "cowboys don't cry"…[But] change will take generations because sexism and the understanding of gender roles are so ingrained'.

In the meantime, women, who are the group most affected by, and most vulnerable to, HIV/AIDS, continue to carry the brunt of the burden of care for all affected by the AIDS epidemic, including children. For them to be able to do that, we need first of all to put an end to what Lewis describes as 'a continuing pattern of sexual carnage among young women'. Given the lack of progress in other areas, such as developing a vaccine or finding a cure for the disease, he places great hope for women in the advent of microbiocides, not only as a means of preventing infection but also in giving them control over their sexual activity. That, however, is still five to ten years away. In the meantime, a wholehearted commitment by the government to a comprehensive roll-out of ARVs would help.

A more fundamental government intervention would be to take steps to close the income gap between men and women. Desmond (2002) argues:

> The greater the income inequality between men and women the greater the power men have over women. If, as it is assumed, men prefer more partners to fewer, the greater the power men have the more sexual partners they will have, placing themselves and their partners at greater risk of infection. An increase in the income inequality between men and women in favour of men will, therefore, increase the risk of the entire group. A distribution of income towards women, while maintaining the same average income for the group, would reduce the risk of the entire group by reducing the power of men within that group.

Who else is there?

A father's absence from the household would be a concern even in the absence of HIV/AIDS. But in the context of the epidemic the father's presence, or at least involvement, is important also prior to either parent's death. There is an increase in the need for care and support for sick adults and cohabitant children. If a mother is ill, the presence of the father could be a key supporting factor for the children (see Chapter 19, this volume).

In addition to exacerbating the need for care prior to death, HIV/AIDS increases mortality rates. HIV/AIDS will increase the need for care for children, and so it is important to ask who will care for a child if either parent dies. Table 8 suggests that the presence of the second parent is lower than the norm in households with children who have lost one parent.

Table 8 If one parent has died, is the surviving parent in the household?[4]

Surviving parent in the household	Percentage
Mother not alive, percentage of surviving fathers present	30
Father not alive, percentage of surviving mothers present	71

Source: Own estimates (based on GHS, 2002).

These results show even lower parental presence than the results for the population as a whole (see Table 7). This does not necessarily mean that when one parent dies the other is likely to desert his/her child/ren. It may well be the case that factors that increase mortality among parents, such as poverty, are also associated with higher parental absence. For example, children in poor communities are likely to have parents with higher mortality rates and higher absenteeism rates associated with labour migration. This is an example of how the impacts of the epidemic on children are intertwined with pre-existing social problems.

If, following a mother's death, the father is not living with the child, who is likely to take care of the child? The question of who cares for the child following the mother's death is also relevant when not only the father is absent but also dead which, given the sexual nature of the transmission of HIV, is often likely to be the case. The focus of the following discussion, however, is on who cares for the child when the mother is dead and the father is alive but absent. This raises the question again as to whether we are using our existing resources to maximum effect; that is, could some of the care needs of children not be filled by men in general, and their fathers in particular?

Table 9 Relationship to household head among children whose mother is not alive and whose father is absent[5]

Relationship to household head	Percentage
Grandchild	68
Brother/sister	7
Son/daughter	3
Other relative	16
Other	6
Total	100

Source: Own estimates (based on GHS, 2002).

Table 9 shows what is commonly known; that the majority of children whose mothers die are in the care of their grandparents or another female relative. What is not shown in this table, however, is that women head most of the households that are caring for maternal orphans. Of the households caring for children who had lost their mother, and whose father was absent, 62 per cent were headed by women.

While still showing a female bias, the results do suggest that at least some men are taking a role, as the remaining 38 per cent of households are headed by men. What is interesting to note, however, is that in 96 per cent of the households headed by men, a female spouse of the head was also present, compared to only 21 per cent of female-headed households that had a male partner of the head present.

It would appear, therefore, that the burden of care for children, both before a mother's death and following it, falls on women. The burden on female relatives occurs even when the father is still alive.

Why are the fathers absent?

The data presented in this chapter and elsewhere in the book suggest that fathers have, on average, a comparatively low level of involvement in the care of their children. Again, as has been discussed elsewhere in the book, even without HIV/AIDS there would be a need for action to rectify this imbalance. For example, Linda Richter, in this volume, points out the benefits to men of involvement with children. In the context of HIV/AIDS, however, that need and almost every conclusion in this book, is amplified. Does the increased urgency created by the epidemic mean that programmatic efforts to support families and increase the role of fathers should be strengthened? Certainly. But can we afford to stop there?

There is not much that can be learned from the national survey data available in South Africa about why fathers are not present, although small-scale in-depth studies provide insights, as is illustrated in several chapters in this book. There are certainly fathers who simply do not want to be involved in their children's lives. There are those, as has been mentioned in this volume, whose roles as fathers have been shaped more by circumstance than choice. While a detailed discussion of why fathers are not present is beyond the scope of this chapter and is dealt with more appropriately elsewhere in this volume, a review of Table 10 raises some pertinent issues.

Table 10 Percentage of fathers who are alive and resident by household expenditure categories[6]

Expenditure category in SA Rand	African households	All households
R0–R399	37	38
R400–R799	35	37
R800–R1 199	46	49
R1 200–1 799	53	57
R1 800–R2 499	58	65
R2 500–R4 999	64	74
R5 000–R9 999	73	84
R10 000+	85	93

Source: Own estimations based on GHS 2002.

Table 10 shows a linear relationship between income and the likelihood of a father being alive and resident with his children. Does this mean that households are wealthier when fathers stay at home or that fathers stay at home because the household is wealthier? Probably a bit of both. There are certainly factors other than economic considerations that lead to the separation of men from their families and from the children they sire, but the data in Table 10 does imply that, given a more inclusive economic situation, fathers are likely to be found alive and at home more often.

It could be argued that, given the racial aspects of income distribution, the increase in fathers present in the household is in part associated with cultural differences between the groups that occupy primarily the upper categories, namely whites and Indians, and those who occupy the lower expenditure categories, namely Africans and coloureds. This might seem to suggest that white and Indian households are more likely to have fathers alive and at home than coloured and African households, because of cultural or social differences, and that the income trend is a coincidence resulting simply from white and Indian households being wealthier. This argument is, however, flawed, because the results hold even when the analysis is repeated within race groups. For example, Table 10 shows the upward trend, with household expenditure, of fathers present in the household when examined among African households only. This suggests that, aside from other factors, income appears to be related to fathers being at home, although the direction of causality is more difficult to determine.

The problems and challenges associated with the impacts of HIV/AIDS on children are intertwined with existing social problems. This means that responses need to go beyond specific programmes for children, even though these also have their place. There is a need for fundamental social change if we want fathers to be more involved with their children.

Conclusions

The most obvious way to mitigate the impact of HIV/AIDS on children is to slow the course of the epidemic through prevention and treatment and, by so doing, keep parents alive or at least prolong the time they can support and be with their children. Success in this has, unfortunately, been limited. United Nations Secretary-General, Kofi Annan, acknowledged this at the opening of the AIDS Conference in Bangkok in 2004. He said 'We are not on track to begin reducing the scale and impact of the epidemic by 2005, as we had promised'. He outlined three areas to focus on: scale up infrastructure to support both treatment and prevention; empower women and girls to protect themselves against the virus; and provide stronger leadership at every level – including at the top.[7]

South Africa's bid to host the 2010 Soccer World Cup managed to convince the Federation of International Football Associations (FIFA) that it had, or could develop, the infrastructure needed for the event, including medical facilities near all the venues. It was able to do this largely because of the support that it received from the government, both in terms of giving guarantees of financial support and in the personal involvement of the president, former president Nelson Mandela, and other top people. However, such support is sadly lacking in the fight against HIV/AIDS in South Africa. Uganda, Botswana and Brazil, among other countries, have shown the importance of political leadership in this fight. Without it there is little hope of success.

It is not, however, simply the denialism, and consequent lack of political commit-ment of the president and the minister of health that is to blame. It is doubtful that any really effective government intervention could be made within the confines of the Growth, Employment and Redistribution (GEAR) macro-economic policy, with its Thatcherite aversion to expenditure on social security – even though both poverty and, perhaps even more importantly, inequality seem to be increasing.

While treatment should be a major part of the response to the needs of children associated with the impact of HIV/AIDS, it should be only one part of this response. Even with treatment, many parents and other caregivers will still become ill, find it difficult to work, and eventually die – and the care of orphans and other children in difficult circumstances will still fall primarily to women. Greater involvement of men has the potential to reduce this burden and to assist in ameliorating the damaging impacts of the HIV/AIDS epidemic on children.

The greater involvement of men brings with it greater access to income and other resources, as men, on average, have higher rates of employment and higher earnings. In addition to greater access to resources, higher rates of involvement by men in childcare, that is by both fathers and other men, in particular male relatives, increases the supply of household labour.

Greater involvement of men may seem like a pipe dream. As has already been mentioned, there are a host of reasons for the current lack of involvement. These range from social and economic conditions to accepted roles for men and women in the home. Whether it is even reasonable to consider this as an option is an issue in itself. That said, the response to HIV/AIDS and its impacts on children is only one of many areas where greater male involvement with children would be beneficial. While the task may seem huge, the potential may well be worth the effort. Moreover, many of the impediments to male involvement are social ills with many negative consequences, and should arguably be addressed independently of their impact on male involvement with children, such as the migrant labour system. However, it may also be the case that as men become more involved with children, this in itself will assist in efforts to redress other social problems.

Currently the burden of childcare falls on women. Even after a mother's death it is likely that living fathers will not be present and that the role of caregiver will be taken on by a female relative, most often a grandmother. HIV/AIDS is worsening an already difficult environment for many children. The involvement of their fathers and other male relatives could go a long way to alleviating the impact on children.

Chris Desmond graduated from the University of Natal in Economics, where he worked as a Research Fellow for the Health Economics and HIV/AIDS Research Division. His research involves considering the economic impact of HIV/AIDS and the planning for responses to such impacts. Recent work has focused on methods of costing different models of childcare and measuring the effectiveness of different options for its provision. Other work has dealt with costs of interventions, such as the prevention of mother-to-child transmission. In addition to research, he has been involved in both planning and teaching workshops as part of his commitment to the Mobil Task Team on the impact of HIV/AIDS on education. He is also the co-editor of a recent UNICEF-sponsored publication, 'Impacts and Interventions: The HIV/AIDS Epidemic and the Children of South Africa'. Chris has been with the HSRC since 2003, and is currently reading for a PhD at the London School of Economics.

Cos Desmond is Chris Desmond's father.

Notes

1   Submission to the Portfolio Commission for Social Development from HIV/AIDS sector.

2   Posel and Devey, in Chaper 4 of this volume, discuss the difficulties in using this data as well as its limitations.

3   Typically household surveys include a household listing which relates each member to the head. In many types of household this makes the identification of parents difficult unless the parent is the head. The GHS, however, asks if a member's parent is resident in the household and, if they are, which member it is. The survey also asks if the parent is alive. This allows for the identification of mothers and fathers in the household. While the question does relate to biological parents, it is possible that other definitions are used in responses and so some caution should be taken. The estimates in this table reflect the percentage of children who responded positively to the question regarding parental presence in the household.

4   As mentioned previously, the GHS asks, of each member of the household, for each biological parent, whether the parent is alive and if they are, whether they are present in the same household. This table presents the results of cross tabulations of one parent dead one parent alive, with parental presence, firstly for 'mother not alive and father still alive' and, secondly, for 'father not alive and mother still alive'.

5   Tabulation of relationship to head of household for children whose biological mother was listed as dead and whose biological father was listed as alive but not present in the same household. As mentioned previously, this does not mean that the father is not involved. In this analysis, absence or presence is simply used as an indicator of care and/or responsibility for children.

6   The households classified as having a father resident were those with one or more resident fathers. There are cases where there are children in a household with different fathers. If any of the fathers is present the household is classified as having a father resident. There will, of course, be household size effects in these data. The trends illustrated nonetheless hold up for per capita expenditure and per capita adult equivalent household expenditure.

7   Press Release SG/T/2416. 15 July 2004.

References

Actuarial Society of South Africa. (2000). *AIDS demographic model*. Cape Town: Actuarial Society of South Africa.

Actuarial Society of South Africa. (2002). *AIDS demographic model*. Cape Town: Actuarial Society of South Africa.

Desmond, C. (2002). The role of absolute and relative income in the spread of HIV. Working paper prepared for UNICEF by the Child, Youth and Family Development Research Programme of the HSRC, Durban.

Duggan, Sr M. (2000). Behaviour change is the best prevention. *ChildrenFIRST, 4, 31*, 29–31.

Lewis, S. (2004). Address to the Microbiocides Conference in London. Available at http://www.coreinitiative.org/pub/20040916UNPressbriefingonUgandaandLesotho.pdf (accessed April 2004).

Maharaj, P., Kaufman, C., & Richter, L. (1998). Fosterage and children's schooling in South Africa. In L. Richter (Ed.), *In view of school: Preparation for and adjustment to school under rapidly changing social conditions* (pp. 58–81). Johannesburg: The Goethe Institute.

Statistics South Africa (2002). *General Household Survey*. Pretoria: Government Printer.

CHAPTER 19

Absent fathers: why do men not feature in stories of families affected by HIV/AIDS in KwaZulu-Natal?

Philippe Denis and Radikobo Ntsimane

This chapter discusses the experience that a group of South African children have of their fathers in the context of the HIV/AIDS epidemic. Thirty-three families affected by HIV/AIDS in KwaZulu-Natal were interviewed in the study. In these families, only 27 per cent of the fathers regularly resided with their children, or had resided with their children if the interviews were conducted after their death. A slightly higher percentage of fathers (34%) were giving some form of support – material or emotional – to their children. The actual percentage may be higher, given that not all interviews provided information on the fathers' whereabouts. We can assume, however, that the men who were never mentioned in the interviews were probably completely absent from the life of the household. This means that nearly three-quarters of these biological fathers had not had sustained contact with their children.

This research is based on 31 group interviews conducted between 2001 and 2003 in the Durban area and in the Natal Midlands. The group interviews were conducted by Nokhaya Makiwane and Sibongile Mafu, two fieldworkers – or 'memory facilitators', as they are often called – of the Memory Box Programme, a research and development project run by the Sinomlando Centre for Oral History and Memory Work of the University of KwaZulu-Natal (Denis, 2004; 2005; Denis & Makiwane, 2003; Denis, in press).

In this chapter, the word 'father' refers to the biological father as opposed to a child's younger and older paternal uncles who, in isiZulu, are respectively referred to as *ubab'omncane*, (younger father) or *ubab'omkhulu* (elder father). These uncles are expected to assume the role of the biological father in his absence.

The crisis of marriage

In the literature on family life and gender in South Africa, little is to be found on the problem of absent fathers per se. However, studies on related topics throw light on the subject. Before moving to the analysis of the interviews, we review selected studies on marriage, illegitimacy, *tsotsi* culture and masculinity which deal, albeit indirectly, with absent fathers.

In 2002, Mark Hunter interviewed 21 elderly people living in *imizi* (homesteads) in a semi-rural area called Ekufundeni near Mandini, KwaZulu-Natal. Most of his informants were born in the 1920s, 1930s and 1940s. He also interviewed a group of young men from the nearby township of Sundumbili, most of whom were born in the 1980s. A student of masculinity, he wanted to understand why so many men in contemporary Southern Africa, have multiple concurrent sexual partners – a practice that contributes to the spread of HIV/AIDS.

Hunter's research confirms what the Sinomlando memory facilitators observe every day. In large sectors of the population, particularly among the poor, the institution of marriage is not the dominant regulator of relations between men and women. Marriage rates have been declining and family units are increasingly unsettled. Most children are raised by single mothers, and seldom see their biological father even if they are lucky enough to know who he is. Hunter presented his findings as follows:

> Around one-third of the elderly informants had a father who had married polygamously. These polygamists will probably be born from the beginning of the century to the 1920s. All of the 33 men over 60 whom I spoke with had married one wife with the exception of one informant who remained unmarried. However, virtually none of the under-35 men from whom I collected data on in Ekufundeni, or knew personally in Mandeni, were married or substantially advanced in the process of marrying. (Hunter, 2004)

What Hunter describes in Mandini is the crisis of marriage as an institution. Both types of marriage are affected by this crisis; customary marriage and western marriage, which is often a Christian marriage celebrated in church, since many ministers of religion are marriage officers. But is marriage the issue? For children, the real issue is not the crisis of marriage but the fact that often their fathers – and sometimes their mothers – leave them to live with relatives or desert them. In addition, paternal uncles or other significant male adults do not replace the fathers, at least not permanently. There may be stepfathers of sorts – the mother's boyfriend of the day – but these rarely play a meaningful role in the lives of the children.

Long periods of absence

There is no national study that quantifies children's separation from parents. A small-scale, Cape Town-based study by Sean Jones, however, provides some sense of the extent to which fathers are absent in an impoverished African community (Jones, 1992 & 1993).

His fieldwork spanned a period of eight months, in 1989, while he was engaged as a voluntary teaching assistant at a self-help primary school. He studied the life circumstances of 24 children, all of rural origin, who resided in a complex of migrant workers' hostels some 40 to 50 kilometres from Cape Town. Each life story was compiled from three interviews, two with the child and one with the child's parents or guardians. All but four children had a paternal affiliation. In some cases the father of the child had obtained rights over his wife and her children by partial or full payment of bride wealth to her family. In others, no marriage between the biological parents was contracted or even contemplated, but the father had redeemed his extramarital child by some kind of payment (*inhlawulo*) to the maternal kin.

Jones found that the domestic histories of the paternally filiated children were characterised by frequent long-term separation from either one or both of their parents:

> All 17 children whose parents were married had lived separately from their fathers at some stage, most of them for very long periods. There was a mean period of separation from fathers among these children of 55 per cent of their childhood years, most having been separated from them for 70 per cent or more of their lives. In all instances children's separation from fathers had taken place as a direct result of the latter's involvement in labour migration. The amounts of time for which children had been separated from mothers were substantially lower, with a mean period of separation of around 22 per cent. (Jones, 1992 & 1993)

These figures are of great interest but, if we want to use them for comparative purposes, we must bear in mind that, by residing in a migrant-worker hostel with a predominantly male population, these children had a better chance than their peers in urban settlements of relating to their father. Jones' statistics indicate a trend, but they cannot be generalised.

Quantitative data on the relationship between fathers and children are also to be found in the statistics of illegitimacy. These statistics, however, are rather scarce, even for recent periods, and only give indirect information on the role played by fathers in the household.

The population data that have been preserved indicate that, since the end of the Second World War, at least a third and, in some cases, up to 80 per cent of all children in black locations were born to unmarried mothers. Commonly used in the primary sources on which we have to rely, the word 'illegitimacy' is questionable because of its moral connotations (Burman & Preston-Whyte, 1992). The so-called illegitimate children may enjoy the support of a father, especially if their mother marries him subsequent to their birth. In any event, as Sean Jones notes, while it is difficult to determine the true status of the relationship between an African child's biological parents, there is no concept of illegitimacy as a legal impediment in traditional African society (1992). It makes more sense to speak of female-headed or – in the case of women who are uterine kin, that is, the grandmother, her daughters and possibly adult granddaughters, and their respective children – female-linked households (Preston-Whyte, 1978).

During the period 1948–1951, according to the birth register compiled by the Institute of Family and Community Health, 235 of 685, (34.5%) of the women who gave birth in Lamontville, Durban, were unmarried. In rural Pholela, during the same period (1943–1950), however, only 11.5 per cent of the mothers were unmarried (Kark & Kark, 2001). In 1963, Pauw found that 42 per cent of the households in East Bank Location in Port Elizabeth, had female heads (1963). An estimate made by the West Rand Bantu Administration Board in 1960 for Soweto, put the proportion of female-headed households at only 14 per cent.

By 1970, however, the proportion of homes registered in the name of women in Soweto had risen to 22 per cent while in Eastern Bantu Township, one of Johannesburg's oldest African areas, a figure of 41 per cent female-headed households had been recorded (Hellmann, 1971). In 1969 Coertze reported that 55 per cent of births in Atteridgeville, Pretoria, were what he termed illegitimate (Coertze, 1969; Preston- Whyte, 1986).

In the late 1970s and early 1980s the figures released by hospitals and clinics in KwaMashu and the greater Durban area suggest that at least 60 per cent and possibly as high as 80 per cent of hospital births were to young unmarried women of whom at least 50 per cent were at school when they became pregnant (Preston-Whyte & Louw, 1986). Household figures from 1986 in Mpumalanga near Hammersdale KwaZulu-Natal show that 40 per cent of the households included the children of an unmarried offspring of the head (Preston-Whyte & Zondi, 1989).

The value of children

It has been suggested that the rise of female-headed households can be explained as a manifestation of the 'uncoupling of marriage and motherhood' (Walker, 1995). A growing number of women have become sceptical about marriage but are not relinquishing their desire to have children. In the African community, an extremely high value is placed on having children. Failing marriage, children still have an intrinsic value that cannot be gainsaid (Preston-Whyte & Zondi, 1989).

The same applies *mutatis mutandis* to males. Men also do not shy away from proving their fertility. But they do not necessarily take responsibility for the children they father. In his study of the *tsotsi* subculture in the Witwatersrand, Clive Glaser noted that it was prestigious for *tsotsis* to father children to prove their manhood. One of his informants, a young man interviewed in 1988, was extremely proud, at the age of sixteen, to have fathered a child with his fifteen-year-old girlfriend. 'We used to boast about our kids.' It was, however, unusual for a *tsotsi* to help support his children. Child rearing belonged to the domestic terrain and, as these young men saw it, this was strictly the woman's responsibility (Glaser, 1992).

These comments do not only apply to *tsotsis* on the Rand. An increasing number of men desert their children. As Eleanor Preston-Whyte observed a quarter of a century ago, this does not mean that men are completely absent from the household. But they no longer head the family. Unattached, they come and go according to circumstances:

> Men are … seldom completely absent from the household since the adult women may have lovers who visit them regularly and even live with them for periods. Though these men give financial and other aid to the women and their children, their role in the household is usually ill defined and transient. Many are married to other women and eventually move away. Their major contribution to the female-linked family is often the protection they provide when living there and the children whom they father. (Preston-Whyte, 1989)

The Sinomlando study

In 2001 Sinomlando conducted a pilot study (Denis & Makiwane, 2003) with Sinosizo Home-Based Care, a Catholic organisation running an HIV/AIDS home-based care programme in ten locations in the Durban metropolitan area. Interviews were conducted with 12 families in the following areas: Emona, Groutville, Lamont-ville, Mount Moriah, Tongaat and Wentworth. In 2002, Sinomlando signed a partnership agreement with a further two AIDS organisations, the Thandanani Children's Foundation in Pietermaritzburg and the Umngeni AIDS Centre in Howick. Twelve family visits were conducted in Sobantu, Pietermaritzburg, the following year as part of the Thandanani community workers' training programme. During the same period, seven family visits were made in the area under the responsibility of the Umngeni AIDS Centre, five in Mpophomeni and two in Cedara.

The primary purpose of the interviews conducted by the Sinomlando memory facilitators was not to gather information about the children's life circumstances and their genealogies. It was to create a space for inter-generational dialogue on family matters as a way of building resilience in the children and their caregivers in the face of AIDS-related illness and death. As a result, the chronology is imprecise and many details in the life stories are missing. The sickness and, when it occurred, the death of the parent(s) were the main focus of the story. With two exceptions, all households included at least one person affected by HIV/AIDS, usually the mother of the children. The people concerned were HIV-positive but asymptomatic, or they had become sick and died of the disease. All were clients of an AIDS organisation with which the Sinomlando Memory Box Programme had signed a partnership agreement.

Following Eleanor Preston-Whyte (Preston-Whyte, 1978), we propose to call households families, whether a father, a mother, another relative or even a child heads it. In practice, most families were female-headed. In only one case – an Indian family in the Durban area – were both parents present during the interview. In all other cases, the mother was the only parent to be interviewed, the children's father(s) being absent. In the event of her death, her own mother and, occasionally, her father, were interviewed. The children, or at least some of them, were always present.

Given these circumstances, we shall call a household headed by a woman – or one headed by her before she died or deserted her children – a family. All interviews but one involved a family thus defined. In this one case, the household included the families of two daughters and one brother all three of whom had died of AIDS. Their parents, a married couple, were raising the orphaned children. In total, 33 mothers, 47 fathers and 65 children were mentioned in the 31 interviews conducted between 2001 and 2003.

Multiple losses

The literature on AIDS insists, and rightly so, on the destabilising effect of AIDS-related deaths on the lives of the orphaned children (Barnett & Whiteside, 2002; Gow & Desmond, 2002; Marcus, 1999). Their life circumstances almost invariably deteriorate and they suffer emotional trauma.

What this research suggests, however, is that the loss caused by AIDS rarely comes alone. In all families examined here, the children suffered multiple losses. Independently of HIV/AIDS their fathers and, in a significant number of cases, their mothers, had deserted them without giving any reason. Added to that was the effect of poverty, which AIDS intensified but did not create. All families could be described as poor despite some disparity in their levels of income and life circumstances. Some interviews were conducted in a shack with bare walls, hardly any furniture and no equipment of any sort. The children were hungry. Other families owned a few sofas, a TV and a fridge. Violence was another source of trauma – several children had lost their father, not to AIDS but to gunfighting.

Seventeen mothers had died by the time the interviews were conducted, in 2002 in Durban and 2003 in Pietermaritzburg and Howick. Six were sick. Several died shortly afterwards, notably in Durban where the first interviews were conducted.

The interviews reveal that 27 mothers resided with their children and supported them at the time of the interview or, if they were dead, until the time of their death. Six mothers, four from Sobantu and two from Mpophomeni, no longer lived with their children. This is a remarkable figure. Between one-fifth and one-sixth of the 31 mothers reviewed here had absconded, probably for reasons which had nothing to do with HIV/AIDS. According to the interviewees, they had either 'left' (*bashiyile*), 'abandoned' (*balahlile*) or 'deserted' (*babhungukile*) their children.

Fatherless homes

While 18 per cent of mothers abandoned their children, a much higher proportion of fathers had done so. Hardly more than a quarter of the 47 fathers mentioned in the life stories were in regular contact with their children at the time the interviews were conducted or, if dead, before their deaths. This suggests an absence rate of 62 per cent. We adopt a broad definition of the word 'present'. We consider, for instance, a father who worked in Johannesburg, but came back to his family at regular intervals to be present.

Where were all the other fathers? As shown in Table 11, five had lived with their children at one stage, but they were no longer part of the family; 14 were said to be absent, without further specification; of the remaining 15 we simply do not have any further information. The family members who participated in the interview did not provide any information. Presumably these fathers were absent as well.

Table 11 Fathers' presence in the family

Fathers' presence in the family	Number	Percentage
Present at the time of interview (or until death)	13	28
Present until divorce or separation	5	10
Absent	14	30
No information	15	32
Total	47	100

In a few cases, the fathers did not live with the children and they did not visit them but they gave them support, if only occasionally. These cases were rare, however, as shown in Table 12. They did not change the picture of a largely absent body of fathers.

Table 12 Fathers supporting children

Fathers supporting their children	Number	Percentage
Emotional or material support to children	16	34
Support until divorce or separation	3	6
No evidence of support	9	19
No information	19	41
Total	47	100

When a father is absent, it is often hard to know whether he is dead or alive. By the time of the interviews, 11 fathers were said to be in good health, one was HIV-positive but asymptomatic, three were sick and 18 had died (see Table 13). No information was provided on the health status of the remaining 14 fathers. Given that AIDS affected 23 of 33 mothers, we can assume that a significant proportion of the fathers about whom we do not have any information were also sick or had died of AIDS.

Table 13 Fathers' health status

Fathers' health status	Number	Percentage
Good health	11	24
Asymptomatic HIV	1	2
Sick	3	6
Dead	18	38
No information	14	30
Total	47	100

By definition, when a father is absent, little is known about him. For example, the following account demonstrates how little is known about some absent fathers:

> When I became older, my friends got me a job in Nyanga where I met Ndumiso, Jabulani's father. Ndumiso left me before Jabulani was born. When I told him that I was pregnant, he went away and I never heard anything about him.[1]

Many life stories collected by the memory facilitators do not say anything about the children's fathers. This does not mean that these men were forgotten. A thorough investigation would probably reveal that their absence caused deep, if repressed, pain in their children. What the interviews show is that these fathers were absent from the children's and their caregivers' discourse. They were, simply, not spoken about. Often they had no name. The mothers of the children probably had some recollections of them, but they preferred to keep silent. The grandmothers, if the mothers had died, would tell the memory facilitators that they had no information about the fathers.

In one case, the paternal grandparents went to the hospital when the news of their son's illness reached them. He had died before they arrived. This was unfortunate, but at least they were in a position to tell their grandchildren that he had died. These children had a father to remember. For the majority of children with an absent father, even that was not possible.

In another interview the mother showed her awareness of the pain experienced by her eldest son, then aged eight, who wanted to know the identity of his father:

> There was nothing I could do because [the boy's father] claimed he was not responsible for the pregnancy. The problem was that my son wanted to know his father. One day, he cried saying his younger brother knew who his father was. He also wanted to visit his father.

The father of the youngest boy, who was three years old when the interview was conducted, did not cohabit with her, but he maintained contact with his child:

> I am not too worried about my youngest son because he knows his father and is known by him and by his family. I am no longer in love with him but there is communication between us.

For obvious reasons, the fathers who had participated in the life of their family – a third of the total – left better memories. This is, for example, how a 15 year-old girl remembered her father when he was coming back from Johannesburg with presents for the children:

> I remember one day when my father arrived and found us eating samp with beans. When we saw him and the briefcase, we all, every one of us, claimed to be full. The mere sight of the briefcase stimulated a savoury smell, whether true or imagined. The smell, the imagined taste, the goodies in the briefcase were irresistible. Usually when my father came home with goodies, he gave them to my mother so that she could share them equally among us. So even though we were claiming to be full, my mother would not open the briefcase until we finished eating samp and beans. We tried very hard to finish what we were eating with our eyes glued on the briefcase. We constantly looked at my father as a way of asking him to plead for us, as we were trying hard to finish our food. 'Papa' (as we would normally call my father) told us to do as 'Na' (as we normally called my mother) had requested us to do (Denis & Makiwane, 2003).

The way a father is remembered, if he has died, seems to have an effect on the well-being of his children. In the group of orphans the memory facilitators were gathering after school in one of the Pietermaritzburg townships in 2003, to teach them life skills, one of the children, a nine-year-old boy, struck them by his kindness, his maturity and his good behaviour. He definitely was a resilient child. His mother was the woman mentioned above. The father, according to the interview, was a good man. He had taken care of the baby. He had once given money for the baby to be taken to the doctor when he was ill. The other children in the house had everything they needed. Contrary to what his nickname – Masoka, the man successful with girls[2] – seemed to suggest, he was a family person. In January 2001, he was arrested after buying a stolen taxi from a friend. He was allegedly severely beaten up by the police and died soon afterwards. Our hypothesis is that the positive image this man had left of himself in the family helped the child to cope with the hardship of his orphaned state.

Other stories involving fathers point to the negative role the paternal side of the family tends to play in the lives of children. The following case was particularly traumatic. Here the problem was not the father's absence – he had died – but rather the abusive behaviour of his brother. In this family in the Durban area, the mother was sick and the father had passed away. The two younger children used to visit their father's family. They would stay over for the holidays. But then, the mother said, things started to go horribly wrong:

> While they were there an incident happened which caused me a lot of pain. The father's brother tried to rape my daughter. Apparently, the family discussed the matter and some sort of solution was found. The

children told me that they had been warned not to tell me anything. No one from the family informed me about the problem.

We should mention here that although many fathers desert their children without bothering about what will happen in their absence, the situation is not irredeemable. Other father-figures can be available – a grandfather, an uncle or even a priest or a teacher. The children also have social fathers in the form of their mothers' or their aunts' live-in-lovers, even if it is for a limited time.

Uncertain unions

Concerning the relationships between the mothers and the fathers of the children, this study fully confirms Hunter's conclusions (2004). Among the poor in contemporary KwaZulu-Natal, marriage has ceased to be an option. Even cohabitation has become unusual. An overwhelming majority of children grow up in female-headed households. Their fathers have casual encounters with their mothers or the parents cohabit only for a short time.

In our sample, only one couple was married. As it happened, it was an Indian family. One couple had been married but had divorced. In three cases, a marriage had been planned but had not materialised because of the death of one of the partners or for some other reason. Four other couples were living together – which brings to seven the number of men and women in a situation of cohabitation. Fifteen households were headed by a female. In one instance, the mother had deserted her children, leaving them in the care of their father – who subsequently died – and of their paternal grandparents. In five other cases, both parents were absent. Another member of the family, often a paternal grandparent, looked after the children (see Table 14).

Table 14 Relationships between parents

Relationships between parents	Number	Percentage
Marriage	1	3
Marriage followed by divorce	1	3
Cohabitation with intention of being married	3	9
Cohabitation	4	12
Cohabitation followed by separation	3	9
Female-headed households	15	46
Male-headed households	1	3
No parents	5	15
Total	33	100

Our overall impression is that, in the families we describe, marriage no longer governs the relationships between parents. We do not only speak here of western marriages. Customary marriage with payment of a bride wealth (*lobola*) to the bride's family has also become obsolete. Only two of 33 couples were or had been married at the time of the interview.

Admittedly, some marriages were mentioned in the interviews. Some men were not taking care of their children because they were married to other women with whom they also had children. And in many cases, surviving grandparents were married. As Hunter indicates, the people born in the 1930s, 1940s and 1950s were still expected to marry at some stage of their lives. In our sample, only a few single mothers could rely on the support of a loving father or, if he had died, could cherish his memories. In several instances, paternal grandfathers took responsibility for the upbringing of their grandchildren on the death of their daughter.

Conclusion

This chapter confirms and quantifies, on the basis of a small sample of families, what other researchers have hinted at. Among the poor, single mothers raise most children. Their biological fathers play a marginal role in their lives. These men do not see the benefit of establishing a permanent relationship with the mothers of their children, and even if they wished to form a stable couple, their life circumstances and the scarcity of jobs would make it difficult for them to reach that goal. Many women have ceased to pursue the ideal of marriage, and the stigma of single motherhood has receded. Many of these single women believe that raising children alone is preferable to suffering the abuse of a violent and unstable man. Short-term associations between men and women are seen as more convenient.

What about the children? It is difficult to believe that this situation is satisfactory from their point of view. Some children express the pain of not living with their father and sometimes of not even knowing their father's name. Not all fathers desert their children, of course. The interviews provide evidence of men who care for their children (or grandchildren) and constitute role models for them. But such men are the exception. One wonders how boys who have been deprived of the presence of a father will ever learn how to become fathers themselves.

Philippe Denis with his son Sandile, 2003

Philippe Denis is Professor at the School of Religion and Theology, University of KwaZulu-Natal. He trained in history at the University of Liège, Belgium, and in Theology at the Universities of Fribourg, Switzerland, and Strasbourg, France. He is the Director of the Sinomlando Centre for Oral History and Memory Work in Africa, University of KwaZulu-Natal. His current areas of research are the methodology of oral history, the history of Christianity in southern Africa, the history of HIV/AIDS in sub-Saharan Africa, memory and resilience in families affected by HIV/AIDS. A single father, he has adopted and is raising five children.

Radikobo Ntsimane is a doctoral student at the School of Religion and Theology, University of KwaZulu-Natal. He trained at the same university. He researches the history of mission hospitals in apartheid South Africa and he is currently working as a researcher at the Sinomlando Centre for Oral History and Memory Work in Africa.

Notes

1 Names have been changed.

2 On the changing meaning of the word *isoka* in KwaZulu-Natal, see Hunter, 2004.

References

Barnett, T., & Whiteside, A. (2002). *AIDS in the twenty-first century. Disease and globalization.* New York: Palgrave Macmillan.

Burman, S. & Preston-Whyte, E. (1992). *Questionable issue: Illegitimacy in South Africa.* Cape Town: Oxford University Press.

Coertze, R. D. (1969). *Atteridgeville: 'n Stedelike Bantoe woonbuurt.* Pretoria: Nasionale Raad vir Sociale Navorsing.

Denis, P. (2004). Enhancing resilience in times of AIDS. The Memory Box Programme of the University of KwaZulu-Natal. *AIDS Bulletin, 13,* 27–35.

Denis, P. (Ed.). (2005). *Never too small to remember. Memory work and resilience in times of AIDS.* Pietermaritzburg: Cluster Publications.

Denis, P. (in press). Are Zulu children allowed to ask questions? Silence, death and memory in the time of AIDS. In B. Carton, J. Sithole & J. Laband (Eds.), *Being Zulu: Contested identities past and present.* Pietermaritzburg: University of KwaZulu-Natal Press.

Denis, P. & Makiwane, N. (2003). Stories of love, pain and courage. AIDS orphans and memory boxes in Kwa-Zulu/Natal, South Africa. *Oral History, 31,* 66–74.

Glaser, C. (1992). The mark of Zorro. Sexuality and gender relations in the *tsotsi* subculture on the Witwatersrand. *African Studies, 51,* 47–67.

Gow, J., & Desmond, C. (Eds.). (2002). *Impacts and Interventions. The HIV/AIDS epidemic and the children of South Africa.* Pietermaritzburg: Natal University Press.

Hellmann, E. (1971). Social change among urban Africans. In H. Adam (Ed.), *South Africa: Sociological perspectives* (pp. 158–176). Cape Town: Oxford University Press.

Hunter, M. (2004). Masculinities and multiple-sexual partners in Kwa-Zulu/Natal: The making and unmaking of *isoka* in KwaZulu/Natal. *Transformation. Critical perspectives on Southern Africa, 54,* 123–153.

Jones, S. (1992). Children on the move: Parenting, mobility and birth status among migrants. In S. Burman & E. Preston-Whyte (Eds.), *Questionable issue: Illegitimacy in South Africa* (pp. 247–281). Cape Town: Oxford University Press.

Jones, S. (1993). *Children's experiences of migrancy and hostel life in South Africa.* Johannesburg: Witwatersrand University Press.

Kark, S., & Kark, E. (2001). *Promoting community health: From Pholela to Jerusalem.* Johannesburg: Witwatersrand University Press.

Marcus, T. (1999). *Living and dying with AIDS.* Pietermaritzburg: CINDI.

Pauw, B. (1963). *The second generation: A study of the family among urbanised Bantu in East London.* Cape Town: Oxford University Press.

Preston-Whyte, E. (1978). Families without marriage: A Zulu case study. In J. Argyle & E. Preston-Whyte (Eds.), *Social system and tradition in southern Africa* (pp. 55–83). Cape Town: Oxford University Press.

Preston-Whyte, E. M., & Louw, J. (1986). The end of childhood. An anthropological vignette. In S. Burman & P. Reynolds (Eds.), *Growing up in a divided society* (pp. 360–392). Johannesburg: Ravan Press.

Preston-Whyte, E. M., & Zondi, M. (1992). African teenage pregnancy: Whose problem? In S. Burman and E. Preston-Whyte (Eds.), *Questionable issue* (pp. 226–246). Cape Town: Oxford University Press.

Walker, C. (1995). Conceptualising motherhood in twentieth-century South Africa. *Journal of Southern African Studies, 21,* 417–437.

CHAPTER 20

Being a father in a man's world: the experiences of goldmine workers

Marlize Rabe

Introduction

The focus of this chapter is on conceptions and experiences of fatherhood amongst black workers in the gold mining industry in South Africa.[1] Mineworkers as a category of men in South Africa are well researched (see Rabe, 2002), but the spotlight is usually on their 'world of work'. This is probably due to a general tendency to see (and study) women as mothers, daughters, wives or sisters, whereas men are not often enough seen (or studied) as sons, husbands and fathers. Furthermore, when mineworkers' families are studied, it is often from the viewpoint of their families (commonly in rural areas), and the focus is frequently on issues of financial support or the lack thereof. In trying to address the bias in information about mineworkers, the focus of *this* chapter is mineworkers' conceptions of fatherhood in general, their relationships with their children and their relationships with their own fathers/father figures.[2]

The fieldwork for this study was carried out during 2002 and 2003 at a mineshaft southwest of Johannesburg. I conducted in-depth interviews with 30 men, at times with the help of a translator. Ten of these original 30 respondents were then re-interviewed after roughly six months, again at times with the help of a translator.[3] It is important to note that being a migrant or a resident father is a fluid status since household structures may change over time. For example, George, one of the mineworkers I interviewed, usually lives in a hostel. However, during our second interview he told me that his wife had come to stay with him for six months. They were renting a room in a nearby township for the six months, after which George would return to the hostel. He said that there was no specific reason for her visit, but indicated that they wanted more children (they were married according to customary law and already had three children). Interestingly, George and his wife (from Bushbuckridge) had never before stayed together for so long a period. Similarly, other men also changed their household arrangements from time to time. Although the fluidity is recognised, for the sake of clarity the categories are largely used in static terms here.

The analysis of this study points to a distinction between *migrant fathers*, who do not live with their children and female partners on a daily basis, and *resident fathers*, who reside with their female partners and children in one household, in relation to their respective conceptions of fatherhood and relationships with children. In the first part of the chapter, the migrant fathers and resident fathers are therefore discussed separately. Although variations were found regarding the father–child relationships amongst migrants, resident fathers generally expressed closer ties with children compared to migrant fathers. In the second part of the chapter, which considers the experiences of the mineworkers' own fathers/father-figures, no distinction is drawn between migrant fathers and resident fathers. It was found that migrant and resident fathers had similar experiences and that no distinction can be made between them with regard to their experiences of their fathers.

Fatherhood: conceptions and experiences

Understandings of fatherhood vary and there is no generally agreed definition of the concept amongst researchers. The men in this study were therefore not approached with a ready-made definition of fatherhood; rather, they were asked about their understandings of fatherhood and what a good father is.[4]

In this section, migrant fathers are discussed separately from resident fathers. Some background is first given on migrant fathers and thereafter their conceptions and experiences with their children are discussed. The same pattern is then followed with resident fathers. Comparative observations regarding migrant and resident fathers conclude this section.

The category of 'migrant fathers': background

In the South African gold mining industry, migrant labour began early, in the late nineteenth century, and became an integral and institutionalised part of the industry during the twentieth century. Initially, young able-bodied men entered wage labour for short periods in order, for example, to help to sustain their extended family or to pay for some important family matter or responsibility (Mayer & Mayer, 1974). The expression that they were at the mine 'on business', showed that they wanted to obtain the necessary money for a specific task and then return to their rural homestead (Moodie & Ndatshe, 1994, p. 139). The cash the mineworkers brought home was welcomed, but it did not immediately become the main means of livelihood. Rural families thus became part of the cash economy but remained within a subsistence economy until the mid-1950s when cash became necessary for survival (Simkins, 1980).

The mineworkers themselves, their families and the mine owners found the oscillating migrant pattern initially preferable to mineworkers settling on the mines. For mine owners, migrancy was a cheap form of labour. The mineworkers' lives were still mainly oriented towards their families, and the lives of these families were at the rural homesteads. However, this arrangement resulted in continuous shortages of labour on the mines. In the early twentieth century, mine management sought the South African state's help in securing the supply of large numbers of unskilled labourers. The state obliged by imposing taxes on black people to force them to seek work in order to pay these taxes. At the same time, the Natives Land Act of 1913 restricted black people's access to land, and therefore people could no longer rely entirely on farming in the rural areas for their livelihood (Horwitz, 2001; Lurie, 2000).

This process, of having less land and depending increasingly on wages, escalated and, in the 1970s, longer contract periods for mine work became common. This resulted in some mineworkers being less invested in their rural homesteads (Crush, Jeeves & Yudelman, 1991) and they began to develop relationships with and have children by urban women. At the same time, families in the rural areas saw less of the mineworkers yet their economic dependence on them was greater than ever before (Lurie, 2000). This meant that the father and head of household could be gone for long periods, but his contribution to the family was essential. Under these circumstances, it is easy to imagine why the absence of men might be endured by their children and wives (as well as other dependent family members), even though the emotional and social burden of this absence might be heavy.

In early twenty-first century South Africa, despite changed legislation, many mineworkers are still migrating and the majority of these migrants continue to live in single-sex hostels. A major reason for the continuation of migrancy is the constant (and realistic) fear of retrenchment amongst workers in the goldmine industry. Mineworkers do not want to invest in a house if they are not sure that they will have a job in that area in the future. Second, some mineworkers prefer migrancy because they own land far from the mine, and their families live there. Third, there is a housing shortage in urban areas and, although some mineworkers have moved into squatter camps that have developed alongside mines, not all mineworkers want to live under such conditions. Fourth, the hostels still offer cheap accommodation for men who want to save money for specific purposes (Horwitz, 2001; Seidman, 1995; Simkins, 1986; Smit, 2001). Another possible motivation for preferring migrancy is the belief that children can be raised best according to traditional customs in the rural areas, whereas children easily become economic burdens in urban areas (see Mayer & Mayer, 1974). Moreover, many mineworkers prefer to keep their families in rural areas as it provides a place for them to return to if they become economically inactive because of health reasons, retirement or lay-offs. The desire to set up or maintain a homestead in a rural area is a wish that is expressed by other migrant workers as well (Bozzoli, 1991; Møller, 1986; Spiegel, Watson, & Wilkinson, 1996). In this study, similar ideas were expressed; for example:

> 'I don't see the reason why she should come this side [referring to mine environment] because once she comes this side it means my home there [in Mozambique] would not exist any longer' (Winfred) and 'No, you

see there I have already erected a house [in a rural area], I can't say that she [his wife] must come and stay here' (Nelson,[5] who owns 25 cattle).

Although legal restrictions on the settlement of mineworkers with their families near the mines have been lifted, practical and other considerations still divide families residentially. As early as the 1970s Møller & Schlemmer (in Simkins, 1986) suggested that the removal of laws would not result in a residential re-unification of all families. Spiegel & Mehlwana (1997) later suggested that 'oscillating migrancy will continue long after apartheid's demise and may…become quite permanent.'

Living as a migrant

The concept of a 'stretched' household as articulated by Spiegel, Watson, & Wilkinson (1996) is helpful in describing migrants' household structures. They note that four criteria had traditionally been associated with households, namely 'co-residence, productive co-operation, income sharing and commensality'. In industrialised countries, production generally takes place outside the household; therefore this criterion is usually not applicable. Furthermore, co-residence and commensality are not applicable either, since these migrants live in single-sex hostels and do not share meals with their household members. The remaining criterion of a household is 'shared income and its expenditure'. Even though migrants live far away from their households, they remain a part of that household as long as they have a commitment to contribute financially to that household on an ongoing basis.

These characteristics of a 'stretched' household were particularly relevant to mineworkers who saw their families only once a year. Over the last two decades, however, migrant goldmine workers have been able to visit rural homesteads more regularly than used to be the case. The main reason for these more frequent visits is improved leave arrangements, although better transport systems also play a role. In addition, wives can now visit their husbands in the hostel, as rooms are set aside for men to share with their visiting wives. However, a woman's stay may not exceed two weeks and, at times, there is a waiting list for these rooms in the hostel at the particular mine where I conducted the interviews (Pheti & Professor, personal communication, 7 July 2003).

As a result of these more flexible living arrangements on the mine, it is now not uncommon for men, even those from Mozambique or Swaziland, to travel to their rural families at least once, or even twice a month. Indeed, some men never have to make special arrangements to send money back home, as now they can carry the money home during their monthly visits themselves. However, there are also men who go home less often, but then for longer periods at a time. I would therefore amend the criteria for the term 'stretched households' related to migrant goldmine workers today, by adding periodic contact with their families, which would imply at least two (but usually more frequent) annual home visits. Personal relations between household members are reinforced during these visits. In practice, this means that men can fulfil certain roles associated with being a father and a husband more readily than used to be the case in the past. Examples include taking an active interest in children's general development and schoolwork, and having sexual relations with wives.

During the interviews for this study, various themes regarding fatherhood emerged among migrant fathers – such as caring for one's family, giving financial support to family members, not engaging in unacceptable behaviour such as beating children severely, and guiding children towards acceptable behaviour and setting an example. Here are some examples of migrants' answers to the question: 'How would you describe a good father in general?'

> A good father is a father who cares about his family. (Sebastian[5])

> It is a man who supports his family. He is also working. I think a good father is like that. (Timothy)

> A good father is a father who takes responsibility for his children. A good father is a father who does not abuse his children by shouting at them or by beating them. (Mandla)

> A good father is the one who corrects you from doing wrong things. (George)

> A good father is a father who cares about his children and who has discipline. (Thabo)

> A good father is the one who takes care of you, good behaviour. (Mac)

> A good father is a father who does not always beat his children; he does not do bad things. A good father is a father who always looks after his family. (Simpiwe)

> He is the one who will give you everything you want, he is the right father. (Fernardo)

> He supports his kids, he looks after his home, he supports his wives, and even the neighbours will like him as a father. (Jerome)

> He is the one who loves his kids. When they have a problem, he solves the problem, eh…even if there is a problem at the school; he goes as far as to go to the school to sort it out. I think that he is a caring father. (Winfred)

Below are examples of migrant fathers who express their relationships with their children. Some attest to close and loving relationships but there are also examples of a relationship with a child with little interaction. Winfred says:

'No, we have a good relationship, like the one who is in standard 10 now, he is trying to educate me to speak English because I can't speak English. They love me, I love my kids.'

Winfred portrays himself as an involved father. Other men describe similar aspects, such as Mathew, who relates how his children are always happy to see him, and that he does not think they are happy when he is away. When he is there, he tells them stories about Johannesburg and life there. Along the same lines, Simon describes the relationship between himself and his children as 'good…because I try to teach them right'. He makes an effort to play with his children and to talk with them.

These representations seem in stark contrast to Thabo, who appears to have little involvement in his children's lives:

Question: How would you describe the relationship between yourself and your children?

Response: No, our relationship is very sound.

Question: Do you tell your children stories?

Response: No.

Question: Do you play with them?

Response: No, I cannot play with children [laughs a little].

It does not seem as if any other form of interaction occurs between Thabo and his children. In addition, Thabo has another child with a girlfriend, of whom his wife is not aware. He has not seen this child in over a year. Compared to some of the other migrant workers, Thabo thus appears distant in his relationships with his children.

Migrant men also describe other forms of interaction with their children, such is the case with Richard: 'I work with my children and then I teach them how to work…we make plastics, we create boxes to put things in, maybe clothing'. He can describe his children's daily lives in detail, and mentions the following themes in their family discussions: 'We talk about life, how my parents lived – they passed away, the children do not have grandparents – we talk about school – the brother [presumably the eldest son in grade 12] sometimes teaches us, he tells us what he learned at school'. They are a religious family, and Richard is a lay preacher. The church seems to play an important role in the family, and much of the communication between himself and his children is on religious matters. It is thus clear from Richard's life that, despite migrancy, fathers can have a variety of interactions with their children, and that these links seem to coincide with close family relationships.

It is clear that, despite the physical distance between men and their children, there is great variation in the relationships men have with their children. Even within a migrant setting it is possible to trace 'involved fatherhood' and a more 'distant fatherhood'. Many migrant fathers are interested in their children's education; some play with their children; some watch television with them; several tell their children stories or have discussions with them; a few work with their children at home; some have religious gatherings, and a few younger fathers are involved in the physical care of their young children (mainly when their wives are occupied elsewhere). Yet, in practice, all of these activities can only take place when the father is physically present and, for the greater part of these children's lives, their fathers are not present. The greatest contribution a migrant father can make to his family therefore remains financial support. Financial support can be seen daily in the food that is eaten, the clothes that are worn, and the school that is attended. Financial support from the father is therefore visible, whether he is physically present or not.

The category of 'resident fathers': background

As stated, the gold mining industry in South Africa has historically been closely associated with migrant workers (moving between urban employment and rural homesteads) who lived in single-sex hostels on the mine premises for the greater part of the year. Up until the 1980s the mines were heavily dependent on foreign labour (Jeeves & Crush, 1995) but, in the mid-1980s, the mines began to recruit workers close to the mines with more vigour (Crush, 1995). In 1986 the influx control laws were abolished and other restrictions on black people's movements (such as the Group Areas Act and squatting laws) were also later removed (James, 1992; Oliver-Evans, 1991). One result of all these changes towards the end of the twentieth century, was that some mineworkers now lived with their families near the mines and some have never lived in a hostel.

Living with children

In 2003, the South African Chamber of Mines[6] and the National Union of Mineworkers[7] signed agreements regarding housing in the goldmine sector. The agreements aimed at improving the standards of accommodation for mineworkers, stating specifically that '50% of employees should be in a position to exercise accommodation options, including family accommodation, by the end of 2009' (Kebeni, representative of the national union mineworkers' Housing Unit, personal communication, 11 March 2004).

At the mineshaft where I conducted my research, 40 per cent of mineworkers live in single-sex hostels (E. Motlhokwane, Human Resource officer at mineshaft where research was conducted, personal communication, 14 May 2003). The remaining mineworkers live in private dwellings, many with their families. Some have never lived in the hostels. Those not residing in any form of mine accommodation receive a 'living-out wage' from the mine. Mineworkers thus now live in a variety of household structures.

At the end of work shifts, taxis congregate at a particular point to transport mineworkers to their various destinations. A few travel by car, bicycle or walk. Many of these men not living in the hostels are not originally from the surrounding areas and, in several cases, they still live apart from their families. There are, however, a substantial number of black mineworkers who live outside the mine hostels, with their wives or girlfriends and/or with their children (and, in some cases, other family members). The statistics available from this shaft do not include details of those people with whom a mineworker lives.

The dynamics of these households stand in stark contrast to the 'stretched households' of the migrants working at the same mineshaft. Many of these men live in nuclear households, normally consisting of a man and woman together with their dependent children, but it may also include other family members, such as grandparents. In some cases, however, mineworkers live in extended households.

These men leave their houses very early in the morning to start their shifts, but many of them spend their late afternoons and evenings at home. They may occupy themselves with various household chores (at times in collaboration with their children), the supervision of their children's homework, and they may watch television with their children. During weekends they may visit family members, go to church or eat out on occasion. Interaction with their children is thus frequent.

In this study some of the resident fathers responded as follows when asked: 'How would you describe a good father in general?'

> If you are a good father it is better that you are working, you get money, if you are working you go to your wife and you plan the money, so you are a good father and when you don't go with the money, you are not a good father you see? (Lukas)

> It is one who does not fight with kids, treats his wife well, the one who loves beautiful things, who is not a drunkard. (Anthony)

> A good father? A good father is one who is always look after the child, play with his children, buying for his children and help them right. Maybe he is happy all the time, stick to your wife. (Isaac)

> Well if your child is asking for something you see, if you give him or her what she want, I think you are a good father. Even the homeworks if you help I think you are a good father. (Stuart)

> A good father is a father to be responsible, that is the first thing. To take care of their family and to take all the responsibility as a father at home. (Steven)

> A good father try to treat his children very well and then try to support them very well and then you show them love and you say to them: I love you. (Dean)

A good father is a father who cares about his family and he must talk to his children. He must help them when they come from school and help with what problems they may have concerning their education. He must play with his children, he must take them out to the beach and to the restaurants. If they got enough money, they must go out with children and with the wife as well, that is a good father. There must be good communication between the children and the wife. If they are doing that even God can bless them. The father must not have girlfriends, the mother must not have boyfriends. (Bernard)

A good father is a father who cares about his wife, his home and his children. He does not have some bad ways. (Ivan)

The answers here reveal similar themes to those of the migrant fathers regarding 'good fatherhood' – care and support of children, not engaging in abuse and other forms of 'bad' behaviour. However, communication with children, spending time together and expressing love are far more frequently mentioned by resident fathers. The reason for the greater prominence of these latter themes can be ascribed to the fact that resident fathers have more opportunity to interact with their children. It can be deduced that their experiences with their children influence the ways in which they view fatherhood in general.

I have shown that, relatively speaking, involved and distant fathers can be distinguished within the migrant context, yet involved fathering is far easier when daily contact with children is possible. This more frequent contact fosters a closer bond with children, which may then also be expressed in the general discourse on a 'good father'. In this general discourse, it seems that resident fathers place far more emphasis on communicating and loving children, compared to migrant fathers.

The reported practices of fatherhood: like father, like son?

In this section, a few short examples are presented to indicate how experiences of a mineworker's own father, father-figure or lack thereof impacts on his relationship with his children. No significant differences were found between the experiences of migrant and resident fathers in this regard, and therefore the men are discussed collectively for this purpose. In some cases, references are made to relations with fathers over the life course, or to how relationships with fathers change over the years. All the men, migrant fathers and resident fathers, came from diverse family back-grounds: some grew up in households where the father or father-figure was always present, while others almost never saw their fathers, or their fathers died when they were still young, leaving nobody to fill their fathers' shoes (in this study, four of the men's fathers died when they were still babies/toddlers with little involvement from other male adults thereafter). The presence of a father or father-figure could cause friction, could have positive effects, or could have very little effect on the children.

Some men had particularly fond memories of their own fathers, such as Mathew, who remembered his father as follows: 'He was loving me. And he had a lot of cattle. *Ja*, even today I am still thinking about my father, *ja*'. Winfred remembers his father thus:

> He loved his kids. He had two wives, my mother was the elderly one, and thereafter he got married to the other one. But we were staying in one home, the kids from the other wife were also staying with us. There was no difference in supporting, he would send money, buy food for us. He even took us a little bit to school…eh…and then he became old and he took pension now.

Winfred still has a good relationship with his father, and he visits him when he goes home, even though his father lives in another province with his younger wife (Winfred's father practised polygyny and his mother died the year before our first interview). Similar relationships exist between Winfred and his own children.

A number of migrant men believe their fathers were too strict, and they used to get beatings as children when their fathers deemed it necessary. Some believe that these beatings were justified, but others highlight the fact that they do not make use of physical punishment when dealing with their children's misdemeanours. Instead of corporal punishment, many prefer talking with their children or reprimanding them. Sam, for example, remembers his father as a drunkard who used to beat his mother as well as the children. He has very different views on raising his own children, though:

> *Ja* but I sit down with her [his wife] and I said don't beat her [their eldest daughter], if you beat them you don't teach your child, you don't teach like that, when she is doing something wrong, don't beat. Sit down and discuss with them, tell them you did wrong here and there. You beat, you don't teach, *ja*, and she will never understand nothing.

The financial support that a father provides is a recurrent theme amongst mine-workers. Men whose fathers failed to provide adequate support for them as children consciously or unconsciously attempt to lead their lives differently. For example Richard, who respects his father, nevertheless says:

> I was really suffering. My father had two wives; we were 16 all of us. Yes, it was bad, I even had to sell some of the things so that I could get money to go to school. It was difficult. That is what made me realise that I must recognise my children. I have four children and I don't want others to suffer because of what I experienced when I was a child.

Others have even less fond memories of their own fathers, such as Jerome: 'My father did nothing good for me because he had a lot of kids, that is why I said I was suffering…I don't remember anything good about my father'. In a second interview he continued to present his father as failing him as a child, as he had to grow up in poverty: 'Yes, he [his father] didn't play a big role because he had three wives and my mother passed away. Although he was there, he did not play a big role because he used to drink a lot'. He continued: 'No we didn't do that [look after cattle or goats], since my father was a drunkard we didn't have anything, we did not have cows, goats or anything.'

Jerome presents himself as a very different kind of father. He has a large family (two wives, 12 children and six grandchildren), and he supports the family together with his two sons, who also work as mineworkers. In addition, he exhibits initiative in agricultural matters. For example, he explained in detail how he constructed a water reservoir to catch enough rainwater to last the household the entire year.

Some of the men did not have particularly positive or negative experiences of fatherhood, although they judge their fathers to have raised them as well as could be expected. A father who was able to provide for the family's needs was well regarded overall; for example George, who says, 'He was a good father as I can remember because he supported us'.

Even Mandla, who remembers his father as a distant figure, says, 'He was a very quiet somebody, he was not strict but he did not like to speak to children, but we were not afraid of him'; later he adds, 'There is nothing good that I can say [about my father] but he did support us'. Mandla has an almost forgiving tone when he mentions his father honouring financial obligations towards his children, even though he did not have much involvement with them otherwise.

The mixed feelings associated with a father are demonstrated by Steven's reminiscences:

> Eh he was a very strict somebody and according in our culture you know the father is like a lion, you understand, he thinks there is no chance to smile and to joke and do that. When he arrives at home, he just sitting down like this [he demonstrates] with the questions: 'What, what? Why is it not like this and this?' So when you see he comes you run away because he is going to ask us a lot of things 'Why did you not do this, why did you not do this?'…but usually it was not so bad.

Later on, Steven recalls good and bad memories from his childhood:

> The best thing that I remember from my father is to assisting us with clothes and foods is some of the things, we never suffered like other children. That was a very good thing so it was to take the responsibility of their children. So the children never suffered so much although the money that he gave, he was never earning such a good salary but he was trying his level best so that his children could have food at home like other children, so that is the very good thing that I can remember.

In response to a further question, he continues:

> Mm *ja*, some of the bad thing is most of the time is he drinking and trying to hit us and all of those things…the bad thing of our father, he didn't give us that love, the relationship was not so good when we were growing to guiding us: 'don't do this, do this, that is a bad thing, do this'. That is some of the bad things that was not *oraait*. *Ja*, because a child really needs guidance from the father sometimes, not only the mother, but the father also. He must guide the child, especially a boy; there are some things he can't discuss with the mother. The father must play a role when growing up as a boy, so times go on with this decision and this decision and you must do one, two, three, four, five. *Ja*, that is some of the things I didn't see with my father, my father was ignoring, some of, a lot of things where he was supposed to play a role with us.

Steven has amicable relations with his father now that he is a grown man. His father was 82 years old at the time of our first interview and, although his father had had a stroke a few years prior to our discussion, he could still walk one or two kilometres at a time, and he continues to show an interest in the lives of his children and grandchildren. Steven, however, makes statements such as, '…I was telling myself I don't want to behave like my father…' When I asked him later on if he consciously tries to be different from his father, he answered, 'Yes, I tell myself I want to be different from the way my father behaved, to give my child the love and responsibility and all other things.'

Many men reported that their fathers drank heavily. Nevertheless, some of these fathers managed to support their families, while others did not. Some men became violent when they were drunk; others did not. It seems that only when lack of financial support or violence accompanied their drinking, do the children (the present interviewees) object to or criticise their fathers. None of them seems to be concerned about the drinking in itself. I found divergent views on how much drinking would make a person a drunkard. There is a difference between spending all of one's wages on liquor, with no money left for one's children, and getting drunk over weekends after having too much beer. This fits with the general sentiment that a father should be able to support his children financially. It is clear that many men not only expect a father to offer financial support to his family (love and guidance are also mentioned frequently), but that this is regarded as the minimum that a father should do.

Conclusion

The discourses of the interviewees on fatherhood revealed similar themes relating to fatherhood for migrant fathers and resident fathers These themes include supporting families financially, caring for children, and not exhibiting unacceptable behaviour such as violence towards children. Resident fathers were, however, more likely to identify communication with children and loving children as salient themes. Their experiences with their own fathers varied, and some mineworkers wanted to be different from their fathers, while others wanted to continue along the same lines as their fathers. Fathers who did not provide for their families financially are portrayed in a particularly negative light.

For migrants it still holds true that a 'good' father will work in the mines and send his wages home regularly. The reality of migrancy and distance from home is important as it excludes many practices often associated with good fatherhood. It should, however, be noted that despite the restrictions placed on migrant fathers, some still manage to build relatively involved relationships with their children by making the most of the little time they do spend with them. Even such limited contact can make a difference in children's lives. Isaac, for example, shares a household for the first time with his parents now that they are old and sick. He saw his father only occassionaly when he was growing up yet he says his father 'encourage[s] me to do my own life, today I am a priest in the church because of him...[t]hat is why today I sit with him and look after him because of the way he guided me'.

Since all the men in this study are employed, they are able to conform to their vision of a good father by providing financial support. Even though financial support is not the sole criterion identified by these mineworkers, it is central to their understanding of a good father. But their capacity to fulfil the fatherhood role also exposes the limitations of this understanding. Many fathers are under- or unemployed. The following words of a contract mineworker (quoted in Crush, 2001) resonate in this regard: 'Life is so unfair. I found myself bound to work for a contractor although it pays so little because I could not face my children and tell them I had no job, that is why I could not provide them with clothing and food. It made me feel irresponsible'. This suggests that alternative understandings of responsible fatherhood might be necessary to allow for more fathers to embrace the role of fatherhood.

Marlize Rabe teaches in the Department of Sociology at the University of South Africa. Previously she taught Sociology at the Sebokeng and Pretoria Distance Education campuses of Vista University. She studied Sociology and Psychology at the Universities of Johannesburg, Pretoria, South Africa, and the Witwatersrand. Her doctoral study focuses on fatherhood in the context of the goldmining industry.

Notes

1   This chapter is a shortened version of a paper with the same title, read at the Symposium on Manhood and Masculinities, hosted by WISER, University of the Witwatersrand, on 7 September 2004.

2   See Rabe (2004) for the impact of the mother–father relationship on fatherhood in this study.

3   The verbatim quotes from the mineworkers are based on translations done 'on the spot', or they consist of mineworkers' expressions, while conversing in English, which may be their second, third or fourth language. The verbatim reports in this chapter should therefore be seen as a tribute to multilingualism and not a manifestation of low levels of formal education.

4   Walker (1995, p. 424) has similarly argued about motherhood: 'there appears to be a powerful but unexamined assumption at work that motherhood is so familiar an institution and experience that it does not need rigorous definition'.

5   Pseudonyms were given to all interviewees to ensure their anonymity.

6   The Chamber of Mines is a representative body of management structures of major mine companies in South Africa, established in 1887 (Davenport & Saunders, 2000, p. 610).

7   The National Union of Mineworkers (NUM) was established at the end of 1982 (National Union of Mineworkers, 2003), and it is generally acknowledged as the 'voice' of the mineworkers.

References

Bozzoli, B. (1991). *Women of Phokeng.* Johannesburg: Ravan Press.

Crush, J., Jeeves, A., & Yudelman, D. (1991). *South Africa's labor empire. A history of black migrancy to the gold mines.* Cape Town/Boulder: David Phillip/Westview Press.

Crush, J. (1995). Mine migrancy in the contemporary era. In D. McDonald (Ed.), *Borders: Perspectives on international migration in southern Africa* (pp. 14–32). Cape Town: Southern African Migration Project.

Crush, J. (2001). Undermining labour. *Journal of Southern African Studies, 27,* 5–31.

Davenport, T. R. H., & Saunders, C. (2000). *South Africa: A modern history.* (5th edn). Hampshire: MacMillan Press.

Horwitz, S. (2001). Migrancy and HIV/AIDS – A historical perspective. Paper read at the AIDS in Context International Conference at Wits University, South Africa.

James, W. G. (1992). *Our precious metal. African labour in South Africa's gold industry, 1970–990.* Cape Town: David Phillip.

Jeeves, A., & Crush, J. (1995). The failure of stabilisation experiments on South African gold mines. In J. Crush & W. James (Eds.), *Crossing boundaries: Mine migrancy in a democratic South Africa* (pp. 2–13). Cape Town: Institute for Democracy in South Africa.

Lurie, M. (2000). Migration and AIDS in southern Africa. *South African Journal of Science, 96,* 343–347.

Mayer, P., & Mayer, I. (1974). *Townsmen or tribesman.* (2nd ed.). Cape Town: Oxford University Press.

Møller, V. (1986). Perceptions of return migration and development: A case study of migrant views prior to the lifting of influx control measures. *Development Southern Africa, 3,* 562–582.

Moodie, D., & Ndatshe, V. (1994). *Going for gold: Men, mines and migration.* Johannesburg: Witwatersrand University Press.

National Union of Mineworkers (2003). Homepage. Accessed from http://www.num.org.za/.

Oliver-Evans, C. (1991). The implications of the abolition of influx control legislation in the Western Cape. Unpublished Master's Dissertation, University of Cape Town.

Rabe, M. E. (2002). Southern African mine migrants and fatherhood. Unpublished paper read at the International Sociological Association's Congress in Brisbane, Australia.

Rabe, M. E. (2004). My children, your children, our children? The impact of the mother–father relationship on fatherhood. Unpublished paper read at the South African Sociological Association's Congress in Bloemfontein, South Africa.

Seidman, G. W. (1995). Shafted: The social impact of downscaling in the OFS goldfields. In J. Crush & C. Simkins, (Eds.), *Crossing boundaries. Mine migrancy in a democratic South Africa* (pp. 176–184). Cape Town: IDASA.

Simkins, C. (1980). Agricultural production in the African Reserves of South Africa, 1918–1969. *Journal of Southern African Studies, 7,* 256–283.

Simkins, C. (1986). Household composition and structure in South Africa. In S. Burman & P. Reynolds (Eds.), *Growing up in a divided society* (pp. 16–24). Johannesburg: Ravan Press.

Smit, R. (2001). The impact of labour migration on African families in South Africa: Yesterday and today. *Journal of Comparative Family Studies, 32,* 533–548.

Spiegel, A. D., Watson, V., & Wilkinson, P. (1996). Domestic diversity and fluidity among some African households in Greater Cape Town. *Social Dynamics, 22,* 7–30.

Spiegel, A. D., & Mehlwana, A. M. (1997). *Family and social network: Kinship and sporadic migrancy in Western Cape's Khayelitsha*, Co-operative Research Programme on marriage and family life. Pretoria: HSRC report HG/MF-31.

Walker, C. (1995). Conceptualising motherhood in twentieth-century South Africa. *Journal of Southern African Studies, 21,* 417–437.

CHAPTER 21
Fathers don't stand a chance: experiences of custody, access and maintenance

Grace Khunou

Introduction

'Fathers are not interested in their children especially when they do not marry their mothers.' This is the kind of statement one hears in the corridors of the maintenance courts, in taxis and in general conversation between men and women in the streets of Jozi.[1] However, since I began a research project on masculinities and maintenance in April 2002, I have come to question these sentiments.

In the three years of my research I have encountered fathers who demonstrate their love for their children, irrespective of the status of their relationship with the children's mother. On the other hand, I have also found cases where mothers struggle financially because fathers do not comply with maintenance orders.

It may come as a surprise, but many fathers – divorced, unmarried, and single – love their children and want to spend as much time as possible with them. Unfortunately, courts and law enforcers often overlook this and treat fathers simply as providers of financial support and discipline.

In this chapter I show that there is more to fathers than this. I also argue that for fatherhood[2] to be more appreciated, policymakers and law enforcers need to shift their attitudes and break their silence on the interests and needs of fathers. Most of the fathers with whom I have come into contact are more concerned about being involved in decisions that impact on their children's daily lives and having more access to their children, than they are with issues concerning maintenance. This chapter shows that for these fathers, paying maintenance is not a problem, though they feel that paying without reciprocal recognition of their needs and interests in their children is not acceptable.

The chapter is divided into three sections. The first briefly discusses the methodology of the study, and the second provides a theoretical discussion of maintenance and fatherhood. The third section presents the findings and is followed by concluding remarks.

Methodology

This chapter is a product of ongoing research that focuses on the relations between fathers, mothers and their involvement in the maintenance system, and how this influences their experience of fatherhood and motherhood.

Initially the project used the Johannesburg Maintenance Court[3] as the research site. This was for purposes of identifying participants for the study. Subsequently, I expanded the scope of the study to include a number of organisations dealing with maintenance and other related matters, such as divorce, access and custody. This resulted in the study including people who live in Johannesburg, irrespective of the maintenance courts they used.

The research combined interviews with fathers as well as an examination of court records. A total of 237 maintenance court files from the year 2002 were examined. This is from a total of approximately 9 000 files for the above-mentioned year.[4] The rationale for the period took into account the time lapse between the passing of the Maintenance Act 99 of 1998 and its implementation.[5] Questions raised and issues looked at were influenced by a broader examination of the maintenance system, interviews with both mothers and fathers, a reading of the Act, and interviews with court officials, policymakers and relevant civil society organisations.

The chapter is primarily based on 10 interviews conducted with white fathers between June 2003 and August 2004. They were aged between 39 and 50, and were both Afrikaans- and English-speaking. Looking at the amount of maintenance they paid, which ranged from R3 000 to R12 000 per year, and the jobs they held, I come to the conclusion that almost all of them were middle class with one or two in the upper working class. According to their accounts, there were times during the divorce proceedings when one or two of them were unemployed; however, at the time of the interview all of them were employed. All the fathers had been married at the time their first child was born, with the exception of one; this man was married to someone other than the mother of his son. Nine of the fathers went through, or were still going through, the process of divorce when I talked to them. This process decides issues of custody and access as well as child maintenance. All of them defined fatherhood as more than financial support and protection of their children. They have a strong sense of family and believe in the father–child bond. They all argued that the Justice Department prevents them from nurturing the bonds that they have with their children.

With one exception, none of the fathers had custody of their children; however they all had rights of access. These rights were limited, largely as a result of the divorce negotiations which had taken place when their relationships with their ex-partners had been strained. At the time of the interviews, it seemed that the fathers were coming to a point where their relationships with their ex-partners were improving with regard to communication about access and maintenance. In cases where the relationship is still sour, the relationships between children and their fathers remains very difficult.

The maintenance system

There are two sides to the South African maintenance system. There is, firstly, the judicial maintenance system which is based on the legal duty to support one's dependants. Secondly, there is the State Maintenance Grant,[6] which is meant to act as a safeguard by providing support where the judicial maintenance system fails. In South Africa the terms 'maintenance', 'support' and 'alimony' are used inter-changeably. But there is a clear legal distinction between maintenance and alimony, with the former being payment for children, while the latter is payment to one's ex-spouse. In general, they both refer to a duty to support – which extends to accommodation, food, clothes, medical and dental attention, and other necessities of life on a scale in line with the social position, lifestyle and financial resources of the parties.[7] However, at the time of writing, the scope of maintenance is always determined by the standard of living of the non-custodial parent.[8]

In 1996 the Lund Committee on Child and Family Support was set up to look at the various issues relating to the maintenance system. One of its challenges was to examine problems with the Maintenance Act of 1963 and come up with recommen-dations and solutions to make it work better. The problems identified in this Act included: high default rates of maintenance payment by non-custodial parents (Lund Committee, 1996), administrative and legislative discretion by maintenance officers and clerks, lack of training of maintenance officers, and negative attitudes within the legal fraternity towards maintenance.

This investigation was followed by the introduction of Maintenance Act No. 99 of 1998, which is said to be progressive and in line with the Constitution. This Act makes the following provisions as a means to resolve some of the problems identified: automatic attachment of emolument orders, the introduction of main-tenance investigators, the issuing of maintenance orders by default, computerisation of payments and claims, and improved training of maintenance personnel. The rationale for these provisions is to make it easier for 'claimants' to use the courts and access the money they need for child support. One of the most interesting features of the Act is that it acknowledges social parenting. Therefore it allows other caregivers to claim maintenance, including fathers and grandfathers.

Claiming maintenance

My study revealed that in 2002, 90.3 per cent of those who initiated maintenance claims were mothers, 1.7 per cent were fathers, and about 9.5 per cent were other caregivers, including older children who made claims against their fathers.

The process of claiming maintenance for divorced parents and parents of children born out of wedlock might follow different formats[9] given the process of the particular divorce. However, the process captured here is the most general one followed at the maintenance courts. Maintenance claims usually go through the following process:

- The applicant (usually the mother) fills in a form;
- A court date is set, and the respondent (usually the father) is notified by letter;
- Both parties are supposed to be informed that they should bring documentation as proof of income and expenses;
- Once the parties appear at the court, there is an informal inquiry before a maintenance clerk (officer). At this meeting, the clerk tries to establish if the parties can come to a settlement;
- If all the information is available, and the parties come to an agreement, an order could be made at this point;
- If there is information missing and the parties do not agree, the matter is postponed for further inquiry in front of a prosecutor and then a magistrate;
- At this stage, a few things could happen:
  - An order could be made;
  - If the respondent is unemployed, the court can order the father to find employment. If the respondent fails to find employment (and can prove this by presenting a form signed by potential employers indicating that they were approached but were unable to hire him), the case may be reopened after a couple of months for further inquiry;
  - The respondent could disappear for months, and not show up for further inquiry;
- If a respondent defaults in the maintenance payments after a few months, the applicant has to come back to the court. A summons will then be issued calling the respondent to court;
- A warrant of arrest might be issued;
- When the respondent comes to court, he might be fined, arrested periodically, and/or have his income garnisheed; and
- The court could also make an order to attach his property (Burman & Wamhoff, 2002).

This list does not begin to capture the obstacles faced by maintenance claimants. The provisions listed in the Act are not necessarily available to all who use the courts. Furthermore, these provisions are still not preferred by maintenance officers, therefore their implementation is not strict. Many applicants either don't know their rights regarding maintenance or lack knowledge as to how the system is supposed to work. Critics of the maintenance system justifiably argue that the law still privileges fathers and makes it difficult for mothers to access maintenance for their children. In the next section, the access of fathers to their children will be discussed as a way of balancing arguments about the gender bias of current laws and legal practices.

Fathers, fatherhood and the law

A particular conception of father – as provider – has influenced the direction of social policy on families. Ideas about fatherhood have changed in the last 30 years and, particularly in the developed world, the engagement of fathers with young children has been encouraged. Fathers in many parts of the world are no longer seen only as providers. The affective side of fathering has become much more important, especially for middle-class fathers for whom the challenge of financial provision is not acute.

In spite of this, the law has not kept up with the fatherhood revolution. The law has a tendency to react slowly to social changes. Barber (1975, p. 119) acknowledges this shortcoming:

> it is important to establish that the manifold inadequacies in the law as it concerns…fathers today, were not deliberately designed, nor, indeed, are the courts to blame for them. Courts are only concerned to enforce existing laws, and the relevant ones are adequate to the traditional needs and views of the…father.

While Barber was discussing the plight of unmarried fathers, his words are just as relevant to divorced fathers' experiences today.

The conception of fatherhood in South Africa and other southern African countries was strongly, but not exclusively, influenced by the British legal system (Armstrong, 1992). Roman–Dutch and English common law have both left their mark although, in South Africa, customary law has also played a role.

Legally fathers have long stood in a dominant position with regard to their families and their legitimate children, in particular. According to both British and customary law, custody arrangements later came to favour the mother. However, with the introduction of a child welfare principle in the late 1800s, came the legal demand for fathers to pay maintenance, which was argued to be based on structural economic inequalities. Maintenance payment was not directly linked to the question of the father's access to his children and this was negotiated at the time of divorce through the courts.

This situation pertained even though access was defined as, 'the right, granted automatically to divorced or separated fathers, to see the child' (Engelbrecht & Rencken-Wentzel, 1999). In such situations, the court makes an order for reasonable access that leaves the parents free to make detailed arrangements. In situations where the parents do not agree, which is most of the time as shown in my study, the court will then specify times and frequency of access. These, also, are not strictly followed in most cases.

Custody refers to the arrangement by which the responsibility for the care of a child is given to a parent or parents. This arrangement determines with whom the child resides, and who is given responsibility for the child on all counts (Barber, 1975). The courts usually award custody to the mother or to both parents (an increasingly common practice in the developed world and, more recently, in South Africa). This gives both parents active participation in making decisions about the child's education or living arrangements, even when the parent is not living with the child.

There are two diverging tendencies in law. The first is moving in the direction of encouraging fathers to develop relationships with their children and to acknowledge their interest in the welfare of their children. This can be seen in international developments around paternity leave and, in South Africa, in the passage of the Natural Fathers of Children Born out of Wedlock Act No. 86 of 1998. On the other hand, some feminists argue that fatherhood rights should not automatically be ceded to men. In terms of this view, men pose a potential risk to children because of their tendency to violence. For Susan Crean (1988), the fact that men remain the perpetrators of violence and sexual abuse in the family should be a significant factor when policymakers consider fathers' custody and access needs. She also suggests that new custody and access laws that view fathers as interested and capable will be detrimental to mothers and the struggle for women's rights. Attempts by fathers to secure access to their children are often viewed in an unsympathetic manner and, by feminists, as part of fathers' attempts to assert patriarchal control over women and children.

The findings: 'fathers don't stand a chance...'

While the media frequently highlight the shortcomings of fathers in meeting maintenance payments and in retaining links with their children, the fathers in this study expressed acute frustration concerning the obstacles placed in their way by their ex-partners and by legal processes. Eight of the fathers referred to in this chapter have tried numerous strategies to get their ex-partners to allow them what they call reasonable access to their children.

The fathers interviewed have all attempted to gain increased access to their children. This has in some cases involved litigation, which most have experienced as a stressful and painful process that has damaged their relationships with their ex-partners. But this is only one of the strategies that the fathers have been forced to adopt in order to gain access to their children. Eric, one of the fathers who was accused of abusing his daughter, went through a long process of investigation to finally get access. The process included the intervention of psychologists, judges, social workers and it took place over a long period of time. What was common with this case and with the experience of litigation more generally, is the assumption that fathers are irresponsible and uncaring unless they prove the opposite. Eric had this to say:

> And the accusations, I mean they were rubbish. You know there is no
> come back on her, it's only me that can go to jail if I do something
> wrong, but she can just accuse, accuse, accuse, with no truth. And
> nothing happens to her. Nothing! And it costs me money, time and
> pain to go to lawyers, to write a letter, to defend myself against the lying.
> Not for her to prove that I'm guilty. She can just say any rubbish she
> wants to and people believe it. (Interview with Eric,[10] Auckland Park,
> Johannesburg, 1 June 2004)

Almost all of the men I interviewed argued that they do not stand a chance because women are never suspected of lying and are given the benefit of the doubt. On the other hand, the honesty of the fathers is always questioned in a way that, over the long term, undermines their confidence in their parenting capacity. The general portrayal of men as abusive by the media and society in general leaves most of these fathers feeling unsure of themselves. George, another father, said this:

> Now you know that, I know that, and every judge knows that. Yet my
> attorneys said to me you dare lay charges against her for assault or for
> anything else, let it go, because if you do anything you will be seen to be
> the aggressor and ultimately it would be used against you. And I know
> that. It just happens time and time again. We do not stand a chance. We
> do not. As a man, as a father in this country you have no chance
> whatsoever. (Interview with George, Braamfontein, 25 June 2004)

Family laws that take into account the capabilities and interests of fathers should not be damaging to feminist gains, yet there has been some resistance over the years to including fathers in the lives of their children. In the 1980s, calling into question the credentials of fathers was considered by some as contributing to the feminist campaign against the patriarchal dominance of women. Making allegations of sexual abuse and violence during access and custody cases was thus considered a legitimate, politically-inspired move. Bitter maintenance disputes still feature in such allegations, as well as male counter-allegations of mothers not being fit to care for their children. Without exception, such disputes have a detrimental effect on the relationship between children and their fathers. Prince, another father, had this to say:

> For me the blow has been two-fold, whilst the mother claimed domestic
> violence and abuse; me, I had to defend myself which cost more than
> R12 000 in legal and psychologist fees. And in the process I was denied
> access to my son for 6 weeks. And that meant no phone calls, nothing.
> When the psychologist report went against her, the state declined to
> prosecute – and she suffered no consequences. I tell you, the mother has
> the ability to destroy the relationship between the child and his father.
> And that I'm afraid is incredibly dangerous. (Interview with Prince,
> Johannesburg, 3 July 2004)

Allowing such situations to continue unchecked may send the wrong message about the use of the justice system. People might think it can be used to settle scores, when really the goal should be to find a situation in which the child gets the best that both parents have to offer.

Striking a balance: paying maintenance and seeing the kids

The fathers in this study were, for the most part, very keen to have frequent contact with their children. They did not see their obligations as fathers ending with paying maintenance. Being a provider was only part of their fatherhood role. They wanted to be integrally involved in the upbringing of their children – they wanted to be involved in deciding which schools the children went to, the subjects they chose, and the sports they played.

It surprised me that the experience of paying maintenance for a majority of these fathers made them actually realise and begin to feel that they were not an integral part of their children's lives. They miss being a father in the everyday sense, making decisions about school activities, getting to know the child's world including their child's friends, tastes, joys and disappointments. Fathers wanted to make an impact on the kinds of people their children will become. These fathers were not against paying maintenance, but against not having control over how the maintenance benefits their children. Fathers pointed out that their objections should not be construed as suggesting that their ex-partners were not good mothers. Their concerns were that their contribution to raising the children should not be measured only in financial terms, but should include their being part of the decision-making process.

> [W]ell I don't mind paying maintenance for my daughter, but when I see what she writes, what her justification is for spending, I have a big problem with that, because she is now claiming for all sorts of stuff that we never had in our lives. Trying to live like a king. (Interview with Eric, Auckland Park, Johannesburg, 1 June 2004).

On the same issues, Prince had this to say:

> I'm busy negotiating a maintenance settlement now, that I have the right to pay expenses directly. So for example, she says school fees is a thousand rand, and I pay a thousand rand to the school, and I know it is a good school. (interview with Prince, Johannesburg, 3 July 2004)

Fathers seem happy to pay maintenance if they are satisfied that it is being used for the benefit of their children. But many question whether their maintenance payments are being used for this purpose, especially when their ex-partners are in good jobs, have new partners and appear to be living lavish lifestyles. In situations where suspicion exists between mother and father, fathers want maintenance issues to be discussed together with issues of access and decision-making. Attempts should be made in legal processes to accommodate holistic attempts to promote the involvement of fathers in the lives of their children.

'Visitor fathers'

The fathers in this study argue that it is not enough to see their children only on their birthdays and on Fathers' Day; they want to read their children bedtime stories and listen to them say the dandiest things.

The issue of time spent with one's child came up frequently in the interviews. It seems fathers really want to be a bigger part of their children's lives. Seeing one's children once or twice a week was not enough for these fathers. Eric endured a number of court cases in order to clear his name so that he could see his daughter more often. His story captures the typical experience of all these fathers, especially with regard to the use of legislation that aims to protect women and children from abuse.

Eric's story

Eric was married for ten years. The problems in his marriage started when his wife fell pregnant. She was not happy with him when he showed an interest in the pregnancy, and as the months went by she became unhappy. His struggle started with him wanting to be present at the birth; he had to fight to be there. He did not know that this was the beginning of a long and costly struggle. A few months after the baby was born his wife moved out with the child and did not allow him to see the child. For six months after that, he did not see his child. He tried several things including therapy, the church and mediation to try and sort out the marriage and their differences. Eventually, they filed for divorce, which had not been finalised when I talked to him in June 2004. In the two-and-a-half years since the separation, there have been continued fights over access to the child. These have been coupled with accusations of abuse and molestation of the child, leading to court orders of all shapes and sizes and barring him from seeing his daughter, from coming to the mother's house, and all sorts of restrictions. These led to interventions by psychologists, lawyers and the courts in general. However, at the time of the interview Eric had regular access to his three-and-a-half-year-old daughter. His voice reveals his distress and mistrust of the law and its mechanics. For example Eric does not understand why the police did not, at any point of his interaction with them, give him the benefit of the doubt. He wonders why they took it for granted that everything his ex-wife said was taken as it was, without further investigation, and why everything he said was treated with disbelief. He sounded very angry and frustrated that he had to spend so much money, time and professional intervention trying to be a father.[11]

Another father, Steve, had this to say when asked whether he still has a relationship with his children:

> It's still not enough, because I only can do homework with them once a week. It's an important time, it's an important thing to have a couple of days continuously, because you find the first and the second day you may be rushed, there may be school activities, it's choir, it's a netball match, it's this, and their friends come over. If at least you have two or three or four days in succession regularly, consistently then the relationship chills out and they open up to you, and you find that quiet quality time with them and you know you can read them stories when they go to bed. And then they ask you things about where the universe ends…you can be a meaningful part of their lives. (Interview with Steve, Johannesburg, 25 May 2004)

Access was a very significant issue for the fathers in this study and was frequently linked to issues of wanting to contribute to the history of the child: 'wanting them to think of you when they need to laugh or when they need to know everything will be all right'. This, they pointed out, is difficult to achieve when you are not available. When asked how he feels about his access arrangements, Eric had this to say:

> You know, you feel like you're visiting your child's life. You are not a parent…that is very hard emotionally. And I love her dearly, and to be cut out like that it's not right. (Interview with Eric, Auckland Park, Johannesburg, 1 June 2004)

Fathers are unhappy to have their roles reduced to birthday playmates for their children. Although all of them agreed that they played with their children and wanted to be with them on birthdays and special days, this was not enough. They all felt it was important to be involved more in their children's daily lives and that the access arrangements they had were making it difficult.

Conclusion

This chapter is based on the testimonies of ten middle-class white men. It cannot therefore claim to be anything more than a snapshot of a much broader and more complex situation that involves fathers who no longer have direct access to their children.

In this chapter, I show how the desire of men to forge close relationships with their children has been frustrated by the gender assumptions of the law, by the officials who administer the law, and by their ex-partners.

No study of fathers should sidestep the issue that in financial and economic terms, men in South Africa are still generally in more powerful positions than women. For this reason among others, men often have the leverage to dictate the terms of post-divorce life. In this study, however, I have shown how the economic power of men has not translated into relational power against their former wives. On the contrary, the responsible discharge of the obligation to pay maintenance has not smoothed the path to easier relationships with their children and they have often found themselves blocked from developing closer relationships. This has been to their detriment as well as to that of their children. This chapter argues that the contributions of mothers and fathers are equally central to the needs of the child. Therefore, policymakers on family issues should take these into account when formulating such policy.

Finally, concerns about gender equity can best be pursued by working with fathers and in reshaping ideas about fatherhood, rather than by trying to cut them out, preventing them from seeing their children, and treating them as the problem.

Grace Khunou is a PhD fellow at the Wits Institute for Social and Economic Research (WISER), at the University of the Witwatersrand. She is currently completing research on the maintenance system and South African notions of fatherhood. Her other research interests include social policy, the labour market, economic sociology and gender.

Notes

1   This is the slang for Johannesburg – the capital city of Gauteng. It houses about 3.2 million people, with the majority of its white population living in the suburbs while Africans are concentrated in the townships, city centre and the flatlands of Hillbrow, Berea and Yeoville.

2   Fatherhood here refers to the role that men play in the lives of children, even if these children are not their own. The concept 'father', on the other hand, is limited to the biological relationship that men have with their children. The justice system, in general, and the maintenance system, in particular, use a biological understanding of 'father' in their deliberations (see Chapter 16, this volume).

3   This court has eight maintenance officers who deal with more than 100 cases per day and who are assisted by one maintenance investigator. The court services areas from Soweto, Kliptown, Lenasia, Langlaagte, and Johannesburg including Hillbrow, Berea and Yeoville. I was also told that the court has only one fax machine servicing four floors, including the Domestic Violence and Child Care Centre in the same building.

4   I found one of the challenges of studying the files in the Maintenance Courts was the unpredictability of their availability at particular and predictable times. Maintenance Court files are documents that are constantly being consulted and one is never in a position to know exactly how many files are going to be available because they are never in the file room all at one time.

5   Key provisions of this Act are noted in the discussion on the maintenance system that follows.

6   Under the apartheid government white, coloured and a few urban African mothers without partners were awarded a State Maintenance Grant to assist them with support of their

children. This grant was set at about R350 per month for children up to the age of 18. Due to its limitations, the system was reviewed in 1996 so as to include African women, especially those in rural areas. In 1998 a new maintenance system was introduced. The Child Support Grant was phased in. It paid to single mothers (or the equivalent primary caregiver) R75 per month for each child up to the age of seven years, and subsequently it has been increased to R170 per child for children up to the age of ten years.

7   Maintenance Act No. 99 of 1998.

8   The non-custodial parent is found to be the father in most cases. However, recently a number of fathers have been successful in getting custody of their children. A workshop hosted by Tshwaranang Legal Advocacy Centre to End Violence against Women on 20 October 2004 raised concerns about the formula used to determine the amount of maintenance to be paid by particular parents. It was pointed out in the workshop that magistrates seemed to use their discretion in this regard, therefore creating problems.

9   For parents who are divorcing, maintenance is incorporated into the parties' decree of divorce as part of the settlement agreement. Due to problems in the system, and to the nature of claiming maintenance, the process usually ends up at the Maintenance Court; for example, when one of the parents applies for a variation order (to increase or decrease the maintenance amount).

10 All the names used to refer to fathers are pseudonyms.

11 The story presented here has not been validated; however, I have no reason to disbelieve it. This is because it resonates with a lot of what some of the other fathers had experienced.

References

Armstrong, A. (1992). *Struggling over scarce resources: Women and maintenance in southern Africa.* Regional Report: Phase One, Women and Law in Southern Africa Research Trust. Harare: University of Zimbabwe Publications.

Barber, D. (1975). *Unmarried fathers.* London: Hutchinson.

Burman, S., & Wamhoff, S. (2002). Parental maintenance for children: How the private maintenance system might be improved. *Social Dynamics, 28,* 146–176.

Crean, S. (1988). *In the name of the fathers: The story behind child custody.* Toronto Canada: Amanita Enterprises.

Crow, G., & Hardey, M. (1992). Diversity and ambiguity among lone-parent households in modern Britain. In C. Marsh & S. Arber (Eds.), *Families and households: Divisions and change* (pp. 142–156). London: Macmillan Press.

Collins, R. (1992). Pursuing errant fathers: Maintenance systems in three western countries. In P. Close (Ed.), *The state and caring* (pp. 72–85). London: Macmillan Press.

Engelbrecht, R., & Rencken-Wentzel, A. (1999). *Divorce: a South African Guide.* Johannesburg: Zebra Press.

Landsberg, M. (1988). Introduction. In S. Crean (Ed.), *In the name of the fathers: The story behind child custody* (pp. 9–11). Toronto Canada: Amanita Enterprises.

Motara, E. (1999). *Improving women's access to justice: A gender critique of the problems experienced by women in the maintenance system, with special reference to the problems experienced with maintenance officers, and to determine whether there is need for specific training and career tracking of maintenance officers* (Research Report No. 1). Pretoria: European Union Foundation for Human Rights in South Africa.

Report of the Lund Committee on Child and Family Support. (1996). Pretoria: Department of Social Development.

Local and international policies and programmes

Martin with his son Sewell, Wentworth, 2003 by Jenny Gordon, professional photographer

CHAPTER 22

The new gender platforms and fatherhood

Dean Peacock and Mbuyiselo Botha

I can say that to be a man you have to have strength. I do not mean strength in terms of muscles. No. I mean [strength] in that you have to be the one taking care of the family; you must be the one maintaining the law. That kind of a man is good in my community. (Man in focus-group discussion, Soweto, October 2003)

There is no such a thing as the father is the head of the house! That thing destroyed our grandfathers and fathers. Today there is nothing like that. Instead a man should say 'my wife has gone to work, let me also take responsibility and help her by doing household chores, look after the children, change the nappies…' (Woman in focus-group discussion, Soweto, October 2003, quoted in CASE, 2004)

I have two daughters and, I tend to see them as my friends. It's also sending a message that it's possible for them to actually have a much more fulfilled relationship with a man, that is not based on hierarchies of power. (Male gender activist interviewed in February 2005, quoted in Peacock, 2005)

Historical context

In South Africa, as in many parts of the world, gender roles are in flux. As the quotes above illustrate, rigid gender roles are being contested in complex and complicated ways by women – and sometimes also by men.

As neo-liberalism and an increasingly unequal and globalised world change traditional modes of production and forms of employment, men and women's roles are forced to change. Similarly, the HIV/AIDS pandemic is forcing dramatic changes on men and women, boys and girls. As more and more people become ill and struggle to gain access to life-saving medication, men and boys are increasingly being called upon to share the tremendous burden of caring for and supporting the ill and dying, previously borne primarily by women and girls.

Entrenched gender inequality and constructive male involvement

While gender roles are indeed shifting, gender inequality remains entrenched and continues to devastate women's lives. It is now well established that the HIV/AIDS epidemic disproportionately affects women's lives both in terms of rates of infection and the burden of care and support they carry for those with AIDS-related illnesses. Young women are much more likely to be infected than men. A recent report conducted by the University of the Witwatersrand in April 2004 indicates that women make up 77 per cent of the 10 per cent of South African youth between the ages of 15–24 who are infected with HIV/AIDS (Pettifor, Rees & Stevens, 2004).

Women's greater vulnerability to HIV/AIDS is in part explained by the very high levels of sexual and domestic violence reported across the country – some of the highest levels reported anywhere in the world. For instance, in the same study, almost one-third of sexually experienced women (31%) reported that they had not wanted to have their first sexual encounter and that they were coerced into sex.

Women's economic dependency exacerbates their vulnerability to violence and to HIV/AIDS and its associated impacts, making it difficult for women to leave abusive and/or sexually coercive relationships. Despite the changes in government and the significant increase in the number of women represented in government, according to Gelb (2003), the gender gap in real wages has widened substantially. This is illustrated by the fact that women's hourly wage as a percentage of men's dropped from 77.9 per cent to 65.6 per cent in 1999. The following figures reinforce just how precarious many South African women's economic position is. According to Gelb, women's participation in the labour force is much lower than that of men. In 1995, only 17 per cent of African females were in wage employment, compared with 43 per cent of African men, while 45 per cent of white women were in the labour force, compared with 63 per cent of white men.

Men working to promote gender equality

Across the world, in addition to the efforts needed to ensure women's rights, there is growing recognition that men's full and active support is necessary to achieve gender equality, end violence against women, and mitigate the impact of HIV/AIDS. Indeed, in many communities worldwide, men work creatively to end men's violence against women and children, prevent HIV/AIDS and to foster gender equity. In Nicaragua, the Men's Group of Managua recently launched a national campaign making the connection between Hurricane Mitch and increased male violence against women. Their theme: 'Violence against women: A disaster that men CAN do something about' (Peacock, 2000). In Kenya, the Male Initiative of the Society for Women on AIDS encourages men to support their partners' full participation in prevention of HIV mother-to-child-transmission programs. And in Brazil, Instituto Promundo works with young men in the urban slums or '*favelas*' surrounding Rio de Janeiro and São Paulo to promote gender-equitable values and practices.

Many of these initiatives draw upon three interconnected principles, each related to an understanding of the many negative ways in which the unequal balance of power between men and women plays itself out. First, contemporary gender roles are seen as conferring on men the ability to influence and/or determine the reproductive health choices made by women – whether these choices be about utilisation of health care services, family planning, condom use or sexual abstinence. Second, contemporary gender roles are viewed as also compromising men's health by encouraging men to equate a range of risky behaviours – the use of violence, alcohol and drugs, the pursuit of multiple sexual partners, and the domination of women – with being manly, while simultaneously encouraging men to view health-seeking behaviours as a sign of weakness. Such gender roles leave men especially vulnerable to HIV infection, decrease the likelihood that they will seek HIV testing, and increase the likelihood of contributing to actions and situations that facilitate the spread of the virus. Third, men are seen as having a personal investment in challenging the current gender order because it is in their health interests to do so, and also because they often care deeply about women placed at risk of violence and ill-health by the consequences of these gender role constellations.

What efforts have been made in South Africa to involve men in promoting gender equality, ending violence against women and children, and playing a more active role in reducing the spread and impact of HIV/AIDS? In answering this question, we will also seek to understand how men's very mixed experiences of fatherhood – as sons and as fathers – and their frequently expressed desire to be engaged, responsible and admired fathers, might serve as an important vantage point from which to work with men to promote more equitable, healthy and enjoyable models of masculinity.

Promoting constructive male involvement in South Africa

In the 1990s, South Africa experienced an unprecedented level of violence perpetrated by men against women and children. What made this type of violence peculiar was that women, together with men, were in the forefront of efforts to democratise the society. The violence shocked and paralysed South Africans from all walks of life. People asked themselves 'Why now? What can be done? Can our society afford to sit back and fold its arms in the face of this brutalisation? Can we watch the fruit of our democracy go to waste?'

Young babies were being raped at an alarming rate and in some instances brutally killed. Mamokgethi in Katlehong, as she came to be known, was raped, killed and buried in a shallow grave – just one of many stories that shocked the public. The man who raped her was known to the innocent girl and her family. It was the trust that this man betrayed which angered the local community and mobilised it into doing something concrete about her death. Baby Tshepang, a six-month-old child from the Northern Cape was also brutally raped by her mother's former boyfriend. Such horrific incidents were viewed by many as an indictment of all men, including those who stood by, quiet, aloof and indifferent to the plight of women and children. The irony of it all was that men and women mobilised and galvanised each other towards redefining what manhood, fatherhood and masculinity was all about in the face of this brutality.

Different strategies and approaches have been developed to involve men actively in ensuring that the stereotypes that have guided and defined men are challenged and redefined as a means towards achieving a more egalitarian society. It is these efforts, by men in particular, that have debunked the myth that all men are the same. This work is testimony to the fact that most men are not violent by nature, but that men are also victims of how they themselves were socialised in a social and political system that encouraged and promoted violence as a way of life, and provided them with few other role models for masculinity.

South Africa has seen some men taking the issue of gender equality as seriously as they took the struggle for the liberation of the oppressed masses. In an interview conducted in 2000 and quoted in Peacock (2003, p. 327), Farid Esack, former member of the Commission on Gender Equality in the Western Cape and a prominent Muslim theologian, gave voice to this commitment and made clear the analogy between the anti-apartheid struggle and the struggle for gender equality, by arguing that:

> 'There isn't a problem of women. In the apartheid years (people) spoke of a 'black problem' and there wasn't a black problem. There was a white problem…And so there isn't a women's problem. Men are sitting with the problem. Of course it becomes a women's problem…Women are quite literally the victims of all of this in the multifarious, insidious, all pervasive forms of violence against women. So women do end up with problems. But women aren't the problem. If we do not address issues of men and men's violence against women, and machismo and male insecurity and the question of masculinities as opposed to a very oppressive, homogenous understanding of a man, we will really be sitting with problems eternally.'

Men's involvement in efforts to promote gender equality, end violence against women and define healthier and more responsible models of masculinity, have taken many forms. Among the earliest and most visible public manifestations of these efforts are the various men's marches launched since 1997 that have drawn thousands of men out into the streets in a public repudiation of men's violence against women and children. Attended by men from all walks of life, these marches have represented the public face of dozens of other initiatives across South Africa that strive to bring about a major shift in the social norms that jeopardise the health and safety of women and men, girls and boys, and society in general.

Since the first men's march organised by ADAPT (Agisanang Domestic Abuse Prevention and Training), the South African NGO Coalition (SANGOCO) and the South African Men's Forum (SAMF) in 1997, both government and civil society have demonstrated considerable commitment to increasing men's involvement in efforts to promote gender equality, end gender-based violence, promote responsible fatherhood, and increase male involvement in HIV/AIDS-related prevention, care and support activities.

The issue of fatherhood and paternal responsibility has more recently become the focus of considerable attention. There are signs that many young fathers are rejecting notions of fatherhood and manhood that have for many years put them in a box and dictated how they should be 'real men'. The following quote bears powerful testimony to this:

> I attended a workshop in which there was an activity looking at positive role models for men, and participants mentioned Mandela and people like that. The facilitator asked us to 'bring it home' and to think of role models in our own lives. And I couldn't find any in my life. I thought of my father, I thought of my uncle, I thought of the men around me, and I was blown away because I could not come up with a man as a positive role model. That challenged me a lot. It was very hard to think that I might be associated with the bad image that men have – as perpetrators and so on. I was really impacted by the bad image of men as the perpetrators of violence, men are the rapists. So I said, I want to change, I want to make a difference, I want to play a positive role in other young boy's lives. (Peacock & Levack, 2004)

There is growing support among men to dismantle patriarchal practices that demean women. Most men have embraced the emancipation of women as part and parcel of their own emancipation from oppressive societal expectations of how 'men' behave or what they ideally should be. And there is growing opposition to men who engage in or promote abusive practices in the name of culture. The tide is indeed beginning to turn against the seemingly rigid meaning and interpretation of manhood and fatherhood, as understood by previous generations of men. The HIV/AIDS pandemic is also prompting new forms of fatherhood as the following quote illustrates:

> Being infected with HIV can be very confusing for a father. Initially I was afraid to touch my children thinking 'what if I will infect them?' You don't know if you should tell your kids or not. If you tell them, you do not know how they would respond. You also don't know at which age it is appropriate for them to be told. But as time went on I got the courage to tell my three boys and they understood the situation. Last October my wife passed on due to HIV and AIDS. I relate to my boys just like any other man or father, I cook, clean them, and do laundry and any house

chores that are there. It has been one of the most difficult times for me and my three boys. Now, though, life is starting to get back to normal, we often talk about her with the boys as a healing process. Sometimes we cry together holding hands when we do this. (*EngenderHealth*, 2004)

The following descriptions of initiatives currently underway across the country provide evidence of this growing commitment. The organisations and initiatives described below were designed to address and interrogate men's power, patriarchy, culture, religion and the violation of women's human rights in South Africa's new democratic dispensation.

Government

Government in South Africa, whether at the local, provincial or national level, has an important role to play in supporting constructive male involvement. In his inaugural speech in 2004, President Thabo Mbeki stressed the importance of gender equality and of the need to end discrimination against women. He said, 'as we engaged in struggle to end racist domination, we also said that we could not speak of genuine liberation without integrating within that the emancipation of women…No government in South Africa could ever claim to represent the will of the people if it failed to address the central task of the emancipation of women in all its elements, and that includes the government we are privileged to lead.' Days later, President Mbeki added substance to his speech by appointing an unprecedented number of women to his Cabinet and to four out of the nine provincial Premier's offices.

The Office on the Status of Women

The Office on the Status of Women (OSW) in the presidency has played an important role in drawing attention to the need for government to promote men's active and constructive involvement in the fight against women's oppression. Following on from its participation in the 2004 Commission on the Status of Women at the United Nations, which focused on the role of men and boys in achieving gender equality, the OSW convened a meeting of key stakeholders in May 2004. This brought together senior representatives from national departments and civil society to discuss the formation and mandate of a National Gender Machinery (NGM) Co-ordinating Committee on Men and Gender Equality. Pending ratification by the full NGM, the co-ordinating committee will be tasked with promoting effective collaboration and co-ordination on issues related to men and gender equality, both amongst government departments and between government and civil society. Few countries in the world can boast of the existence of a co-ordinating body of this sort.

The Commission on Gender Equality

The Commission on Gender Equality (CGE) is a constitutional body established by the Commission on Gender Equality Act 39 of 1996 to support the development and implementation of democracy. Its constitutional mandate is to promote, protect and monitor gender equality in South Africa. The CGE is committed to creating a society free from gender discrimination and other forms of oppression, a society where people will have the opportunities and means to realise their potential regardless of gender, race, class, religion, disability or geographic location. Part of its mandate involves a countrywide men's programme to advance gender equality in all nine provinces. Together with the South African Men's Forum, the Moral Regeneration Movement (MRM) and the National Council of Churches (NCC), the CGE has recently launched a series of dialogues entitled 'Unmasking Patriarchy' which explore men's roles and responsibilities in achieving gender equality.

The Department of Health's Men in Partnership Against AIDS Programme

In October 2002, under the slogan 'South African Men Care Enough to Act', a National Men's *Imbizo*[1] was held bringing together some 400 men from around the country to raise awareness of the need for men's involvement in preventing and mitigating HIV/AIDS. At this meeting, an Interim National Task Team was elected as a first organisational step towards the formation of a broad-based countrywide men's forum. Co-ordinating the responses of the men's sector is considered paramount to developing effective strategies in the four priority areas identified in the HIV/AIDS and STD Strategic Plan for South Africa (2000–2005) – prevention; treatment, care and support; human and legal rights; and research, monitoring and evaluation.

Based on outcomes of the *Imbizo* (Gobind, 2005), the decision was taken to further engage the men's sector through a series of consultative workshops at the provincial level. Through the establishment of provincially co-ordinated men's networks, the Men in Partnership Against AIDS Programme (MIPAA) mobilised men in each of the nine provinces and organised a series of regional men's marches culminating in a national men's march in Durban in March 2004. Provincial workshops are planned with the aim of providing men with an opportunity to develop coherent plans to guide their actions as individuals, as groups, and as partners with other sectors.

Civil society

Civil society organisations in South Africa working to promote constructive male involvement and responsible fatherhood are active and increasingly successful at enlisting men and creating awareness. At an organisational level, in communities across the country, in trade unions and faith-based organisations, within houses of traditional leadership and within Community-Based Organisations (CBOs) and non-governmental organisations (NGOs), many innovative programmes are working together to promote men's involvement. Of these, some organisations, such as Fathers Speak Out, the Men as Partners Programme, and the South African Men's Forum, have as their primary focus reaching men and fathers. Others, such as the trade union federations and affiliates or faith-based organisations, have only more recently begun to include a focus on men. Some organisations, for example the House of Traditional Leaders, are relatively new to conversations about men and gender equality but are of vital significance given their positions of influence, especially in rural communities.

Space constraints prevent a full description of all the constructive male involvement work currently being done across the country. However, a few examples of some of the better-established and more comprehensive programmes are used to illustrate the richness of these initiatives.

Agisanang Domestic Abuse Prevention and Training (ADAPT)

ADAPT was established in Alexandra township outside Johannesburg by Mmatshilo Motsei, who argued that it was important to address the role of men in stopping violence against women. Alexandra, like almost all black townships in South Africa, is beset by high rates of unemployment, homelessness, and domestic violence. ADAPT's programmes, such as 'Adopt a Father', the 'Best Father Competition', and the 'Men's Prison Programme' all seek to address the role that men can and should play in bringing about a violence-free society. ADAPT's men's programmes offer diverse services involving counselling and mentorship on what the modern man can and should be to his children and his family.

The Five in Six Project and the Everyday Hero Campaign

The Cape Town-based Five in Six Project was named for the five men out of six who, by extrapolation from available data, are not violent with their partners. Consistent with their vision of engaging men as part of the solution by offering men both an opportunity to end violence and to reconnect with their own humanity, the Five in Six Project launched a campaign in 1999 that attempted to enlist men as 'everyday heroes' uniquely situated to end violence against women. In its Everyday Hero Campaign, Five in Six attempted to educate men about the price all men pay when some men enact violence against women and children, and articulated their vision of men as vital and willing allies in the struggle to end such violence. Five in Six attempted to saturate the popular media with posters that encouraged readers to nominate a man they viewed as an everyday hero. Their poster read ' Five in six men want to stop domestic violence. That's an overwhelming majority…We're asking you to give [them] a decisive thumbs up in the form of a poem or letter, the most inspiring to be published in the Cape Argus. Go on, give that man in your life exactly what he deserves. Recognition'. From this call, posted also in supermarkets and on corner stores, Five in Six received 50 000 'everyday hero' nominations. Most often written by women – girlfriends, wives, daughters and sisters – but also by sons and brothers, and usually handwritten on notebook paper, these thousands of pages bore testimony to men who in their everyday lives are seen as allies in the struggle to create a non-violent South Africa. In response, Five in Six staff and volunteers wrote letters congratulating each 'everyday hero', and visited those nominees who lived in or near Cape Town. During these visits, they encouraged men to organise neighbourhood groups and provided these groups with training in the hope that each group would engage in activism to create communities that guarantee safety and justice for women and girls.

Gender, Education and Training Network (GETNET)

GETNET was one of the first training organisations in the voluntary sector to initiate men's gender training. The GETNET training programme aims to enable men to play a positive role in organisational and institutional change. GETNET emphasises that transformation of power relations flows from partnerships between women and men. This organisation continues to play a critical role in promoting dialogue about constructive male involvement through conferences and workshops.

The Men as Partners (MAP) Network

MAP was developed by EngenderHealth and the Planned Parenthood Association (PPA) of South Africa, and is now co-ordinated by EngenderHealth. The MAP Network is made up of nearly 30 member organisations working in most of South Africa's nine provinces. These organisations vary in size and scope. At one end of the spectrum, MAP Network partners include large national organisations such as the AIDS Consortium, Hope Worldwide, PPA, the SAMF, the Solidarity Centre and their trade union partners the Congress of South African Trade Unions (COSATU), the Federation of Unions of South Africa (FEDUSA) and the National Council of Trade Unions (NACTU). At the other end of the spectrum, MAP partners include small, local CBOs and NGOs reaching men, women and youth in communities across Gauteng such as the Youth Channel Group in Tembisa, Sabelani Life Skills in Thokoza, HIVSA based at the Chris Hani-Baragwanath Hospital, and the Township AIDS Project based in Soweto.

Using a variety of strategies, all organisations collaborating with MAP attempt to reduce the spread and impact of HIV/AIDS by encouraging men to take a stand against violence against women and children and to become more involved in HIV/AIDS-related prevention, care and support activities. Across the country, every month thousands of men participate in week-long MAP workshops. These workshops often conclude with men expressing a keen interest in integrating the insights they have gained about their lives and their communities. To ensure that this commitment endures, organisations within the MAP Network provide men with ongoing support and a menu of possible activities for constructive community-based male involvement. Currently the MAP Network is developing an Action Kit to be used by men in local communities as well as exploring a range of sustainable livelihood strategies to keep men involved.

The South African Men's Forum (SAMF)

In 1997 Dr Bongani Khumalo challenged all men in South Africa to 'restore the soul of the nation', out of which the South African Men's Forum was born. During its launch he said, 'the prevailing negative trends in our society, the status of men as a common denominator in crime and violence, and the moral slide away which is threatening the soul of our nation makes it imperative for all of us to get involved as men to be agents of change'. Since its inception, the purpose of the SAMF has been to mobilise and galvanise men and boys to change their mindset about gender roles and to work to bring about equality. The SAMF has a number of programmes focused on redefining men's roles in the family and in broader society. The Fatherhood Project is a collaboration between the South African Men's Forum (SAMF) and the Human Sciences Research Council (HSRC) and it encourages men to play an active role in their children's lives by presenting positive images of men in nurturing roles in relationship to children. The Religious Men's Guilds Project has been established by the SAMF in various churches and seeks to challenge religious stereotypes of men and women's roles by engaging with religious leaders. For example, during activities with churches, men are asked to examine the role of fathers as portrayed by the Bible and to contextualise the important role that fathers in the church should play in bonding emotionally with their children. Similarly, the Shebeen Project hosts monthly men's conversations in shebeens and taverns focusing on a variety of topics, including rape, alcohol and violence. Shebeens have also provided important opportunities to engage men about fatherhood. During shebeen talks, men are challenged to explore their relationships with their children and asked to consider their own relationships with their fathers.

Room for optimism

At the time of writing, a series of domestic violence murders took place in which men killed their entire families and themselves. These serve to remind us how much work still needs to be done with men to end violence against women and children and to secure men's full support for more gender-equitable models of masculinity and fatherhood. At the same time, and despite these tragic killings, the growing numbers of men attending men's marches, celebrations of responsible fatherhood, or quietly playing more involved roles in the lives of their families and children, provides room for optimism. The words of one male gender activist bear witness to the ways in which efforts to redefine men's roles can enrich men's lives:

> I am a casualty of the past. I come from a violent family, a violent society that has impacted [upon] my life. Being involved in this work has helped me to understand what is it that is human [and allowed me] to see the beauty of life, I must say. And it has helped me with my family and my extended family as well – to challenge my grandparents, to challenge my brothers and sisters so they understand the fullness of life. (quoted in Peacock, 2004)

Another male gender activist emphasises similar themes saying:

> I've seen a lot of changes in my personal life. My relationship with my kids prior to this was more of, 'I provide and give you money – that's it! What more do you want?' Today, all of my kids are my friends…That keeps me going! (quoted in Peacock, 2005)

Mbuyiselo Botha works as a General Secretary of the South African Men's Forum (SAMF). Before that he was the Dissemination Officer of the South African Red Cross. This work entailed teaching different institutions, schools, universities, technikons, teacher training colleges, private companies and the general public about the Red Cross. Mbuyiselo studied the International Red Cross/Crescent at the Henry Dunant institute in Geneva, Switzerland. His current work is with men in the area of gender-based violence as a trainer/facilitator on the following topics: masculinity; gender-based violence and its causes; religion and how men and women are portrayed; culture, tradition and women; patriarchy, power/control and dominance; and the socialisation of the boy-child and men.

Dean Peacock has worked in South Africa, the United States and Latin America for the last 11 years to end men's violence and to promote egalitarian, non-abusive models of masculinity that improve the lives of men, women and children and contribute to a more just society. He is the South Africa Programme Manager for EngenderHealth where he co-ordinates the Men as Partners (MAP) Network and also provides ongoing training and technical assistance to a wide range of organisations on the development and implementation of the MAP programme. After working in Washington DC as a co-author of the *Agenda For the Nation to End Violence Against Women*, he developed and co-ordinated the *Building Partnerships Initiative to End Men's Violence*, for the Family Violence Prevention Fund.

Note

1   A gathering of people, usually convened by a traditional authority.

References

Community Agency for Social Enquiry (CASE). (2004). Men as partners: a diagnostic study. Unpublished study, Johannesburg, August.

EngenderHealth (2004). Unpublished report on Father's Day event, held June 2004.

Gelb, S. (2003). *Inequality in South Africa: Nature, causes and responses.* Johannesburg: The Edge Institute.

Gobind, R. (2005). South African men care enough to act against HIV/AIDS. *Agenda,* Special Focus, 144–145.

Peacock, D. (2003). Building on a legacy of social justice activism: Enlisting men as gender justice activists in South Africa. *Journal of Men and Masculinities, 5,* 328.

Peacock, D. (2004). Men as partners: South African men respond to violence against women and HIV/AIDS. A description of accomplishments, challenges and possible next step*s*. Unpublished masters thesis.

Peacock, D. (2005). 'Democratising our relationships': Voices of male gender activists working to promote gender equality in southern Africa: An interview with Rodney Fortuin, Boitshepo Lesetedi, Dumisani Rebombo, Mbuyiselo Botha and Regis Mtutu. In S. Wilson (Ed.) (forthcoming). *Young feminist voices for now and the future? The borders and disorders of the current global order.* London: Zed Books.

Peacock, D., & Levack, A. (2004). The Men as Partners Program in South Africa: Reaching men to end gender based violence and promote sexual and reproductive health. *International Journal of Men's Health, 3,* 178.

Pettifor, A., Rees, H., & Stevens, A. (2004). *HIV and sexual behaviour among young South Africans: A national survey of 15–24 year olds.* Johannesburg: Wits University Press.

President Thabo Mbeki's inaugural speech, 27 April 2004. Available at: www.gov.za (accessed July 2004).

CHAPTER 23

The child's right to shared parenting

Patrice Engle, Tom Beardshaw, Craig R. Loftin

In a highland village in Peru, an extra bench in the antenatal clinic means that the father comes with his wife to her check-up and, as a result, he makes sure that his wife takes her iron tablets. Women in the village look with pleasure at a photograph on a poster, taken in their village, in which a man places his hand affectionately on his wife's pregnant belly – sending the message that he cares. In Honduras, a father finds out that his unborn child responds differently to his voice compared to the voice of a stranger – his child already recognises him!

These are small changes that encourage fathers and other men to be more involved with their young children. Fathers can be involved in all phases of parenting, but it requires effort, commitment and opportunity. These efforts must also incorporate strategies to increase gender equality, women's autonomy and, at the same time, respect gender differences in the expectations for fathering behaviour. In this chapter, we briefly review recent research on the importance of fathers for children, discuss child rights, and describe the United Nations Children's Fund (UNICEF's) history of programming for fathers as well as current efforts by two groups – Fathers Direct in the United Kingdom and UNICEF – to develop programmes that recognise that men make a difference in the lives of children.

The impact of fathers on children

The role of men in families and as fathers has appeared in reference to gender equity, reproductive health, HIV/AIDS, childcare and child welfare debates. This trend is likely to continue as social and economic changes around the world focus attention on fatherhood. The increasing numbers of women working outside the home, changes in the structure of employment, a growing awareness of the impact fathers and father-figures have on child development, and the numbers of fathers who live away from their children, mean that fatherhood is likely to be of increasing concern in coming years.

For most children, the presence or involvement of a father or father-figure in their lives has a positive effect on their life chances, educational outcomes, health and physical, emotional and cognitive development (see for example, Lamb & Lewis, 2004). Father involvement is associated with children developing higher-level cognitive skills in the early years, being more sociable with their peers and adults, less stressed and anxious, and better adjusted. Macro-analyses of studies that track paternal influence on children show that the quality of father–child relationships is positively associated with a range of measures of child outcomes, including educational attainment, levels of criminal behaviour and substance abuse and long-term measures of psychosocial well-being such as feelings of satisfaction in adult children's spousal relationships and self-reported parenting skills (see also Chapter 5, this volume).

Men, in their role as fathers, often hold decision-making power and resource control over the wellbeing of children. Despite this, interventions to promote children's health and wellbeing continue to target solely women who may have no authority to put these recommendations into practice. In one state in India, about 20 per cent of fathers made the decision about when their children would get their first food, yet all of the available nutritional messages are directed toward women. Fathers make decisions about what girls can do, how much freedom they have, and whether they can go to school.

But it is not the mere presence of the father in the household that counts. The nature of the relationship between a man and his children is often more important. Many studies show that income in the hands of women is more likely to be used for imme-diate child wellbeing than is income in the hands of men. However, where men do contribute to their children's care and education, their children do better than those who play little or no role in their children's upbringing. (Engle, 1995b). The same effect is found when fathers become closely involved with their children. For example, fathers who live apart from their children but see them frequently tend to contribute more resources to their upbringing than less involved dads, both in terms of the provi-sion of food, clothing and other materials bought for the children, as well as through the contribution of child maintenance paid to mothers (Graham & Beller, 2002).

Biological fathers are not the only men important to children. In many countries and cultures, grandfathers, uncles and older brothers are important father-figures.

Good fathering: the child's right and the state's obligation

Is the experience of knowing a father a child's right? In 1989 the Convention on the Rights of the Child (CRC) proclaimed that every child has the right to know and be cared for by his or her parents (Article 7). States have the obligation to recognise that both parents have common responsibilities for the upbringing and development of the child (Article 18) and to 'render appropriate assistance to parents and legal guardians in the performance of their child-rearing responsibilities'. It would seem reasonable that this obligation would extend to ensuring the child's right to have both parents responsible for his or her care.

How well has the commitment to shared parenting been supported by government action? In general, not well at all. Some countries have tried to support fatherhood and promote a culture of shared responsibility for children between men and women by focusing on systems of parental leave. In many European countries maternity leave can be taken by either men or women. The uptake of this provision is variable, depending on downstream support and commitment by government, employers and families (see Chapter 17, this volume). While there have been a number of projects working within government and non-government services to deliver information and support to fathers as well as mothers, there has been little sustained effort by states to strategically reform national institutional programmes that deliver support to families. This remains largely targeted at mothers only.

In March 2004, the Commission on the Status of Women made a strong statement in support of men's roles not only in achieving gender equality but also in supporting children's growth and development:

> The Commission on the Status of Women recalls and reiterates that the Beijing Declaration and Platform for Action encouraged men to participate fully in all actions towards gender equality and urged the establishment of the principle of shared power and responsibility between women and men at home, in the community, in the workplace and in the wider national and international communities. The Commission also recalls and reiterates the outcome document adopted at the twenty-third special session of the General Assembly entitled 'Gender equality, development and peace in the twenty-first century' which emphasised that men must take joint responsibility with women for the promotion of gender equality.

The Commission urges governments, organisations, civil society and the UN system to take the following actions regarding men's roles as fathers:
- Create and improve training and education programmes to enhance awareness and knowledge among men and women on their roles as parents, legal guardians and caregivers and the importance of sharing family responsibilities, and include fathers as well as mothers in programmes that teach infant childcare development;
- Develop and include in education programmes for parents, legal guardians and other caregivers' information on ways and means to increase the capacity of men to raise children in a manner oriented towards gender equality.

The Commission also recognises that the participation of men and boys in achieving gender equality must be consistent with the empowerment of women and girls and acknowledges that efforts must be made to address the undervaluing of many types of work, abilities and roles associated with women. In this regard, it is important that resources for gender equality initiatives for men and boys do not compromise equal opportunities and resources for women and girls. (Commission on the Status of Women, 2004)

It is also important to recognise that domestic violence and child abuse make homes dangerous places for millions of women and children. In addition to supporting men's involvement with children, there must be an effort to protect women and children and, when there is no other recourse, to assist them in leaving negative relationships with abusive men.

What do we know about how to reach fathers?

Given the importance of men for children's health and wellbeing, how can fathers be reached and included in programmes to promote children's development? Some answers to this question emerged from the International Fatherhood Summit (IFS) which was hosted by Fathers Direct at Christ Church, Oxford, in the United Kingdom during March 2003. The IFS brought together specialists working on fatherhood issues in the UK, Mexico, Brazil, New Zealand, Jamaica, Australia, USA, Sweden, Egypt, Israel, Turkey, Russia, Netherlands, South Africa, Cameroon, Chile, Belgium, Peru and India.[1]

The conference concluded that despite an increasing worldwide focus on men in families, and a strong research base confirming the positive outcomes of father-involvement for children, politicians and policymakers have been slow to recognise the effects of a wide range of public institutions and policy on fathering. In many countries, and from many different perspectives, ad hoc attempts are currently being made to develop policy approaches to encourage fathers' greater participation and investment in the care, health and education of their children. Further work is needed to develop and evaluate these efforts, and to increase the impact of multiple public policy measures on men as fathers.

The past decade has seen the emergence of expertise and best practices to support father–child relationships. This work has usually been embedded in mainstream programmes to enhance outcomes for children, women and families. However, most of this work is poorly funded and has operated at the margins of mainstream services, rather than as part of an integrated strategy to support father–child relationships. Nevertheless, there is a growing body of practice that shows great promise in encouraging men to engage positively with their children, and for improving outcomes for child development and gender equity.

Programmes around the world that have made conscious efforts to support father involvement include reproductive health and teen pregnancy prevention, broad-based peri-natal services for children, infant and child health and nutrition, early years services, parenting education, and employment programmes that support men's relationships with their children. There is an increasing emphasis on involving fathers in children's learning (for example, in schools) and on working with the fathers of young offenders. Increasingly, domestic violence and substance abuse programmes are recognising the value of engaging men in their parenting role. There has been a lot of work with fathers in prison (which is beginning to extend to the resettlement of offenders), as well as work with refugee fathers and some resettlement support for fathers returning from war. Children who are living apart from their fathers (due to separation or divorce, migrant work or war) are seen as a particularly high-need group.

This work, carried out internationally by a growing body of practitioners, demonstrates that there are benefits for children, women, men and society if community support is also offered to fathers as they engage in the important work of child-rearing alongside mothers. There is great potential to be realised by programmes incorporating the role of fathers into strategic planning processes and implementation, where fathers in families influence the health, education and protection of children.

The technical expertise for helping agencies to develop strategies to engage fathers and the training and resources that are often a necessary part of this strategic change, is emerging in many parts of the world. Very often, what is needed is relatively inexpensive adjustment to mainstream practice, rather than dedicated service streams.

In the UK, Fathers Direct has published *Working with fathers: A guide for everyone working with families* (Burgess & Bartlett, 2004). This organisation, along with others in the UK, USA, Caribbean, Latin America and Europe, offers training and strategic development in father-friendly practice. Attempts to influence professional training (for example, for social workers and midwives) have begun and, in the United States, the first textbook about working with fathers, developed for students working with young children and their families, has been published (Fagan & Palm, 2004).

One example of how these changes might be realised across the broad range of social programmes and policies that influence fathering behaviour, comes from the organisers of the Oxford Summit, Fathers Direct (UK), which in 2004 launched 'The Charter for Father Friendly Britain'.

The Charter promotes policies, services and practices that support the active engagement of fathers in caring for children. It is working in partnership with the national government and UK-based NGOs in maternity services, schools, business and employment, child protection programmes, domestic violence services, prisons and youth offending teams, youth services, mental health services and social services supporting separated families. Working groups in each sector are developing practical tools for change (benchmarks, audit tools, core skill specifications, specialised training), publicly promoting good practice, and developing a policy framework that articulates both the changes required within individual sectors and an overarching policy narrative on active fatherhood.

How do we put this into practice? UNICEF's history of work with men in families

Prior to 1994, the International Year of the Family, UNICEF had not played a major role in supporting fathering. Even the well-known UNICEF logo, often interpreted as a mother–child dyad, seemed to suggest that the father was not a major focus of the agency's work. But this has changed during the last decade.

A series of conferences and papers have outlined the major issues related to men in families from 1993 to 1997, including a report on families with the Population Council (Bruce, Lloyd, & Leonard, 1995), an Innocenti Seminar in 1995 (Engle, 1995a; Richardson, 1995); and a major publication in 1997 – *The role of men in the lives of children* (UNICEF, 1997). These seminars and publications identified the critical contribution that men (including uncles, grandparents and other relatives) can make to the lives of children, and emphasise that men and not just 'fathers' should be the focus of programmatic and policy work. These meetings also developed strategies to help men develop their skills and esteem for domestic activities so that they can ease the double burden of work that women and girls are facing. 'It is necessary to identify strategies that will help people to view sharing in domestic work as a positive component of masculinity' (UNICEF, 1997).

In the last eight years, UNICEF's focus has turned to the family as a whole, focusing on strengthening families' roles in the care and support of their children. Fathers are seen as critical but activities have not specifically targeted them. Nonetheless, many UNICEF country offices have developed approaches to increasing the involvement of fathers. The following data come from the annual Country Office 2002 and 2003 reports that summarise the activities of each of the 126 offices of UNICEF in developing countries in seven regions around the world.

Supporting the role of men and fathers in parenting

UNICEF and its government and civil society partners support parenting programmes in 73 of the 158 countries with which it works. Examples include groups of parents going through the *Better Parenting Initiative* materials in the Middle Eastern and Central European region; the parenting component of pre-school and community-based childcare centres (Cameroon, Nepal, Romania, FYR Macedonia, Ghana, Burundi, Burkina Faso, Myanmar); and media approaches (TV spots in Tunisia, phone hot-line counselling in Yugoslavia, using mass media in Vietnam, Bangladesh, Maldives, and South Africa, and radio spots in Chile). Nepal works through women's income generation projects to provide parenting information and support, and Bolivia uses literacy classes.

In 2002, ten countries reported activities to enhance the role of fathers in children's care. This number increased dramatically in 2003 when 28 countries reported activities specifically focusing on fathers. Of these, 11 have been collecting data in order to understand and develop strategies for increasing the role of fathers; 17 have developed programmes, and of these, seven already have some evaluation data.

Namibia, Bangladesh, and Togo have collected data to find ways to increase men's participation. El Salvador, Guyana, the Gambia, Lebanon, South Africa, Chile, and Jamaica are using surveys, focus groups, previous experience, and networks to develop strategies for reaching fathers. Although most countries report difficulties in getting men involved, in two countries fathers have demanded a more active role. In the Caribbean region, fathers sought more active roles in childcare but said that they were constrained by non-father-friendly services and by women's attitudes; and in Bosnia and Herzegovina, fathers-to-be wanted to be included in pregnancy classes (and they were).

A variety of approaches have been used to increase fathers' roles. In Costa Rica, all children are ensured the right to recognition and support from their fathers. A paternity law has been enacted requiring a man to submit to DNA testing or to publicly acknowledge his parental role if a child's mother has named him as father. Similar statutes are being explored in other countries in the region. Nicaragua, Belarus, Bolivia, Macedonia, and Jordan developed strategies to increase men's roles in parent education and support programmes. In Vietnam communications media have been developed to reinforce the 'positive deviant' practices of male caregivers from specific ethnic groups and to use these men as spokespersons and advocates. The Maldives has held workshops for fathers who were separated from their children due to work, and Sri Lanka has worked with 30,000 families with migrant worker mothers and where fathers take care of their children. In several countries interventions focused on fathers: for birth registration in Benin and Bolivia, pregnancy classes in Bosnia and Hercegovina, for infant and young child feeding in Honduras and Ghana, and to help girls enter and stay in school in Uruguay and the Maldives. Guyana used Father's Day to highlight children's issues, Panama encouraged the government to support a Responsible Parenthood law, Albania created fathers' boards in local areas to support local government in early childhood development, and Bolivia used male adult literacy classes to teach parenting.

In the Gambia, a community-based programme to increase breastfeeding set up teams of eight in each community to work with breastfeeding women to support exclusive breastfeeding for six months. The team, which initially consisted of women only, is now comprised of almost 50 per cent men, including community leaders, fathers and health workers. These men are given training and are well informed about the benefits of breastfeeding. The programme is highly successful, and now these men acknowledge some of the additional benefits of breastfeeding, such as fewer trips to the health clinic for the child, for example (National Nutrition Agency, 2003).

Getting men involved with young children, particularly in patriarchal systems, has been a challenge right across the board. Exceptions were the parenting classes in the Maldives, in which attendance was twice that expected. Based on focus group research, Jordan developed strategies to involve men, such as designing shorter modules specifically for men, and specific to their role.

In six countries, significant changes in fathers' behaviour were observed, and these changes seem to have had positive impacts on children. In Malawi, in nine districts, a community-based Integrated Management of Childhood Illnesses (IMCI) programme that stressed the role of men in supporting children's survival, growth and development (including encouraging men to make toys for their children), resulted in a significant change in fathers' reported involvement with young children. Infant and young child feeding practices in Ghana improved significantly, in part because fathers as well as mothers were the targets of the communication strategy. In Honduras, the Integrated Early Childhood Development (IECD) interventions targeted heads of families, and the result was strong father involvement. The impact on children of such initiatives has not yet been measured. In the Maldives, the father orientation and communications campaign resulted in reports of an increase in the success of girls attending school as well as greater involvement and improved communication of those fathers living apart from their young children.

The Life Start programme, a community-based early learning programme, reached 10,000 families in Macedonia and increased men's involvement in their children's care. The evaluation of this programme showed that children's entry and performance in the first grade was significantly better than that of other children who had not participated in any other early childhood programme. Mothers gained knowledge and improved parenting skills and became more confident and involved in the decision-making processes concerning their children (their status and participation in family and community life also improved). Families as a whole benefited from the greater involvement of all family members, especially fathers, in raising their children. The wider community became more aware of and empowered in influencing decisions and taking actions related to issues of common concern. Success was predominantly attributed to the project's roots in the community, and with the close support of local NGOs and authorities.

In the Philippines, the ERPAT (Empowerment and Re-affirmation of Paternal Abilities) programme aims to engage fathers to become effective and responsive. It emphasises fathers' paternal roles, responsibilities and abilities. It aims to achieve shared parenting tasks in the performance of familial responsibilities (UNICEF, 2003). Under the guidance of the Department of Social Welfare and Development, and with the support of UNICEF, ERPAT develops father–leaders in each *baranguay*.[2] ERPAT was initiated in 1995 in response to the non-involvement of men in parenting, and it has since been through several revisions. The programme is popular and is expanding.

In Peru, the Buen Inicio programme aims to improve ante-natal care, child nutrition and development in the four poorest districts of the country, where economic disparities are extreme and often linked with cultural differences. Nutrition indicators and practices improved in four marginalised districts as a result of community interaction, dialogue and improved integrated training of the health-care workers.

Effect indicators include improved access to quality services for pregnant women and children, exclusive and continued breastfeeding, complementary feeding and psycho-affective practices at the family and community level, and the father's participation in care for women and children (UNICEF, 2003).

In addition to improving health services, the Peru programme sought to empower parents to recognise that there were things that they could do to improve the life chances of their children, even without additional funds – such as breastfeeding or improving the learning environment for the child. Increasing the involvement of fathers in ante-natal care, and taking children for growth and development monitoring, were two goals of the programme.

Although the father attendance rates were still low (for example, 8–14 percent of pregnant women had husbands attend the clinic with them), the rate increased significantly, as did children's birth weights. One explanation for this change was that the father and other family members helped the pregnant woman care for herself during pregnancy (by resting, trying to eat healthily, and taking iron supplements). The project also relied heavily on the support of local authorities and health promoters, who were usually men.

UNICEF Brazil, in conjunction with the government, created a set of goals and materials for strengthening 'family competencies'. In supporting and strengthening the capacity of families to provide holistic, integral care to their young children, the office identified core family competencies applicable to all Brazilian families in a collaborative process that took 18 months. The 28 identified competencies were validated through existing international research on family care practices that promote children's survival, development, protection and participation.

The competencies can be loosely organised into three categories: interacting directly with the child; organising the family to care and advocate for the young child, and strengthening family interactions with and promoting the organisation of services to care for the integral needs of the young child. The family competencies were then translated into an interactive kit for families entitled *Strengthening Brazilian families: Unifying actions for integrated early childhood development*. This kit was developed during 2003 in collaboration with 29 key partners (government, NGOs, and UN agencies).[3] It did not focus specifically on fathers, but rather on the family context for care.

Conclusions

Fathers are a critical resource for children. Many fathers are the primary source of financial support for their children, but they are also an important resource in other ways – through the time and skills they bring into the household, through the support they provide to mothers, through their social networks (friends, workmates and extended family). Fathers can protect and educate their children, play with and care for them, tell them stories, help them settle to sleep, worry about them every day, and love them for life. Fathers' involvement and investment is one of the greatest yet most under-utilised sources of support available to children in our world today. A child whose father does not take on the responsibilities of father-hood, for reasons in or out of his or her control, suffers a resource deficit that is often irreplaceable. The father also experiences the loss with as yet unassessed decrements in health and social participation.

We know something about how to involve men in the care of children, but we need to learn to do it better and the programmes need to expand. Getting fathers involved requires commitment and expertise from those involved in service design, as well as innovative policies. Practitioners need education and support, clear strategic direction, backup from managers, a knowledge base of research on fathers in their locality, resources for programmes and sometimes training to develop the skills necessary for engaging fathers and developing sensitivity to their needs. Network support for those involved in this field to reduce isolation, spread good practice and avoid 'reinventing the wheel' is a priority. Small regional networks of practitioners are developing, and bodies that support national networks are being formed. A logical next step would be to establish a small international network capable of spreading good practice and linking activists in the field with each other.

As the Commission for the Status of Women noted, these actions must not under-mine gender equality nor devalue the activities of girls and women. These efforts must also continue to protect women and children from the abuse – physical, sexual, and emotional – that many experience in the home at the hands of men.

The barriers to fathers becoming involved, confident and competent as parents are manifold. These barriers exist within institutions and in virtually all policies that impact on family life. Gender stereotypes of fathers as uninterested, uncaring and incapable are reflected in the practices of institutions such as health and education programmes that target only mothers, even when fathers are present and active in their children's lives and are making key decisions affecting children's futures. Developing strategies to include fathers in such programmes, as recommended by the Commission on the Status of Women, constitutes a vital first step in maximising the potential of fathers to improve the lives of children and to promote the sharing of responsibility for children between mothers and fathers. It is not always easy to reach fathers and men in families, but innovative strategies, such as using sport, religious leaders and the military, can work. Where it has worked, the pay-off for children is substantial.

Stereotypical images and behaviours of masculinity and culturally-defined roles within the family structure are obstacles to change. But, as evidenced from work in several UNICEF Country Offices including South Africa, the Maldives, Vietnam and Bangladesh, redefining 'masculinity' and demonstrating to men how their children benefit from their positive involvement and nurturing can have an impact.

Shared parenting is a child's right, and countries need to do more to ensure that this right is fulfilled for every child. The Commission on the Status of Women has recommended that countries do their best to support men's roles in gender equity and care for children, at the same time that they empower women. Countries can move forward by supporting specific actions like those described in this chapter that will, on the one hand, provide men with more opportunities for caring for their children and, on the other hand, support gender equality in the home, community, and society.

Tom Beardshaw is Network Director of Fathers Direct in the United Kingdom. He trained in Social Anthropology at the London School of Economics, and in Social Ethics at Cardiff University in Wales. He writes and speaks extensively on fatherhood and public policy, runs Fathers Direct's website, leads their international work and co-ordinates Europe's largest conference on fatherhood – 'Working with Fathers', which takes place annually in London. He is the father of two sons: Bonga, who lives in the Natal Midlands in South Africa, and Cole, who lives with Tom in Cardiff, in the United Kingdom.

Patrice Engle is Senior Adviser for Early Childhood Development at UNICEF in New York. She was chief of Nutrition and Child Development in India for UNICEF, and prior to that, was professor of psychology and child development at Cal Poly State University in San Luis Obsipo, California. She is a developmental psychologist specialising in the relationships between nutrition and development. Her research includes the impact of women's work on child outcomes, the role of men in families, and the psychological context of feeding in malnourished populations. She has consulted for WHO and the World Bank, and received her PhD from Stanford University.

Craig Loftin is a Senior Programme Officer at UNICEF's headquarters in New York where he is concentrating on establishing a new area, the Large Child Population Country Initiative – Every Child Counts. He has promoted fathers' involvement in the lives of their children as a means of achieving mutually beneficial outcomes since the mid-1970s when he was the director of the Home Start Training Center for the Administration of Children, Youth and Families (ACYF) Region V in the United States. After completing his PhD in psychology from Utah State University, he spent 16 years working with international organisations throughout Latin America, most recently as UNICEF's Deputy Representative for Brazil.

Notes

1   The full report from the International Fatherhood Summit ('Supporting Fathers') is available from the website of the Bernard Van Leer Foundation (www.bernardvanleer.org).

2   Small village.

3   This kit can be viewed electronically at http://64.233.179.104/search?q=cache:g3I7kg3XQtsJ:www.unicef.org/childfamily/files/JoeJu ddFamily_presentation_on_Dec_6.doc+Strengthening+Brazilian+families&hl=en (accessed May 2004).

References

Bruce, J., Lloyd, C. B., & Leonard, A. with Engle, P. L., & Duffy, N. (1995). *Families in focus: New perspectives on mothers, fathers and children*. New York: Population Council (also published in Spanish in 1998).

Burgess, A., & Bartlett, D. (2004). *Working with fathers: A guide for everyone working with families*. London: Fathers Direct.

Commission on the Status of Women. (2004). *Agreed conclusions on the role of men and boys in achieving gender equality*. New York: United Nations.

Engle, P. L. (1995a). *Men in families: Report of a consultation on the role of males and fathers in achieving gender equity*. Evaluation and Research Conference Reports. New York: UNICEF.

Engle, P. L. (1995b). Mother's money, father's money, and parental commitment: Guatemala & Nicaragua. In R. Blumberg, C. A. Rakowski, I. Tinker & M. Monteón (Eds.), *Engendering wealth and well being* (pp. 155–180). Boulder, Colorado: Westview.

Engle, P., & Breaux, C. (1998). Fathers' responsibility for children: A cross-cultural perspective. *Social Policy Report of the Society for Research in Child Development, 12*, 1–23.

Fagan, J., & Palm, G. (2004). *Fathers and early childhood programs*. New York: Delmar.

Graham, J., & Beller, A. (2002). Nonresident fathers and their children: Child support and visitation from an economic perspective. In C. Tamis-LeMonda & N. Cabrera (Eds.), *Handbook of father involvement: Multidisciplinary perspectives* (pp. 431–459). New York: Lawrence Erlbaum.

Lamb, M., & Lewis, C. (2004). Fathers: The research perspective. In *Supporting fathers: Contributions from the international fatherhood summit*. The Hague: Bernard Van Leer Foundation.

National Nutrition Agency (Gambia). (2003). *The baby-friendly community initiative: An expanded vision for integrated early childhood development in the Gambia*. Banjul, Gambia: National Nutrition Agency.

Richardson, J. (1995). Achieving gender equality in families: The role of males. *Innocenti Global Seminar Report*. Florence: UNICEF Innocenti Research Centre.

UNICEF. (1997). *The role of men in the lives of children: A study of how improving knowledge about men in families helps strengthen programming for children and women.* New York: UNICEF.

UNICEF. (2003). ERPAT: *A manual for implementers and father-volunteers.* Manila: Department of Social Welfare and Development with UNICEF. Electronic version available at http://www.acpf.org/WC7th/PapersItem5/PpPhilippinesBalanonItem5.htm (accessed May 2004).

UNICEF. (2003). *Noveno informe de progreso: Cooperation UNICEF–USAID.* Lima: UNICEF.

CHAPTER 24

Taking forward work with men in families

Tom Beardshaw

The ideas set out in this chapter derive from discussions held by the leading international researchers and practitioners in the fatherhood field, and are based on an analysis of the current state of work and the needs of the field. Suggestions for taking forward work with men in families are outlined in three main areas: research, policy and programmes.

Research

There are a number of substantial gaps in the international research literature on fatherhood and men's roles in families. In particular, there is a lack of data from the majority-world countries and almost all studies of fatherhood have concentrated on white, middle-class North American, European and Australasian families, with a few exceptions (including a recent increase in research from Latin America and the Caribbean).

There is a desperate need for further research in Africa, the Middle East and Asia, where data on fathers are almost non-existent. Fathers in these areas have remained largely invisible on researchers' agendas; moreover they have not featured on the budgets of research funders. There are four major areas of work in the research field that should be undertaken:

Demographic studies

Demographic studies of men in families would assist in helping substitute hard data for speculative assumptions, particularly for those parts of the world that remain understudied. To further develop the understanding of factors which bear on the diversity of patterns observed among and within nations around the world, researchers need to record basic information such as:
- The longevity and fertility of fathers;
- Union status and co-residential patterns;
- Religious, ethnic and intra-national differences; and
- Socio-economic factors, employment and poverty statistics.

National and regional case studies

National and regional case studies are necessary to provide more detailed analyses of fathering behaviour within a given country or region and of the impact of fathering roles on areas of particular national, regional and international concern. For example:

- The impacts of taxation, benefits, childcare and parental leave regimes on family decision-making about the division of labour between mothers and fathers;
- The roles of fathers in influencing reproductive health outcomes for women and infants;
- The roles of fathers in influencing children's health outcomes;
- The roles of fathers in influencing education outcomes for their children;
- The impact of HIV/AIDS on fathering roles and responsibilities;
- The impact of labour market policies and workplace cultures on the accessibility of flexible 'family-friendly' work for men and women, and the degree to which they provide incentives for stereotyped or equitable gender relations;
- Explorations of the diversity of men's thoughts and aspirations in relation to their children and partners to develop greater understanding of what motivates men in families;
- Research on children's perceptions of their fathers and their aspirations for their relationship with their fathers;
- Documentation of 'fair families', which have adopted more equal models of family responsibilities, and the conditions that have influenced them;
- Research on the roles of men in decision-making about family members' access to education opportunities, health services, transport, finance, and so on;
- Time-use surveys documenting the use of time by fathers and mothers across domestic, caring, leisure and working activities;
- Research on the impact of policies and legislation related to paternity recognition, divorce, separation, contact and child support on child–father relationships;
- An analysis of professional and vocational training for social and health care staff to assess how 'father-friendly' it is;
- The impact of fathering behaviours on attitudes towards gender among their children; and
- Longitudinal studies of fathering across the family cycle, measuring changes in fathering attitudes and behaviour across generations, and the transmission of fathering skills and ideas.

Cross-cultural studies

We need cross-cultural thematic studies that make use of international, regional and national data to explore the impact of patterns of father involvement, divorce, separation, new partners/step-parents, social fathers and father absence (as well as policies and programmes that affect these variables) on:

- Opportunities and constraints for women to engage in paid employment and public life;
- Opportunities and constraints for men to be involved in the lives of their children;
- The impact of fathering behaviour on women's health and reproductive health, in particular;
- The impact of men's roles in families, including their caring for children, on the health of their infants and children;
- The influence that fathers have on the education of their children;
- The influence of fathers on the attitudes of their children towards gender; and
- Changes in fathering attitudes and behaviour over time and across generations.

Dissemination of research

Research needs to be disseminated to promote greater understanding of research on fathering by national and international policymakers and programme planners:
- Support should be given to efforts by the international community of researchers and other actors in the fatherhood field to develop an international network with research-disseminating capacity;
- There should be a series of international technical workshops/conferences to present the latest research findings on the relationships between men's roles in families and:
  - child development;
  - labour market, taxation, benefits, childcare and parental leave policies;
  - women's health, including reproductive health;
  - children's education;
  - infant and children's health;
  - gender equality within families; and
  - policies on paternity recognition, divorce and separation, contact and child support.

Policy

In recent years, there have been moves in a number of countries to develop policies that seek to encourage the active participation of fathers in domestic and family life. Lessons have been, and are continuing to be, learnt about what is effective in strengthening fatherhood within a gender-equitable policy framework. Recommendations are made in five major areas of national policymaking, namely: the labour market, education, health, family law and social services.

Labour market

Taxation, benefits, employment, childcare and parental leave regimes influence the gender distribution of labour within the economy, and household decision-making affects the employment and caring opportunities of men and women. Imbalances within labour markets, such as the existence of a pay gap between men and women, restrict women's opportunities in paid employment, and also men's opportunities to engage in domestic and caring activities. To create real opportunities for involved fatherhood, countries should:

- Seek to base their taxation, benefits, employment, childcare and parental leave systems on the principle that both fathers and mothers are jointly responsible for children's economic, physical, cognitive, social and developmental wellbeing;
- Ensure that women are not disadvantaged in the labour market by the incentives that influence families' decision-making as a result of the balance of taxation, benefits, employment, childcare and parental leave regimes;
- Use legislation, regulatory authority and wage bargaining to reduce income inequality between men and women;
- Introduce or expand childcare and parental leave policies, providing for both men and women in such a way as to reflect the diversity of aspirations of men and women and ensuring that women's opportunities in the labour market are not damaged and men's opportunities to care for their children are not restricted;
- Develop family-friendly employment policies that acknowledge the diversity of working practices to which men and women aspire;
- Use promotion policies, leadership, flexible working practices and anti-discrimination laws to support the development of workplace cultures that enable men to share domestic work and care responsibilities with their partners;
- Develop and use gender-sensitive policies in the informal economy to promote men and women's opportunities for both domestic/care work and employment.

Education

Education policies have the potential to influence young people's thinking about the roles of mothers and fathers and, in many countries, fathers are critical decision-makers about which family members receive the benefits of education services. Fathers' direct involvement and support of children's education work can also bring benefits to a child's education achievement. National goverments should:

- Develop national education programmes for children that promote the sharing of working, domestic and caring responsibilities between men and women for future generations;
- Develop curricula that include a consideration of men's potential as carers to complement work on women's potential in public life, as part of efforts designed to reduce gender role stereotyping; and

- Portray the diversity of fatherhood, including fathers as responsible and active participants in their children's lives, in all relevant parts of the curriculum. For example, if sex education is offered for boys, this should include substantial reflections on fatherhood, and if childcare and parenting skills are part of the curriculum, both boys and girls should be encouraged to actively participate in these classes. If not, we must look for ways to include these skills in the curriculum.

Programmes aimed at increasing the levels of participation in education (for example, girls' access to education) should build on research to develop appropriate strategies that help strengthen the commitment of fathers to all of their children's education.

Education policies should assume that mothers and fathers have equal responsibility for their children's education and recognise that they both have the potential to influence educational outcomes for both sons and daughters. This needs to be reflected in the training of all staff involved in schools, and in the ways in which relationships are established with parents. Schools need to:

- Develop policies and practices that enable education staff to recognise the barriers to fathers being actively involved and develop appropriate engagement techniques, for example, for homework, meetings with teachers, attendance at school functions and activities;
- Include both fathers and mothers, where possible, in all communications with parents; and
- Inform fathers and mothers of the value of their involvement in their children's education (both informally, at home; and formally, at school).

Adult education policies should recognise that involving fathers in their children's education can be a route into further education for fathers. For teenage fathers with low educational attainment, education and training should be a particular focus.

Health

Health policies have a profound impact on fathering behaviour, primarily through the degree of inclusion or exclusion of expectant fathers from maternity (pre-natal, birth and post-natal) services. This communicates powerful messages to fathers about society's expectations of fathering behaviour. Fathers also affect health outcomes for family members, often by virtue of their role in family decision-making about access to healthy diets and health services. Including fathers in health policy thinking has the potential to improve health outcomes for children, mothers and fathers. Health policies should:

- Recognise the influence of men's roles in families in affecting health outcomes for mothers, fathers and children.

- Include men in pre- and post-natal services to encourage greater levels of father involvement and improve health outcomes for infants and mothers. The birth of a child is often the best opportunity to engage with fathers. At this time, fathers are usually physically available to health services, and have strong aspirations for their role as a father, their child and their family. The development of practices within mainstream services that support and inform men about child and maternal welfare during pregnancy and birth, and the optimal roles for fathers, can have a huge impact on family outcomes.

- Include men in strategies to promote breastfeeding, to educate and inform them about the advantages of breastfeeding and provide information and skills to enable them to support their partners.

- Include fathers in programmes to deliver health benefits to children to ensure that fathers as well as mothers receive information about infant care, hygiene, disease prevention, recognition and treatment, dehydration, diet and nutrition, access to health services, and other information that all parents need in order to take responsibility for their children's health.

- Communicate to men in families the importance of women's access to health services, especially in areas where men influence women's access to transport, finance, etc. Practice should be developed to ensure there is communication with men as well as women about the benefits of health services, and that men are engaged in dialogue to explore and resolve any barriers to women's access to health services.

- Address fathers' physical and mental health, and health behaviours (for example, smoking, diet, sexual activity), as these can impact profoundly on their partners', babies' and children's wellbeing. Health policies that focus specifically on men as fathers are needed to ensure this issue is addressed effectively.

- Include fathers in policies and practices relating to post-natal depression: men may contribute to the development or persistence of depression in their partners. Alternatively, they may provide valuable support in its treatment. Research indicates that some men also experience post-natal depression, which can impact on their partner's mental health.

- Develop specific strategies to support men as the primary carers of children in areas where they take on such roles (especially in areas of high levels of HIV/AIDS infection – areas with high levels of maternal mortality).

- Emphasise the development of policies to support couple relationships and marriage (for example, by giving funding priority to agencies that develop creative ways to engage men in this process – men traditionally are less likely to access relationship education or therapeutic services). The quality of the couple relationship is central to parents' physical and mental health and wellbeing, and also to the health and wellbeing of their offspring.

- Ensure that men are fully informed about methods for avoiding HIV/AIDS transmission.

Family law

Family law and the institutions that implement the law have a powerful influence on the level of involvement and responsibility that fathers have in their children's lives, particularly when the parents of a child separate or divorce. Family law in this area needs to be clearly based on the twin aspirations of guaranteeing children's rights and achieving gender equality. Family law should:

- Institute clear systems for paternity recognition within birth registration systems;
- Ensure that a child's right to know and be cared for by both parents is protected as far as possible, regardless of the age, sex, economic or political status, union status, ethnic or religious background of his or her parents;
- Conduct a review of agencies that have contact with families experiencing stress and relationship breakdown, in order to find ways of ensuring that the best interest of the child is kept in mind at all times, and to balance the interests of both parents;
- Provide support, wherever possible, for a child's relationship with his or her biological father while at the same time supporting positive relationships with stepfathers and other father-figures;
- Develop culturally-appropriate systemic interventions in families with dependent children, to provide active support for child–mother, child–father and mother–father relationships at regular intervals;
- Continue this support after family breakdown, particularly at key transition points (for example, geographical relocation; re-partnering; birth of half-siblings);
- Institute and develop appropriate child maintenance collection regimes;
- Develop systems for identifying parents in the process of separating early on, perhaps via school, welfare or child maintenance 'entry points', and provide information, counselling and/or mediation services;
- Develop systems to 'fast track' the examination of cases where violence or child abuse is proven or alleged and ensure family and relationship repair as the case unfolds;
- Provide appropriate accommodation for family members fleeing violence within the family;
- Seek to identify and support the child's 'community' – that is, supportive relationships with extended family members, friends, parents of friends, community leaders or workers, and other relevant professionals;
- Support parents in practical and emotional terms to devise post-separation parenting routines (including appropriate housing in nearby locations) that will optimise the chances of children spending substantial quality time in both parents' households;
- Recognise that children's relationships with the parent that they do not live with may need particular support at this time;

- Develop systems for immediate intervention when a parent is not maintaining contact as promised, or is being prevented from seeing his or her child;
- Draft the primary legislation in such a way that the expectation of substantial parenting time with both parents after separation or divorce is made clear, and cannot be easily compromised;
- Develop and operate 'parenting time' guidelines for children of different ages, who have parents living in different households.

Social services

Services for vulnerable children, such as family and community services, are not only failing to engage with fathers, but are actively (if often unconsciously) erecting barriers to fathers' involvement with vulnerable children. A key finding is that family professionals may not record the biological father's name, even if he is co-resident with the child; and typically fail to seek clarification of the relationship-to-child of men living in the child's household or visiting regularly. Thus fathers are essentially invisible. Policies that could enable family and community service providers to engage effectively with fathers and other male carers, without putting children or women at risk, include:

- Defining, as a core objective, support for strong and positive relationships between men and their children;
- Emphasising the importance of local services collecting data about men in families: their names (and other contact details), their relationships with children and their needs for support;
- Instituting quality standards for 'father-friendliness' in family, children's and community services;
- Setting targets to increase the numbers of men employed, and volunteering in such services;
- Routine (and in-service) training for family service personnel working with men;
- Routine (and in-service) training for family service personnel in working with couple relationships and marriages;
- Designing and implementing validated risk-assessments when abuse is indicated and encouraging the development of child protection services that take into account the potential role of biological and social fathers;
- The development and evaluation of a range of innovative services to work with abusive men in families;
- The development of workshops/materials to help men and women examine the roots of distrust in their relationships, violence in relationships, and the implications of relationships that include children.

Programmes

In recent years, a number of programmes that explicitly seek to increase the involvement of fathers in childcare and domestic responsibilities have been developed around the world. This field has developed a number of practices and training capacities that need to be further strengthened, evaluated and disseminated. It is important to emphasise that many of the skills and much of the knowledge required to engage successfully with fathers is unique to this form of activity and not part of existing core training for workers in health, education and social welfare programmes. To further the development of international, national and local capacities to increase the participation of fathers in domestic and childcare responsibilities, four main activities should be promoted:

Firstly, pilot projects that test emerging father-friendly practice within mainstream programmes need to be developed in diverse settings. Such programmes should be rooted in existing practice and supported at the highest level to ensure sufficient funding, technical expertise and a knowledge base from which to work. Pilot programmes should be developed in the following areas:

- Provision of work-based daycare centres in all enterprises with a certain number of employees that include men as well as women in calculations of childcare needs;
- Education curricula that explore the roles of fathers and men's potential to engage in caring and domestic activities;
- Working with men in families to increase girls' participation in education;
- Increasing men's involvement with their children's education;
- Ensuring that fathers are included in all communications with parents;
- Supporting men in the pre-natal period by providing them with information on maternal and infant health and care;
- Informing fathers about the benefits of breastfeeding;
- Explicitly including men in families in strategies to disseminate information about infant care, hygiene, disease prevention, recognition and treatment, dehydration, diet and nutrition and access to health services;
- Communicating to men about women's health needs and attempting to resolve barriers to women's access to health services;
- Services to support men's physical and mental health, and health behaviours;
- HIV-transmission prevention strategies that develop and evaluate methodologies for including and involving men in information programmes;
- Methods for promoting father involvement to mothers, developed within services traditionally accessing large numbers of mothers;
- Support services that work to promote positive relationships and co-operative parenting with separated parents;
- Providing skills-based education for couple relationships and for marriage;

- Identifying, documenting and supporting gender-equitable models of fatherhood and fathering behaviour within communities;
- Providing routine (and in-service) training in working with fathers, for court and other personnel working with separating, separated and blended families.

All programmes should develop performance and quality systems (audit, performance review, inspections and so on) that capture the extent to which agencies, services and staff are effectively strengthening father–child relationships.

Secondly, evaluation research is a critical component in the development of pilot projects that aim to increase the participation and responsibility of fathers in domestic and childcare activities. Evaluation programmes need to take account of:

- Existing research on measuring fathering behaviour;
- The ability of the programmes to change fathering behaviour;
- The impact of the programmes on the agencies' core objectives (for example, maternal health outcomes, breastfeeding rates, infant mortality, early years development, children's attitudes towards gender and so on);
- Their impact on the relationships between children and their fathers;
- Their impact on the relationship between fathers and mothers;
- Their impact on strengthening families.

Thirdly, training capacities need to be developed in order to spread the development of the skills and knowledge base among programme planners and workers. Successful work with fathers requires access to research, technical and knowledge bases that are being developed around the world, but as yet are not widely available. Such training capacities are already being developed in the USA, Europe, Australasia and some parts of Latin America. These capacities need strengthening. There is also a need to disseminate these skills and knowledge more widely to other areas of the world for adaptation and development in diverse local contexts. The following activities, in particular, would help to develop training capacities around the world:

- Efforts by the international community of researchers and other actors in the fatherhood field to develop an international network with a training capacity should be supported; and
- A series of international technical workshops to train trainers within national, international and regional agencies should be held in order to spread and strengthen training capacity in the following areas:
  - working with men within pre- and post-natal services;
  - working with fathers in education services;
  - working with men in health programmes;
  - provision of relationship and marriage education and support; and
  - supporting children's relationships with their parents in separated families.

And finally, dissemination of good practice is essential to the development of services and practices that promote fathers' involvement in domestic and childcare responsibilities. This dissemination involves:

- The interpretation of evaluation and academic research for practitioners;
- The integration of the lessons learnt from such research into training programmes; and
- Ongoing dialogue between actors working on fatherhood issues worldwide.

The key activity that is required to ensure that good practice is disseminated internationally is support for the efforts of researchers, programme planners and other key actors in the fatherhood field to develop an international network with a capacity for developing:

- Evaluation and academic research interpretation and worldwide dissemination;
- Training capacity;
- Ongoing dialogue between leading actors in the field;
- Joint initiatives and ongoing networking; and
- Advocacy and technical consultation to international, regional and national agencies.

A proposal for such a network has been developed by leading actors in the fatherhood field at the International Fatherhood Summit, which took place in Oxford in the United Kingdom in March 2003.

Tom Beardshaw with his son

Tom Beardshaw is Network Director of Fathers Direct in the United Kingdom. He trained in Social Anthropology at the London School of Economics, and in Social Ethics at Cardiff University in Wales. He writes and speaks extensively on fatherhood and public policy, runs Fathers Direct's website, leads their international work and co-ordinates Europe's largest conference on fatherhood – 'Working with Fathers', which takes place annually in London. He is the father of two sons: Bonga, who lives in the Natal Midlands in South Africa, and Cole, who lives with Tom in Cardiff, in the United Kingdom.

Index

Untitled by Mukelwa Mthembu aged 11 years, KZN

Index